Edward Gibbon

and the

Decline and Fall of the Roman Empire

EDWARD GIBBON Esqr. born the 8th May 1737.

Engraved by Jno Hall from an Original Picture painted by Sir Joshua Reynolds.

London. Published as the Act directs Feb 7th 1780 by W. Strahan & T. Cadell.

Edward Gibbon, Esq. An engraving by John
Hall from a painting by Sir Joshua Reynolds.
By permission of the Harvard College Library.

Edward Gibbon
and the
Decline and Fall of the Roman Empire

Edited by

G. W. Bowersock

John Clive

Stephen R. Graubard

Harvard University Press
Cambridge, Massachusetts
and London, England
1977

Copyright © 1976 by the American Academy of Arts and Sciences

Introduction Copyright © 1977 by the President and Fellows of Harvard College
All rights reserved
Printed in the United States of America

Library of Congress Cataloging in Publication Data

Main entry under title:

Edward Gibbon and the decline and fall of the Roman
    Empire.

    Includes bibliographical references and index.
    1. Gibbon, Edward, 1737–1794—Addresses, essays,
lectures. 2. Rome—Historiography—Addresses, essays,
lectures.   I. Bowersock, Glen Warren.   II. Clive,
John.   III. Graubard, Stephen Richards.
DG206.G5E37   1977   937'.06'072024   76-48192
ISBN 0-674-23940-7

Contents

MYRON GILMORE

Introduction

The Conference in Rome, January 6–10, 1976

The centenary of the death of Edward Gibbon was marked by a public commemoration held in London on November 15, 1894, under the auspices of the Royal Historical Society. The president of the committee charged with planning this observance was the Earl of Sheffield, grandson of Gibbon's great friend to whom he had left all his letters and papers. The first Lord Sheffield outlived Gibbon by twenty-seven years, and during that time published in several editions a version of the *Memoirs* and the *Miscellaneous Works*. On his death his will forbade any further publication from the Gibbon manuscripts unless he should have left a special authorization. As there was no such authorization, the manuscripts were locked up and seen in the nineteenth century only by Dean Milman when he was preparing a new edition of the *Decline and Fall*. The interest aroused by the commemoration of 1894 persuaded the third Lord Sheffield to remove his grandfather's restriction, and in 1896 he presented the Gibbon papers to the nation, depositing them in the British Museum.

The consequence of this decision was the publication of *The Private Letters of Edward Gibbon*, edited by R. E. Prothero in two volumes in 1896, and the six and a half drafts of the *Autobiographies* edited by John Murray in 1897. The twentieth century has seen new editions of these sources: the *Letters* with additional correspondence from other collections, edited by J. E. Norton in three volumes in 1956, and the *Memoirs* edited with a critical apparatus by Georges Bonnard in 1966. Furthermore, most of Gibbon's *juvenilia*, diaries, and notes have now been published: *Gibbon's Journal to January 28, 1763: My Journal I, II, III and Ephemerides*, edited by D. M. Low (New York, 1929); *Le Journal de Gibbon à Lausanne*, edited by Georges Bonnard (Lausanne, 1945); *Miscellanea Gibboniana*, edited by Georges Bonnard, G. R. De Beer, and L. Junod (Lausanne, 1952); *Gibbon's Journey from Geneva to Rome: His Journal from 20 April to 2 October, 1764*, edited by Georges Bonnard (London, 1961); and *The English Essays of Edward Gibbon*, edited by Patricia B. Craddock (Oxford, 1972) with additional material never before made public.

With these publications most of Gibbon's papers have been made available in scholarly editions, and it cannot be expected that future commemorations will concentrate on the small amount of material still to be edited.

Thus in 1976, which marked the two-hundredth anniversary of the publication of the first volume of *The Decline and Fall of the Roman Empire*, interest was centered on the analysis of Gibbon's character and achievement, his intellectual background, and the influence of his *History*, from the perspective of twentieth century scholarship.

In 1974 John Clive conceived the idea of commemorating the Gibbon bicentennial and first approached Glen Bowersock about the possibility of a conference composed of scholars whose professional interests were directly related to some aspect of Gibbon's achievement as historian of the Roman Empire. Clive then raised the matter with Stephen Graubard, who agreed to consider the organization of a conference under the auspices of the American Academy of Arts and Sciences. Bowersock, Clive, and Graubard then undertook to secure financial support from foundations and to issue invitations to participants. Grants were received from The American Council of Learned Societies, The Loeb Classical Library Foundation, and the Andrew W. Mellon Foundation, and it was possible to hold the conference in Rome. On January 7, 1976, there assembled in Rome for three days of sessions twenty scholars, eighteen of whom had been invited to submit prepared papers and two who were present as interlocutors, one of whom was myself.

The first session was held on the Campidoglio in sight of the steps of Aracoeli, on which or near which Gibbon sat when, according to his account in the *Memoirs*, he conceived his plan for writing the history of Rome. Subsequent sessions were held in Palazzo Paganica by courtesy of Dr. Vincenzo Cappelletti, Director of the Istituto della Enciclopedia Italiana. Stephen Graubard presided over the animated discussions which took place at the morning and evening sessions. The papers were published in *Daedalus* under the title *Edward Gibbon and the Decline and Fall of the Roman Empire*, volume 105, no. 3, of the *Proceedings of the American Academy of Arts and Sciences*.

These essays, written by authorities in a variety of different disciplines, offer new perspectives not only on the personality of Gibbon but also on his historical writing, on the age in which he lived, and on the relevance of the *Decline and Fall* today. I am not a specialist in any of the subjects considered, but in introducing this volume I should like to attempt to summarize briefly what seem to me the most important contributions of this conference.

The Man

It has often been said that Gibbon wrote about himself in just the way he wrote about the Roman Empire. The image that emerged from such famous phrases as "I sighed as a lover, I obeyed as a son" and "The enthusiasm which I do not feel, I have ever scorned to affect" was that of the serene historian whose life had moved in an ordered sequence of events to the completion of his great work. The papers and discussion concerned with Gibbon's character and personality modified this image in several important respects. For example, it now seems clear to me that, whatever the reality of the experience on the steps of Aracoeli in Rome on October 15, 1764, it was not at the time the momentous turning point which Gibbon makes of it in the *Autobiography*. This is but one instance of the art Gibbon applied to the characterization of the figure he wished to present to the world. The conference brought vividly before me the reality behind the figure, all the elements of emotional deprivation, incongruity, and contradiction in Gibbon's personality, raising interesting questions on how far the analysis of character can be applied to the "explanation" of achievement. I have not much confidence in the methods of psychohistory, now so widely practiced, and, indeed, the participants in the conference did not do more than touch on the possibilities of exploring Gibbon's inner emotional life in psychoanalytic terms, but the following pages do contain data and suggestions which help us understand the complex interplay between character and situation that lay behind the creation of his masterpiece.

The History

Participants in the conference were privileged to hear critical discussions by highly qualified authorities on particular areas in the vast panorama of *The Decline and Fall of the Roman Empire*. These areas include the early Empire, the later Empire, the Italian Middle Ages, Byzantium, and Islam. In each of these cases there was a new consideration of the sources or the use of the sources as well as an analysis of the presuppositions and prejudices within the framework of which the narrative moves forward. I found particularly interesting the account of Gibbon's relation to Tacitus on the theme of civil war and rebellion in the early Empire. The analysis of the famous description of the origin and development of monasticism and the growth of the early church throws new light on Gibbon's philosophy of history. It is also of great value to have a survey of his treatment of Byzantium and Islam from the point of view of contemporary scholarship with an analysis of his strengths and weaknesses in areas that have often been neglected because of the concentration of interest on the chapters on Christianity and the fall of the western Empire. Several chapters bring new clarifications to the great sociological themes of the history, the phenomena of decline, barbarism, despotism, religious enthusiasm, survival, and revival and thus give us new perspectives on the complexities of Gibbon's conception of the nature of historical explanation, to which he himself did not do justice in the "General Observations on the Fall of the Roman Empire in the West." Particularly stimulating is the novel suggestion that perhaps Gibbon intended to apply the famous phrase "the triumph of barbarism and religion" to the Arabs rather than to the Germans and to Islam rather than to Christianity.

The Age

It is sometimes said, and I think with truth, that Gibbon tells us more about the mind of the eighteenth century than he does about the Roman Empire. Much has been written on his assimilation of the ideas of his contemporaries and predecessors, but I have never before encountered a description of the intellectual influences that shaped his thought so comprehensive, so detailed, and so carefully shaded as is provided in this book. These influences extend in time from the Renaissance to the Enlightenment and include Renaissance humanists, scholars, historians, literary critics, political theorists, and philosophers. The theme of decline was already a subject of speculation in Renaissance Italy and was subsequently applied both to ancient and to contemporary European experience. For the first time we have an important account of the relationship of Gibbon to the heritage of Machiavelli. For his ecclesiastical history he depended on the church historians, who first appeared in opposing camps after the Reformation and were succeeded by the learned Jansenists and Jesuits of the seventeenth century. The careful survey here presented of Gibbon's relationship to these sources, both Catholic and Protestant, enlightens us on his own religious opinions and on his constant quest for freedom from bias. Among the most original contributions is the detailed tracing by more than one writer of Gibbon's response to French thought from the *érudits* of the seventeenth century to the *philosophes* of the eighteenth. We have here what is certainly the most complete picture yet provided of the complexities of Gibbon's relationship to the French authors he read or met.

The importance of the Scottish Enlightenment is also clearly brought out, with particular emphasis on the influence of Hume in supplying a model of philosophical history in respect to both method and moral judgment. Some of these sources, combined with Gibbon's experience of the political life of the Swiss communes, suggested possible topics for historical investigation and the account of these early projects, before he committed himself to his grand design, gives a new perspective on the germination of his historical vision. Fascinating also are the reflections of several contributors on Gibbon's response to the public events of his time, especially the American and French Revolutions. The analysis of Gibbon in the context of his age has thus produced a volume that must be counted a major contribution to the understanding of many aspects of the intellectual history of the eighteenth century.

The Heritage

Several of the contributors have made interesting suggestions about the influence of Gibbon on later historical writing in the nineteenth and twentieth centuries. Among the most valuable pages in this volume for the student of historiography are those that describe the genesis and nature of Gibbon's conception of "philosophic history," and on this subject there was general agreement. How far and in what specific ways he may be said to have been a precursor of such nineteenth century historians as Sismondi, Michelet, Taine, and Renan will continue to be debated. Contrasting opinions were offered on the effect on certain fields of his presuppositions and prejudices that were said to have inhibited the development of Byzantine scholarship but opened the way for advances in the study of Muhammad and Islam. Two chapters of particular interest and originality deal directly with specific aspects of Gibbon's influence in the nineteenth century, one on art history and the other on Italy.

Gibbon's *Journal* of the tour to Italy reveals his sensitivity to the visual arts, although he does not use evidence from this source in the *Decline and Fall*. A French art historian and connoisseur, Seroux d'Agincourt, was directly inspired by his reading of Gibbon to produce a monumental history of painting, sculpture, and architecture from the decadence in the third century to the renewal of the arts in the fifteenth. In this he adopted Gibbon's chronological framework as well as his conceptions of cultural decline and revival.

The chapter on the place of Gibbon in the historiography of modern Italy points out that Gibbon's account of the decline of Rome, the barbarian invasions, and the rise of the medieval *communes* had a great influence on nineteenth century Italian historians and helped establish a tradition, especially in the work of Sismondi, the effects of which continued to be evident in the studies by twentieth century medievalists. The author observes, however, that the chapters on Christianity had always been neglected and his interesting conclusion is that "Gibbon's fortunes in Italy are therefore part of one of the most significant aspects of Italian culture, the refusal to examine critically the problems of the origin and value of Christianity."

Beyond the consideration of specific examples of Gibbon's influence, however, it may be said that this whole volume testifies to the ways in which Gibbon and his work continue to be relevant to us today. He analyzed the nature and results of despotic regimes in Rome and in the eastern empires; we have seen such regimes spread over a large part of the globe and Gibbon's analysis, although it may increase our pessimism, will also enlarge our understanding. Similarly suggestive is his treatment of political liberty, between illusion and reality in the declining days of the Roman Republic, present as a redeeming feature in the savage German tribes, and reappearing in institutional forms in the Italian and Swiss communal republics and the civil politics of Europe. We live in an age when comparative history and sociology are cultivated as never before, and how can we not learn from the vast number of radically different societies encompassed in the range of Gibbon's historical vision? It is true that we no longer find it possible to accept the extreme statement on the increase of "the wealth, the happiness, and perhaps the virtue of the human race," with which he closed the "General Observations on the Fall of the Roman Empire in the West." On the other hand we are in a position to share with empathy his later apprehensions, when, under the impact of the French Revolution, he saw the threat of the "new Barbarians who labour to confound the order and happiness of society, and who, in the opinion of thinking men, are not less enemies of subjects than of kings."

Yet in the end it may be that Gibbon has most to teach us not through uniformities and analogies in his work which we may think applicable to our situation today but through his conception of the nature and limits of historical explanation, so different from ours and so profoundly characteristic of the man and his age.

"The Limits of Nature and History"

Gibbon's outlook on man and society has often been described as one of "practical common sense," that of a "down-to-earth man," able to "distinguish between the real and the unreal." No passage from the *Decline and Fall* was more often cited at the Rome conference than the one in which Gibbon celebrated the durability of the mechanical arts in contrast to the folly of enthusiasts and the idle speculations of philosophers and theologians, assuring his readers that "the scythe still continued annually to mow the harvests of Italy." This same quality which is rightly said to underlie his irony and humor, is responsible for the many occasions on which he rejects a fantastic or exaggerated account in one of his sources.

A splendid example of the application of this criterion is Gibbon's treatment of Saint Jerome's description of the devastation of the Illyrian provinces by the Gothic invasion. The saint depicted the terrible scenes of rape and pillage by the barbarian horde and maintained that afterwards "nothing was left but earth and sky; not only was the human race extirpated but also the beasts, birds, and fish." Gibbon's reply to this rhetoric is, first, that it was known that the Illyrian provinces continued for centuries to supply new material for subsequent invaders and, second, that even if it were to be supposed that human life and domestic animals had been completely eliminated, still "the beasts of the forest would multiply in their solitary domain." But the heart of his argument is magnificently expressed: "The saint is surely transported beyond the *limits of nature and history* [italics mine] . . . The various tribes that people the air, or the waters, are still less connected with the fate of the human species [than the beasts of the forest]; and it is highly probable that the fish of the Danube would have felt more terror and distress from the approach of a voracious pike than from the inroad of a Gothic army."

The conviction that the "limits of nature and history" existed and could be understood by rational men was a quality of the eighteenth century mind. Other ages have been more conscious of events like miracles, which were outside the course of nature, or catastrophes so overwhelming that they seemed outside the course of history. Perhaps it was this belief in limits that helped Gibbon find continuity through more than a millennium of the history of Europe and also gave him and his friend David Hume the serenity (sometimes complacency) and self-confidence reflected in their autobiographies.

Hume's account of his life ends with his last illness and his expression of equanimity before his imminent dissolution. His friend Adam Smith has recorded their last conversation. Hume had been reading Lucian's *Dialogues of the Dead*. "Among all the excuses which are alleged to Charon for not entering readily into his boat, he could not find one that fitted him: he had no house to finish, he had no daughter to provide for, he had no enemies on whom he wished to revenge himself . . . 'I have done everything of consequence which I ever meant to do, and I could at no time expect to leave my relations and friends in a better situation than that in which I am now likely to leave them. I therefore have all reason to die contented.' He then diverted himself with inventing several jocular excuses which he supposed he might make to Charon, and with imagining the very surly answers which it might suit the character of Charon to return to them. 'Upon further consideration,' said he, 'I thought I might say to him, 'Good Charon, I have been correcting my works for a new edition. Allow me a little time, that I may see how the public receives the alterations.' But Charon would answer, 'When you have seen the effect of these, you will be for making other alterations. There will be no end of such excuses. So, honest friend, please step into the boat.' But I might still urge, 'Have a little patience, good Charon. I have been endeavoring to open the eyes of the public. If I live a few years longer, I may have the satisfaction of seeing the downfall of some of the prevailing systems of superstition.' But Charon would then lose all temper and decency. 'You loitering rogue, that will not happen these many hundred years. Do you fancy I will grant you a leave for such a term? Get into the boat this instant.' "

Gibbon had seen Hume in his last illness in London and recorded that "he died the death of a philosopher." It is not difficult to imagine Gibbon presenting a similar excuse to Charon to have "the satisfaction of seeing . . . the downfall of superstition."

The various drafts of Gibbon's autobiography remain unfinished. In the version that takes the story furthest he contemplates that "the laws of probability, so true in general, so fallacious in particular, still allow me about fifteen years, and I shall soon enter into the period which, as the most agreeable of his long life, was selected by the judgment and experience of the sage Fontenelle."

When Gibbon reached his own final illness so much earlier than he had calculated, Lord Sheffield has recorded on the testimony of his servant that "he was quite tranquil . . . and did not show the least sign of alarm or apprehension of death; and it does not appear that he ever thought himself in danger unless his desire to speak to Mr. Barell [the friend and relation for whom he had sent] may be considered in that light."

Gibbon wrote in one version of his autobiography: "In old age, the consolation of hope is reserved for the tenderness of parents, who commence a new life in their children; the faith of enthusiasts who sing Hallelujahs above the clouds; and the vanity of authors who presume the immortality of their name and writing."

How keen a sense of the immortality of literature Gibbon had is evident from his celebrated remark on Fielding's *Tom Jones*: "The romance of *Tom Jones*, that exquisite picture of human manners, will outlive the palace of the Escurial and the Imperial Eagle of the House of Austria." He could take comfort from the conviction that no less would be true of *The Decline and Fall of the Roman Empire* and its author. The present volume testifies to the validity of this conviction and fittingly commemorates the lively interest in both the author and the book after the passage of two hundred years.

Edward Gibbon

and the

Decline and Fall of the Roman Empire

Bibliographical Note

Because no modern edition of *The History of the Decline and Fall of the Roman Empire* conforms to Gibbon's original division of it into volumes, all volume numbers have been omitted from the references to the *Decline and Fall* at the end of each chapter. In studying Gibbon's thought, the reader might do well to keep in mind the original volumes and their dates of publication: Volume I was published in 1776 and comprised chapters 1 through 16; Volumes II and III, in 1781, comprised chapters 17 through 38 (including the "General Observations on the Fall of the Roman Empire in the West"); and Volumes IV, V, and VI, in 1788, included all the remaining chapters.

References in the individual chapters are to Gibbon's chapter numbers and to the page numbers of the edition used by each author. The edition used is identified at the head of the list of references in chapters where citations of the *Decline and Fall* are numerous, and in the first citation, where they are few. The work is throughout abbreviated *DF*.

DAVID P. JORDAN

Edward Gibbon: The Historian of the Roman Empire

THE COST OF GENIUS IS HIGH. Some are condemned to pay the price incessantly in the agony of their lives. Others, like Edward Gibbon, endowed with a cool, dispassionate temperament and the gift of irony, are able, through a supreme effort of the will, to transmute the pain into an art that breathes the spirit of happiness and a life that seems a model of self-awareness and control. Gibbon's serene spirit, free of the passionate disruptions that plagued so many of his contemporaries, finds its natural expression in the *Decline and Fall of the Roman Empire*: the history, one of the architectural wonders of historical writing, was built, patiently and elegantly, out of the learning of the ages; his unique vision of the emergence of European civilization, out of his inimitable style and the ruins of Rome. His other masterpiece, *Memoirs of My Life*, was built out of less promising materials. Gibbon left his *Memoirs* unfinished, but from its six and a half drafts we can see the historian wresting serenity from frustration and trying to give to his life the same order he bestowed on the Roman Empire. But here and there the incongruities show through, and the self-apotheosis of "the historian of the Roman empire" remains incomplete.

It is incongruous that Mr. Gibbon, Sr., the historian's capricious and irresponsible father, should have reared England's great historian. It is incongruous that the sickly and misshapen boy who pored over massive tomes of scholarship and spent sleepless nights reconciling the chronologies of antiquity or remembering the dynasties of Egypt and Assyria should have written a great book. It is incongruous that the man who prided himself on the elegance and correctness of his manners, the probity of his sentiments, the tastefulness of his appearance, the eloquence of his conversation, should have been a subject of fun, even of caricature. It is incongruous that the short, fat little man should have called attention to his ridiculous physique with extravagant clothes, or carried his Frenchified manners, which verged on parody, into English society, or cultivated a style of conversation that closely resembled a French theatrical declamation. It is incongruous that Gibbon was a literary genius; more incongruous still that he should have devoted his gifts to historical writing. It is incongruous that England's most remarkable gentleman-scholar should have been self-educated, or that insular England with its parochial squirearchy should have produced so cosmopolitan a writer. Above all, it is incongruous that Europe's history, through more than a thousand years, should have been mirrored in the mind of an eighteenth-century English gentleman.

Nowhere are these incongruities more obvious than in his portraits. The most

1

famous was painted in 1779 by Gibbon's friend, Sir Joshua Reynolds. It was the historian's favorite and hung in his study for years. Gibbon enjoyed contemplating himself as he paced back and forth, casting his magnificient paragraphs in his mind before setting them down. Sir Joshua's portrait is flattering, a fit monument to an intellectual hero. Gibbon sat for the artist in a red coat, "the national colour of our military ensigns and uniforms," and Sir Joshua has successfully harmonized Gibbon's irregular features to complement his martial pose. The historian looks out at us with a steady, even arrogant, gaze. He is formidable, dignified, aloof. His huge forehead seems almost a symbol for the massive erudition of the *Decline and Fall.*

I prefer, as Gibbon did not, the less formal portraits: Henry Walton's intimate Gibbon as man about town, with his lively eyes and amused look; Mrs. Brown's silhouette of a short (he was apparently under five feet), fat little man with an overly large head, standing on spindly legs and about to take a pinch of snuff; Lady Diana Beauclerk's pen drawing, actually a caricature, emphasizing Gibbon's huge forehead and equally huge double chin, with the sober historian ridiculously crowned with an olive wreath. But most revealing of all is Michel-Vincent Brandoin's drawing, done in the last decade of the historian's life. Gibbon is seated on a square plinth in the garden of La Grotte, his Lausanne home. In the background is Lake Leman and, beyond it, the Alps. His pose is informal but regal, for Gibbon thought of himself as "the king of the place" and referred to La Grotte as "Gibbon Castle."

Obese, short, his head too large for his body, disfigured by a hydrocele, his left arm akimbo, his right hand resting on a walking stick with his index finger extended to punctuate an anecdote, he seems about to speak, perhaps about the garden he himself designed. The round, resolute mouth is petulant rather than sneering while his delicate feet, in buckled pumps, look too small and fragile to support his grotesque bulk. Here is "the Gibbon"—he never minded the ironic sobriquet—in the autumn of his life, basking contentedly and a bit foolishly in the glory won by twenty years' labor on the *Decline and Fall.* Here is the man we occasionally glimpse through the lush and beautiful foliage of his rhetoric: pompous, vain, self-satisfied, a bit ridiculous, even ugly, but indifferent to the absurdity of his appearance and perhaps absorbed in contemplating his own genius.

Gibbon loved to sit for his portrait, but lest his many admirers pay homage incorrectly he decided to do his own portrait by writing his *Memoirs.* And his self-portrait more resembles Sir Joshua's oil than Brandoin's sketch. It is a portrait of "the historian of the Roman empire" as he liked to call himself, rather than of Edward Gibbon the man. Like the Fairy Godmother, Gibbon swept his magic wand over the incongruities of his life, turning pumpkins into coaches, mice into footmen.

Gibbon was born at Putney, Surrey, April 27, 1737, according to the old calendar: when England finally adopted the Gregorian calendar in the middle of the eighteenth century—most of Western Europe had been using the new calendar by 1587—he celebrated his birthday on May 8. He was the oldest son, as it turned out the only surviving child, of Edward Gibbon, Sr., and Judith Porten. The family fortune had been established by Gibbon's grandfather, a merchant and war profiteer who was ruined by the collapse of the South Sea Bubble (1720), yet managed to amass another fortune. An obscure quarrel between Gibbon's father and grandfather had deprived Mr. Gibbon, Sr., of a more substantial share of the family's wealth, but he was rich enough to lead the life of an English squire. He was incompetent in financial matters, vengeful, capricious, moody, and self-indulgent.

Portrait of Edward Gibbon by Henry Walton.
National Portrait Gallery, London.

Gibbon's mother, apparently a pretty and vivacious woman, found little time for her son. Her willing submission to the eccentricities and confused ambitions of Gibbon's father and a series of pregnancies deprived the child of a mother's love so long as she lived, and the last of these pregnancies killed her when Gibbon was nine. The maternal role was filled by Gibbon's maiden aunt, Catherine Porten, a simple, loving, exceptionally kind woman who encouraged her nephew's precocious and curious intellectual inclinations.

Gibbon was a sickly child, plagued by a succession of mysterious illnesses and ignorant, incompetent doctors. He spent more time confined to bed than at school. His only companion was his Aunt Porten; his only amusement, desultory reading. During one of his few periods of relative good health, he was sent to Westminster School and "purchased," as he put it, a rudimentary knowledge of Latin "at the expense of many tears and some blood." But he hated school. His weak constitution kept him from joining the games of his contemporaries, and they taunted him for his clumsiness and the supposed sins of his Tory family (it was just after the abortive rebellion of 1745). Along with his few scraps of Latin, he carried from childhood a lifelong aversion to schools and doctors.

At the age of fifteen his disorders "most wonderfully vanished," and his father enrolled Gibbon in Magdalen College, Oxford, as a Gentleman Commoner (1752). He arrived there, in his self-mocking description, "with a stock of erudition that might have puzzled a Doctor, and a degree of ignorance of which a school boy would have been ashamed." Gibbon was delighted with his new freedom and loved the velvet cap and silk gown that distinguished a Gentleman Commoner from a plebeian student. But the naïve little boy was as unprepared for Oxford as Oxford was for him. Gibbon later described the tutors of Magdalen as "sunk in port and prejudice," safe and lazy in their sinecures.

At Oxford, Gibbon read a few plays of Terence and was discouraged from learning Arabic before he discovered the secret of the place: the lamest excuse for truancy was readily accepted by his tutor. He was absent from Oxford more often than not. He says his youth and bashfulness kept him from "the taverns and bagnios of Covent Garden" during his frequent elopements to London, but he got himself into mischief of another kind. After reading some controversial books and talking to a Roman Catholic student, Gibbon was converted to Catholicism (1753). He was immediately forced to leave Oxford, and with it he also left the promise of an easy and conventional life.

Scandalized by his son's conversion, Mr. Gibbon, Sr., sent the boy into exile in Lausanne, in the doctrinally correct house of Daniel Pavilliard, a Calvinist minister. Gibbon spent almost five years in Switzerland (1753-58), and was reconverted to Protestantism on Christmas Day, 1754. He was recalled to England on the eve of his twenty-first birthday and settled into his father's country home at Buriton, Hampshire. He quickly made the library his private preserve, a safe refuge from the boring round of country obligations. He also met his new stepmother, Dorothea Patton, of whose existence he learned from a neighbor rather than from his own father.

In Lausanne, Gibbon had become bilingual in French and English, and with the systematic passion of an autodidact had mastered Latin and learned some Greek as well. He would take one of the Latin classics, for example an epistle of Cicero, translate it into French, and then lay it aside for some days or weeks. He would then retranslate it into Latin and compare his version with the original. He also set himself the task of reading a couple of hundred lines of Homer every day, but he never became as comfortable with Greek as he was with Latin. French literature, especially the classical French theater from Corneille to Voltaire and the works of the *philosophes*, filled his hours of study. He was influenced by the ideas of the *philosophes*, but even more he was seduced by their style. His first book, the *Essai sur l'étude de la littérature* (1761) was begun in Lausanne, and Gibbon played the sedulous ape to Montesquieu's pungent, aphoristic style. He was also influenced by Continental scholarship, wrote some essays on abstruse points of ancient history and literature, and entered into a Latin correspondence with several scholars. And he fell in love with a Swiss girl, Suzanne Curchod. He hid his infatuation from his father until he was back in England. When he broached the subject of marriage, his father threw a tantrum. The dutiful son gave up Suzanne and retreated to the library. The years in Lausanne made Gibbon a scholar and a European: by the time he returned to England he aspired to be a man of letters.

In 1760, Gibbon's routine of study and intellectual idleness at Buriton was interrupted by the Seven Years' War. It was not an unwelcome break: Gibbon was not made for the life of a country squire. He neither rode nor hunted, and his Frenchified manners appeared odd to his country neighbors. A few pathetic attempts had been made to launch him in London society, but they had no more success than his father's efforts to make his son a country gentleman. But Mr. Gibbon, Sr., was as stubborn as his son, and, without consulting him, he got Gibbon a captaincy in the Hampshire Militia. The young man spent almost three years (1760-63) marching his recruits up and down the countryside and debauching, too often he thought, with his fellow officers. But all was not idleness and dissipation. Gibbon had a knapsack full of books and found enough time to complete and publish one of his own, or, as he put it, he lost his literary maidenhead.

Mr. Gibbon, Sr., thought the *Essai sur l'étude de la littérature*, the fruit of Gibbon's foreign education, might be put to some practical use. The *Essai* had value for Gibbon's father only as evidence of his son's mastery of French, for it might secure him a diplomatic post. Gibbon was pushed to complete the manuscript and the dutiful son obeyed. Written in graceful, if imitative, French, the *Essai* is a spirited defense of classical literature as the best subject to exercise the mind, improve the critical faculties, and teach a sense of style while inculcating the principles of human nature.

Alas, no diplomatic post was offered, and Mr. Gibbon, Sr., had to resign himself once again to his son's failure to please him. As soon as the war was over and the Hampshire Militia disbanded, Gibbon talked his father into sending him on the grand tour. He arrived in Paris on January 28, 1763, where he stayed until spring. Then he moved on to Lausanne where he spent nearly a year and prepared for the Italian leg of his journey by writing a historical geography of ancient Italy (*Nomina Gentesque Italiae*). When the snows melted, he crossed the Alps and made his way to Rome. The city where he had lived in his imagination for years enthralled him, and he spent several months studying the ruins with a professional antiquary. The tour, however, was cut short by his father's parsimony. After some weeks of financial distress, Gibbon obediently returned to England.

Gibbon once again resumed his country routine and began seriously writing history. In the summer of 1767, he started his *Histoire générale des républiques Suisses* but soon abandoned the project. At about the same time he co-authored, with his friend

Georges Deyverdun, a periodical journal, *Mémoires littéraires de la Grande Bretagne*, of which only two issues appeared. The only other literary project of these years was his first English essay, *Observations on the Sixth Book of the Aeneid* (1770). His father's last illness and death that same year interrupted any further work. Untangling the family's confused finances occupied him for the next two years. When the estate was finally settled, Gibbon moved to London, installed his substantial library, indulged his taste for elegance by acquiring a coach and a couple of servants, and joined the best clubs. In 1773, he started writing the *Decline and Fall*; the following year, he entered Parliament for Liskeard where he supported the government with "many a sincere and *silent* vote."

The first volume of the *Decline and Fall* appeared on February 17, 1776, and was immediately hailed as a masterpiece. The reading public and polite society alike were taken by surprise. "Lo," wrote Horace Walpole, expressing the enthusiasm of London society, "there is just appeared a truly classic work." The first printing of one thousand copies, in boards, was exhausted in a few weeks: second and third editions, not to mention two pirated Irish editions, quickly followed. The second and third volumes were published in 1781, carrying his history down to the fall of the Western Empire. In 1783, Gibbon retired to Lausanne to become the "king" of La Grotte and complete the *Decline and Fall*. His sinecure at the Board of Trade, along with its substantial income, had been suppressed by a government under attack. Gibbon decided to settle where his reduced income would still be adequate to support the domestic comfort he craved. This, at least, is the practical explanation he gives in the *Memoirs*. But retirement to Lausanne, a sleepy yet refined little town, was a virtual retreat from the world. Gibbon had always preferred to move on the fringes of society, finding himself more comfortable among men and women a bit intimidated by his reputation. Retreat to Lausanne also gave the theatrical little man the social importance, even celebrity, he never had in London or Paris. He was the most important Englishman in Lausanne; indeed he was the most important resident Lausanne ever had.

The last three volumes of the *Decline and Fall*, carrying the story down to the fall of Constantinople to the Turks (1453), were finished in late 1787. Publication was delayed until May 8, 1788, to coincide with Gibbon's fifty-first birthday. He lived in Lausanne for the rest of his life, basking in his reputation, enjoying the homage of Swiss neighbors and visiting Englishmen, dabbling with his autobiography and other literary projects, and caring for his garden. In 1793, he set off for England on a mission of mercy and friendship. He wanted to be with his friend, John Holroyd, Lord Sheffield, whose wife had just died.

The journey literally killed him. Afflicted by the gout and his grotesque infection, grossly corpulent and sedentary by nature and choice, he was exhausted by the long winter journey. After some weeks of harried visits and dinners in England, he took to his bed at Sheffield Place (Sussex), complaining of feeling tired and having little appetite. But Gibbon had no intention of dying. Holding court in his room, propped up on pillows, he chatted with visitors, discussing how long he could expect to live— he was only fifty-six—and what literary projects he had planned. On the day of his death (January 16, 1794), he asked to be left alone with Dussaut, his French valet. He apologized to his loyal servant for any difficulties death might cause and hoped Dussaut would never be as sick as his master had been. Then he lay back among the pillows, half dozing, mumbled a few words incoherently—it was the only time in his life he was incoherent—and fell unconscious at about 12:45 in the afternoon. Gibbon returned from Sheffield Place to 76 St. James's Street, London, on January 7. There he died. He was buried in the Sheffield family vault in the little country church in Fletching, Sussex: in death, as in life, the most distinguished resident of an obscure place.

Had Gibbon merely reported the few facts of his "quiet and literary" life, we would know him only from those rare passages in the *Decline and Fall* where he unconsciously spoke about himself. His portrait, for example, of the fourteenth-century scholar, Barlaam of Calabria:

> He is described by Petrarch and Boccace, as a man of a diminutive stature, though truly great in the measure of learning and genius; of a piercing discernment, though of a slow and painful elocution. For many ages (as they affirm) Greece had not produced his equal in the knowledge of history, grammar, and philosophy; and his merit was celebrated in the attestations of the princes and doctors of Constantinople.[1]

But Gibbon wanted to paint a formal portrait of himself. He wanted to present to the public not Edward Gibbon the man, with his deformities, his flaws, his carefully contrived personality, but "the historian of the Roman empire," as unique a creation as was the *Decline and Fall*. By watching Gibbon transform his "quiet and literary" life into a romance, a quest for literary fame, with himself as the hero valiantly overcoming all obstacles, slaying all dragons, we can perhaps see why (and how) he created his *persona*, why and how he forged the incongruities of his life into a satisfying and compelling vision of the man who created the Roman Empire for his age.

Gibbon saw far more pattern and purpose in his own life than he was willing to see in history. But to create "the historian of the Roman empire" Gibbon paid dearly, not in the coin of the realm but in loneliness, frustration, unfulfilled love. He learned to live in books and was only a realized personality in the *Decline and Fall*. His history gave meaning to his life—a life full of false starts and occasional anguish. No wonder that, when he sat down to make a reckoning, fat and famous and lazy at La Grotte, it was easy to pass over the years of pain, to gaze contentedly at the years of achievement.

There are two famous episodes in Gibbon's *Memoirs*, intimately related—his youthful conversion to Catholicism and his mature conversion to pagan Rome—where we can see the autobiographer at work on his self-image. And in Gibbon's relationship with his father, we catch a glimpse of the emotional cost of the *Decline and Fall*.

Gibbon reached Rome on October 2, 1764; he commemorates his arrival in a moving passage in the *Memoirs*. It is one of the few passages in which Gibbon abandoned his customary emotional detachment in favor of an almost romantic attitude:

> My temper is not very susceptible of enthusiasm and the enthusiasm which I do not feel I have ever scorned to affect. But at the distance of twenty five years I can neither forget nor express the strong emotions which agitated my mind as I first approached and entered the *eternal City*. After a sleepless night I trod with a lofty step the ruins of the Forum; each memorable spot where Romulus *stood*, or Tully spoke, or Caesar fell was at once present to my eye; and several days of intoxication were lost or enjoyed before I could descend to a cool and minute investigation.[2]

Were it not for the fascination with pagan antiquity the passage might well be mistaken for the effusions of a Christian pilgrim. Indeed, the whole Roman visit is treated by Gibbon as a kind of religious experience, and this second conversion to Rome can usefully be compared to Gibbon's description of his first conversion, when he was at Oxford. He dismisses his youthful conversion with a carefully contrived apothegm: "I read, I applauded, I believed," he says of his seduction by the arguments of Bishop Bossuet, "I surely fell by a noble hand." He then goes on, at considerable length, to excuse his conversion—he speaks of it as a "religious folly" or a "childish revolt"—reminding himself and his readers that Chillingworth and Bayle had been similarly seduced by Catholicism and *they* were mature men at the time.

Gibbon's first conversion was not only, as he would have it, a lapse of good judgment, a piece of "folly." It was a "childish revolt." But against what? Gibbon was not a pious man, nor had he ever had a strong Protestant faith to lose. It was, I think, a revolt against his father, against Oxford, even, perhaps, against English society. Gibbon certainly hated Oxford. Indeed that institution has probably never suffered so much insult and scorn as Gibbon poured on his would-be alma mater. As we will shortly see, he also hated his father. Conversion to Catholicism on the part of a young Englishman interested in religious controversy was probably a barely conscious way of disobeying his father and getting out of Oxford. And conversion, despite the unanticipated severity of Mr. Gibbon, Sr., had the great attraction of not being a definitive revolt. It was only "childish." As soon as Gibbon returned to the church of his father, he was readmitted to the family, restored to society. Conversion to Catholicism in post-Reformation England was a disgrace, but not an unusual one. It was as if English history had created a traditional form of revolt against family, friends, institutions, society itself, and through the relatively broad tolerance of the Anglican Church left the door open to forgiveness.

Gibbon's second conversion to Rome is another matter. It is enthusiastically celebrated in the *Memoirs*, and the contrast between the two conversions is surely intentional:

> It was at Rome, on the fifteenth of October, 1764, as I sat musing amidst the ruins of the Capitol while the barefooted fryars were singing Vespers in the Temple of Jupiter, that the idea of writing the decline and fall of the City first started to my mind.[3]

It is almost too perfect; not just the elegance of expression but the event itself: it is so obviously the kind of experience "the historian of the Roman empire" should have had, so obviously the kind of experience that would have appealed to Gibbon's keen sense of drama. The passage has a history.

Gibbon kept a journal of his grand tour. The account of his entry into Rome is matter-of-fact: he entered the city over the Milvian Bridge, absorbed in a dream of antiquity which was interrupted by the customs officials. Twenty-five years later this germ became the famous moment of inspiration for the *Decline and Fall*. There is no evidence to suggest that Gibbon invented the chanting friars who interrupted his melancholic reverie on the Capitol, but there is evidence that he worked the passage up for the greatest effect and, in doing so, altered facts. Gibbon wrote two earlier versions of his moment of inspiration, the first in January, 1790, the second some months later:

> In my Journal the place and moment of conception are recorded; the fifteenth of October 1764, in the close of evening, as I sat musing in the Church of the Zoccolanti or Franciscan fryars, while they were singing Vespers in the Temple of Jupiter on the ruins of the Capitol.[4]

It was on the fifteenth of October, in the gloom of evening, as I sat musing on the Capitol, while the barefooted fryars were chanting their litanies in the temple of Jupiter, that I conceived the first thought of my history.[5]

Gibbon's final version of the episode is superior to the first two in style and impact, but not necessarily in truth. And the addition and subtraction of details, the altering of facts, are more important than changes in diction. Perhaps Gibbon did have a vision on the Capitol—although it is difficult to know where he sat on the fateful October evening, for the romantic "ruins of the Capitol" no longer existed in the eighteenth century—but I think it more likely that his memory either betrayed him or led him to gather into a single dramatic moment discrete impressions from his weeks in Rome. The *Decline and Fall* was the central activity in Gibbon's life; its creation gave coherence and meaning to all that had gone before. It is not difficult to imagine Gibbon bending or stretching the truth in order to explain the genesis of his history.

Had Gibbon been less of an artist, had he had an identity outside the *Decline and Fall*, he might have told the story of his inspiration more prosaically. For years he had been a student of Rome, for years he had subordinated everything in his life to his obsession with writing a great book. The idea of writing Rome's history had long been on his mind. He had even sketched—sometime between 1758 and 1763—the outlines of the *Decline and Fall* in his "Outline of the History of the World." No moment of illumination was necessary, but Gibbon could not attribute so great an achievement to such mundane causes.

If Gibbon created himself, or rather created "the historian of the Roman empire," he had good reason to do so. He had, so to speak, retreated from English society, taken refuge in his history, as earlier he had taken refuge in the Buriton library. But it was, in many ways, Mr. Gibbon, Sr., and the accident of a lonely childhood caused by poor health and neglect that started Gibbon on his journey into himself.

Mr. Gibbon, Sr., always disapproved of his son and intimidated him. Apparently Gibbon could do nothing right. Dependent on his father for money and emotional sustenance, Gibbon found himself a stranger, an outcast, in his father's house. In 1760, for example, while Gibbon was living at Buriton, he wrote his father a letter asking that the fifteen hundred pounds Mr. Gibbon, Sr., was anxious to spend on buying his son a seat in Parliament be used to send him on the grand tour: "An address in writing, from a person who has the pleasure of being with you every day may appear singular. However I have preferred this method, as upon paper I can speak without a blush and be heard without interruption."[6] This was not the first time Gibbon had tried to explain himself to his father, but it was the most pathetic. His father apparently ignored the letter, for the whole question of the grand tour comes up again in 1763.

Gibbon's father was "neither a bigot nor a philosopher," but he was passionately attached to the values of his class. He could not understand why his own son took no pleasure in the life and values of an English squire, why a seemingly cruel fate had given him a sickly, clumsy, timid, Frenchified son who would rather read a book than ride to hounds, rather take the grand tour than sit in Parliament, rather write history than be a gentleman farmer. He made Gibbon's life hellish. Everything the boy did was seen as a deliberate act of disobedience. Mr. Gibbon, Sr., struck back at his son by withholding his affection and his money. Even when he acted with apparent generosity, his real motives were selfish and capricious. Having ignored his son's pathetic letters from Lausanne, Mr. Gibbon, Sr., after almost five years, summoned the exile home. But it was not so much out of love as out of the need for money. Gibbon had just reached his majority and could now break the entail on the family lands. "The priests and the altar had been prepared," writes Gibbon of his homecoming, "and the victim was unconscious of the impending stroke."

As long as his father was alive, every important event in Gibbon's life was controlled, and the son was repeatedly subject to the kind of emotional blackmail that only an insensitive parent can use against a child. He sent Gibbon into exile, he called him home to break the entail, he forbade his marriage, he remarried without telling him, he pushed him to publish the *Essai sur l'étude de la littérature*, he enlisted him in the Hampshire Militia, he insisted Gibbon live at Buriton, he reneged on his commitment to finance the grand tour, he tried to force his son into Parliament: in a word he tried to make Gibbon what he imagined he ought to be. Fortunately, for historical literature at least and for Gibbon himself, the son was as stubborn as his father. After his youthful conversion to Catholicism, Gibbon avoided direct confrontations with his father. But despite his external complacency he tenaciously pursued his studies, obstinately refusing to become the gentleman his father wanted.

Only as his father lay virtually blind and dying, sunk in a deep depression, did Gibbon find out how the tyrant's incompetence had ruined the family fortune and seriously compromised Gibbon's future. During the last months of his father's life, Gibbon tried to restore some order to the chaos created by his father's incompetence. But the old man had lost or misplaced important papers and viciously attacked Gibbon's integrity whenever he asked for a document or a signature. He refused to face the truth: only a serious amputation could save what remained of the Gibbon fortune, one half the property had to be sold to pay the mortgages on the other half. Mr. Gibbon, Sr., resisted to the end. Then he died—without a will!

But the long summer of 1770, during which Gibbon struggled almost daily with his father, gave the historian a new sense of himself. Gibbon was thirty-three when his father died, a magical age for any student of antiquity. At least he was free, and he suddenly found himself able to do all the things he had been incapable of doing when his father was alive. Gibbon's energy and self-confidence in the years after 1770 are astonishing. With his father dead, he had "the first of earthly blessings, Independence." The new Gibbon, "the historian of the Roman empire," for years stifled by Mr. Gibbon, Sr., was about to emerge.

Somehow the years of paternal oppression had not crushed Gibbon, or rather they had forced upon him the creation of a unique personality. He remained resilient. The *Decline and Fall* testifies not only to Gibbon's genius, but to his tenacity as well. The twenty years he spent writing his history were but one manifestation of his stubborn will. The twenty years he spent in single-minded preparation for that work, all the while badgered and humiliated by his father, are at least as impressive, if not astonishing.

Gibbon's triumph was that of genius and will over his father, his society, his physical disabilities, and chance itself. Genius, someone has said, is the ability to think about a problem until it is solved. Trained to self-amusement by his sickly childhood, inured to loneliness by his years in Lausanne, bookish by nature (and for self-defense), Gibbon fixed his attention, concentrated his extraordinary gifts, on the problem of Europe's genesis. He himself recognized that some of his achievement was a matter of luck:

When I contemplate the common lot of mortality, I must acknowledge that I have drawn a high prize in the lottery of life. The far greater part of the globe is overspread with barbarism or slavery: in the civilized world the most numerous class is condemned to ignorance and poverty; and the double fortune of my birth in a free and enlightened country in an honourable and wealthy family is the lucky chance of an unit against millions.[7]

But it was not all luck. Gibbon's triumph went beyond the cosmic odds that so fascinated him in his last years. He indeed had the leisure to spend most of his life brooding over Roman history, but he paid for his leisure. Gibbon's struggle was different from that of most of his contemporaries.

Of all the Englishmen of his generation who achieved some intellectual distinction—with the obvious exception of Horace Walpole, that "elegant trifler"—none came from the squirearchy. Scotsmen such as Boswell, Hume, William Robertson, and Adam Smith, Irishmen such as Edmund Burke, poor boys such as Dr. Johnson, David Garrick, Oliver Goldsmith, and the poet Thomas Gray had to struggle to make their way in English society by their wits or by connecting themselves to a patron. Gibbon was spared such a struggle. He had the ironic task of overcoming the stultifying obligations of "a high prize in the lottery of life."

Gibbon created two works of art: his history and "the historian of the Roman empire." And he cherished both as only a creator can. Yet the crude bricks and mortar that support the dazzling façade—like the masonry of a Roman temple, masked by beautiful marble—he deliberately hid from public view. His person he enveloped in extravagant clothes, and his ideas he enveloped in an ironic style. The man and his work are rich in ambiguities and incongruities. Only now and then do we catch a glimpse of Gibbon, for he was an extremely self-protective man. Unlike Oscar Wilde, who put his genius into his life and his talent into his books, Gibbon was able to put his genius into both.

"Style," said Gibbon, "is the image of character," and he used his style, carefully refined over the years, to put a patina of self-satisfaction and rational happiness over the incongruities of his life and his achievement. The inveterate theater-goer—and Gibbon preferred the refinement and formality of the French classical theater—donned his *persona* before appearing in public (or in print).

If the price of genius was high, Gibbon paid it willingly. By the time he sat down to dabble with his *Memoirs*, he could scarcely remember the early years of pain and anguish and loneliness. He had become "the historian of the Roman empire," and, reflecting on his satisfying life, it was easy for him to celebrate his becoming as an inevitable, if meandering, process. From the fourteen-year-old boy "immersed in the passage of the Goths over the Danube" when "the summons of the dinner-bell reluctantly dragged me from my intellectual feast" to the author of the greatest and most imposing history of his age doubtless seemed to Gibbon a logical development. He had merged himself into his history, and as he created his Roman Empire he also created himself. Now, in retirement from the world and from the strains of scholarship and composition, he could sit back and enjoy his work.

REFERENCES

[1]*The History of the Decline and Fall of the Roman Empire*, ed. J. B. Bury, 7 volumes (5th edition, London, 1909), chap. 46, p. 118.

[2]*Memoirs of My Life*, ed. Georges A. Bonnard (London, 1966), p. 134 (hereafter cited as *Memoirs*).

³*Memoirs*, p. 136, n. 7, and p. 305.

⁴*Memoirs*, p. 136.

⁵*Memoirs*, p. 304.

⁶*The Letters of Edward Gibbon*, ed. J. E. Norton, 3 vols. (New York, 1956), I, p. 123. The letter is undated, but was written in the summer of 1760.

⁷*Memoirs*, p. 186.

MARTINE WATSON BROWNLEY

Gibbon: The Formation of Mind and Character

SAMUEL JOHNSON COMMENTS in his *Life of Sprat* that "the history of the Royal Society is now read, not with the wish to know what they were then doing, but how their Transactions are exhibited by Sprat,"[1] and the same kind of remark could be made about Edward Gibbon's great history of Rome. The *Decline and Fall of the Roman Empire* continues to be read, not for the precise dates of various emperors, but for Gibbon's own unique historical perspective; the enduring success of the work seems to rest on the singular and powerful imprint of Gibbon's mind on his materials. The same attitudes that enabled Gibbon to cope with the problems of his own life and shape it as closely as possible to his wishes allowed him to confront the raw materials of centuries of history and mold the mass into a coherent narrative.

In a letter to his stepmother two years before his death, Gibbon summarizes his life: "Although I have been long a spectator of the great World, my unambitious temper has been content with the occupations and rewards of study. . . ."[2] Gibbon's entire life was marked by his preference for watching rather than participating, and no single tendency is more apparent in the man than a certain detachment, a refusal to commit himself to an active role in events. Gibbon's parliamentary career, although problematical in many ways for the student of Gibbon's character, provides striking evidence of this detachment.

During his final years in Lausanne, Gibbon expresses delight in his letters at having escaped from "the tiresome suspense of . . . incomprehensible politics," "the scramble for power and profit at Westminster or St. James's," and "the narrow and dirty circle of English Politics."[3] In his relief, he begins to insinuate that his friends rather than his personal desires led him into politics, and he apparently finally convinced himself that others were entirely responsible for forcing him into a way of life totally uncongenial to him. However, references in earlier letters clearly show that, at least in the beginning, the interest in obtaining a seat in Parliament was Gibbon's own. A letter written in 1773 to his friend John Holroyd expresses his strong desire for one of the seats controlled by John Eliot, a relative of the Gibbon family, and in the next year, after Eliot has offered him the seat and an election had been unexpectedly called, Gibbon writes to his stepmother: "Before his offer I could have contentedly borne my exclusion; but I could not now support the disappointment; and were it to happen, I would instantly and forever leave this Kingdom."[4] This unusually bold and direct expression of feeling, so uncharacteristic of Gibbon, underlines his eagerness to enter Parliament. His enthusiasm continued after the

13

election. He sacrificed both time and effort to obtain as much information as possible about issues before Parliament, and constant political comments, especially on America, in his letters show his full understanding of the importance of current problems.

Gibbon's friends and relatives eagerly awaited his first address to the House of Commons, and his letters to them tell his story. Writing to Holroyd of the first meeting of Parliament, Gibbon disdainfully comments on the maiden speeches of others and reports himself "well pleased that I resisted the premature temptation."[5] Almost two months later, he seems less sure of himself, although still expecting to speak eventually: "If my confidence was equal to my eloquence and my eloquence to my knowledge, perhaps I might make no very intolerable speaker. At all events I fancy I shall try to expose myself."[6] The slight hesitation in the words is underlined by a quotation from Juvenal that Gibbon includes—*Semper ego auditor tantum, numquamne reponam?*—which suggests the anxiety he was beginning to feel. A week later he tells Holroyd defensively that an "inundation" of speakers has left no time for him to speak, but by the end of the month he confesses honestly: "I am still a mute, it is more tremendous than I imagined; the great speakers fill me with despair, the bad ones with terror."[7] As the yearly parliamentary sessions were concluding, a verbal slip in a letter to Holroyd vividly portrays the frustration Gibbon felt. He writes that he has "alas" remained silent "and notwithstanding all my efforts chained down to my place by some invisible unknown invisible [*sic*] power."[8] The inability to sustain an active role in public haunts Gibbon throughout his eight sessions in Parliament. The historian who should have known more than any other man present about the forces that create and destroy empires never spoke to the House of Commons as it confronted the fateful events that led to the loss of one of the British Empire's most important possessions.

Years later, recalling his parliamentary experience in his *Memoirs*, Gibbon explains: "Prudence condemned me to acquiesce in the humble station of a mute" and, without oratorical talents, "timidity was fortified by pride; and even the success of my pen discouraged the trial of my voice."[9] This kind of statement indicates that his lack of oratorical talents and his basically apolitical temperament cannot sufficiently explain his failure to speak out. The "prudence," the psychological impediment which so effectively blocked him from action during his years in Parliament, was again evident at the end of his life in another political context. Despite his intense fear and hatred of the French Revolution, Gibbon, while living in Lausanne, did not wear mourning after the death of the King of France. Just as in Parliament, he was "tempted" to reveal his position, but, as Maria Josepha Holroyd, the daughter of Gibbon's close friend, angrily explains, he did not because "he, as the only Englishman of any note, was afraid of being singular."[10] His detachment remained firm; he had found it better, easier, and above all safer to remain a spectator.

A second significant example of Gibbon's particular detachment, his unwillingness or inability to commit himself personally, can be found in his actions in affairs of the heart. A decision not to marry is hardly unusual, and in a century boasting of such eminent literary bachelors as Pope, Swift, Gray, Cowper, Reynolds, and Walpole, to focus on Gibbon's bachelorhood as singular would obviously be ridiculous. However, once more his *Memoirs* and letters illuminate a certain ambivalence in his attitude. Gibbon enjoyed feminine companionship throughout his life; describing his first visit to Paris in the *Memoirs*, he writes that he has "reserved for the last the most exquisite blessing of life—a female friend who received me every evening with a smile of confidence and joy."[11] At least once, in his youthful romance with Suzanne Curchod in Switzerland, Gibbon's ability to feel deeply enough to make a commitment to a woman was shown. Five years after that affair ended, Gibbon indicated in a letter to his father that he did not think he would marry, and in another letter to his father the following year he cites "my circumstances, my constitution, and a way of thinking grounded upon reasoning and strengthened by experience and habit"[12] as the reasons keeping him from matrimony. Yet Gibbon's decision against marriage was a personal rather than a general one; for example, he assures Sheffield in a fine Johnsonian manner: "I am convinced that if celibacy is exposed to fewer miseries, marriage can alone promise real happiness, since domestic enjoyments are the source of every other good."[13] The possibility of marriage arises occasionally throughout Gibbon's life. In the middle years of the seventeen-seventies, Gibbon several times discusses "candidates" with Mrs. Gibbon in fairly serious terms and shows varying amounts of interest. Toward the end of his life, letters from Lausanne show him again toying with the idea of marriage, basically for the purpose of procuring a companion to alleviate his loneliness. That Gibbon felt the temptation to marry is clear; yet once again he dabbled without committing himself.

Many external considerations undoubtedly influenced Gibbon's choice of a single life. From his parents' marriage he had seen graphically the financial and emotional cost of matrimony. Moreover, finding a suitable wife would have been difficult for such a man; as he notes of one candidate, "she has been talked of for me, but tho' she will have a noble fortune, I must have a wife I can speak to."[14] Though the romance with Suzanne Curchod had revealed to him the feelings of which he was capable, there is no evidence that he ever let himself feel that way again. In fact, much later he writes in the *Memoirs* that he is "rather proud, that [he] was once capable of feeling such a pure and exalted sentiment."[15]

Gibbon was essentially a man of no strong passions. In addition, the problems that the youthful affair created, both with his father and with Suzanne Curchod herself, could well have made a more hardy sort than Gibbon wary of future involvements. Most probably, however, the feelings caused by the experience itself were not nearly so frightening to Gibbon as the hitherto dormant attitudes within himself that the experience activated. His fear surfaces in the *Memoirs* as he writes: "A matrimonial alliance has ever been the object of my terror rather than my wishes."[16] The depth and intensity, and perhaps part of the basis, of Gibbon's "terror" of close association with women is most revealingly shown again in the *Memoirs* when he speaks of his deep and sincere regret that his sister's death destroyed his only chance to experience "the sole species of Platonic love that can be indulged with truth and without danger."[17] Gibbon's close relationship with Georges Deyverdun has also been focused on by some as an explanation for his attitudes toward women and his failure to marry. Whatever the explanation or combination of explanations, love and the emotional and personal commitments it required were too threatening to Gibbon; the only safety lay in the kind of detachment that marked his character. In the end, in love as well as politics, Gibbon was content after an initial period of enthusiasm to confine himself to sporadic and basically half-hearted attempts and to remain a spectator. Characteristically enough, however, he remained a flirt throughout his life.

A survey of Gibbon's life presents several possible explanations for his personal detachment and concomitant reluctance to commit himself. Gibbon's childhood was marked by physical disabilities and by a lack of companionship with either family or friends. A sickly baby who matured only to suffer from a plethora of childhood illnesses, Gibbon received practically no attention from a mother whose energies were drained by constant pregnancies and whose interests were focused almost exclusively on her husband and on his never ending rounds of social activities. The devotions of a maiden aunt provided Gibbon's childhood consolations and companionship. Catherine Porten's position as the sole figure of any importance to him in his youth is emphasized in the *Memoirs* when he writes, on being sent to Lausanne at the age of fifteen, "I had few objects to remember and fewer to regret in the British islands" and adds, on his return from Switzerland at twenty-one, "[Mrs. Porten] was the only person of whom I had cherished a tender remembrance, whose kind embraces I was impatient to seek."[18] Aside from her and his Swiss master Pavilliard, no one took any real interest in Gibbon in his youth. The boy had few with whom to talk seriously except those two, and though, in the *Memoirs*, he lauds the goodness of heart and abilities of mind of both these people, he clearly indicates that they were in no sense his intellectual equals. Pavilliard and Mrs. Porten could show and suggest more than they could actively lead or teach the frail and precocious child entrusted to them by default.

Gibbon's shy and reserved temper was either created or reinforced by his lonely childhood. When he was finally well enough to attend school, the timid boy found himself an outsider, disqualified from sports by his physical disabilities and "reviled and buffeted for the sins of [his] Tory ancestors."[19] Formal schooling was constantly interrupted by his continuing illnesses. Under such conditions Gibbon's reaction seems natural enough: "Instead of repining at my long and frequent confinement to the chamber or the couch, I secretly rejoiced in those infirmities which delivered me from the exercises of school and the society of my equals."[20] He describes "the Dynasties of Egypt and Syria" as "my top and cricket-ball"; small wonder that in the *Memoirs* he protests against "the trite and lavish praise of the happiness of our boyish years" and asserts that "according to a just computation we should begin to reckon our life from the age of puberty."[21]

Gibbon's father was understandably perplexed over what to do with such a child. However, his capriciously irresponsible decision to deal with the situation by packing his son off to Oxford only aggravated the damage already done. At Magdalen College, Gibbon remained behind and on the outskirts. Younger than most of the students, odd in appearance and habits, he was still separated from his fellows, and, typically enough for a child reared with only adults for company, he preferred his tutor's companionship to that of his fellow students. The lack of supervision of Oxford students again left the lonely boy with little effective guidance. His removal from Oxford to Lausanne as a result of his father's outrage at his conversion to Roman Catholicism forced on Gibbon yet another experience of isolation, initially almost complete, because of the foreign language and manners.

The pattern of isolation continued when Gibbon finally returned home. More cosmopolitan because of his exposure to Continental culture and his assumption of French manners, he confronted a native land which seemed alien and provincial to him. At his father's house in the country at Buriton, he kept to himself as much as possible. In a typical account in his journal of one visit there, he lists his only entertainments as himself, his books, and family conversations, adding "but to me these were great resources."[22] A family servant corrects the picture by noting that

Gibbon not only ignored the people of his own age in the neighborhood, but did not "even afford his father or mother much of his company; his beloved books riveted his attention, and to books he sacrificed all the amusements of youth."[23] Months spent in London improved his lonely existence only a little. His father had been living in the country for many years, and paternal social connections in the city had been almost completely lost. Gibbon tells in the *Memoirs* of his shyness and diffidence in social situations and of his solitary evenings spent over his books while coaches rattled through the streets below, emphasizing, however, that "in each of the twenty-five years of my acquaintance with London (1758–1783) the prospect gradually brightened: and this unfavorable picture most properly belongs to the first period after my return from Switzerland."[24] Yet London life was never entirely satisfactory to him. After his final retirement to Switzerland, during a period when he was suffering from the gout, Gibbon, in a letter to his old friend Holroyd (by then Lord Sheffield), praises his life at Lausanne by comparing it to the one he had led in London:

> Either in health or sickness I find it far more comfortable than your huge metropolis. In London my confinement was sad and solitary: the many forgot my existence when they saw me no more at Brookes's; and the few who sometimes cast a thought or an eye on their friend were detained by business or pleasure, the distance of the way or the hours of the house of commons; and I was proud and happy if I could prevail on Elmsley [the bookseller] to enliven the dullness of the Evening. Here the objects are nearer and more distinct, and I myself am an object of much larger magnitude.[25]

Financial problems increased Gibbon's isolation throughout his life. In his first banishment to Lausanne, when for punishment his father had intentionally limited his support, Gibbon says that his poverty and resulting pride estranged him from the English there: "I soon felt the impossibility of associating with them on equal terms, and after the departure of my first acquaintance I held a cold and civil correspondence with their successors."[26] Under his father's irresponsible control the family fortune and holdings continued to diminish, and from the time that Gibbon was recalled from Lausanne to break the entail, the family faced steadily deteriorating financial prospects. Financial considerations contributed to his isolation from life in London. In the *Memoirs*, Gibbon comments that his annuity was "inadequate to the style of a young Englishman of fashion in the most wealthy Metropolis of Europe," although he hastens to add defensively, "[I was] rich in my indifference or more properly my aversion for the active and costly pleasures of my age and country."[27] The pleasures of young adulthood were thus forfeited along with childhood fun.

His painful and constant scrimping is revealed when he writes after his father's death: "I no longer numbered with the same anxious parsimony my dinners at the club or tavern."[28] Financial problems played a part in the termination of his plans for marrying Suzanne Curchod, and they disrupted his youthful schemes for living in Europe with his friend Deyverdun. For several years before and after his father's death, Gibbon was forced to devote almost all his energies to straightening out the family fortunes, and it was not until the final years of his life that the financial problems inherited from his father were finally settled. Pecuniary concerns ultimately banished Gibbon entirely from England. Forced to leave the expensive life of London for Lausanne so that he could live within his income, Gibbon at last found a place where money no longer limited his participation in society.

Thus, from his early years reserved in temperament, accustomed to living nearly always alone, and limited in financial means, Gibbon grew to maturity as a man set somewhat apart. Even at Lausanne, where throughout his life he felt most comfortable, he remained a foreigner. Ever the outsider, he became accustomed to separation in some way from the life around him, and the psychological adjustments forced on him by circumstances gradually formed ways of thinking and of viewing the world that became habitual. His detachment was reinforced by the experiences that occurred when he occasionally broke out of his usual reserve and committed himself unequivocally to a course of action. The immediate results of Gibbon's early strong personal commitments or attempts to be a part of society were usually disastrous. He wholeheartedly embraced the Catholic faith at Oxford and was immediately exiled to Lausanne for his pains. Trying to participate in the English social life at Lausanne, he gambled, ran up a debt he could not pay, fled to Geneva in order to depart for London to raise money for the debt, and had to be fetched home ignominiously by Pavilliard. Later he committed himself to Suzanne Curchod and found that insurmountable problems were his reward. Although he came to consider (or at least to depict) several of the experiences as blessings in disguise—"Whatsoever have been the fruits of my education, they must be ascribed to the fortunate shipwreck which cast me on the shores of the Leman lake"[29]—they could hardly have encouraged a man like Gibbon to involve himself in further questionable ventures.

Moreover, Gibbon lived for far too long completely under the control of others to become accustomed to making his own decisions and commitments. The capricious commands of an inconsistent father had taught him that prudence and obedience were in most cases, and particularly in the face of parental orders, synonymous. When Gibbon returned from his European travels, his father continued to plan his life for him. At his father's behest he joined the militia, made an abortive attempt at a parliamentary race, and published his *Essai sur l'étude de la littérature*. His father's fiscal mismanagement also ensured that Gibbon would continue to feel paternal influence for twenty years after his parent's death. Gibbon was continually forced to wait for others to act before his own plans could prosper. His cousin Eliot commanded the parliamentary seat that Gibbon wanted, and, after he finally gained the seat, ministers controlled the additional sinecures that he desperately needed for financial stability. After experiencing so many situations that found him unable actively to promote his own welfare, Gibbon cultivated a detachment that allowed him to function as he waited—and waited. He became in some sense accustomed to consider any efforts on his part as fundamentally useless. By the time he was free of his father's domination, he was thirty-three years old and had settled into a passive pattern. Accustomed to being alone and to avoiding commitments, he found it easier and safer to remain an onlooker, a bachelor, a mute in Parliament. Although he struggled valiantly for a time with financial matters, the man accustomed to another's control almost instinctively located in Lord Sheffield a valuable friend who could ease the burden. Soon enough Gibbon was sending unopened letters which he thought contained unpleasant financial news to Sheffield Place for the peer to handle.

Desiring to keep himself safely uncommitted as he adapted himself to a world never entirely friendly, Gibbon fortified his personal detachment by a dependence on the intellectual and by a corresponding emotional independence. He focused on one of the greatest benefits of his lonely position and set his priorities accordingly: "Freedom is the first wish of our heart; freedom is the first blessing of our nature: and, unless we bind ourselves with the voluntary chains of interest or passion, we advance in freedom as we advance in years."[30] He fiercely protected his autonomy. When Lord Sheffield was called away and Gibbon remained with Lady Sheffield, he described himself as "almost in the servile state of a married man"[31]—an attitude that, incidentally, goes far to explain his failure to marry.

To protect his personal freedom, Gibbon cultivated emotional independence. J. W. Johnson describes him as "an emotional Houyhnhnm among the Lilliputians and Brobdingnagians," [32] and Gibbon in his *Memoirs* describes a nature distinctly unemotional when he cites his "moderate sensibility" and mentions that his "nerves are not tremblingly alive."[33] With his past experiences, he came finally to distrust emotion and to avoid its complications whenever possible. Even in so minor a matter as theatrical taste, Gibbon's dislike of feeling is apparent: while visiting in Paris he notes, "Two famous actresses then divided the public applause: for my own part I preferred the consummate art of the Clairon, to the intemperate sallies of the Dumesnil which were extolled by her admirers as the genuine voice of nature and passion."[34] Gibbon was not totally without enthusiasm, but in his personality a strong tendency to the intellectual almost immediately succeeded initial emotion. The original impetus for his conversion was probably an emotional need to assert himself and to end his isolation; however, his subsequent wide reading in controversialists and his own theological reasoning were what finally determined his decision to turn Catholic. His experience with the Roman Empire is similar. The euphoria which he records in his *Memoirs* as dominating his first days in the city of Rome undoubtedly was a sort of basic inspiration for his great work, but the *Decline and Fall* really emerged from his extensive reading both before and after the journey.

At the age of twenty-five, Gibbon assesses his character in his journal as "proud, violent, and disagreeable in society,"[35] and his problems in dealing with people were both a cause and a result of his carefully cultivated emotional independence. A lonely childhood deprived him of much of the knowledge of other men that early experience normally provides; he formed assumptions about character from books. For example, in the *Memoirs* he writes that on his journey to meet his stepmother, his mind dwelt on the hateful Latin epithets for a stepmother, on a particular line from Virgil ending *injusta noverca*, and on the *odium novercale* "proverbial in the language of antiquity."[36] Another serious disadvantage for Gibbon lay in the character of his father, that irascible, charming, and monumentally irresponsible and inconstant man. Paternal authority, of course, placed Gibbon in a weak position; he had no allies to assist him against his father's whims, and at an early age he undoubtedly decided that the most effective way to cope with them was to avoid direct confrontations. His predilection for indirect action and his highly developed instinct for the political, apparent in many of his letters, probably evolved from stratagems for dealing with his father. Prudence perhaps formed so prominent a part of Gibbon's character because of his reaction to his father's model of irrational impetuosity. This caution became a habit with Gibbon in dealing with others, and he carefully preserved a safe distance. To this distance that he fostered can be attributed some of the lack of sympathy and shortsighted coldness which occasionally surfaces in Gibbon's character. He complains that French refugees in Lausanne after the Revolution "are entitled to our pity; they may claim our esteem; but they cannot, in the present state of their mind and fortune, much contribute to our amusement."[37] Yet the same distanced view of men, which produced at times such a lack of sympathy and prohibited intimate relationships, also resulted in Gibbon's talent for friendship. To Lord Sheffield and his family, to Deyverdun, to his stepmother, and to the de Severys, Gibbon proved a constantly energetic and faithful friend. Within the more limited demands that friendship made, he could retain his independence and his basic detachment while enjoying beneficial and stimulating relationships.

Because he preserved a distance from people, Gibbon grew to care very much about social externals that might compensate for, and disguise, his physical and psychological limitations. Short, very corpulent and hardly handsome after his youth, Gibbon overdressed elaborately. He was careful to calculate the effects of his every move in company; an early journal entry notes that "an idle fear of appearing too particular" had prevented his asking the name of an attractive woman.[38] The six drafts of the autobiography he was writing when he died show his relentless striving to interpret facts and events in a way that would present the best possible face to the world. Despite his careful assertions that he was being completely honest and candid in his account, anyone who approaches the *Memoirs* expecting to find that "truth, naked unblushing truth" that Gibbon terms "the sole recommendation of this personal narrative"[39] is far more naïve than the author of the work—who might well smile even as he internally registered intense satisfaction at such a response on the part of the reader. Significantly, Gibbon almost immediately abandons his remarks on the importance of truth in autobiography, for the statement appears only in the first draft.

How Gibbon molds history in his favor in the *Memoirs* can be seen in a chronological comparison of several versions of his reasons for publishing his youthful *Essai sur l'étude de la littérature*. He first states:

Two years elapsed in silence; but in the spring of 1761 I yielded to the authority of a parent, and complied, like a pious son, with the wish of my own heart.

In the next version he carefully justifies any personal impulses to publish that he might have felt and then emphatically denies any such motivation:

If I had yielded to the impulse of youthful vanity, if I had given my Manuscript to the World, because I was tired of keeping it in my closet, the venial sin might be honestly confessed, and would be easily pardoned. But I can affirm, in truth and conscience, that it was forced from my reluctant hands by the advice and authority of my father.

He adds two more authorities and their credentials to give weight in the third draft:

My *Essai sur l'étude de la Littérature* still reposed in my desk, and I might long have balanced between the fears and wishes of virgin modesty, had not my father's pressing exhortation been enforced by the advice of Dr. Maty, the author of the *Journal Britannique*, and of Mr. Mallet, whose name still lives among the English poets.

In the last draft, Gibbon seems to think that the names are enough without the accomplishments:

In the midst of this military life, I published my *Essai sur l'étude de la Littérature*, which was extorted from me by my father's authority, and the advice of Dr. Maty and Mr. Mallett, after it had slept two or three years in my desk.[40]

Gibbon's final draft ceases before this incident, and one wonders what the definitive account would have been—not to mention what the truth actually was. Could his ingeniously artistic invention and selectivity have found an even more flattering light to cast upon the publishing?

Unsure of himself in his relationships with people, Gibbon loved external marks of social acceptance. He was proud of his memberships in many of London's clubs and of his seat in Parliament. Unwilling and unable to rely on his personality for a place in society, he paid great attention to distinctions of rank. In the *Memoirs* he emphasized that his patrimony was "always sufficient to support the rank of a Gentleman, and to satisfy the desires of a philosopher,"[41] and the order of priorities is revealing. This kind of remark underlines the psychological validity of Lord Chesterfield's astute reminder to his son that the great politician Richelieu always preferred to be thought of as a poet. References to rank are ubiquitous throughout the *Memoirs*; Gibbon delights both in his own rank and in the positions of those around him. Gibbon's happiness in Switzerland was unquestionably due partly to his clear preeminence in that secluded society. His dislike of equal interchanges and his desire to operate from a detached position can be seen in his attitude toward social conversations. He wrote to Sheffield, and undoubtedly made clear to others, that he always sought conversation for amusement rather than information.[42] Even thus fortified against excessive expectations of his conversation from listeners, Gibbon felt safer in solitary domination through lecturing. One is not surprised to find that there is no record of any conversations between Gibbon and Johnson at meetings of The Club.

Gibbon's preoccupation with appearance, assumed to ease social intercourse, ironically enough caused many of his social problems. Because he felt secure in his work, the narrative self in the *Decline and Fall* is presented easily, naturally, and very pleasantly. In social situations, however, Gibbon too often overcompensated and thus entirely missed his desired effect. Viewed from the distance that he always retained between himself and others, the careful attention to appearance seemed vanity, the painstakingly formed poses and manners verged on pomposity, and the detachment hiding reserved shyness could be mistaken for pride. The drive toward emotional independence led Gibbon to cover natural inadequacies with unnaturally acquired faults.

For Gibbon, a dependence on the intellectual filled the void in his life which was created by his emotional independence. The compensation for a solitary life was the pleasure of his own intellect: "I might say with truth that I was never less alone than when by myself."[43] If feelings misled him, knowledge provided unceasing joy without personally disturbing difficulties. Gibbon found the safety he required in his devotion to the life of the mind, the one commitment that he could make completely. Under the most adverse conditions—military duty, the bustle of London life, financial struggles—he persevered in his studies. The intensity of his love for books was to him so palpable a sensation that he constantly discussed it in metaphors of taste: the dinner bell "dragged me from my intellectual feast"; "after this long fast [during his militia service], the longest which I have ever known, I once more tasted at Dover the pleasures of reading and thinking, and the hungry appetite with which I opened a volume of Tully's philosophical works is still present to my memory"; book sales in London "afforded a plentiful feast, at which my literary hunger was provoked and gratified."[44] His was the kind of intellectual passion intense enough to lead to the dedication always required for producing a great book.

Gibbon's mind focused on the concrete and the earthbound. He disliked philosophy and metaphysics, had no ear for music, and espoused fairly pedestrian views of sculpture and painting. His love for the little fact, the concrete detail, surfaces constantly in his personal writings. From his love for, and reliance on, fact came Gibbon's practicality, his hard dedication to the real and the actual. When French armies threatened Switzerland, Gibbon's response was philosophical and political indignation, backed by his provision for himself of "two strong horses and a hundred Louis in gold."[45] Gibbon's focus on the factual combined with his lack of certain emotional sympathies sometimes produced an honesty as direct as it was cold. In letters he anticipates the death of his stepmother (for whom he had a real fondness) and the resulting financial benefits for himself with a calm detachment slightly unnerving to the reader. The *Memoirs* presents his composed reaction to his father's death as a typical and justifiable filial response. No emotional considerations disturb the serenely relentless dedication to uncomfortable but irrefutable fact.

From his trust in fact also came Gibbon's tremendous intellectual self-sufficiency. Lonely in his life, he also worked alone. In his first years at Lausanne, a course on the law of Nature and Nations was taught in the academy by a Mr. Vicat, a man of some reputation. Gibbon heard about the lectures, "but instead of attending his public or private course, I preferred, in my closet, the lessons of his masters and my own reason."[46] In writing the *Decline and Fall* he was intimidated neither by the achievements of other historians nor by the mountains of material he had to confront. Successfully managing the difficult dual roles of author and critic, he early abandoned the practice of reading his manuscript to friends for their comments.

The basis of his intellectual self-confidence is shown in the *Memoirs* when Gibbon discusses his attitudes while awaiting publication of the first volume of the history: "During this awful interval I was neither elated by the ambition of fame; nor depressed by the apprehension of contempt. My diligence and accuracy were attested by my own conscience."[47] Though his calmness is probably overstated here for effect, his confidence in facts is not. By the end of his history, he could proudly note that his first rough manuscript for the last volumes had been sent to the printer with no changes whatsoever, and he could proclaim confidently that "the faults and the merits are exclusively my own."[48] To a certain extent he was most comfortable with himself where his work was concerned; fortified by his trust in fact and his dedication to factual accuracy, he felt completely safe in defining himself in terms of his work. It is hardly surprising that Gibbon rests his apologia or justification of himself in the *Memoirs* mainly on the intellectual powers on which he had placed a lifelong dependence.

Gibbon's practical bent led him to order and control his life very strictly. The man who for so many years had been under another's control enjoyed exercising fierce control in very limited areas. Maria Josepha Holroyd describes him as "clockwork"[49] because of his inflexible punctuality; he made a daily allotment of time for every task and expected his servants to adhere to the same kind of rigid schedule. (Surprisingly, they are reported to have adored him.) In good or bad health, he took medicine on the first day of every month.[50] Both in the *Memoirs* and in journals he gives obsessively careful accounts of his time and activities, in a balanced manner strangely reminiscent of a bank statement. His tendency to discuss the immaterial in financial terms can be seen in the letters, where he speaks several times of the "market" for wives and notes that, because many Parisians summered in the country, "many valuable acquisitions have escaped me."[51] But Gibbon's most successful method for controlling his life was to accept the reality of a given situation gracefully, lower his expectations if necessary, and make the best of circumstances. In a letter to his stepmother, he mentions as a gift of nature his "propensity to view and to enjoy every object in the most favorable light," a tendency which "has been exercised on the most unfavorable materials."[52] This natural tendency was undoubtedly fortified by intellectual reflection and probably by philosophic reading of classical literature. Calm phrases of acceptance dot the letters: "Human felicity is seldom without alloy"; "a state of perfect happiness is not to [be] found here below"; "human life is perpetually checkered with good and evil."[53] For Gibbon, these were not empty platitudes; he lived his philosophy, retaining final control over his life by continual flexibility.

Gibbon's whole life was composed of constant adjustments of his expectations; it is little wonder that he settled for "the solid comforts of life, a convenient well-furnished house, a domestic table, half a dozen chosen servants, my own carriage, and all those decent luxuries whose value is the more sensibly felt the longer they are enjoyed."[54] This apparent materialism is simply another reflection of Gibbon's acquiescence in the possible, not a final verdict on ultimate values. "Agreeable" is one of the adjectives most frequently employed in the letters, and for Gibbon, the man of limited enthusiasm and of hopes often thwarted, the agreeable was a sufficient goal toward which to aspire. How well he succeeded in making the best of life by controlling, not events, but his reactions to events can be seen in the comments of biographers. Leslie Stephen finds a "singular felicity" in Gibbon's life, while Lytton Strachey writes: "With Gibbon there was never any struggle: everything came naturally to him. . . ."[55] Such attitudes, fairly widespread among commentators, are an indication of Gibbon's ultimate success in measuring, limiting, and controlling his own impressions and those of others. Whatever pain was involved remains hidden.

Thus the detachment which shaped Gibbon's view was derived from his love of freedom, his emotional independence, and his dependence on the intellectual. In the end the detachment resulted in a self-distance which made it difficult for him to face the personal, as the *Memoirs* show. David Jordan notes: "But it is instructive that the man who experienced no difficulty in writing six volumes on Roman history, the man who could turn out a volume of history in less than three years, should have been unable to finish a short book about himself."[56] Unquestionably, part of his problem was the purely intellectual one of finding the proper scale and proportion for his autobiography. Nevertheless, Gibbon's drafts show him often reluctant to examine his own life directly. The first time he tries to write of his militia experiences he begins: "From the general idea of a militia, I shall descend to the militia of England in the war before the last; to the state of the Regiment in which I served, and to the influence of that service on my personal situation and character."[57] Throughout the various drafts of the *Memoirs*, the reader sees Gibbon's veering into the general and the abstract, and again and again having to force himself back to the personal and the concrete.

Gibbon's genius derives from confinement to the possible and the factual, a recognition of, and capitalization on, his own limits. The strength marshaled from personal limitation involved sacrifices; "the original soil has been highly improved by labor and manure: but it may be questioned whether some flowers of fancy, some grateful errors, have not been eradicated with the weeds of prejudice."[58] In all of Gibbon's writings, few expressions of regret for these lost "flowers of fancy" occur, and it is impossible to know how much pain he suffered in achieving his ends. The limitations of the man and consequently of the mind are painfully obvious. Yet had Gibbon not consciously and unconsciously limited his life by his massively complete insistence on freedom and on emotional independence and a compensatory dependence on the intellectual, he could never have produced a work of the magnitude of the *Decline and Fall*.

REFERENCES

Note: Most of the references to the *Memoirs* are to Georges A. Bonnard's definitive edition, but J. M. Murray's edition has been used for certain quotations from sections of the autobiographical drafts not included in Bonnard's text or notes.

[1] Samuel Johnson, *Life of Sprat*, in *Lives of the English Poets* (New York, 1925), I, p. 304.

[2] Edward Gibbon, *The Letters of Edward Gibbon*, ed. J. E. Norton (London, 1956), III, p. 266. Hereafter cited as *Letters*.

[3] *Letters*, II, p. 401; III, p. 25; III, p. 12.

[4] *Letters*, II, p. 36.

[5] *Ibid.*, p. 45.

[6] *Ibid.*, p. 57.

[7] *Ibid.*, pp. 59, 61.

[8] *Ibid.*, p. 64.

[9] Edward Gibbon, *Memoirs of My Life*, ed. Georges A. Bonnard (London, 1966), p. 156. Hereafter cited as *Memoirs*.

[10] J. H. Adeane, ed., *The Girlhood of Maria Josepha Holroyd* (London, 1896), p. 212.

[11] Edward Gibbon, *The Autobiographies of Edward Gibbon*, ed, John Murray (London, 1896), p. 263. Hereafter cited as Murray.

[12] *Letters*, I, 187.

[13] *Ibid.*, pp. 213-14.

[14] Edward Gibbon, *Gibbon's Journal to January 28th, 1763: My Journal, I, II, & III and Ephemerides*, ed. D. M. Low (New York, 1929), p. 83. Hereafter cited as *Journal*.

[15] *Memoirs*, p. 84.

[16] *Ibid.*, p. 140.

[17] *Ibid.*, p. 24.

[18] *Ibid.*, p. 210.

[19] *Ibid.*, p. 33.

[20] *Ibid.*, p. 41.

[21] *Ibid.*, pp. 43, 27.

[22] *Journal*, p. 44.

[23] Meredith Read, *Historic Studies in Vaud, Berne, and Savoy* (London, 1897), II, p. 372.

[24] *Memoirs*, p. 94.

[25] *Letters*, III. p. 33.

[26] *Memoirs*, p. 71.

[27] *Ibid.*, p. 90.

[28] *Ibid.*, p. 151.

[29] *Ibid.*, p. 209.

[30] *Ibid.*, p. 45.

[31] *Letters*, II, p. 283.

[32] J. W. Johnson, *The Formation of English Neo-Classical Thought* (Princeton, 1967), p. 197.

[33] *Memoirs*, pp. 186, 188.

[34] *Ibid.*, p. 127.

[35] *Journal*, p. 69.

[36] *Memoirs*, pp. 91-92.

[37] *Ibid.*, p. 185.

[38] *Journal*, p. 34.

[39] *Memoirs*, p. 1.

[40] Murray, pp. 169, 254-55, 402, 300.

[41] *Memoirs*, p. 154.

[42] *Letters*, III, p. 185.

[43] *Memoirs*, pp. 95-96.

[44] *Ibid.*, pp. 42, 117, 248.

[45] *Letters*, III, p. 282.

[46] *Memoirs*, p. 78.

[47]*Ibid.*, p. 157.

[48]*Ibid.*, p. 180.

[49]Adeane, p. 239.

[50]Gavin de Beer, *Gibbon and His World* (London, 1968), p. 96.

[51]*Letters.*, II, pp. 54, 57, 161.

[52]*Letters*, III, p. 386.

[53]*Letters*, III, pp. 297, 311; II, p. 373.

[54]*Memoirs*, p. 154.

[55]Leslie Stephen, *Studies of a Biographer* (New York, 1898), p. 157; Lytton Strachey, *Portraits in Miniature and Other Essays* (New York, 1931), p. 156.

[56]David Jordan, *Gibbon and His Roman Empire* (Urbana, Illinois, 1971), p. 7.

[57]*Memoirs*, p. 107.

[58]*Ibid.*, p. 186.

G. W. BOWERSOCK

Gibbon on Civil War and Rebellion in the Decline of the Roman Empire

NEAR THE BEGINNING OF THE TWENTY-SIXTH CHAPTER of the *Decline and Fall*, Gibbon alludes to "the disastrous period of the fall of the Roman empire, which may justly be dated from the reign of Valens." While he thereby inaugurates the fall some four centuries after the time of Caesar Augustus, his own narration of the decline opens, as everyone knows, with the dissolution of the supposed Antonine peace. In the winter of 1790–91, Gibbon realized that he had made a terrible mistake: he had misapprehended the causes of decline and in so doing had started his great work at the wrong point. But it was too late. Gibbon's papers for a seventh volume which was to contain revisions of the *Decline and Fall* preserve the following eloquent words: "Should I not have deduced the decline of the Empire from the Civil Wars, that ensued after the fall of Nero or even from the tyranny which succeeded the reign of Augustus? Alas! I should: but of what avail is this tardy knowledge? Where error is irretrievable, repentance is useless."[1] It is a strange irony that Gibbon's admired Roman predecessor, Tacitus, "the first of historians who applied the science of philosophy to the study of facts,"[2] had similarly recognized, though not when it was too late, that his initial work on imperial Rome had to be supplemented by another on the preceding reigns. By late 1790, Gibbon had seen two major uprisings, one in America and one in France, and we may imagine that he was moved enough to attach more importance than before to civil war and social tumult. The readjustment was difficult for Gibbon, who by 1793 had abandoned all hope for the French rebels, now become in his judgment "the new barbarians."[3] But they rose from within and did not invade from without.

If one reads Gibbon's chapters on the decline of Rome with an eye to his observations on civil war and uprisings, it becomes easy to see why this great and scrupulous historian came to castigate his own work so unambiguously. Gibbon's vast reading and philosophic reflection had served only to persuade him that disturbances in society were but an ugly disfigurement—a stain on the social fabric or a wound in the body politic. They were essentially external; they were disagreeable but susceptible of cleansing or healing. It is not impossible that Gibbon's sharp mind had been dulled by the potency of his own metaphors.

The stain and the wound occur with almost equal frequency and in contexts which rarely represent the historian's most profound thought. For example, in chapter 3 we find one of Gibbon's most breathtaking inaccuracies (to which we shall return): "Excepting only this short, though violent eruption of military licence [A.D. 69], the two centuries from Augustus to Commodus passed away unstained with civil

27

blood, and undisturbed by revolutions."[4] In chapter 4 we are told that because of the love of power "almost every page of history has been stained with civil blood."[5] The old Gordian in chapter 7 begs his supporters to let him die "without staining his feeble age with civil blood."[6] And in chapter 26 Gibbon declares that the cause of a successful aspirant to power "is frequently stained by the guilt of conspiracy or civil war."[7]

For Gibbon, the Roman Empire was "that great body,"[8] like the *immensum imperii corpus* of Galba's speech in Tacitus's *Histories*.[9] It could be wounded, but the wounds could be healed. Augustus "hoped that the wounds of civil discord would be completely healed."[10] The Emperor Tacitus in the third century "studied to heal the wounds which imperial pride, civil discord, and military violence had inflicted on the constitution."[11] In the last years of Constantius, barbarians moved into Gaul "before the wounds of civil discord could be healed."[12] In one important passage, concerning the establishment of Septimius Severus as emperor, Gibbon acknowledged that appearances could be deceptive: "Although the wounds of civil war appeared completely healed,"[13] they were not. A "mortal poison" was left in the vitals of the constitution,"[14] and with this remark the "slow and secret poison," which had been introduced "into the vitals of the empire" well before Severus, received a booster shot.[15] It may be that Gibbon himself was not altogether free from the fault he discovered in Ammianus: "It is not easy to distinguish his facts from his metaphors."[16]

Disruptive, disfiguring, even poisonous on occasion, civil strife and social upheaval in the period of Rome's decline rarely seemed to Gibbon much more than a superficial occurrence due to a widespread love of power. A consideration of the relevant occurrences, as they are chronicled by Gibbon, makes his attitude embarrassingly clear. To take a particularly striking example, from A.D. 132 to 135 the Jews, under the leadership of Bar Kochba, rose in a mighty rebellion against Roman authority. The uprising was fierce and protracted, ultimately requiring the presence of the Emperor Hadrian himself. By its end, Jerusalem was transformed into the Roman colony of Aelia Capitolina. No historian would deny the significance of these events not only in the annals of Rome but also of European civilization down to the present. In the opening pages of his *Decline and Fall*, Gibbon appears to have forgotten completely about this four-year war: "If we except a few slight hostilities that served to exercise the legions of the frontier, the reigns of Hadrian and Antoninus Pius offer the fair prospect of universal peace."[17] But Judaea was not on the frontier, nor were the hostilities slight. Gibbon certainly knew about the rebellion of Bar Kochba, and when in the course of his work his subject drifted close to the history of the Jews he was able to write in chapter 15: "But at length, under the reign of Hadrian, the desperate fanaticism of the Jews filled up the measure of their calamities."[18] By chapter 16, Gibbon refers to "that furious war which was terminated only by the ruin of Jerusalem," and he labels it "that memorable rebellion."[19] Yet he himself had not remembered it when he was writing the text of chapter 1.

Gibbon was perfectly capable of distinguishing popular uprisings and revolts from "those civil wars which are artificially supported for the benefit of a few factious and designing leaders."[20] On the whole, he neither liked nor trusted the people. He attributed the peace and prosperity of Europe in 1776 to a general recognition of "the superior prerogative of birth," which he declared to be "the plainest and least invidious of all distinctions among mankind."[21] He had no patience with the tensions and disturbances of the highly complex society of ancient Alexandria: "The most trifling occasion, a transient scarcity of flesh or lentils, the neglect of an accustomed salutation, a mistake of precedency in the public baths, or even a religious dispute, were at any time sufficient to kindle a sedition among that vast multitude, whose resentments were furious and implacable."[22] Gibbon's outlook coalesced easily and naturally with that of his model and predecessor, Tacitus, who scorned the *plebs sordida et circo ac theatris sueta*.[23] For Tacitus, the mob abused the body of Vitellius with the same perversity (*pravitas*) with which they had fawned upon him as emperor;[24] the enthusiasms of the Roman people were short-lived and ill-omened (*breves et infaustos populi Romani amores*).[25] Compare Gibbon: "The resolutions of the multitude generally depend upon a moment; and the caprice of passion might equally determine the seditious legion to lay down their arms at the emperor's feet, or to plunge them into his breast."[26]

Gibbon's opinion of the movements of multitudes caused him to dismiss one of the more significant events in the social history of the later Roman Empire. The peasant revolt of the so-called Bagaudae in Gaul began under the Tetrarchy and had long-lasting influence. Gibbon introduces the subject by making a facile and false comparison of the Bagaudae insurrection with "those which in the fourteenth century successively afflicted both France and England";[27] he then observes drily: "They asserted the natural rights of men, but they asserted those rights with the most savage cruelty."[28] When they yielded to the armies of Rome, "the strength of union and discipline obtained an easy victory over a licentious and divided multitude."[29] It is impossible to tell from reading Gibbon that in the peasant revolt under the Tetrarchy lay the origins of an independent Brittany ruled by the Bagaudae in the fifth century. When Gibbon himself finally reaches, at the end of chapter 35,[30] the fortunes of Brittany, or Armorica as it was called, he shows no sign of recalling that "the confederations of the Bagaudae" who created the "disorderly independence" in the fifth century were the descendants of the licentious multitude he has already written about. It is simply not true to say of the revolt of Armorica, "the Imperial ministers pursued with proscriptive laws, and ineffectual arms, the rebels whom they had made." It was the revolt of America, not Armorica, which Gibbon had in mind as he concluded chapter 35. As we know, for example, from his celebrated "General Observations on the Fall of the Roman Empire in the West," Gibbon relished making parallels and predictions; but, owing to some fundamental attitudes, he was not always at his most perceptive in doing so. Although contemporary affairs interested and moved him, he responded to them as the man of letters he was, insulated by his library. Gibbon's seat in Parliament exposed him directly to the excitement of current history and yet never altered his bookish temperament.

If Gibbon was contemptuous of popular rebellions and upheavals, he viewed with equal contempt the efforts of Roman factional leaders to raise the standard of revolt and to curry favor with the people or with the legions. It is astonishing that he could describe the two centuries from Augustus to Commodus as "unstained with civil blood, and undisturbed by revolutions"—with the sole exception of the "military licence" of A.D. 69.[31] Gibbon goes on to admit that he is aware of "three inconsiderable rebellions," which he enumerates in a footnote. Yet the rebellion of Camillus Scribonianus was a sinister adumbration of the coming proclamations of claimants to the throne as they served at the head of legions in the provinces. The rebellion of Antonius Saturninus under Domitian signaled the alliance of Roman usurpers with

primitive tribes on the frontiers. And the rebellion of Avidius Cassius in Syria in
A.D. 175 marked the first attempt of a provincial Roman to exploit the allegiance of
his home territory in making a desperate claim to the purple. How could Gibbon miss
all this? For him the uprisings are inconsiderable for one reason only: they failed.
They "were all suppressed in a few months, and without even the hazard of a battle."

The view of almost uninterrupted peace from Augustus to Commodus depends
not only on the depreciation of disturbances Gibbon mentions but on the omission
of others. We have already noted the absence of the Jewish revolt in Gibbon's account
of Hadrian; he likewise omits, in his survey of the first century A.D., the Jewish
revolt which broke out in A.D. 66 and ended with the Fall of Masada. We hear
nothing of the revolt of Tacfarinas in Africa under Tiberius, nothing of the great
popular support for the pretenders who claimed to be Nero after Nero was dead,
nothing of the uprising of the Jewish diaspora at the end of Trajan's reign (now better
documented through archaeology but amply attested in sources which Gibbon knew).
Gibbon's deep persuasion that the early centuries of the Roman Empire were a time
of relatively unviolated peace can perhaps best be traced to the author he revered,
Tacitus. Gibbon's language is like his—*immota quippe aut modice lacessita pax*.[32] In
composing the *Annals*, covering A.D. 14-68, Tacitus could say this with a certain
aptness, especially as a reinforcement of his view that the price of peace was
monarchy: Augustus gave *iura quis pace et principe uteremur; acriora ex eo vincla*.[33] While
valuing monarchy more highly, Gibbon fully imbibed this lesson and these words.
Yet not even Tacitus himself would have described the years from 68 to 96 as *modice
lacessita pax*, as the opening chapters of his *Histories* make very plain.

Gibbon took Tacitus as the model of a philosophic historian, blending *érudit* and
philosophe before the opposition had ever been thought of. We are in no doubt as to
what a philosophic historian should, in Gibbon's view, be able to accomplish,
namely, to discover secret causes and connections. When the soldiery submitted to
Severus Alexander, Gibbon was moved to remark, "Perhaps, if the singular transac-
tion had been investigated by the penetration of a philosopher, we should discover the
secret causes which on that occasion authorized the boldness of the prince and
commanded the obedience of the troops."[34] Later, in reviewing ancient assessments
of the character of Theodosius, Gibbon wrote: "There are few observers who possess
a clear and comprehensive view of the revolutions of society; and who are capable of
discovering the nice and secret springs of action which impel, in the same uniform
direction, the blind and capricious passions of a multitude of individuals."[35] This
conception of the philosophic role of a historian was firmly rooted in Gibbon and
appears clearly articulated in his early *Essai sur l'étude de la littérature*, published in
1761 but written in 1758-59. There the young Gibbon dilates upon *l'esprit philosophique*
and designates Tacitus as its embodiment: "Je ne connois que Tacite qui ait rempli
mon idée de cet historien philosophe."[36] Only the philosopher can perceive amid the
chaotic mass of historical facts "ceux qui dominent dans le système générale, qui y
sont liés intimément, et qui en ont fait mouvoir les ressorts."[37] Montesquieu is singled
out, not surprisingly, for particular praise. Gibbon's conviction that there were
always secret springs of action in human history naturally inclined him to consider
events so public and obvious as civil war or rebellion to be purely external,
superficial, and ultimately insignificant. These were to be numbered among the
innumerable facts "qui ne prouvent rien au-delà de leur propre existence."[38] In
alluding to Constantius's struggle with Magnentius, Gibbon opens a sentence, "As

long as the civil war suspended the fate of the Roman world. . . ."[39] The war merely interrupted the fulfillment of a fate set in motion by hidden causes; it is presented as external to them.

In writing the *Decline and Fall*, Gibbon's search for the hidden springs of action not only diverted his attention from tumultuous events but also led him to postulate a secret cause for the whole decline of Rome. Gibbon, as often, turned to metaphor: "This long peace, and the uniform government of the Romans, introduced a slow and secret poison into the vitals of the empire."[40] Although the visible decline did not begin before Commodus, Gibbon is obliged to explain what happened then in terms of the poison of peace. By the end of the fourth century a kindred poison is transfused from one organism to another: "The effeminate luxury which infected the manners of courts and cities had instilled a secret and destructive poison into the camps of the legions."[41] And we can recall that, between the long peace and the effeminacy of the Theodosian court, Septimius Severus had added a "mortal poison" from the civil wars of 193—not, however, a secret poison. It is remarkable enough that Gibbon should have considered the disturbances of 193 poisonous at all in view of his dismissive attitude toward the comparable vexations of 69. But Gibbon was by no means consistent in his vast work, and he had a special reason to give more weight to 193. With the death of Commodus at the end of the preceding year and the eventual emergence of Severus at the end of the civil strife of· 193, the visible decline of Rome, in Gibbonian terms, was launched. The era of public felicity was over, and Gibbon saw in Severus "the principal author of the decline of the Roman empire."[42] Gibbon had forced himself into this remarkable opinion.

By the time of the "General Observations" in chapter 38, Gibbon's notions of Roman decline had changed noticeably in favor of an interpretation redolent of Montesquieu: "The decline of Rome was the natural and inevitable effect of immoderate greatness." There is no word of the secret poisons of peace and effeminacy, no harking back to the impact of Septimius Severus. Barbarians and Christianity had come to engage Gibbon's attention. The secret cause he had tried to find eluded him. His problem consisted in the continuing search for a single secret cause. Had he looked only for various secret springs of action, his interpretations might have cohered better. It is unclear why Gibbon's concept of the philosophic spirit kept driving him to find a secret poison, a single hidden cause to explain the whole story of Rome's decline. But one can hazard a guess. It may once again have been Gibbon's great evil genius, Tacitus.

In chapter 4 of the first book of his *Histories*, Tacitus declared that at the death of Nero the secret of the Empire was revealed: *Evulgato imperii arcano posse principem alibi quam Romae fieri*. Gibbon, misjudging the influence of the legionary troops which made it possible for emperors to be raised up in the provinces, tried to go beyond Tacitus's identification of the *arcanum imperii*; but, just as with the *modice lacessita pax*, Tacitus's formulation seemed to have been embedded in his thought. There had to be, for the historian of Rome's decline, an *arcanum imperii*. Refusing to see in civil war and revolt anything secret, Gibbon had to look elsewhere. As he did so and as his reflections naturally found expression in metaphor, the *arcanum imperii* of Tacitus became transformed into a *venenum adfusum*, afflicting the *immensum imperii corpus*.[43]

Naturally it would not have been necessary for Gibbon to look to Tacitus for the concept of a secret cause. The thought of the eighteenth century was full of it, as is evident not least in Gibbon's early *Essai sur l'étude de la littérature*, where he discusses the importance—which he later forgot—of searching for many hidden causes rather than one.[44] While Tacitus himself had a powerful influence in shaping post-Renaissance theories of causation, it is more significant that Gibbon worked closely from the original ancient sources.[45] His renewed study of Tacitus for the *Decline and Fall* was more than sufficient to put him in search of a secret cause for Rome's decline. Gibbon's intellectual heritage was imperceptibly metamorphosed into the attitude of his classical master.

It may be, too, that somewhere in Gibbon's extraordinary mind there echoed the *tam grande secretum* proclaimed by the eloquent fourth-century pagan, Symmachus. But Gibbon's treatment of Symmachus's pleading discourages such a notion: "Even scepticism is made to supply an apology for superstition. The great and incomprehensible *secret* of the universe eludes the enquiry of man."[46] That was obviously not the kind of secret a philosophic historian labored to discover. The *arcanum imperii* was.

It has sometimes been said that between the discussion of *l'esprit philosophique* in the *Essai* and the *Decline and Fall* Gibbon passed through a phase, connected with his Italian journey, of almost pure antiquarianism. Yet the journal does not bear this out. It reveals a voracious scholar, reading and digesting every learned treatise he could lay his hands on, but doing so with an admirable sense of the ultimate objectives of research: "C'est un travail sec and ingrat, mais quand on construit un édifice il faut en creuser les fondements. L'on est obligé de faire le rôle de maçon aussi bien que celui d'architecte."[47] Of the epigraphical collections of Muratori, Reinesius, and Gruter, Gibbon wrote: "Elles me fourniront surtout beaucoup pour les moeurs, les usages, des curieuses anecdotes, et toute cette histoire intéressante qui est cachée dans l'histoire ordinaire."[48] These reflections, written in Florence in the summer of 1764, display an arresting, even startling, sense of the historian's task. The concept of hidden history (*qui est cachée*) betrays the philosophic writer still mindful of his duty, but the attention to social behavior and customs illustrates a maturity absent from the *Essai*. At the same time Gibbon was busy with work on the geography and economy of Roman Italy as the direct result of an intensive study of Muratori's dissertation on an inscription, recently uncovered at Veleia, which provided precious details about the alimentation system of Trajan. Gibbon even fancied that he could improve on Muratori, whom he much admired. The inscription provides "des lumières très utiles sur l'histoire, le géographie, et l'économie de ce siècle."[49]

It is evident that the philosophic historian was at work on Roman history before he even reached Rome in the year 1764. His plan had been to compose *Recueils géographiques sur l'Italie*, but that original plan was gradually altered during the summer of 1764 as Gibbon was studying his inscriptions and observing the art of Italy. On the thirtieth of August he wrote in his journal about texts which would be useful "pour mes Desseins sur la géographie de l'Italie qui subsistent toujours quoique le plan en soit un peu changé."[50] It was on the same day that he penned his lines on the revelations of society concealed *dans l'histoire ordinaire*. By the time Gibbon reached Rome, the thought of a larger history of Rome and its empire may well have been in his head. If we must reject as romantic fiction Gibbon's later account of what started to his mind amid the ruins of the Capitol on October 15, 1764, it is nevertheless by no means impossible that the *Decline and Fall* had its origins in Gibbon's labors and ruminations on the Italian journey.

Gibbon's approach to the subject at that time was, as we can readily judge from the diary, substantially different from what was to appear in 1776. One finds, to be sure, the same scrupulous attention to ancient sources, the same taste for geography, the same alert wit, the authentic Gibbonian tone. But the deep interest in society and economic life is unparalleled in the *Decline and Fall*. Gibbon's painstaking work on the inscription of Veleia finds no resonance in his later masterpiece, where there is not even a passing allusion to Trajan's alimentation scheme. In the *Decline and Fall*, there is little sign of the sifting of *histoire ordinaire* to recover the secret history of society. The gulf between the would-be historian of 1764 and the author of the *Decline and Fall* is nowhere so apparent as in the following lines written at Turin on May 3, 1764: "une cour est à la fois pour moi un objet de curiosité et de dégoût. La servilité des courtisans me révolte, et je vois avec horreur la magnificence des palais qui sont cimentés du sang des peuples."[51] With these remarks may be compared Gibbon's reaction to a bust of Nero at Florence: "Dois-je le dire et le dire ici? Néron ne m'a jamais révolté autant que Tibère, Caligula, ou Domitien. Il avoit beaucoup de vices, mais il n'étoit pas sans vertus."[52] Gibbon had studied too much ancient history not to have known the high esteem in which people and soldiers held the Emperor Nero. In 1764, Gibbon would not have ignored completely the three pretenders to Nero's name and their supporters. In 1764, Gibbon's attitude to an imperial court, to the first-century Roman emperors, to social history in general was manifestly not that of 1776. The Bagaudae might have held more interest for a historian who viewed with horror the magnificence of palaces "qui sont cimentés du sang des peuples."

What caused the change? Gibbon's personal circumstances may properly be invoked, particularly his social position in London and his seat in Parliament. But again there is Tacitus. To write his *Decline and Fall*, Gibbon steeped himself in the works of a writer with whom he must have felt increasingly sympathetic and whom he had judged since the days of the *Essai* to be the very model of a philosophic historian: "The revolution of ages may bring round the same calamities; but ages may revolve without producing a Tacitus to describe them."[53] Under the spell of the old Roman, Gibbon moved away from the sympathies and interests of the Italian journey. The Roman court and its vivid personalities, on which Tacitus laid such brilliant emphasis, enliven many of the most polished pages of Gibbon. His scorn of the multitude resembles that of Tacitus and underlies his refusal, which is not Tacitean, to allow any special importance to the upheavals of society. Revolts and civil wars play an often colorful but essentially superficial role. When they occur in Gibbon's narrative, fate is suspended, history stained, the body politic wounded; but for him they have almost nothing to do with the explanation of decline.

Yet, sometime after the outbreak of the French Revolution—and conceivably under its influence—Gibbon was moved to write that he had been wrong to trace the decline of Rome from the collapse of the Antonines. He had attempted to write the history of the Roman Empire from the end of that era of felicity at which Tacitus had left off.[54] But instead, by his own admission, he should have "deduced the decline of the Empire" either from the civil wars of A.D. 69 or perhaps even from "the tyranny which succeeded the reign of Augustus" in A.D. 14. This constitutes an entirely new assessment of the first century A.D. and attaches a significance to the civil wars and "inconsiderable" rebellions altogether alien to Gibbon's earlier outlook. Yet the confession of irretrievable error has a curious and chilling aspect. It is not the bold declaration of rethinking which it seems at first to be. In minimizing the civil war after Nero's death, Gibbon had parted company with his Roman mentor in search of a more profound *arcanum*. When, in the winter of 1790-91, he acknowledged that he ought to have begun at one of those two first-century dates, he did no less than make the ultimate submission to Tacitus; for Tacitus had actually begun one major work, the *Histories*, with the civil wars of 69, and the other, the *Annals*, with "the tyranny which succeeded the reign of Augustus." In the shadow of the American and French revolutions, the old Roman claimed his disciple.

REFERENCES

Note: References to the *Decline and Fall* (*DF*) are given by chapter number and page in the seven-volume edition of J. B. Bury (New York, 1914).

[1] *The English Essays of Edward Gibbon*, ed. P. B. Craddock (Oxford, 1972), p. 338. On the date of these notes, see Craddock, p. 211.

[2] *DF*, chap. 9, p. 230.

[3] *The Letters of Edward Gibbon*, ed. J. E. Norton (London, 1956), III, p. 321. This extreme judgment comes at the end of the crescendo of despair which follows Gibbon's initially sympathetic reaction to the revolutionaries. Already in December, 1789, he wrote, "How many years must elapse before France can recover any vigour, or recover her station among the powers of Europe? (*Letters*, III, p. 184).

[4] *DF*, chap. 3, p. 80.

[5] *DF*, chap. 4, p. 93.

[6] *DF*, chap. 7, p. 189.

[7] *DF*, chap. 26, p. 127.

[8] *DF*, chap. 15, p. 1.

[9] Tacitus, *Hist.* 1.16. Neither Gibbon in modern times nor Tacitus in ancient was alone in preferring this imagery for the state. See my remark in note 43 below.

[10] *DF*, chap. 3, p. 68.

[11] *DF*, chap. 12, p. 346.

[12] *DF*, chap. 19, p. 271.

[13] *DF*, chap. 5, p. 133.

[14] *Ibid.*

[15] *DF*, chap. 2, p. 62.

[16] *DF*, chap. 26, p. 72, n. 1.

[17] *DF*, chap. 1, p. 9. In the footnote he wrote for this text Gibbon somewhat lamely reminded himself and his reader of the omission of Bar Kochba's revolt.

[18] *DF*, chap. 15, p. 10.

[19] *DF*, chap. 16, p. 89.

[20] *DF*, chap. 7, p. 194.

[21] *Ibid.*, p. 182.

[22] *DF*, chap. 10, p. 301.

[23] Tacitus, *Hist.* 1.4.

[24] Tacitus, *Hist.* 3.85.

[25] Tacitus, *Ann.* 2.41.

[26] *DF*, chap. 6, p. 170.

[27] *DF*, chap. 13, p. 383.

[28] *Ibid.*, p. 384.

[29] *Ibid.*

[30] *DF*, chap. 35, p. 507.

[31] *DF*, chap. 3, p. 80.

[32] Tacitus, *Ann.* 4.32.

[33] Tacitus, *Ann.* 3.28.

[34] *DF*, chap. 6, p. 170.

[35] *DF*, chap. 27, p. 196.

[36] *Essai*, chap. 52.

[37] *Essai*, chap. 49.

[38] *Ibid.*

[39] *DF*, chap. 19, p. 265.

[40] *DF*, chap. 2, p. 62.

[41] *DF*, chap. 27, p. 196.

[42] *DF*, chap. 5, p. 137.

[43] Cf., for the phraseology *venenum adfusum* (in a different context), Tacitus, *Ann.* 1.10. I am not, of course, suggesting that Gibbon owed the idea to Tacitus, but rather that a writer imbued with Tacitean language would choose this terminology from the diction of decline.

[44]*Essai*, chap. 49, "ce n'est qu'en rassemblant qu'on peut juger."

[45]I will return to this subject, with reference to Julian, in my contribution to the *Actes du Colloque Gibbon à Lausanne*, June, 1976.

[46]*DF*, chap. 28, p. 202.

[47]*Gibbon's Journey from Geneva to Rome: His Journal from 20 April to 2 October 1764*, ed. Georges A. Bonnard (Edinburgh, 1961), p. 129. I have, to some extent, normalized Gibbon's French.

[48]*Ibid.*, p. 221.

[49]*Ibid.*, p. 122. The Veleia inscription is no. 6675 in H. Dessau's *Inscriptiones Latinae Selectae*.

[50]*Gibbon's Journey*, p. 221. It has sometimes been wrongly assumed that Gibbon's description of Italy was completed before he visited the country, since the work was started as a preparation for the visit. But it is clear from the passage in the *Journal* as well as from a letter written in Florence on June 20, 1764 (*Letters* [see note 3 above], p. 181) that he continued to work on the project, begun in Lausanne, during his Italian tour.

[51]*Gibbon's Journey*, p. 18.

[52]*Ibid.*, p. 168.

[53]*DF*, chap. 36, p. 49, n. 119.

[54]Observe Tacitus on his own time at *Agricola* 3 (*felicitatem temporum*) and *Hist.* 1.1 (*rara temporum felicitate*). The wording of Gibbon's celebrated judgment of the Antonine age is remarkably parallel to Robertson's reference to the century and a half after Theodosius: "If a man were called to fix upon the period in the history of the world during which the condition of the human race was most calamitous and afflicted, he would without hesitation name that which elapsed from the death of Theodosius the Great to the establishment of the Lombards in Italy" (*History of the Emperor Charles V* [1769], I, p. 10). I am inclined to think this parallel more significant for style than substance. Cf. D. Jordan, *Gibbon and His Roman Empire* (Urbana, Illinois, 1971), p. 216, n. 8.

PETER BROWN

Gibbon's Views on Culture and Society in the Fifth and Sixth Centuries

MINE IS AN UNGRATEFUL TASK. For, to examine Gibbon's ideas on culture and society in the fifth and sixth centuries after Christ, I must begin the *Decline and Fall* at a point where Horace Walpole had already begun to chafe:

> Then having both the Eastern and Western Empires in his hands at once, and nobody but *imbéciles* and their eunuchs at the head, one is confused with two subjects, that are quite alike, though quite distinct; and in the midst of this distraction enters a deluge of Alans, Huns, Goths, Ostrogoths and Visigoths, who with the same features and characters are to be described in different terms, without any substantial variety, and he is to bring you acquainted with them when you wish them all at the bottom of the Red Sea.[1]

Yet, to follow Gibbon through the centuries after he had brought the Roman monarchy to an end in Western Europe is to appreciate in him far more than a majestic narrator who can span the centuries. For we can seize in those chapters a perspective that made Gibbon's work the peak of a century of scholarship conducted in the belief that the study of the declining Roman Empire was also the study of the origins of modern Europe. Exclusive preoccupation by classical scholars with the initial sections of the *Decline and Fall* seriously restricts the range and the relevance to present-day scholarship of Gibbon's concerns. Gibbon was very much the heir of Pietro Giannone. As a young student in Naples, Giannone had already realized that the "immense and boring" work that lay before him on the legal writings of the later Roman Empire, as he set to work in 1702 on studies that would culminate in his *Istoria civile del Regno di Napoli* of 1723,

> . . . non l'avea come fine, ma l'indirizzava come efficaci mezzi per intendere le origini ed i cangiamenti dell' Impero romano e come, poi ruinao, fossero surti tanti nuovi domini, tante nuove leggi, nuovi costumi e nuovi regni e repubbliche in Europa.[2]

It is not only the range of Gibbon's work and the preoccupations that lie behind such a range that have to concern us: Gibbon's criteria of what is relevant to the study of late antiquity and the early Middle Ages are also laid bare in his treatment of this period. These would repay attention. The modern specialist who is invited to offer an opinion on the merits and possible relevance to modern studies of the *Decline and Fall* tends to register, with varying degrees of self-satisfaction, those points on which our information and, to an even greater extent, our historical sensibility have gone beyond Gibbon. Yet, such a treatment obtains only partial results and is liable to obscure the extent of Gibbon's relevance to modern research. We are, indeed, better informed than Gibbon; and, at first sight, our sympathies appear to be wider. We are more capable of that whole-hearted empathy for late-antique men which, in our generation at least, has been held to be the touchstone of historical skill. But in laying bare Gibbon's limitations, we often fail to allow the exercise to provoke us to scrutinize our own. Put bluntly: we may differ from Gibbon largely in the degree of our unclarity on what is relevant to the study of late antiquity.

If Gibbon seems, at first reading, to be different from ourselves, it is because he embarked upon his enterprise with a deeply premeditated criterion of relevance. The iron discipline which enabled him to carry through so great a work was based upon this criterion. It was built up by innumerable acts of renunciation. Volumes could be filled with what Gibbon was in a position to put into the *Decline and Fall* and yet decided to leave out: Basnage "might have added from the canons of the Spanish councils and the laws of the Visigoths many curious circumstances, essential to his subject, though foreign to mine."[3] We first meet him in Italy, quietly absorbing the artistic and archaeological evidence which modern scholars now use for the cultural history of late antiquity. Only very seldom is it the stereotype of the eighteenth-century gentleman who stands before a statue, as in the Villa Ludovisi: "He stabs himself with spirit but a good deal too high, . . . she sinks down with a most beautiful faintness. I think the story is taken a moment too late."[4]

But in the galleries of Turin and Florence, it is an eye as alert as that of any modern scholar which lights up: an *ossuarium*, "c'est bien là qu'on prend une idée de la *domus exilis Plutonis*";[5] conclusions for social history are drawn from a collection of *missiones honestae*;[6] two inscriptions detrimental to the reputation of a mother-in-law;[7] syncretism on a medal of Sarapis—"Je pense que les Egyptiens (qui commençoient à raffiner sur le paganisme pour le fortifier contre les attaques des chrétiens) . . .";[8] a coin of the Palaeologi—"La gravure ne ressemble qu'à la première et la plus ancienne sculpture. Tel est le cercle des arts";[9] the Velleia Tablet is diligently copied out:

> C'est un travail sec et ingrat, mais quand on construit un Édifice il faut en creuser les fondements. L'on est obligé de faire le rôle de maçon aussi bien que celui d'Architecte. J'espère pouvoir tirer quelque chose de cette espèce de recensement.[10]

Gibbon, therefore, possessed a visual sensitivity to precisely those material objects the interpretation of which by archaeologists and art historians has been regarded as a unique achievement of modern late-Roman scholarship. Yet little or nothing of his awareness of that particular aspect of late antique culture survives into the pages of the *Decline and Fall*. Thus, much of what we value as central to our access to the cultural and social life of late antiquity was appreciated by Gibbon, and yet it was regarded as irrelevant to the theme of the *Decline and Fall*. It may well be that it is in those aspects which make Gibbon appear to be most alien to the sympathies of modern scholars that he has remained most relevant: for behind his dismissal of much of the evidence and many of the phenomena that have come to interest us, there lies a theory of the relation between the ideas and society of a large empire which still merits our careful attention.

In the first place, even to cut Gibbon's history into periods and areas may be unwise. Few writers illustrate so magnificently the ideal of the universal historian. Gibbon was convinced that societies widely scattered in space and time were comparable and that their rhythms of growth and decay and the patterns of the exercise of power within them followed a roughly similar course. When he deals with the crisis of the Roman Empire in the third century, he writes that "though he [the historian] ought never to place his conjectures in the rank of facts, yet the knowledge of human nature, and of the sure operation of its fierce and unrestrained passions, might, on some occasions, supply the want of historical materials."[11] This meant more for Gibbon than the imaginative reconstruction of certain incidents in the past: "the knowledge of human nature" demanded a knowledge of societies from the whole breadth of the Eurasian landmass. Such knowledge nourished and attuned Gibbon's awareness of the decline and fall of the Roman Empire. He was always prepared to see in the Roman Empire a paradigm of the universal dilemma of empires. Gibbon, "the historian of the Roman empire," frequently emerges as something more. He is a sociologist of empire; and we must be prepared to meet him and learn from him on that high level.

Gibbon is at his best when he is analyzing the accumulation and manifestation of despotic power over an extended geographical area. Readers of the *Decline and Fall* will relish the brilliant dissection of the Augustan constitution. The contrast between the canny veiling of absolutism by Augustus and the equally premeditated ostentation of Diocletian marks a turning point in the narrative and recurs like a musical "subject" at widely differing stages of the decline of the Empire. Yet Gibbon appears to have come to this problem from a period and an area far removed from the Roman world. A comparison of the Achaemenid Empire of the sixth century B.C. with the rise of Tamerlane in the fourteenth century A.D. enabled him to perceive a similar pattern in the rise to power of Cyrus. Getting behind the flat picture of Cyrus presented in the *Cyropaedia* of Xenophon, Gibbon is able to conjure up a three-dimensional picture of the creation of an absolute monarchy. The resultant portrait of Cyrus in the *Essai sur la monarchie des Mèdes*[12] is a triumph of binocular vision. It was the fruit of an intimate knowledge of two millennia of empire-building in the Near East. We are dealing, therefore, with a historian who treads with certainty and clear eyes on any ground where any empire has risen and declined in the Eurasian landmass.

To take a small example from the period under discussion: Gibbon was impatient of a purely diplomatic and military narrative of Byzantine-Sassanian relations in the late sixth century:

> Lamenting the barren superfluity of materials, I have studied to compress the narrative of these uninteresting transactions; but the just Nushirvan is still applauded as the model of oriental kings, and the ambition of his grandson prepared the revolution of the East.[13]

We know that we are due for yet another majestic unfolding of the decline of the empire:

> By the fatal vicissitude of human affairs, the same scenes were renewed at Ctesiphon, which had been exhibited in Rome after the death of Marcus Aurelius.[14]

Just as the changing position of the monarch in the delicate weave of Roman society provided Gibbon with the leitmotif for his account of the third-century crisis of the Roman Empire, so a spasm of despotism tore apart the society of late-sixth-century Iran:

. . . the intermediate powers between the throne and the people were abolished; and the childish vanity of Hormouz, who affected the daily use of the tiara, was fond of declaring that he alone would be the judge as well as the master of his kingdom.[15]

A great Empire, subject to the same tensions, Iran is viewed with an impartial curiosity, unclouded by any romantic sense of the exotic. We meet the legendary vizir Buzurg Mihr:

Buzurg Mihr may be considered, in his character and station, as the Seneca of the East; but his virtues, and perhaps his faults, are less known than those of the Roman, who appears to have been much more loquacious.[16]

In one of his implacable square brackets, Professor Bury adds: "Buzurg Mihr is a favorite figure in rhetorical literature, but is unknown to strict history. Cp. Nöldeke, *Tabari* p. 251"—a saddening victory of nineteenth-century criticism and Europocentrism.

Faced with the phenomenon of such effortless universality, we must attempt to analyze not so much Gibbon's account of the culture and society of the Roman Empire and barbarian Western Europe in the fifth and sixth centuries as that firm constellation of insights on culture and society in general that enabled Gibbon to write about it as he did.

It would be best to start with culture. Here, we come up against a sternly maintained barrier of relevance. A vast amount of what men have shown themselves capable of thinking and dreaming, and hence of what survives in their writings, has no relevance whatsoever. For such thoughts and dreams find no outlet in the society around them. Large tracts of Christian dogmatic history are irrelevant to the historian:

The oriental philosophy of the Gnostics, the dark abyss of predestination and grace, and the strange transformations of the Eucharist from the sign to the substance of Christ's body, I have purposely abandoned to the curiosity of speculative divines.[17]

The reason Gibbon offers for so strict a delimitation is misleadingly trenchant: "I have reviewed, with diligence and pleasure, the objects of ecclesiastical history, by which the decline and fall of the Roman empire were materially affected . . . ."[18]

What lay at the root of his approach is a firm distinction between the "real" and the "unreal"—between what was concrete and useful and what he would often call "folly." At a given moment in the development of a society, an "unreal" force—a body of religious ideas or a train of metaphysical speculation—might become active. At other times, "folly" was effectively excluded or kept within narrow bounds. For Gibbon, the study of society and culture was very largely the study of the meeting point of a "real" texture of society with the forces of "folly" in its various manifestations—human vanity, passion, and superstition. Some topics belonged too much to the world of the "unreal" to admit a meeting point. His tone can be *cassant* with such intruders: "The Church of St. Autonomous (whom I have not the honour to know)";[19] the monk Antiochus, "whose one hundred and twenty homilies are still extant, if what no one reads may be said to be extant."[20] History viewed by Gibbon is punctuated by exuberant outbursts of unreality. What angers him, for instance, about the Middle Ages is less that it was an Age of Ignorance, than that it became an Age of Folly. The Arabs had "bewildered themselves very ingeniously in the maze of metaphysics"; but they had, at least, "improved the more useful sciences of physic, astronomy and the mathematics."[21] In the twelfth century, however, "with the Liberty of Europe its genius awoke; but the first efforts of its growing strength were consumed in vain and fruitless pursuits. Ignorance was succeeded by error."[22] "Universities arose in every part of Europe, and thousands of students employed their lives upon these grave follies. The love songs of the Troubadours, or Provençal bards, were follies of a more pleasing nature. . . ."[23] Gibbon's insistence on what was relevant to his own history of society and culture, therefore, was the product of a sense of the unbounded capacity of human beings for irrelevance.[24]

Behind such an attitude lay a century of philosophical skepticism and empiricism; these had already been allied, in the case of Pietro Giannone and the historians of the Scots Enlightenment (whose relevance to Gibbon has been lucidly demonstrated by Professor Giarrizzo), with a direct concern for the study of the past in terms of the problems raised by the impact of the "unreal" on the "real." As a result of this attitude, a more modern dichotomy of social and cultural forces in a society is alien to Gibbon. For Gibbon transcends this dichotomy. "Ideas" and "society" do not exist over against each other, still less are they to be studied separately—as has happened far too often in the course of recent late-Roman scholarship—for the simple reason that most ideas do not exist: they are fine-spun cobwebs brushing against the solid tissue of society. Yet, once these ideas harden into "prejudices" they take on weight and interest for Gibbon.

It is, therefore, the society and its behavior that give flesh and blood to the wraiths of fantasy and metaphysics. This is as true of religion as of any other aspect of society. In the mid-fourth century, Roman society could still make the gods live:

> Our familiar knowledge of their names and characters, their forms and attributes, *seems* to bestow on these airy beings a real and substantial existence. . . . In the age of Julian, every circumstance contributed to prolong and fortify the illusion: the magnificent temples of Greece and Asia; the works of those artists which had expressed, in painting and in sculptures, the divine conceptions of the poet; the pomp of festivals and sacrifices; the successful art of divination; the popular traditions of oracles and prodigies; and the ancient practise of two thousand years.[25]

Gibbon was the last man to dismiss "airy beings," once belief in them was woven into society in so solid and intricate a manner. Merciless on Christian metaphysical folly, he is more tolerant than we might think of Christian ceremonial:

> Experience had shewn him [Pope Gregory the Great] the efficacy of these solemn and pompous rites, to soothe the distress, to confirm the faith, to mitigate the fierceness, and to dispel the dark enthusiasm, of the vulgar. . . .[26]

For what was visible and concrete, even if it was superstitious, could be controlled and modified. It was the "folly" that welled up from the isolated intellect that both disgusted and frightened him. The anxieties of the first pagan observers of Christianity were his own:

> . . . they supposed that any popular mode of faith and worship which presumed to disclaim the assistance of the senses would, in proportion as it receded from superstition, find itself incapable of restraining the wanderings of the fancy and the vision of fanaticism. The careless glance which men of wit and learning condescended to cast on the Christian served only to confirm their hasty opinion, and to persuade them that the

principle, which they might have revered of the Divine Unity, was defaced by the wild enthusiasm, and annihilated by the airy speculations of the new sectaries.[27]

"Inside every fat man," Cyril Connolly once remarked, "there is a thin man crying to be let out." In the young Gibbon, the thin man cried ever louder. It was possible to credit him with the following exchange with his beloved Aunt Catherine: "Once, it was said (but Gibbon declined to confirm the story), he proposed to kill her. 'You see,' he explained, 'you are perfectly good now, so if you die you will go to heaven. If you live you may become wicked and go to hell.' 'But where do you expect to go if you kill me?' 'That,' he replied, 'my godfather will answer for. I have not been confirmed . . . ,' "[28] nor "had the elastic spring been totally broken by the weight of the Atmosphere of Oxford. The blind activity of idleness encouraged me to advance without armour into the dangerous maze of controversy."[29] He arrived in Lausanne: "a thin little figure with a large head, disputing and urging, with the greatest ability, all the best arguments that had ever been used in favour of popery." The slow reweaving of the web of reality around the angular young Gibbon by Pavilliard, a man "rational because he was moderate," is a microcosm of the concern of Gibbon's lifework. Seldom has a historian watched with such close attention in the distant past the tragic working out of forces which had once strained so dangerously on the leash within himself. His history of the society and culture of late antiquity is a study of how the hard bones of speculative "folly" came to push through the wasted flesh of the Empire.

More is involved in this, however, than Gibbon's attitude toward Christian controversy and Christian otherworldliness. For these were merely paradigms of the more general tension between reality and "folly" in society as a whole. To be effective, in Gibbon's view, institutions and legal systems had to be firmly swaddled in an integument of prejudices and values. This integument kept them in touch with reality and exposed them to the modifying influence of human contact. Cut it, and the enduring human propensity for "folly"—for vanity, for cruelty, for fanaticism—will be released. Thus, religious and institutional experiences can be congruent: in both a religious and a political system, decline and breakdown take the form of a kind of "folly," whether this is speculative theology or tyrannical vanity, bursting out of the net of controls in which it had been held. The imperial court, once it had burst its way out of the delicate restraints of the Augustan settlement, came to exist in as great an isolation from the modifying influences of humane society as did any Christian hermit.

Though the tearing of the web of reality may often be brutal and dramatic, as with the emergence of the monks, this tearing is preceded by a long and insidious process. This process might be seen as a "leakage of reality": what is natural and spontaneous insensibly passes to the artificial, and the artificial in turn gives way to "folly." The process is at no time irreversible: it admits no sudden, catastrophic breaks; and a frequent reweaving of the broken web of restraints on "folly" occurs, if often in this period, at a more primitive level. Individuals and institutions are allowed by Gibbon to tremble for generations on a knife edge between artifice and unreality. Hence a sense of tension and movement runs through the *Decline and Fall*.

Let us examine aspects of Gibbon's attitude to the irruption of "folly" in the fifth- and sixth-century Roman world in terms of this "leakage of reality." First, let us consider the religious evolution of the period. In this, Gibbon is the heir of a long tradition. We still share his problem. The rise of the Christian church is the story of the rise to great power in this world of an institution whose basis was a claim to be interested only in the other world. By Gibbon's time, however, the problem had changed. What to later medieval and Reformation thinkers had appeared as a religious and moral incongruity had become a problem strictly of religious and cultural history. For not only could the Christian church be said to have abandoned its otherworldly vocation, it had actually risen to greater and greater power by inflating belief in the other world. With Pietro Giannone, for instance, we already have a man wrestling with the problem of the religious psychology of the late-antique world. How had the mercifully pedestrian attitudes of the ancient Hebrews to the afterlife, joined by the reverential simplicity of the authors of the Gospels, blossomed into that rank growth of fantasy on which the Christian church had built its power in society?[30]

It is from this standpoint that we can best appreciate Gibbon's contribution. Where Giannone had looked with fascinated horror at the growth of the plant, Gibbon, not in any way surprised to find such a weed in the human mind, looked to the remissness of the gardeners. His thought on the role of religion in society draws its nuances from a deep pessimism. Superstition and the vanity of metaphysicians being an ineradicable part of the human condition, what mattered was the system of social constraints that ensured that these did not get out of hand and that might yet, *per impossibile*, channel them into useful functions. Hence his attitude to the paganism of the Roman world. He was untouched by romantic regret for the pagan past. Paganism was a system of belief mercifully deprived, by its incoherence, of the power to build up those strong imaginative and speculative structures beneath whose pressure the tissue of society might yield: it was a world of "faint and imperfect impressions."[31]

In any case, these impressions would have met their match in the system of social restraints that characterized the social and religious establishment of the Roman Empire. Writers whose works keep modern experts in *Religionsgeschichte* busy for a lifetime on the second century after Christ are dismissed in one curt footnote: "I do not pretend to assert that, in this irreligious age, the natural terrors of superstition, dreams, omens, apparitions, &c. had lost their efficacy."[32] They existed, but they did not impinge.

Religious phenomena which the modern historian might regard in isolation as symptoms of irreversible changes in mentality are held by Gibbon in a network of checks and balances. If anything, the irrational rises to the surface less rapidly in Gibbon's narrative than in many modern treatments of the religious world of late antiquity. In his highly differentiated account of the Emperor Julian, for instance, Gibbon gives us something far more satisfying than the usual balance sheet of "superstitious" and "public-spirited": his portrait has the fascination of allowing us to see the tissue of reality giving and springing back under pressure from a world of dreams and visions, and so allows us to appreciate all the more fully how much of it had already given way among Julian's contemporaries:

> These sleeping or waking visions, the ordinary effects of abstinence and fasting, would almost degrade the Emperor to the level of an Egyptian monk. But the useless lives of Anthony or Pachomius were consumed in these vain occupations. Julian could break from the dream of superstition to arm himself for battle.[33]

Hence the horror of the ascetic movement for Gibbon and the consequent change of tone when he described the Christological controversies and those Christian groupings that were increasingly presided over by monks in the fifth and sixth centuries. For, with the appearance of the monks, the restrained irony with which Gibbon traces the rise of the Christian church breaks down. The irony had reflected a tension in Gibbon's own thought. The rise of an institution within an institution still held out the remote promise of weaving, if from the coarse thread of Christian belief, yet another web of social control. Gibbon's attitude to the church in the early centuries has retained its fertility because it was developed under a perpetual question mark. Despite a heavy indictment, the Christian bishops were let out on parole:

> Yet party-spirit, however pernicious or absurd, is a principle of union as well as of dissension. The bishops, from eighteen hundred pulpits, inculcated the duty of passive obedience to a lawful and orthodox sovereign; their frequent assemblies, and perpetual correspondence, maintained the communion of distant churches: and the benevolent temper of the gospel was strengthened, though confined, by the spiritual alliance of the Catholics.[34]

With the monks, however, Gibbon is confronted by men who had finally destroyed the knife-edge balance between superstition and the social constraints which the Christian church might have woven from its own institutions. The monk ceased to be a man because he had burst free from the merciful integument of society.

After all, superstition is not the only disruptive and potentially brutalizing component of the human mind. Sexuality, if unmellowed by society, can have similar effects. The Emperor Heliogabalus was not only debauched: he was debauched in a particular way. "A rational voluptuary," however, "adheres with invariable respect to the temperate dictates of nature and improves the gratification of the senses by social intercourse, enduring commitments and the soft coloring of taste and imagination."[35] The monk was a Heliogabalus of the spirit: "The lives of the primitive monks were consumed in penance and solitude, undisturbed by the various occupations which fill the time, and exercise the faculties, of reasonable, active, and social beings."[36] A culture of monks was a culture of non-men: "glorious was the *man* (I abuse that name). . . ."[37] It is the sharpest phrase in the *Decline and Fall*.

The rise of the ascetic movement, therefore, represents a nadir of depletion. The tissues that had held even the Christian bishops in a web still woven with the firm ironies of social existence had snapped. The point is driven home by a magisterial juxtaposition. The same chapter in which Gibbon describes the unraveling of the web of civilized life at the hands of the monks ends with a warm appreciation of how the Christian Gothic Bishop Ulfilas and the later Catholic bishops of the West patiently took up again those tattered shreds to weave, albeit unconsciously, yet another web of civilized living around the barbarians of the north: "while they studied the divine truth, their minds were insensibly enlarged by the distant view of history, of nature, of the arts, and of society."[38] Seldom does Gibbon's irony stretch to such a courageous assertion of the silent craftsmanship of civilization.

This brings us to the social dimensions of the "leakage of reality" in the Roman world. For if the monks are depleted men, it is not merely because of their ideas; it is because they are paradigms of the change that had insensibly made the Roman Empire a depleted society. We return, by this roundabout route, to Gibbon the sociologist of empire. For the "leakage of reality" that had loosened the web of social restraint around the individual fantasy was mirrored in Rome, as in every great empire, by the dissolution of those tissues that had once held the Empire together as a balanced commonwealth.

Gibbon transferred the new awareness of the texture of society, exemplified in the work of Montesquieu, from the study of small and organic units, to a gigantic empire. Furthermore, he treated the Roman Empire as only one in a wide typology of empires. In so doing, he gained the sense of scale and analytic skill that enabled him to write the *Decline and Fall*. Early on, Gibbon appears to have realized the quantitative differences that the sheer size of the Empire would impose on the interpretative tools available to him. The vast geographical erudition of Gibbon is in itself evidence for his sense of the problem of scale in empires. It is an alertness that he carried with him on his journeys: the style of a cameo, he observed, betrays a fifty-year time-lag in the spread of taste to the frontiers of the Empire.[39] When he arrived in Rome, it is far from certain what actually passed through his mind as he viewed its ruins. I suspect that it was not only a sad appreciation of the beauties of classical architecture. Our "philosophic historian" was already thinking of the problems of empire made manifest in building. As he wrote of the ruins of Persepolis: these could only have been erected at the apogee of the Achaemenid Empire, not earlier, as Caylus had suggested:

> . . . je ne sais s'il a assez réfléchi sur la combinaison de la puissance despotique avec la grandeur, les trésors, et la résolution de triompher sur tous les obstacles. J'ai encore devant les yeux les restes augustes de l'amphithéâtre de Vespasien, des bains de Tibère, de la colonne de Trajane.[40]

Yet it is precisely in his sociology of empire that Gibbon's subtlety tends to elude us. For in his "General Observations on the Fall of the Empire in the West" he dangerously simplified his own perspective:

> The rise of a city, which swelled into an Empire, may deserve, as a singular prodigy, the reflection of a philosophic mind. But the decline of Rome was the natural and inevitable effect of immoderate greatness. Prosperity ripened the principle of decay; the causes of destruction multiplied with the extent of conquest; and, as soon as time or accident had removed the artificial supports, the stupendous fabric yielded to the pressure of its own weight. The story of its ruin is simple and obvious; and, instead of inquiring why the Roman empire was destroyed, we should rather be surprised that it had subsisted so long.[41]

This statement has been used by modern historians as carte blanche for reducing the problem of the decline of the Roman Empire to manageable proportions. It has enabled them to direct attention to those developments in late-Roman society that can be documented with reassuring precision—the increasing weight of taxation and the rapid expansion, in the fourth century, of the governmental and ecclesiastical superstructure of the Empire. Yet, I suspect that Gibbon's attitude has been subtly simplified by such appeals to his authority. The remarks of the "General Observations" derive their deceptive simplicity from having been framed in terms of a comparison between the Roman Empire and the Europe of Gibbon's own day. The emphasis on the "immoderate greatness" of the Roman Empire is made in terms of qualities that this Empire did not have in common with the more realistically based states of modern Europe. But just because one trait is highlighted by comparison with other societies, it does not follow that this is a privileged cause of the weakness of that society. In his narrative, the size of the Empire alone does not seem to have satisfied

Gibbon as an explanation, and the growth, in the late third and fourth centuries, of the relative size of its superstructure—which happened as a comparatively late development in terms of the problems which, in Gibbon's view, had faced the Empire since the reign of Augustus—seems to have satisfied him even less.

For what concerned Gibbon was not the size of the Empire as such, but its cohesion. The relative weight of its superstructure concerned him less than the extent to which this superstructure threatened to detach itself from the web of social relations whose tenacity and differentiation, in the age of Augustus and even of the Antonines, had distinguished the Roman Empire from all other despotisms. With this we return to the leitmotif of the "leakage of reality." The declining Roman Empire is marked by a slow and largely irreversible process of the weakening of the tissue of prejudices and interests which, in Gibbon's view, had enabled the already unlimited power of Augustus to be exercised decorously and, as a result, both effectively and in a civilized manner.

This is as much a cultural as an institutional problem. For the "prejudices" which made for cohesion were expressed and carried by cultural, quite as much as by institutional, means. Our starting point is Gibbon's view of the small society. In such a society, artifice, the thin end of the wedge of "folly," has only limited freedom of play: strong "impressions" fit closely to manageable institutions. We find this best expressed in a remarkable note by Gibbon on the religious beliefs of the Germanic tribes at the time of their settlement in the Mediterranean world, written as a comment on Mallet's *History of Denmark*. The German conquerors of the Roman provinces did not, in his opinion, convert to Christianity in order to fit more easily into the social system of the conquered. Rather, Gibbon preferred to trace the process of acculturation that followed to their loss of local spontaneous roots. A North African scene, with the Vandals helplessly exposed to a zealous Catholic community "tout jusqu'à leur maîtresses qui meloient les caresses et la controverse,"[42] is a straightforward enough Gibbonian tableau. Less accustomed, but more revealing of Gibbon, is the brief analysis of the local nature of Scandinavian religion:

> Toutes les religions sont locales, jusqu'à un certain point. . . . Mais chez les nations savantes, les livres et la reflexion et chez les peuples de l'Orient une Imagination échauffée suppléent à la présence actuelle des objets. . . . Les idées ou les images étoient trop subtiles pour ne pas échapper à la dureté tranquille et phlegmatique des Scandinaves. . . . Ce temple d'Upsal où ils avoient acheté la faveur d'Odin par des milliers de victimes humains, ces rochers que les anciens Scaldes avoient couvert de caractères Runiques. . .tous ces objets frappoient son Esprit parce qu'ils avoient frappé les sens.[43]

The problem of empire is at the opposite end of the scale from this state of quasi-physical immediacy. In an empire, the spontaneous is attenuated and replaced by artifice. Yet Gibbon was not a man to reject artifice. Part of the conviction that Gibbon's account of the Roman Empire in the age of Antonines carries derives from his sober sense of the necessity of artifice and of its viability in an extended society. In his opinion, no large society is doomed merely because it has lost the virtues appropriate to a small community. The classical Roman Empire functioned well enough on an ersatz for public spirit; the entropy from artifice to unreality was slow and complex.

Play-acting, we should remember, struck Gibbon as a necessary social discipline.

For some people to wear a mask did no harm. The portrait of Augustus owes its three-dimensional quality to this assumption. Many other figures in Gibbon's narrative learned to act their parts on the stage of Roman life: Maximin Thrax "displayed on every occasion a valour equal to his strength; and his native fierceness was soon tempered or disguised by the knowledge of the world."[44] When Gibbon uses the imagery of the theater, as he often does, he uses it with a full-blooded sense of the necessity of role-playing in a complex society. Without it, for instance, the religious establishment of the pagan world would not have functioned the way it did; "sometimes condescending to act a part on the theatre of superstition, they concealed the sentiments of an Atheist under the sacerdotal robes."[45] Some actors acted in better plays than others:

> Like the modesty affected by Augustus, the state maintained by Diocletian was a theatrical representation; but it must be confessed that, of the two comedies, the former was of a more liberal and manly character than the latter. It was the aim of the one to disguise, and the object of the other to display, the unbounded power which the emperors possessed over the Roman world.[46]

Once again, the studied ambiguity of Gibbon's attitude to the tissue of society enabled Gibbon to place the new court life of the age, as he placed the Christian church, on parole. It was not inevitable that the balance should tilt irreversibly toward the mere show against the substance of power. Hence the vital importance for Gibbon of Constantine. In the *Decline and Fall*, it is not Constantine the convert of the Milvian Bridge who holds the center of the stage, it is Constantine the victorious autocrat of the period after 324. The reign of Constantine emerges as of crucial significance in the history of the formation of late-Roman absolutism: for with Constantine the balance shifted from role-playing to fantasy. This, and not his relations with the Christian church, is what gives Constantine his place in the *Decline and Fall*. "Diocletian was a man of sense, who, in the course of private as well as public life, had formed a just estimate both of himself and of mankind: nor is it easy to conceive that, in substituting the manners of Persia to those of Rome, he was seriously actuated by so mean a principle as that of vanity."[47] Constantine, however, was spun into the illusion which his great predecessor had manipulated: "The Asiatic pomp, which had been adopted by the pride of Diocletian, assumed an air of soft effeminacy in the person of Constantine."[48]

> In the life of Augustus, we behold the tyrant of the republic converted, almost by imperceptible degrees, into the father of his country and of human kind. In that of Constantine, we may contemplate a hero, who had long inspired his subjects with love and his enemies with terror, degenerating into a cruel and dissolute monarch, corrupted by his fortune or raised by conquest above the necessity of dissimulation.[49]

From that time onward, Gibbon's eyes remain on the court. This is not because he was interested solely in politicians, nor because he regarded the court and its demands as the main cause of the decline of the Empire. Rather, the rise of a court, for Gibbon, was the paradigm of the weakening of the tissues of Roman society. This is shown by the differentiated quality of his attitudes toward courts and court ceremonial. The phenomenon fascinated and repelled him. He met his first and most impressive one in Turin:

Une cour est à la fois pour moi un objet de curiosité et de dégout. La servilité des courtisans me révolte et je vois avec horreur la Magnificence des palais qui sont cimentés du sang du peuple. . . . Dans chaque chambre dorée je crois voir un village de Savoyards prêts à périr de faim, de froid et de misère.[50]

Yet his moral outrage does not blind him to the subtler ramifications of a court society: "The architecture and government of Turin presented the same aspect of tame and tiresome uniformity.[51] Such an observation prepares us for the dying fall in his summary of the age of the Antonines: "This long peace, and the uniform' government of the Romans, introduced a slow and secret poison into the vitals of the Empire."[52] The ceremonial of a court itself is a measure of its increasing isolation from reality. "The most brilliant shows in courts, the carousals of Lewis XIV or the festivities of the Dukes of Wurtemberg attested the wealth, and sometimes the taste, of princes"; this contrasts with the more cohesive society of the Roman Republic: "In the triumph, every circumstance was great and interesting. To receive its full impression, it was enough to be a man and a Roman. With the eyes of citizens, the spectators saw the image, or rather the reality of the public glory."[53]

Byzantine society is repugnant to Gibbon less through any reputed limitation in his sympathies and knowledge than precisely because he saw with singular clarity the most obtrusive feature of that society as it was faithfully reflected in the historical sources available to him. It was the Byzantine historiographical tradition itself, often the work of courtiers or of writers who purveyed court slander, that betrayed Byzantium to this regular and critical attendant at the stage play of autocracy. Byzantium, a society of monks and courtiers, represented the final weakening, on both the religious and the institutional plane, of the merciful restraints of civilized society. The development of the Holy Roman Empire, by contrast, poignantly illustrated the other aspect of this process of depletion. The "leakage of reality" reaches its height at the imperial court of Charles IV of Bohemia:

If we annihilate the interval of time and space between Augustus and Charles, strong will be the contrast between the two Caesars: the Bohemian, who concealed his weakness under the mask of ostentation, and the Roman, who disguised his strength under the semblance of modesty.[54]

Gibbon's attitude is best illustrated by the manner in which two young scholars of our time have corrected it. The resilience of the provincial aristocracies of the Western Empire has recently been studied by John Matthews. His book leaves little room for Gibbon's picture of the social structure of the later Empire: this was not, in fact, a society reduced to uniformity beneath an all-powerful court.[55] The pioneering studies by Sabine MacCormack of the relation between imperial art, ceremonial, and panegyric show a court culture that was far less concerned than Gibbon had thought merely with the display of the unlimited power of the emperor: far from it— what emerges from such differentiated studies is a picture of an imperial autocracy, still subject to a continuous, discreet pressure from below, whose panegyrics could be used to stress the traditional limitations of the imperial office and whose ceremonies were very often ceremonies that left room for a large measure of consensus and popular participation.[56]

These works show that to go beyond Gibbon in his views on the weakening of the traditional texture of Roman society and the consequent loosening of traditional restraints on the court may be the more fruitful manner of meeting his views on the causes of the decline and fall of the Roman Empire. Merely to appeal to the authority of Gibbon's "General Observations" in emphasizing the oppressive weight of the governmental superstructure of the Empire gets us less far than we might think. The deeper problem remains: by what means and with what success were local groupings and particular vested interests within the Empire induced for so many centuries— deep into the late antique period, in fact—to lend their support to the "stupendous fabric"?

To turn to the barbarian states of Western Europe is to have this impression confirmed. Here, Gibbon saw a society which, though primitive, was somehow less exposed to a "leakage of reality" than the Empire had been. "Folly" was not so strong a thread in the fabric of social life. The Latin church had always been protected "by propitious ignorance"[57] from the metaphysical rigors of the East. Even in the fourth century, "the inhabitants of the West were of a less inquisitive spirit; their passions were not forcibly moved by invisible objects."[58] In such a society the Christian church could exercise the cohesive role which Gibbon had always been prepared to allot it. For "the Franks and the Visigoths were disposed to embrace, with equal submission, the inherent evils, and the accidental benefits, of superstition."[59] "The bishops of Spain respected themselves and were respected by the public; their indissoluble union disguised their vices and confirmed their authority; and the regular discipline of the Church introduced peace, order and stability into the government of the state."[60]

In a similar manner, the "entropy of reality" was avoided by the barbarian societies which occupied the former provinces of the Empire. Here, we find Gibbon at his most differentiated, because at his most pragmatic. Any system that did violence to the observed quality of human nature in a given society repelled him. In an essay on the origins of the feudal system in France, he declared his methods: "Je combine l'expérience avec le raisonnement. J'ouvre les codes de ces peuples qui renversoient l'empire. . . . J'ouvre leurs annales. . . . Enfin j'aperçois l'aurore de la nouvelle institution." Again, this is conducted with Gibbon's breathtaking sense of scale; the whole quality of barbarian society is involved: "Tel est l'esprit qui s'est répandu du nord au midi, depuis les frontières de la Chine jusqu'au fond de l'Afrique."[61]

The method brings unexpected warmth and texture to his treatment of the barbarian societies of the West. To take one example, that of the Lombards in Italy: Giannone and, before him, Grotius had stressed the essentially secular, non-clerical nature of the legislation of the Lombards. This, wrote Giannone, was sufficient merit in itself; it proved the independence of the laws of the original Italian states from the law of the church. Gibbon follows Giannone, and yet he draws a subtly different conclusion. The absence of bishops meant the absence of Romans. Not being clericalized, the Lombards were not Romanized, and so their laws reflected the essential spirit of their society: they were "the genuine fruits of the reason of the barbarians."[62] Faithful to his methods, Gibbon brings alive this "reason of the barbarians." Hence his preference for Paul the Deacon: "His pictures of national manners, though rudely sketched, are more lively and faithful than those of Bede or Gregory of Tours."[63] And so we are treated, as an *apéritif* to the laws, to a story from Paul: "the adventurous gallantry of Autharis, which breathes the true spirit of chivalry and romance."[64]

Yet Gibbon was no romantic. He could react with seismographic sensitivity to the slightest tremor of romanticism in Montesquieu. When Montesquieu "condescended to explain and excuse *la manière de penser de nos pères* on the subject of judicial combats . . . , the philosopher is sometimes lost in the antiquarian."[65] Gibbon regarded romantic empathy as a shortcut. When it came to understanding the irrational elements in barbarian law, Gibbon was firm: rationality was a long, hard road, and no amount of special pleading could excuse a Frank of the sixth century from having to travel it, nor make him travel any faster than his general level of culture and manners could allow him: "the fierce and illiterate chieftain was seldom qualified to discharge the duties of a judge, which require all the faculties of a philosophic mind, laboriously cultivated by experience and study. . . ."[66]

What impressed Gibbon, therefore, about barbarian society was less any exotic or romantic qualities it might have possessed than the manner in which its institutions avoided the "leakage of reality" that weakened the structure of extended empires. The comparison of Western Europe with the sixth-century Byzantine state makes this plain:

> In the Salic laws and the Pandects of Justinian we may compare the first rudiments and the full maturity of civil wisdom; and, whatever prejudices may be suggested in favour of Barbarism, our calmer reflections will ascribe to the Romans the superior advantages, not only of science and reason, but of humanity and justice. Yet the laws of the Barbarians were adapted to their wants and desires, their occupations, and their capacity; and they all contributed to preserve the peace, and promote the improvements, of the society for whose use they were originally established.[67]

"The *Decline and Fall* is probably the most majestic work of history ever written."[68] But its author was a down-to-earth man. The intricate craftsmanship with which men can be observed to weave the web of civilized society concerned him more deeply than systems. We have followed him through the period in the history of Europe when the web seemed to lie in tatters. Only a few strands of what had once been so rich a weave are being replaited by unskilled hands. Yet how much of this web has actually been broken? Gibbon's sense of civilization and of its resilience goes far deeper than the mere study of courts and churches:

> Private genius and public industry may be extirpated; but these hardy plants survive the tempest, and strike an everlasting root into the most unfavourable soil. The splendid days of Augustus and Trajan were eclipsed by a cloud of ignorance; and the Barbarians subverted the laws and palaces of Rome. But the scythe, the invention or emblem of Saturn, still continued annually to mow the harvests of Italy; and the human feasts of the Laestrygons have never been renewed on the coast of Campania.[69]

If the modern historiography of late antiquity can relive some of Gibbon's anxious alertness to the weaving and reweaving of the restraining web of society, can reintroduce into its analysis of the social structure of the later Roman Empire and of the role of religion in this structure something of Gibbon's sense of the irony of a complex society, and, when faced with the overwhelming mass of material for the religious and cultural history of the age, be prepared to follow Gibbon in his many acts of silent renunciation, then we may move yet again from an age of erudition to an age of "philosophic" history.

REFERENCES

Note: All references to the *History of the Decline and Fall of the Roman Empire* (*DF*) are to chapter and page of the seven-volume Bury edition (London, 1914; 2nd ed, 1929).

[1]*The Letters of Horace Walpole*, ed. P. Toynbee (Oxford, 1934), pp. 408-9. Walpole to the Reverend William Mason, March 3, 1781.

[2]Pietro Giannone, *Vita scritta da lui medesimo*, ed. S. Bertelli (Milan, 1960), p. 14.

[3]*DF*, chap. 37, p. 104, n. 143.

[4]*Gibbon's Journey from Geneva to Rome*, ed. G. A. Bonnard (London, 1961), p. 247.

[5]*Ibid.*, p. 24.

[6]*Ibid.*, pp. 148-51.

[7]*Ibid.*, p. 156.

[8]*Ibid.*, p. 200.

[9]*Ibid.*, p. 202.

[10]*Ibid.*, p. 129, which was done—and very well—in 1974; see Ramsay MacMullen, *Roman Social Relations* (New Haven, 1974), p. 98, fig 2.

[11]*DF*, chap. 10, p. 256.

[12]*Collected Works*, III, at pp. 132 sq.

[13]*DF*, chap. 46, p. 43.

[14]*Ibid.*, p. 46.

[15]*Ibid.*, p. 47. Whether Gibbon's picture of Hormizd IV is correct is another matter. What struck him, in Roman terms, as "childish vanity" was a manifestation of the "personalisation of power" peculiar to Sasanian Iran that is not strictly comparable to Roman practice; see P. Brown, "The Sasanian Empire in the Near East," *Iran* (to appear).

[16]*DF*, chap. 46, p. 46, n. 11.

[17]*DF*, chap. 49, p. 261.

[18]*Ibid.*

[19]*DF*, chap. 46, p. 66, n. 55.

[20]*Ibid.*, p. 75, n. 73.

[21]"Outlines of the History of the World," *Collected Works*, III, p. 4.

[22]*Ibid.*, p. 19.

[23]*Ibid.*, p. 29.

[24]Gibbon's attitude is admirably summed up by Professor Giarrizzo: "La giustificazione consapevole di questi limite è dato dalla convinzione che essi non toccherebbero la decadenza e caduta dell'impero. La realtà è che essi non toccano sopratutto a Gibbon: laddove non gli riesce di sentire, dietro un pronunciamento teologico o una formula dommatica l'interesse 'politico' che traduce la credenza superstitziosa in un pregiudizio per farne trama del tessuto connettivo della società" (G. Giarrizzo, *Edward Gibbon e la cultura europea del settecento* [Naples, 1954], p. 302).

[25]*DF*, chap. 23, p. 460.

[26]*DF*, chap. 45, p. 38.

[27]*DF*, chap. 16, p. 82, n. 11.

[28]G. M. Young, *Gibbon* (2nd ed., London, 1948), p. 12.

[29]*The Autobiography of Edward Gibbon*, ed. John Murray (London, 1896), p. 84 F.

[30]P. Giannone, *Vita*, pp. 199-210.

[31]*DF*, chap. 15, p. 59.

[32]*DF*, chap. 2, p. 34, n. 8.

[33]*DF*, chap. 23, p. 466.

[34]*DF*, chap. 38, p. 175.

[35]*DF*, chap. 6, p. 159.

[36]*DF*, chap. 37, p. 76.

[37]*Ibid.*, p. 79

[38]*Ibid.*, pp. 85-86.

[39]*Gibbon's Journey*, p. 194.

[40]"Sur la Monarchie des Mèdes," *Collected Works*.

[41]*DF*, chap. 38, pp. 173-74.

[42]*Gibbon's Journey*, p. 164.

[43]*Ibid.*, p. 163.

[44]*DF*, chap. 7, p. 183.

[45]*DF*, chap. 2, p. 34.

[46]*DF*, chap. 13, p. 413.

[47]*Ibid.*, p. 412.

[48]*DF*, chap. 18, p. 217.

[49]*Ibid.*, p. 216.

[50]*Gibbon's Journey*, p. 23.

[51]*Autobiography*, p. 266 C.

[52]*DF*, chap. 2, p. 62.

[53]"On the Triumphal Shows of the Romans," *Collected Works*, IV, pp. 394-95.

[54]*DF*, chap. 49, p. 330.

[55]John Matthews, *Western Aristocracies and Imperial Court, A.D. 364-425* (Oxford, 1975).

[56]Sabine G. MacCormack, "Change and Continuity in Late Antiquity: The Ceremony of Adventus," *Historia*, XXXI (1972), pp. 721-52: "Latin Prose Panegyrics," *Empire and Aftermath* (*Silver Latin*, II, ed. T. A. Dorey [London, 1975]), pp. 143-205; "Latin Prose Panegyrics: Tradition and Discontinuity in the Later Roman Empire," *Revue des études augustiniennes* (to appear), and "Adventus and Consecratio: Roman Imperial Art and Panegyric from the Late Third to the Sixth Century" (Oxford University, D. Phil Thesis, 1974).

[57]*DF*, chap. 37, p. 103.

[58]*DF*, chap. 21, p. 374.

[59]*DF*, chap 38, p. 152.

[60]*Ibid.*, p. 153.

[61]"Du Gouvernement féodal surtout en France," *Collected Works*, III, p. 189.

[62]*DF*, chap. 45, p. 32.

[63]*Ibid.*, p. 6, n. 10.

[64]*Ibid.*, p. 29.

[65]*DF*, chap. 38, p. 137, n. 86.

[66]*Ibid.*, p. 136.

[67]*Ibid.*, p. 132.

[68]H. Trevor-Roper, *Gibbon: The Great Histories* (New York-London, 1966), p. xxi. This fine introduction is the distillation of a knowledge of Gibbon and the historiography of the Enlightenment, from which I have frequently benefited in personal conversation and to which I wish to acknowledge a debt of gratitude.

[69]*DF*, chap. 38, p. 181.

STEVEN RUNCIMAN

Gibbon and Byzantium

ANY HISTORIAN WHO WRITES A WORK that sweeps over the centuries is bound sooner or later to be obliged to cover a period which he finds unsympathetic and uninteresting. Gibbon reached this moment when he finished the forty-seventh chapter of the *Decline and Fall*. His historical sense told him that he could not end his story there. He knew that the empire which is usually called Byzantine was the lawful continuation of the Roman Empire and that his work must therefore extend to the year 1453, when it was extinguished by the Turks; and he wished to say something about the other co-heirs of Rome, the papacy and the medieval empire in the West and the Moslem caliphate in the East. He planned three more volumes. This obliged a change in the scale of his writing. He had only reached the beginning of the seventh century in his first forty-seven chapters. He had now to cover eight and a half more centuries. He could not treat them in the detailed manner in which he had treated the previous three and a half centuries, nor could he treat them in the same roughly chronological manner, as there was no longer the unity of the Roman imperial theme. But the problem did not weigh on him too heavily. "The historian's eye," he wrote, "shall always be fixed on the city of Constantinople." In fact, he did not wish to look at Constantinople too closely. He had no desire to deal in detail with Byzantium. To do so, he thought, would not provide "the patient reader" with "an adequate reward of instruction or amusement." Byzantine history was to him "a tedious and uniform tale of weakness and misery. On the throne, in the camp, in the schools, we search, perhaps with fruitless diligence, the names and characters that deserve to be rescued from oblivion."[1] The Byzantine historians, after Procopius, seemed to him all to be tedious chroniclers of narrow views and feeble or corrupt judgment. The story had to be told, but it should be told as quickly as possible.

Chapter 48 of the *Decline and Fall*, in which Gibbon races through five centuries of Byzantine history, is, historically speaking, the weakest section of the whole work. Quite apart from the temperamental distaste that he had for a civilization so alien to his eighteenth-century standards, he had certain handicaps that help to explain his failure to understand Byzantium. In the first place, his knowledge of Greek was far less profound than his knowledge of Latin. In his *Memoirs*, he laments that he never worked assiduously enough at Greek studies.[2] While he was thoroughly at ease with medieval Latin, he was not at ease with medieval Greek, of which he disapproved and which he occasionally mistranslated. It is true that Byzantine literary style is all too often affected and verbose. While medieval Latin developed as a language in its own right, medieval Greek authors far too often looked back over their shoulders to their classical predecessors and tried to imitate, with added elaboration and a disregard for the rules of Attic grammar, the works of Thucydides or of Plato. On the whole the best writers in Byzantium were the hymnographers and the theologians. Gibbon was quite uninterested in the former; and, while he read the earlier Greek fathers, with distaste for their matter, he knew nothing of such elegant and humanistic writers as the fourteenth-century mystic, Nicolas Cabasilas. Again, irritation at the piety and pretentiousness of writers such as Anna Comnena or Pachymer made him unwilling to admit that they were good historians. He complained of the paucity as well as of the poor quality of Byzantine historians. For the seventh and eighth centuries, his complaint is justified. They are covered by only two historians, writing—neither of them very well—about the year 800, and both relying upon a source that is lost. But from the ninth century onward the number of historians increases, and many of them were masters of their craft.[3]

It must be remembered that Gibbon was dependent upon sources that were already published and accessible. This meant that for Byzantine historiography he had to rely on the great *Corpus Byzantinae Historiae*, published at the royal press in Paris from 1645 to 1711, originally under the patronage of Louis XIV and Colbert. Additional volumes followed, published in Venice, Rome, and Leipzig; and the whole collection was republished in Venice from 1722 to 1733, in an edition which Gibbon found as magnificent as, but cheaper and more copious than, that of Paris.[4] The texts were accompanied by a Latin translation, which was not always very accurate and which, one suspects, Gibbon often used in preference to the Greek. Many of the volumes were annotated by eminent French seventeenth-century scholars, headed by Philippe Labbé and Charles duFresne du Cange, whose works— on the Latin Empire of Constantinople, on the topography of Constantinople, and on the imperial Byzantine families—Gibbon knew and admired. For the religious history of Byzantium, he relied mainly on another great production of the royal press in Paris, the *Conciliorum Collectio Regia*, whose thirty-six volumes were all first published in 1644, and on the *Ecclesiastical Annals* of Baronius, for which he seems to have used Pagius's edition, published at Lucca in 1738-46. He also depended on compilations by other seventeenth- and early eighteenth-century scholars such as Combefis and Fabricius. Indeed, it was only in such collections that the original sources could be found in print.[5] There was, however, one great compilation that Gibbon ignored, the *Acta Sanctorum* of the Bollandist Fathers; their first volume was published at Antwerp in 1643 and, by Gibbon's time, they had dealt with the saints whose days covered the months from January to October. He could have found useful material in the lives of Byzantine saints included in the series. He made great use of Mosheim's *Ecclesiastical History*, written earlier in the eighteenth century,[6] and he was aware of the huge *Histoire du Bas-Empire*, written by his contemporary, Le Beau, published in twenty-one volumes from 1757 to 1786 and completed in six more volumes after his death; but his only reference to it is to remark that "even le Beau, a gentleman and a scholar, is infected by the odious contagion" of approving of image-worship.[7] He certainly read and admired the four contemptuous chapters on Byzantium which concluded Montesquieu's *Considérations sur les causes de la grandeur des Romains et de leur décadence*, published in 1734.[8]

Considering the amount of time at his disposal, it is remarkable how much Gibbon managed to read. He is not to be blamed if he did not use the *Chronographia* of Michael Psellus, a historian whose wit and vividness might have appealed to him, for it was only published in 1874 (though Combefis did make use of the manuscript in Paris[9]). He could not have known the *Strategicon* of Cecaumenus, a work on military affairs with comments on life in general by a tough, down-to-earth soldier of whom he would have approved. The only manuscript of it was in Moscow and was not published until 1881.[10] Had he been able to use it and other similar material that is now available, he might have avoided such doubtful statements as "the vices of the Byzantine armies were inherent, their victories accidental" which, as his editor, J. B. Bury, pointed out, is the exact reverse of the truth.[11]

Gibbon's chief defect in treating of Byzantine history was, perhaps, due to his keeping his eye too firmly fixed on the city of Constantinople and on the sequence of emperors there. For this, the Byzantine historians themselves were largely to blame, as they tended to concentrate upon affairs in the capital. As a result, he did not see that Byzantine history was not one of steady decline but that it had its periods of vigorous expansion. He did not see that its problems were largely economic and agrarian; and he showed little interest in tracing Byzantine influence over other lands, in particular over the Slavs. Here again he is not to be blamed too sternly: Slavic studies were still in their infancy. For Russian history, he depended upon the *Histoire de la Russie* by Pierre Charles Levesque, published a few decades earlier, and of little value by modern standards.[12] He also read Mosheim on Christianity among the Slavs. But it is remarkable that he makes no mention of Cyril and Methodius, the apostles to the Slavs, who, though their original mission to Central Europe ended in failure, were responsible for a Slavic alphabet and, ultimately, for the establishment of Slavic churches in the Balkans and, later, in Russia. Mosheim had devoted three pages to them, and they were given ample treatment in a note in Pagius's edition of Baronius.[13] They were far more important in European history than was Ulfilas, apostle to the Goths, to whom Gibbon had paid attention. He never mentions Boris, the Bulgarian monarch who brought his people into the Christian fold, and his account of the conversion of Russia is brief and superficial. The whole subject seems not to have interested him, though, at the same time, his insight showed him the importance of the Paulician heresy.[14]

Indeed, even if Gibbon had been better equipped to study Byzantium, it is doubtful if his basic attitude would have been different. In the first place, he clearly found Byzantine history after the seventh century a little parochial and a little too static. It lacked the breadth of the old Roman world. One feels his enjoyment returning when he could deal with the sweeping conquests of the followers of Muhammad, or again when he comes to the great movement of the crusades, "the world's debate," as he called it, or to the career of Tamurlane. Compared to the ruthlessness of the great world conquerors the petty crimes of Byzantium were boring. It was tedious to have to describe palace revolutions in Constantinople, whose frequency he somewhat overstresses, disingenuously for a historian who has recently been dealing with the history of the third century. Compared with such periods as that of the Thirty Tyrants, the Byzantine era, in which he somewhat arbitrarily calculated the emperors' reigns as averaging ten years apiece, shows considerable stability.[15]

Still more, Gibbon was affected by the intellectual climate of his time. To the eighteenth-century gentleman of education the personal qualities that seemed most admirable were those of the Romans in the great days of the Republic. The intellectual and artistic achievements of the Greeks should be appreciated; but, to a good Roman, the Greek character was to be mistrusted. Virgil, Cicero, and Cato had all played their part in this, and Virgil's influence was particularly persistent. He was the one classical writer continuously read in the West throughout the Middle Ages; and the messianic tone of his Fourth Eclogue gave his works the rank almost of Holy Writ. His readers, warned by him of the perfidy of the Greeks, felt justified in disliking the Greeks of their own times, the Byzantines; and their dislike was enhanced by envy of the wealth of Byzantium and by the deepening schism between the churches of Eastern and Western Christendom. Indeed, as Gibbon himself noted, by the fifteenth century it was widely believed that the Turks, the *Turci*, were the same people as the Trojans, the *Teucri*, and that their capture of Constantinople was a just revenge for the Greek capture of Troy some two and half millennia previously. Gibbon smiled at the notion; but his own attitude was not far different.[16]

Sympathy for the Greeks was introduced by the Reformation. The Reformers felt drawn to a church which had suffered from, and resisted, the pretensions of Rome, while the Catholics were alarmed lest so ancient a church should be taken over by the upstart Protestants. During the first half of the seventeenth century, there was a diplomatic struggle in Constantinople between the embassies of the Protestant powers, England and Holland, and of the Catholic powers, France and the Habsburg Empire, to secure the sympathies and the ultimate control of the Orthodox Greek Patriarchate.[17] It was this interest in the Orthodox that led the French scholars, encouraged by their government, to publish the *Corpus* of Byzantine historians, to which Labbé wrote an introduction stressing the significance of Byzantine history and inviting all nations to join in its study.[18] These religio-diplomatic intrigues came to nothing; and when the religious passions of the seventeenth century were replaced by the rationalism of the eighteenth, Father Labbé's words were forgotten, and the publications he inaugurated only served to show up the medieval Greeks as a priest-ridden community with a taste for idols and for servitude to their emperor and their church. Seventeenth-century travelers to the East, such as the Englishmen Thomas Smith and Sir George Wheler or the Frenchman Spon, had been not unsympathetic toward the Greek church. Eighteenth-century travelers found it ridden with bigotry and ignorance, and in truth its standards in the Greek provinces had declined. In such an atmosphere, Byzantine studies could not be expected to flourish, and Byzantium became a byword for servility, superstition, and intrigue.[19]

Once again the French were the pioneers. Voltaire, in his work on the Pyrrhonism of history, after writing critically of imperial Rome and its historians, adds that "there exists another history more ridiculous than the history of Rome after the time of Tacitus; it is the history of Byzantium. This worthless collection contains nothing but declamations and miracles. It is a disgrace to the human mind."[20] Montesquieu, who was a better scholar, rightly saw Byzantium as being the continuation of the Roman Empire, but the chapters that he devotes to its history are written with dislike and disdain. "The history of the Greek Empire is nothing but a tissue of rebellions, sedition and treachery." He finds it puzzling that a polity so corrupt and so riddled with organic defeats should have managed to survive for so many centuries. He decides that it must be due to "unusual outside causes."[21] Montesquieu's writings were widely read, and it was chiefly due to him that the word "Byzantinism" came to mean, as it still means in the journalistic jargon of today, tortuous intrigue and corruption. A little later, Hegel, who had also read Gibbon, says of the Byzantine Empire that "its general aspect presents a disgusting picture of imbecility; wretched, even insane, passions stifle the growth of all that is noble in thoughts, deeds and persons."[22] Napoleon, in his speech to the Assembly during the Hundred Days, begs France not to follow the example of the "Bas-Empire" and become a laughingstock to posterity.[23]

In such an atmosphere, Gibbon could not fail to despise Byzantium. In spite of a liking for the works of Herodotus, Thucydides, and Xenophon, and in spite of a conventional admiration for classical Greek art, he does not seem to have felt much sympathy for the Greeks themselves of any period. He read with interest contemporary books of travel that concerned Grecian lands, but he did not share the interest in their present inhabitants that travelers such as Chandler, whom he admired, were beginning to show, as were the archaeologists sent to the Levant by the Society of Dilettanti. He had no truck with the emergent Philhellene sentiment that was to reach its climax with Byron: though it must be admitted that even the Philhellenes felt little sympathy for the medieval Greeks or the Greeks of Constantinople.[24] But even if Gibbon had liked the Greeks in general, he would not have forgiven them for their church.

It was the distaste that Gibbon felt for what he held to be a superstitious and monk-ridden church that kept him from having any understanding of Byzantine civilization. The virtue of tolerance that he so often praised was not applied by him to its followers. We can read with relish his satirical accounts of the councils, summoned to solve the Christological disputes of the fourth, fifth, and sixth centuries. We can enjoy the irony with which he tells of the character and behavior of such unedifying saints as Cyril of Alexandria and of the jealous rivalries of the great sees of early Christendom. The controversies basically arose out of a genuine attempt to find the proper philosophical terms for the central Christian doctrine of the Incarnation. Gibbon had no strong feelings about the doctrine. He could afford to be impartial. But when we come to the controversy over iconoclasm, in which an understanding of the issues involved is essential for the understanding of Byzantine thought, he was frankly one-sided. He took most of his information from a book by Basnage, of whom he says: "He was a Protestant, but of a manly spirit; and on this head the Protestants are so notoriously in the right that they can afford to be impartial."[25] Gibbon followed up this curiously illogical statement by being wholly partial on the subject. He did not try to understand the arguments of the defenders of images, John of Damascus or Theodore the Studite. The works of the Patriarch Nicephorus dealing with images were not available to him, but one may doubt if he would have bothered with them had he known them. Had he felt any sympathy for Neoplatonic philosophy he might have begun to understand what images meant to their defenders. But he had no use for the Neoplatonists, whom he seems to have considered as superstitious as the Christians and perhaps even sillier.[26]

The Byzantine artists believed with Plotinus that art is concerned not with material forms but with eternal conceptions, and their aim was to interpret the doctrine of the Incarnation in terms of visible beauty and to increase the understanding of the divine through the God-given senses, beyond the finite limits of the human mind. All this would have been nonsense to Gibbon. He had no interest in Byzantine art. Though he conscientiously describes the great church of Saint Sophia from Byzantine literary sources, it is only with a grudging admiration for its size and magnificence.[27] He never saw Byzantine art in its homelands. If he ever visited the Byzantine churches in Rome they made no impression on him. He never went to

Ravenna, and he disliked Venice, considering the Piazza of San Marco to be "a large square decorated with the worst Architecture I ever yet saw."[28] Image-worship to him was sheer superstition. But to condemn it, as he does, because of the adulatory excesses of its more ignorant adherents is as unfair as it would be to condemn the whole Protestant movement because of the vandalism of Cromwell's more fanatical soldiery.

Gibbon's almost phobic dislike of monks made it inevitable that his account of the Hesychast controversy should be wholly one-sided. But many modern historians have followed his example and have based themselves on the hostile writings of Nicephorus Gregoras without reading the rather difficult works of the Hesychasts themselves, which were almost entirely unpublished in Gibbon's time.[29] Less excusable was Gibbon's failure to realize that the monks were not all men who had renounced the world. In Byzantium, as elsewhere in medieval Europe, but more so, the monasteries and convents ran nearly all the orphanages, the elementary schools, the old people's homes, and the hospitals that made Byzantium the most efficient welfare state in the Middle Ages.[30]

Gibbon was also deluded by his interpretation of the endless ceremonial of the Byzantine court, with its prostrations and its stiff etiquette, as a sign of absolute despotism. He did not see that Byzantium still maintained the old Roman imperial constitution, based on the semi-fictitious Lex de Imperio, by which the people of Rome transferred their sovereignty to an elected emperor. In Byzantine times the electors were held to be the people, the senate, and the army, whose endorsement of a new emperor was expressed by acclamation at the time of his coronation. In fact, an informal hereditary system was achieved by the emperor's right, acknowledged since pre-Byzantine days, to nominate a colleague who would succeed to his power; and in default of an emperor it was for the empress to name a successor. But the people consciously retained what the historian Mommsen, writing about the earlier Empire, called "the legal right of revolution." If an emperor was unworthy of his high post he should be dethroned. The failure to see this led Gibbon into inconsistencies, as when he talks of the period in the early eleventh century in which "the Greeks, degraded below the common level of servitude, were transferred like a herd of cattle by the choice or caprice of two impotent females." Yet on the previous page he has described how the people of Constantinople took matters into their own hands to prevent one of those ladies from being driven from the palace by an unworthy emperor whom she had adopted. The impotent females were in fact beloved by their subjects.[31]

The right of revolution extended to the army and to the senate. The army would not long remain faithful to an incompetent general. The civil service, with which the senate may be equated, was quite ready to remove a hopeless administrator from the throne. An emperor who was thought to be breaking the law similarly risked deposition. He might be the source of law, but he was bound by the law. The old Roman respect for the law was never forgotten in Byzantium.

Gibbon should have noted these legal checks on despotism. He would, however, never have comprehended the supplementary constitution of Byzantium, based on the concept of a Christian empire. This was first formulated by Eusebius of Caesarea in the days of Constantine the Great, and it came to be tacitly accepted by every Byzantine, except for a monastic minority that sought complete independence for the church. The Byzantine was deeply religious and sincerely believed that life on this earth was but the prelude to the life everlasting in heaven. The Christian empire on this earth could therefore be no more than a transient copy of the true reality of the Kingdom of Heaven. The emperor was merely the shadow, the fallible viceroy, of God in Heaven, surrounded by his courtiers, ministers, and bishops, just as God was surrounded by the archangels, the angels, and the saints. The adulation given to the emperor—the prostrations and the pompous processions which so irritated Gibbon—was not adulation given to a man but to God through His earthly representative, just as the reverence shown to holy pictures was not given to the picture itself but to the holy figure that it depicted. But the emperor was not only the representative of God before the people. He was also the representative of the people before God, and the people retained its right to remove him should he prove unworthy. All the sacrosanctity of Imperial Majesty would not avail to keep a bad emperor on the throne. This constitution was never fully thought out. It never decided the role of the Patriarch of Constantinople and the ecclesiastical organization. The emperor was generally held to be only the administrator of the church. He could not interfere in theological matters. That was the province of the council of the church. The emperor might be able to dominate and bully the council, but the forms had to be respected.[32]

The arrogant autocracy with its servile subjects which Gibbon attributed to Byzantium never in fact existed. Deeper research might have enlightened him. But it would have been impossible for an educated eighteenth-century gentleman to comprehend the Byzantine character, with its illogical mixture of worldly ambition, cynicism, and intense mystical religion. Anyone who studies Gibbon's chapters on Byzantium must stand amazed at the extent of his reading and his extraordinary ability to extract the essential facts from his sources and to evaluate their worth. But, for all his greatness as a historian, the spirit of Byzantium eluded him. The splendor of his style and the wit of his satire killed Byzantine studies for nearly a century. It is only in recent decades, when the old certainties of life seem to be shattered, that historians have found themselves able to contemplate with sympathy the strange and sad, but not ignoble, history of Byzantium.

REFERENCES

Note: The references to the *History of the Decline and Fall of the Roman Empire (DF)* are to J. B. Bury's seven-volume ninth edition (London, 1925).

[1]*DF*, chap. 6, pp. 169-71.

[2]Gibbon, *Memoirs of My Life*, ed. G. A. Bonnard (London, 1965), p. 77. He returned to Greek studies later, with greater success, *ibid*., p. 164.

[3]*DF*, chap. 6, pp. 169-71. See Bury's Appendix I to Vol. V, pp. 495-509.

[4]*DF*, chap. 68, p. 208, n. 128. He never mentions Labbé.

[5]For Baronius and other church historians, see Professor Chadwick's contribution to this volume.

[6]Along with Mosheim, Gibbon mentions his indebtedness to Petavius, Le Clerc, and Beausobre. *DF*, chap. 47, pp. 96-97, n. 1.

[7]*DF*, chap. 49, p. 276, n.77.

[8]Montesquieu, last four chapters of *Considérations sur les causes de la grandeur des Romains et de leur décadence* (Paris, 1734).

[9]Combefis seems to have translated, but never published, part of the Paris manuscript of Psellus's *Chronographia*, which he used when writing on the origins of Constantinople. Dositheus, Patriarch of Jerusalem, made use of another manuscript, now apparently lost, when he wrote his ecclesiastical history (published in 1713), a book which Gibbon did not know. Busbecq, whose works Gibbon did read, reported the existence of two other manuscripts in the Greek library at Rodosto, which has long since disappeared See the *History of Psellus*, ed. C. Sathas (London, 1899), Preface, pp. viii-ix.

[10]See G. Ostrogorsky, *History of the Byzantine State*, trans. J. Hussey (Oxford, 1956), p. 281.

[11]J. B. Bury, *Selected Essays* (Cambridge, 1930), pp. 222-23, quoting C. Oman, *A History of the Art of War in the Middle Ages* (2nd ed., London, 1924), I, p. 172.

[12]For Levesque, see *DF*, chap. 55, p. 148, n. 57, and notes on subsequent pages. Levesque's chief merit

was that he introduced the so-called *Chronicle of Nestor* to the West, though he used it uncritically. For Russian history, Gibbon also used works by Siegfried Bayer, the geographer d'Anville and the travelers Coxe and Beauplan.

¹³J. L. Mosheim, *An Ecclesiastical History*, trans. A. Maclaine (London, 1768), II, pp. 104-6; Baronius, *Annales, ad ann. 857*, ed. Pagius (Lucca, 1743), XIV, p. 473.

¹⁴For the Paulicians, *DF*, chap. 44, pp. 110-25. Gibbon was one of the first historians to realize the connection of the Paulicians with the Albigensians in France, and so with the Reformation.

¹⁵*DF*, chap. 48, p. 242.

¹⁶See S. Runciman, "Teucri and Turci," *Medieval and Middle Eastern Studies in Honor of Aziz Suryal Atiya* (Leiden, 1972), pp. 344-48. Gibbon, *DF*, chap. 68, p. 193, n. 87, blames the legend on the Byzantine historian Chalcondyles, who seems in fact to have learned it from Western sources.

¹⁷For Western interest in the Greek Orthodox Church, see S. Runciman, *The Great Church in Captivity* (Cambridge, 1968), Book II, chaps. 5-7. Melancthon's pupil Hieronymus Wolf was the first Westerner to edit, rather haphazardly, Byzantine texts. He was followed by the Dutchman Meursius.

¹⁸Labbé's introduction to the *Corpus* is entitled "De byzantinae historiae scriptoribus ad omnes per orbem eruditos," i.e., "appeal."

¹⁹Runciman, *The Great Church*, pp. 308-9, 319.

²⁰Voltaire, *Le Pyrrhonisme de l'histoire, par un bachelier en théologie*, chap. 5.

²¹See above, note 8.

²²Hegel, *Vorlesungen über die Philosophie der Geschichte*, III, part 3, section 3, trans. Sibree, *Lectures on the Philosophy of History* (London, 1890), p. 353.

²³Reported in *Le Moniteur*, June 13, 1815.

²⁴For the background to the attitude of the Philhellenes, see T. Spencer, *Fair Greece, Sad Relic* (London, 1954), esp. chaps. 8 and 10.

²⁵*DF*, chap. 49, p. 246, n. 6.

²⁶*DF*, chap. 13, pp. 392-93.

²⁷*DF*, chap. 40, pp. 244-48.

²⁸*The Letters of Edward Gibbon*, ed. J. E. Norton (London, 1956), I, p. 193, letter 67.

²⁹Gibbon's account of the Hesychasts is given in *DF*, chap. 63, pp 506-8. See Runciman, *The Great Church*, pp. 238-58.

³⁰For Byzantine welfare services, see D. J. Constantelos, *Byzantine Philanthropy and Social Welfare* (New Brunswick, 1968), *passim*.

³¹*DF*, chap. 48, pp. 219-20.

³²For the "Eusebian" conception of the Empire, see N. H. Baynes, "Eusebius and the Christian Empire," in *Byzantine Studies and Other Essays* (London, 1955), pp. 168-72.

BERNARD LEWIS

Gibbon on Muhammad

GIBBON'S INTEREST IN ISLAM seems to have begun at an early date: "Muhammad and his Saracens soon fixed my attention, and some instinct of criticism directed me to the genuine sources. Simon Ockley, an original in every sense, first opened my eyes, and I was led from one book to another, till I had ranged around the circle of Oriental history. Before I was sixteen I had exhausted all that could be learned in English of the Arabs and Persians, the Tartars and Turks, and the same ardor urged me to guess at the French of De Herbelot and to construe the barbarous Latin of Pococke's Abulfaragius."[1]

The interest persisted. As an undergraduate at Oxford, Gibbon was impressed by the tradition of Oriental scholarship in the University: "Since the days of Pococke and Hyde, Oriental learning has always been the pride of Oxford, and I once expressed an inclination to study Arabic. His [Gibbon is here speaking of his tutor] prudence discouraged this childish fancy, but he neglected the fair occasion of directing the ardor of a curious mind."[2] Gibbon never did learn Arabic, but the "instinct of criticism" which he had displayed in his early reading served him well, perhaps the better because his ardor had not been directed by the teachings of early-eighteenth-century Oxford.

It was a time when interesting changes were taking place in the European Christian perception of Islam and its founder. Far from being prepared to recognize any merit or authenticity in Islam as a religion, Christendom had been unwilling even to take cognizance of the fact that it was a religion, as is shown by the persistence of European Christians in designating the Muslims by names which were ethnic rather than religious in connotation. In Greece, the Muslims could be Arabs, Persians, Hagarenes, or even Assyrians; in Russia they were Tatars; in Spain, Moors; in most of Europe, Turks; and in both Eastern and Western Christendom, they were commonly called Saracens, a name of obscure origin but certainly ethnic in meaning, since it is both pre-Christian and pre-Islamic. Only in comparatively recent times did Christians begin to call the followers of Muhammad by a name with a religious connotation. Then, by false analogy, they called them Muhammadans and their religion Muhammadanism, on the totally false assumption that Muslims worshiped Muhammad as Christians worshiped Christ.

Medieval Christendom did, however, study Islam, for the double purpose of protecting Christians from Muslim blandishments and converting Muslims to Christianity. In the course of time it gradually became known that the one was unnecessary and the other impossible. In the meanwhile, a body of literature had grown up concerning the faith, its Prophet, and his book, ·polemic in purpose and often

scurrilous in tone, designed to protect and discourage rather than to inform. Despite
the growth of a somewhat more detached scholarship, writing on this subject was still
dominated by the prejudices and purposes of polemical writing at the time when
Gibbon began to read about Islam.

But if the polemicists still dominated the subject, they no longer monopolized it—
and more than one kind of polemic purpose was now represented. One important
factor of change was the Reformation, which influenced the literature in several ways.
Catholic authors frequently tried to discredit Protestant doctrine by likening it to
Islam—Muhammad was an early Protestant, and the Protestants were latter-day
Saracens. Protestant theologians in turn took up the challenge in several ways:
sometimes by refuting it, and showing that they were as fierce as the Catholics in their
hostility to Islam; sometimes by turning it against their own protesters, such as Deists
and Unitarians;[3] sometimes by accepting the accusation and turning it to their own
advantage. This had some practical aspects in the occasional attempts by Protestant
powers to seek a Turkish alliance against the Catholic empires,[4] and it reached its
extreme in the Unitarian sympathy with Islam, at times even to the point of an
espousal of the Islamic faith.

The Protestants, notably in Holland, England, and, later, Germany, made a
major contribution to Arabic studies. Here again, there were several motives which
impelled them in this direction. One was their concern with the Hebrew Bible and
with the discovery that Arabic and Arabian lore could help in the better understanding of the Hebrew text of the Old Testament. Another was an interest in the Eastern
Christians who were seen as possible allies of the Protestants against the Church of
Rome. A third was the growth of English and Dutch commerce in the Levant, which
required a knowledge of local languages and customs and provided opportunities for
Protestant scholars to spend some time in those parts.

One of the most important European Arabists of the seventeenth century,
Edward Pococke (1604–1691), was the source of much of Gibbon's information, both
directly through his own writings, and indirectly through other later writers who
relied very heavily on his work. Pococke began with Hebrew and Syriac and then
went on to learn Arabic. In 1630 he was appointed by the Levant Company as
Chaplain in Aleppo and remained there until 1636, when he returned to Oxford to
take up the newly created Laudian Chair of Arabic.

These practical and theological interests in Islam and its history were disciplined
and directed by the new kind of philological and textual scholarship which, from the
time of the Renaissance onward, was applied first to classical languages and then to
Hebrew and Arabic.

Despite the practical interest in the Middle East—as a source of the Turkish
danger and as a market for European goods—there was little material encouragement
for scholars working in this field. The Cambridge scholar Simon Ockley (1678–1720),
whose *History of the Saracens* first directed the young Gibbon's interest to this area,
lived in penury. "I was forced," he says, "to take the advantage of the slumbers of my
cares, that never slept when I was awake; and if they did not incessantly interrupt my
studies, were sure to succeed them with no less constancy than night doth the day."[5]
The second volume of his history was produced from Cambridge Castle, where
Ockley was imprisoned for debt. The great German scholar Johann Jakob Reiske
(1716–1774), whom Gibbon compares to Erasmus, Scaliger, and Bentley,[6] was
unable to find a publisher for his Latin translation of the *Annales* of Abu'l-Fida and

had to print it at his own expense. When he had sold barely thirty copies of the first volume, he was compelled to stop the printing.

In a lengthy note on the sources for his chapter on the Prophet,[7] Gibbon names his main sources of information: three translations of the Qur'ān into Latin, French, and English by Marracci, Savary, and Sale; two biographies of Muhammad by Humphrey Prideaux and the Count de Boulainvilliers; the relevant article in d'Herbelot's *Bibliothèque Orientale*; and "the best and most authentic of our guides," Jean Gagnier, "a Frenchman by birth and professor at Oxford of the Oriental tongues" and author of two "elaborate works," one of them an edition with Latin translation and notes of a biography of the Prophet by the Arabic author Isma'il Abu'l-Fida, the other, Gagnier's own biography of Muhammad in three volumes. In addition to these, Gibbon made extensive use of two other important works, a treatise on the Muhammadan religion by the Dutch scholar Adrian Reland, and Pococke's most important work, the *Specimen Historiae Arabum*,[8] an excerpt from an Arabic chronicle by the Syrian Christian author Bar Hebraeus (Abulfaragius), with a Latin translation and hundreds of pages of learned notes. The Arabic text itself occupies a mere fifteen pages and includes an account of the Arab tribes and of pre-Islamic Arabia, a brief biography of the Prophet, and a discussion of the biblical texts alleged by Muslims to prophesy his coming and of the miracles ascribed to him.

Each of the translations of the Qur'ān is introduced by a long "historical discourse" provided by the translator; all three of them, according to Gibbon, "had accurately studied the language and character of their author." In fact, however, of the three translations, only that of Marracci is completely original and based exclusively on the Arabic text. Claude Savary (1758–1788) had some knowledge of colloquial Arabic acquired during a stay in Egypt, but clearly had only a limited command of the written language. His translation is based on those of Marracci and Sale, with some reference to the Arabic text. His introductory biography of the Prophet, like those of most other European scholars of the time, rests in the main on a single Arabic source, the late-medieval chronicle of Abu'l-Fida. His chief difference from his predecessors lies in his approach. "Le philosophe y trouvera," he says, "les moyens qu'un homme appuyé sur son seul génie, a employés pour triompher de l'attachement des Arabes à l'idolatrie et pour leur donner un culte et des lois; il y verra, parmi beaucoup de fables et de répétitions des traits sublimes et un enthousiasme propres à subjuguer des peuples d'un naturel ardent."[9] This evaluation of Muhammad is common to writers of the Enlightenment, and it is one of the determining influences in Gibbon's presentation.

Savary, both in his translation and in his preliminary discourse, relied very heavily on the English scholar George Sale (1697?–1736), the first English Arabist of any consequence who was not a clergyman, and one of the first in Europe. The son of a merchant and himself a practicing solicitor, he pursued the study of Arabic as a hobby and mastered it well enough to be commissioned by the Society for the Promotion of Christian Knowledge to correct an Arabic translation of the New Testament produced for them by a Syrian Christian. His Qur'ān translation, published in 1734,[10] is a major step in the progress of knowledge of Islam in Europe, and was for a long time by far the most widely read and best known. It served as the basis for virtually all other translations into European languages until the nineteenth century. His translation is based on the Arabic text, and he made effective use of his predecessor, Marracci, as well as of one of the major Muslim commentators.

Sale's "preliminary discourse," dealing with pre-Islamic Arabia, the career of the Prophet, and the principles of the Muslim religion, greatly increased both the value and influence of this book. For his biography of the Prophet he relied in the main on Abu'l-Fida and profited greatly from Pococke's *Specimen*. Sale, though not affected by the Enlightenment idealization of the Prophet, was commendably free from the religious prejudices shared by most of his predecessors and many of his successors, and did at least understand, in the words of a modern scholar, "that Arabic writers were the best sources of Arab history, and Muslim commentators the fittest to expound the Qur'ān."[11] Sale himself indicates his approach in the quotation from St. Augustine inscribed on the exergue of his book: "Nulla falsa doctrina est, quae non aliquid veri permisceat."

Sale, like all subsequent translators, relied very heavily on the pioneer work of the Italian priest Lodovico Marracci, published in Padua in 1698;[12] it consisted of a refutation of Islam, previously published in Rome in 1691, and the Arabic text of the Qur'ān with a Latin translation and a very full annotation. Marracci's purpose was frankly polemic, and he devoted forty years of his life to studying the Qur'ān and the Muslim commentators in order to destroy Islam with its own weapons. His refutation of Islam is aptly described by Gibbon as "virulent, but learned."[13] Marracci knew Arabic well, and he consulted a wide range, impressive for that time, of Arabic sources. Many of those whom he cites, however, he knew only at second hand, chiefly from Pococke's *Specimen*. Apart from these, there were some earlier attempts at translating the Qur'ān, which Gibbon seems rightly to have disregarded.

The two biographies of Muhammad by Dr. Humphry Prideaux[14] and by the Count de Boulainvilliers[15] were both polemical in purpose, and their weaknesses are well described by Gibbon: "The adverse wish of finding an impostor or an hero has too often corrupted the learning of the doctor and the ingenuity of the Count."[16] Prideaux's biography, first published in 1697, was enormously successful, being reprinted in numerous editions and translated into French. Its purpose is clear from the title. Prideaux is, of course, perfunctorily concerned to refute the claims of the Muslims—a somewhat unnecessary task in seventeenth-century England—but is more anxious to provide a terrible warning against the dangers of conflict within the church. It was the quarrels and arguments within the Eastern church, according to Prideaux, that "wearied the Patience and Long-Suffering of God" so that

> . . . he raised up the Saracens to be the Instruments of his Wrath . . . who taking Advantage of the Weakness of Power, and the Distractions of Counsels, which these Divisions had caused among them, soon overran with a terrible Devastation all the *Eastern* Provinces of the *Roman* Empire. . . . Have we not Reason to fear, that God may in the same Manner raise up some *Mahomet* against us for our utter Confusion. . . . And by what the *Socinian*, the *Quaker* and the *Deist* begin to advance in this Land, we may have Reason to fear, that Wrath hath some Time since gone forth from the Lord for the Punishment of these our Iniquities and Gainsayings, and that the Plague is already begun among us.[17]

Prideaux was principally alarmed by the Deists, and it is against them that he directs his main arguments. His book, though elaborately documented, is not a work of scholarship. He had no access to untranslated Arabic works and relied principally on three printed Latin translations—that of Pococke's *Specimen*, and two others— while for the Qur'ān he used a twelfth-century Latin translation. His use of his sources is uncritical, and Gibbon is rightly suspicious of his treatment of them.

The French biography of the Prophet by Count Henri de Boulainvilliers (1658–1722), published posthumously in London in 1730, had quite a different purpose.[18] If Prideaux was concerned to refute Deists, Quakers, Socinians, and others who alarmed him, Boulainvilliers used the Prophet and the advent of Islam as a weapon against Christian dogma and the Catholic clergy. Though favorable, his tone is still more than a little patronizing. Muhammad, for Boulainvilliers, was the Prophet of a nation of noble savages, among whom he appeared and for whom he knew how to temper nature with law. In its essentials, his religion was true and reasonable:

> En effect, tout ce qu'il a dit est *vrai*, par rapport aux Dogmes essentiels de la Religion; mais il n'a pas dit tout ce qui est *vrai*: et c'est en cela seul que notre Religion diffère de la sienne, sans la grâce de la Révélation Chrétienne, qui nous éclaire bien au-delà de ce que Mahomed a voulu connoître et savoir, il n'y auroit système de Doctrine si plausible que le sien, si conforme aux lumières de la Raison, si consolant pour les Justes, et si terrible aux Pécheurs volontaires et inappliquez.[19]

Boulainvilliers's Islam was free from all the familiar and reprehensible excesses of religion: "On n'y connoit ni les Macerations, ni les Jeunes, ni les Fouets, ni les Disciplines. . . ."[20] As a further merit, it imposed no mysteries which could constrain reason. The Arabs asked him for miracles, but in this they were irrational, while Muhammad himself was rational in denying the need for them. Muhammad was "un Homme-d'État incomparable et un Législateur supérieur à tous ceux que l'ancienne Grèce avoit produits."[21]

This image of Muhammad as a wise, tolerant, unmystical, and undogmatic ruler became widespread in the period of the Enlightenment, and it finds expression in writers as diverse as Goethe, Condorcet, and Voltaire—who, in some of his writings, condemns Muhammad as the terrible example of fanaticism, but in others praises him for his wisdom, rationality, moderation, and tolerance.[22]

Gibbon, while recognizing the polemic character and purpose of the Count de Boulainvilliers's biography and occasionally commenting with some irony on his methods, was nevertheless himself deeply influenced by it.

The source whom Gibbon describes as "the best and most authentic of our guides" was Jean Gagnier, a French Protestant who settled in England and taught at Oxford. Of his two major works, one was an edition, translation, and commentary of the Arabic Chroncle of Abu'l-Fida, the other a biography of the Prophet in three volumes based in the main on Abu'l-Fida (1273–1331) and on another Arabic Chronicle, that of Abu Muhammad Mustafa ibn al-Hasan al-Jannabi (d. 1590). Gagnier was the first to try to break away from the established habit of uninformed abuse and polemic. In 1723, through his edition and translation of Abu'l-Fida, he made available to European readers for the first time an Arabic biography of the Prophet written by a Muslim. In his own biography published in 1732, he cautiously explained that his purpose was not to depict Muhammad as he really was, but simply to acquaint the European reader with what orthodox Muslims tell and believe about him. This he did by translating long passages from the Muslim sources. His book was the basis of most other European writing on Muhammad until the publication of Gustav Weil's *Mohammed der Prophet* over a century later; its appearance in 1843 marked the beginning of an entirely new era in Islamic studies in Europe.

In addition to Gagnier's writings, two other books served as major sources for Gibbon's discussion of Muhammad. One was Pococke's *Specimen*, a work of epoch-making importance in the development of Arabic and Islamic studies in Europe and the basis of a good deal of subsequent scholarship. Prideaux, Marracci, Sale, and virtually all the other writers consulted by Gibbon relied very heavily on Pococke, who was the only scholar of his time to possess a mastery of the Arabic sources and literature sufficient to be able to read in bulk and cite with authority. The other was the biography of Boulainvilliers. Despite Gibbon's awareness of its defects and occasional caustic comments about them, he nevertheless seems to have been much affected by the presentation of the Prophet and, still more, of the Prophet's time and place in the eighteenth-century mythic version which was first designed by the Count de Boulainvilliers and which became commonplace in the writings of the Enlightenment.

But beyond the work of these seventeenth- and eighteenth-century scholars, one must seek the original Arabic texts on which their presentations or misrepresentations of the Prophet are based. Virtually the only Arabic text known to European scholarship dealing with the subject was the history of Abu'l-Fida. Jannabi was not then—and still has not been—published, and, as Gibbon remarked, "I must observe that both Abu'l-Fida and al-Jannabi are modern historians, and that they cannot appeal to any writers of the first century of the Hegira."[23]

This was precisely the problem. Abu'l-Fida was a Syrian prince who lived seven centuries after the Prophet. His biography of Muhammad, like other parts of his work, is little more than a transcript of the account given by an earlier Arabic historian, Ibn al-Athir, who died in 1233, still a long time after the Prophet. He, in turn, relies almost entirely on a still earlier historian, Muhammad ibn Jarir al-Tabari (d. 923), omitting the chains of authorities and arbitrarily harmonizing variant versions. Tabari, in turn, cites or abridges several earlier authors: Ibn Sa'd (d. 843), who relies on his predecessor and master, al-Waqidi (d. 823); Ibn Hisham (d. 834), who edited the work of his predecessor, Ibn Ishaq (d. 768). These bring us, if not to the first century of the Hijra, at least to a date reasonably near to it. But how reliable is the information which they provide?

In an essay first published in the *Revue de Deux Mondes* in 1851, Ernest Renan remarked that Islam was the last religious creation of mankind and also the best known. The faculty of originating religions, he said, like that of creating languages, has atrophied in our mature and reflective age, making it difficult, if not impossible, for us to understand that lost instinct of the childhood of our race. It is therefore fortunate that the origins of Islam are known to us so well and in such detail, while the origins of other earlier religions are lost in dreams and myths: "La vie de son fondateur nous est aussi bien connue que celle des réformateurs du XVIᵉ siècle. Nous pouvons suivre année par année les fluctuations de sa pensée, ses contradictions, ses faiblesses."[24]

In making these remarks, Renan was referring to the *Sira*, the great traditional biography of the Prophet which has been read and cherished by Muslims for over a thousand years. It was not until the nineteenth century that the *Sira* became known to European scholarship, but the text of Abu'l-Fida, though based on it at several removes, nevertheless retained enough of it to give the reader some idea of its content and character.

The idea of compiling a connected narrative of the life of the Prophet did not appear in the Muslim community until a comparatively late date; when it did, its appearance was caused by factors other than an interest in history. The oldest biographical data concerning the Prophet are to be found in two groups of sources.

One of these is the great corpus of tradition—the record of the actions and utterances attributed to the Prophet. In the years following his death, the Muslims came face to face with all kinds of problems and difficulties which had never arisen during his lifetime and for which the Qur'ān therefore offered no direct guidance. The principle was in time established that not only the Qur'ān, the word of God, was authoritative, but also the example and precept of the Prophet throughout his life. His opinions and sayings were therefore collected, sorted, and compiled in great corpuses of traditions. While the collectors and students of tradition were primarily concerned with material on which to base rulings of law, doctrine, and ritual, the collections also included much that has a narrative or biographical content. In fact, every major collection of traditions contains sections on both the biography and the military campaigns of the Prophet.

This brings us to the second source—the Arabian saga. The peninsular Arabs of pre-Islamic and early Islamic times lived and sang in the heroic style—tribal, nomadic, warlike, obsessed with battle and vengeance, honor and shame, death and destiny, personal, family, and tribal pride. Their poetry and legends mirror the conceptions and preoccupations of a heroic age. Muhammad, the greatest of them all, was not only a prophet; he was also an Arab hero and a warrier of noble birth. Before long, writings appear celebrating the exploits and victories of the Prophet and his companions in their wars against the unbelievers. These works, though nearer to history in character and purpose than the tradition, are still very far from being historiography in the normal sense. They are subjective and episodic, presenting a series of heroic figures and incidents without concern for chronology, sequence, or consistency—in a word, saga rather than history.

While a considerable mass of biographical data was accumulated in these various ways, the impulse for the collection and establishment of the biography of the Prophet came from another source—from the great transformation which had meanwhile been taking place in the personality of Muhammad as conceived in the religious consciousness of the community established by his revelation. In a brilliant monograph,[25] the Swedish scholar Tor Andrae showed how, under the influence of the Christian and Jewish communities with whom they came into contact, the Muslims began to see their Prophet in another light, as founder of their faith, to be compared with Jesus and Moses and, indeed, superior to them since his was the final revelation completing and supplanting those of his predecessors. Thus arose that cult of personal veneration—which Muhammad himself had explicitly rejected—making him an examplar of ethical and religious virtues, the best and noblest of mankind. To meet and outdo the miracles of Jesus and Moses, Muhammad, who had explicitly disclaimed any superhuman powers or attributes, was made the protagonist of a cycle of wonders and marvels stretching back to his early childhood and even to before his birth.

By the beginning of the second century of Islam, the main biographic pattern had been fixed. It was given its classic formulation by Muhammad ibn Ishaq, who was born in Medina about 719. A collector of traditions by training, he devoted himself to the study of the biography of the Prophet, collecting material from all available sources. In doing so he broke away from the formal rules laid down for the science of tradition and used by practitioners of that science to distinguish true from false tradition. He enlarged the scope of the source material and adopted a new and different attitude to it—that of a biographer rather than of a traditionist. This, not surprisingly, aroused the ire and resentment of the men of tradition, and it may have been because of this that Ibn Ishaq was forced to leave his native Arabia and travel, first to Egypt and then to Iraq. He finally settled in Baghdad where he died in 768. It was there, under the patronage of the Caliph al-Mansūr, that he completed his biography of the Prophet.

The work in its original form is lost, but it survives in a later recension by Ibn Hisham, a scholar of Basra who died in 834. In the edition of Ibn Hisham, Ibn Ishaq's biography of Muhammad has acquired almost the status of a sacred book all over the world of Islam. The information which it contains is supplemented by those other texts already mentioned above.

The primary question that will occur to the modern reader is: How far is all this authentic? Among Ibn Ishaq's own contemporaries and co-religionists, the masters of the science of tradition regarded both his objectives and his methods with some suspicion, and there have been not a few since then who have echoed their doubts. The overwhelming majority of Muslims, however, have accepted this book as a true portrait of the life and work of their Prophet. The modern reader will get the impression that Ibn Ishaq, unlike the compilers of some other religious texts, was at least concerned with historical accuracy. He is careful to distinguish between good authorities and poor ones, between those he cites with confidence and those he cites with reserve. He does not hesitate to tell stories which show the Prophet's enemies in a favorable light and—what is still more striking—stories that show the Prophet himself in what is to Western eyes an unfavorable light. One cannot, of course, build too much on this: the picture of the noble and courageous enemy is part of the heroic tradition on which Ibn Ishaq drew, while, on the other hand, much that might seem discreditable to us would not have seemed so to Ibn Ishaq. But we may be fairly sure that Ibn Ishaq's failures are of judgment and not of historical integrity.

The first generation of Western scholars who worked on the biography of Ibn Ishaq adopted, on the whole, a positive attitude. After discounting the obviously legendary and miraculous passages, they were ready to accept most of the remainder as an accurate record of the life and work of Muhammad, whose career, in Renan's words, did indeed seem as well known and as well documented as those of the sixteenth-century Reformers. Since then, however, our knowledge of the life of Muhammad has grown less and less as the progress of scholarly research has called one after another of the data of Muslim tradition into question. The Jesuit Henri Lammens and the positivist Leone Caetani, from their different vantage points, subjected the tradition to minute historical and psychological analysis, while the meticulous scholarship of Tor Andrae was able to show the motives and influences which led the early Muslims to give a new shape and color to their image of the last and greatest of the Prophets. Lammens went so far as to reject the entire biography as no more than a conjectural and tendentious exegesis of a few passages of biographical content in the Qur'ān, devised and elaborated by later generations of believers.[26] Other Western scholars reacted against this extreme formulation and, while agreeing that there is much that is purely legendary in the biography, especially in the passages dealing with the Prophet's early life, were prepared to accept most of the remainder as substantially accurate. Gibbon, equally ignorant of past Muslim and future Western doubts about the authenticity of the *Sira*, used his own critical judgment and was able to achieve a version which at least reflected an early Muslim view.

Eighteenth-century scholarship on Islam in Europe was still subject to many difficulties. Among the most important were the lack of adequate access to major Arabic sources and the lack of tools facilitating access to the Arabic language itself. Even now, Arabists have no historical dictionary or historical grammar of the Arabic language; the task of the seventeenth- or eighteenth-century Arabist, reading manuscript sources with virtually no research aids to assist him, was truly formidable. There were further problems: the remnants of theological prejudice, which still colored the views even of those who personally were free from them and which sometimes made the expression of a more objective opinion physically hazardous; the fables and absurdities inherited from the ignorant past; and—a new feature of the period—the various attempts to present Muhammad and Islam in terms of current controversies in Christendom, between Catholics and Protestants, between Protestants of various persuasions, or between Christians and Deists or freethinkers.

Nevertheless, great progress was made. The more preposterous legends about Muhammad—the trained dove who came to his ear, the coffin suspended in mid-air, and the like—were now abandoned even by the most bigoted of writers. New sources were made available in printed Arabic texts and in Latin translations, and the study of Islam was established as a serious subject worthy of attention and respect. The Muslims were no longer seen purely in ethnic terms as hostile tribes, but as the carriers of a distinctive religion and civilization; their Prophet was no longer a grotesque impostor or a Christian heretic, but the founder of an independent and historically significant religious community.

Gibbon's "instinct of criticism" did not forsake him in dealing with the Arabic sources for the life of the Prophet. There was, indeed, little else to guide him. For Roman history, he could build on the work of Tillemont and a host of lesser historians. For Islam, his main guide was Simon Ockley's *History of the Saracens*, and this begins with the death of the Prophet. Gibbon recognized the late and legendary character of much of the Arabic material made available to him in Latin translations and attempted some critical analysis of its content. However, his own imperfect knowledge and the defective state of European scholarship at the time hampered his work and sometimes blunted the skepticism which he usually brought to the sources and subjects of his historical inquiries. The chapter on Muhammad and on the beginnings of Islam is still much affected by myths, and in this, more visibly than in the chapters on Rome and on Byzantium, Gibbon gives expression to his own prejudices and purposes and those of the circles in which he moved.

There were several layers of myth and misunderstanding in the portrait of the Prophet as depicted in the literature available to him. Medieval Christian denigration of a rival product had little effect on him. Western scholarship was already in the process of demolishing the grosser errors, and Gibbon would have been the least likely of historians to be influenced by them. The Muslim religious myths enshrined in the traditional biographical literature on which all his sources ultimately rest were more difficult for him to detect, and there are failures of perception and analysis excusable in a historian of the time. Sometimes, indeed, he shows rather less than his usual acumen. Thus, his account of pre-Islamic Arabian religion—"liberty of choice . . . each Arab . . . free to elect or to compose his own private religion"[27]—would be difficult to sustain even in the light of the evidence available in the eighteenth century, and is indeed self-evidently absurd. As Gibbon rightly remarked of his approach: "I am ignorant, and I am careless, of the blind mythology of the barbarians."[28]

Gibbon was, of course, well equipped to recognize the propaganda and counterpropaganda of Catholic, Protestant, Christian, and Deist, and he has some amusing comments to offer on this subject. Where he himself is very clearly affected is by the mythology of the Enlightenment—a vision of Islam which seems to have been initiated in the biography of the Prophet by Boulainvilliers, and was widely accepted among the writers of the Enlightenment in various European countries. Europe, it seems, has always needed a myth for purposes of comparison and castigation: Prester John in the Middle Ages, the United States in the nineteenth century, the Soviet Union in the early twentieth. The eighteenth-century Enlightenment had two ideal prototypes, the noble savage and the wise and urbane Oriental. There was some competition for the latter role. For a while the Chinese, held up as a model of moral virtue by the Jesuits and of secular tolerance by the philosophers, filled it to perfection in the Western intellectual shadow play. Then disillusionment set in, and was worsened by the reports of returning travelers whose perceptions of China were shaped by neither Jesuitry nor philosophy, but by experience. By the time Gibbon began to write, there was a vacancy for an Oriental myth. Islam was in many ways suitable. While China was ceasing to impress, Islam no longer terrified, and it had the further advantage of being the intimate enemy of the church. The mythopoeic process began with an attempt by historians to correct the negative stereotypes of the Middle Ages and to recognize the contributions of Islamic civilization to mankind. It developed into a portrait of Muhammad as a wise and tolerant lawgiver, the founder of rational, undogmatic, priest-free religion and society.

The honor and reputation of Islam and its founder were protected in Europe neither by social pressure nor by legal sanction, and they thus served as an admirable vehicle for anti-religious and anti-Christian polemic. Gibbon occasionally accomplishes this purpose by attacking Islam while meaning Christianity, more frequently by praising Islam as an oblique criticism of Christian usage, belief, and practice. Much of his praise would not be acceptable in a Muslim country.

There are several lessons which he tries to draw from the biography of the Prophet and the subsequent history of Islam. One of these is that Islam is a religion with a purely human founder—a point also made by Boulainvilliers. This is, of course, an argument against the Christian doctrine of the divinity of Christ as the Son of God and all that is connected with it. In this, Gibbon and his predecessors in the Enlightenment did rely on something genuinely Islamic, and indeed showed some perspicacity in going back beyond the later and legendary accretions of the Muslim biographies of the Prophet to the authentic historical figure of Muhammad and to the earliest Islamic tradition, which insists that Muhammad, though a Prophet and a Messenger of God, was no more than a human being, mortal like others.

Another point which Gibbon is at some pains to impress upon his readers is the stability and permanence of the Islamic faith in the form in which it was founded by the Prophet—that is to say, it is free from subsequent and local accretions such as have overlaid the message of Christ and retains its pristine content and character. In this, of course, he was greatly mistaken, as he could have ascertained by some attention to Islam as practiced in various parts of the Islamic world in his own day.

Linked with this is his insistence that Islam is a faith with few dogmas and without priesthood or church and, therefore, by implication much freer and better than Christianity, which is heavily burdened with all these. This is slightly better than a half truth. There is indeed no priesthood in the sacerdotal sense—no priestly ordination, office, or mediation; there is, however, a priesthood in the sociological sense, an order of professional men of religion, and these have played a part which, though entirely different from that of the Christian churches, is nevertheless of great importance in the history of Islam. His further argument that Islam has been free from schism and strife is greatly exaggerated. Sectarian strife in Islam never reached the degree of ferocity which became normal in Christendom, but differences existed, and men were ready to kill and die, to suffer and persecute because of them. "The Metaphysical questions on the attributes of God and the liberty of man," says Gibbon, "have been agitated in the schools of the Mahometans as well as in those of the Christians; but among the former they have never engaged the passions of the people or disturbed the tranquillity of the state. The cause of this important difference may be found in the separation or union of the regal and sacerdotal characters."[29] This assessment is so manifestly wrong as to place its author almost on a par with the Persian letter-writers and Turkish spies who enlightened the West about its defects, rather than with serious historians of the East.

On the religious doctrines of Islam, Gibbon has little to say, since it was only in its public and social aspects that religion was of any interest to him. The Islamic creed, that there is no God but God and that Muhammad is his Apostle, he describes as "compounded of an eternal truth and a necessary fiction"—a recognizable echo of Boulainvilliers's "mais il falloit être prophète, ou passer pour tel à quelque prix que ce pût être."[30] The same tolerant acceptance of the necessity of the fiction informs his other comments and asides on the sincerity of the Prophet: "From his earliest youth Mahomet was addicted to religious contemplation; each year, during the month of Ramadan, he withdrew from the world and from the arms of Cadijah [his wife]; in the cave of Hera, three miles from Mecca, he consulted the spirit of fraud or enthusiasm, whose abode is not in the heavens, but in the mind of the prophet."[31] A later passage is somewhat more severe:

> In the spirit of enthusiasm or vanity, the prophet rests the truth of his mission on the merit of his book, audaciously challenges both men and angels to imitate the beauties of a single page, and presumes to assert that God alone could dictate this incomparable performance. . . . The harmony and copiousness of style will not reach, in a version, the European infidel; he will peruse, with impatience, the endless incoherent rhapsody of fable, and precept, and declamation, which seldom excites a sentiment or an idea, which sometimes crawls in the dust and is sometimes lost in the clouds. . . .[32]

On the other hand, "The Mohometan religion is destitute of priesthood or sacrifice; and the independent spirit of fanaticism looks down with contempt on the ministers and slaves of superstition."[33] The final version is moderately severe:

> It may perhaps be expected that I should balance his faults and virtues, that I should decide whether the title of enthusiast or impostor most properly belongs to that extraordinary man. . . . From enthusiasm to imposture the step is perilous and slippery; the daemon of Socrates affords a memorable instance, how a wise man may deceive himself, how a good man may deceive others, how the conscience may slumber in a mixed and middle state between self-illusion and voluntary fraud. Charity may believe that the original motives of Mahomet were those of pure and genuine benevolence; but a human missionary is incapable of cherishing the obstinate unbelievers who reject his claims. . . .[34]

On the subject of tolerance, Gibbon seems undecided. At the beginning of his chapter on the rise of Islam, he describes how "Mahomet," "with the sword in one hand

and the Koran in the other, erected his throne on the ruins of Christianity and of
Rome."[35] "Mahomet," of course, is here used metonymically for the empire of the
Caliphs. Even so, the statement is remarkably inaccurate. Both Christianity and
Rome survived the advent of Islam; the Qur'ān did not become a book until some time
after Muhammad's death; only a left-handed swordsman could brandish both, since
no Muslim would hold the sacred book in the hand reserved for unclean purposes—
and most important of all, there was a third choice, the payment of tribute and
acceptance of Muslim rule.[36]

Gibbon's influence on the Western perception of the Prophet, Islam, and their
place in history was enormous. From recondite and learned books, most of them in
Latin and little known outside the narrow world of clerics and scholars, he was able to
present a picture of the Prophet and the rise of Islam that was clear, elegant, and
above all convincing. Most important of all was that unlike previous writers, including
the Arabists, he saw the rise of Islam not as something separate and isolated, nor as
a regrettable aberration from the onward march of the church, but as a part of human
history, to be understood against the background of Rome and Persia, in the light
of Judaism and Christianity, and in complex interplay with Byzantium, Asia, and
Europe.

REFERENCES

[1]Gibbon, *Autobiography*, ed. Dero A. Saunders (New York, 1961), p. 67.

[2]*Ibid.*, p. 79.

[3]Thus, Catholic polemicists accused Calvin of Islamizing tendencies, and Calvinists in Geneva tried to
bring the same charge against Servetus. See Aldobrandino Malvezzi, *L'Islamismo e la cultura europea*
(Florence, 1956), pp. 246ff.; R. H. Bainton, *Michel Servet, hérétique et martyr* (Geneva, 1953), p. 116.

[4]See Kenneth M. Setton, "Lutheranism and the Turkish Peril," in *Balkan Studies* (Thessaloniki), 3
(1962), pp. 133-68; Dorothy Vaughan, *Europe and the Turk: A Pattern of Alliances* (Liverpool, 1954).

[5]S. Ockley, *History of the Saracens* (Cambridge, 1757), ii, xxxv, cited in P. M. Holt, *Studies in the History
of the Near East* (London, 1973), p. 55.

[6]*The History of the Decline and Fall of the Roman Empire (DF)*, ed. J. B. Bury (London, 1909-14), chap. 7,
p. 135.

[8]Oxford 1648-50; reprinted Oxford, 1806.

[9]Claude Étienne Savary, *Le Coran, traduit de l'Arabe, accompagné de notes et précédé d'un abrégé de la vie de
Mahomet, tiré des écrivains orientaux les plus estimés* (Paris, 1783), Preface.

[10]*The Koran: commonly called the Alcoran of Mohammed; translated into English immediately from the original
Arabic, with explanatory notes . . . to which is prefixed a preliminary discourse* (London, 1734).

[11]Holt (above, note 5), p. 60.

[12]*Alcorani Textus Universus ex correctionibus Arabum exemplaribus summa fide . . . descriptus, eademque fide . . .
ex arabico idiomate in Latinum translatus; oppositis unicuique capitis notis, atque refutatione. . . .*

[13]*DF*, chap. 50, p. 374, note 118.

[14]*The True Nature of Imposture fully Display'd in the Life of Mahomet. With a Discourse annex'd for the
Vindication of Christianity from this Charge. Offered to the Consideration of the Deists of the Present Age* (Oxford,
1697).

[15]*La Vie de Mahomed; avec des réflexions sur les religion Mahometane, et les coutumes des Musulmans* (London,
1730; reprinted Amsterdam, 1731).

[16]*DF*, chap. 50, p. 375, note 119.

[17]Prideaux, Preface, cited in Holt (above note 5), p. 51.

[18]On this work and its influence in Europe, see Massimo Petrocchi, "Il mito de Maometto in
Boulainvilliers," in *Rivista Storica Italiana*, 60 (1948), pp. 367-77.

[19]Boulainvilliers (Amsterdam, 1731), p. 267.

[20]*Ibid.*, p. 85.

[21]*Ibid.*, p. 225.

[22]On this literature, see further Hans Haas, "Das Bild Muhammeds im Wandel der Zeiten," in
Zeitschrift für Missionskunde und Religionswissenschaft, 31 (1916), pp. 161-71, 194-203, 225-39, 258-69, 289-95,
321-33, 353-65; Gustav Pfannmüller, *Handbuch der Islam-Literatur* (Berlin-Leipzig, 1923), pp. 115-206;
Pierre Martino, "Mahomet en France au XVIIe et au XVIIIe siècle," in *Actes du XIVe Congrès international*

des Orientalistes: Alger 1905, part III (Paris, 1907), pp. 206-41; *idem*, *L'Orient dans la littérature française au XVIIᵉ et au XVIIIᵉ siècle* (Pairs, 1906); G. H. Bousquet, "Voltaire et l'Islam," in *Studia Islamica*, fasc. xxviii (1968), pp. 109-26; Djavad Hadidi, *Voltaire et l'Islam* (Paris, 1974). On the history of Arabic scholarship in Europe, see Johann Fück, *Die arabischen Studien in Europa bis in den Anfang des 20. Jahrhunderts* (Leipzig, 1955).

[23]*DF*, chap. 50, p. 375, note 119.

[24]Ernest Renan, *Études d'histoire religieuse* (2nd edition, Paris, 1857), pp. 217ff., especially p. 220. The same desire to observe the visible birth of a prophetic religion inspired the historian of antiquity Eduard Meyer and the Islamicist D. S. Margoliouth to study the history of the Mormons.

[25]Tor Andrae, *Die Person Muhammeds in Lehre und Glauben seiner Gemeinde* (Stockholm, 1917).

[26]More recent scholarship, chiefly in Russia, has questioned the historicity of the Qur'ān and even of Muhammed himself. See N. A. Smirnov. *Očerki istorii izučeniya Islama v SSSR* (Moscow, 1954); English abridgement, *Islam and Russia* (London, 1956).

[27]*DF*, chap. 50, p. 354.

[28]*Ibid.*, p. 349. In spite of this, Gibbon devoted considerable attention to the Arabian background of Muhammad's career, drawing, in addition to his classical and Arabic sources, on the accounts of recent travelers, notably Carsten Niebuhr, for information about the geography of Arabia and the way of life of the Arabs. His treatment of this subject is much colored by his general views on barbarian virtue, and might usefully be compared with his discussion of the pre-Christian Germans and pre-Islamic Turks.

[29]*DF*, chap. 50, p. 420.

[30]Boulainvilliers, p. 343.

[31]*DF*, chap. 50, p. 360.

[32]*Ibid.*, pp. 365-66.

[33]*Ibid.*, p. 376. This distinction between superstition and fanaticism (sometimes equated with enthusiasm) is derived from David Hume, "Of Superstition and Enthusiasm," *Essays*; cf., *Dialogues Concerning Natural Religion*, ed. Norman Kemp Smith (Indianapolis-New York, 1947).

[34]*DF*, chap. 50, pp. 400-1.

[35]*Ibid.*, p. 332.

[36]For a fuller discussion of these points, see G. E. von Grunebaum, "Islam: The Problem of Changing Perspective," in Lynn White, Jr., ed., *The Transformation of the Roman World: Gibbon's Problem After Two Centuries* (Berkeley and Los Angeles, 1966), pp. 147-78.

THE

H I S T O R Y

OF THE

DECLINE AND FALL

OF THE

ROMAN EMPIRE.

VOLUME THE SECOND.

Title page of Volume II of *The Decline and Fall of the Roman Empire*, and facing page with Gibbon's dedication to his Aunt Catherine Porten. By permission of the Harvard College Library.

ARNALDO MOMIGLIANO

Gibbon from an Italian Point of View

I

I HAPPEN TO BE WRITING MY PIECE on Gibbon in Spoleto. It is a challenge, for there are few places in Italy where one is less aware that the Middle Ages were a barbaric parenthesis between the Golden Age of the Antonines and the Renaissance. In the late fourth century, Ammianus Marcellinus chose Spoletium as the symbolic extreme place to which an aged and not very mobile Roman aristocrat would go if he knew that he was to get a present as a guest at a wealthy marriage.[1] Spoleto was exactly the sort of town in which a late-Roman aristocrat could turn up without feeling the shock of a conflict between the old and the new. The city absorbed Christian and pagan events without being much shaken by either. While the edict of Constantine about the church of the Novatiani was signed in Spoleto in A.D. 326,[2] Julian's edict against Christian teachers and doctors was received there on July 29, 362.[3] About A.D. 415 Syrian monks came to occupy the sacred forest (*lucus*) over the city (now Monte Luco) which an archaic Roman law had protected since the third century B.C.[4] At Spoleto the arch of Drusus now stands in the middle of a medieval street, and one of the medieval gates has the reputation, supported by a Renaissance inscription, of having witnessed the successful forays of the Roman colonists against Hannibal. In its turn the medieval cathedral is decorated by one of the masterpieces of Filippo Lippi. As if to emphasize the continuity, Lorenzo de' Medici put Lippi's tomb there with an epigram by Politian. The sense of decay—the contrast between the ancient ruins and the barefooted friars which Gibbon experienced in the Roman Forum in 1764—is absent in Spoleto where, properly speaking, there is no ruin. The direct rule by the popes which began, albeit among conflicts, in 1198 prevented the development of the kind of communal life that is so much more in evidence in neighboring Foligno. Spoleto was kept in its medieval shell until the French Revolution. While handling in the municipal library of Spoleto a copy of the second Pisa edition of the Italian translation of Gibbon—which began to appear exactly in 1789—it was natural to reflect that it was perhaps Gibbon himself who brought the modern age to Spoleto. To say the least, Spoleto is one of those Italian places which compel the reader of Gibbon to question the validity of his assumptions about Italian history.

II

Let us at the outset make clear a fundamental fact: Gibbon's view of Italian medieval history was to a great extent shared by the most enlightened Italians of the eighteenth century—and it could hardly have been otherwise, for that view had been derived by Gibbon from his Italian mentors, Sarpi, Giannone, and·Muratori.[5] Gibbon had two not entirely coherent models for his Middle Ages. One was the Byzantine, about which there was essentially no dispute in his time. It was a model of progressive dissolution through administrative incompetence and theological disputations which led to the Turkish rule over both Constantinople and the Balkans. This model was unrelated to any direct experience; Gibbon never saw the east of Europe. He learned about it from scholars and travelers, mainly English and French, and with their help he went back to the original sources.

The other model was Italian, both in the sense that it was suggested to him by what he saw of Italy and in the sense that it was confirmed by what he learned from those Italian historians and *érudits* he admired. The decline of Rome was first of all a visual experience which an immense amount of literary documentation confirmed and defined in its chronological framework. As a foil to it there were the prosperous and modern cities of northern and central Italy which had long ago rid themselves of feudal lords and, as monarchies or republics, seemed to be committed to a policy of reform. We know from the journal how interested Gibbon was in Turin and its monarchy and how he relished other northern and central Italian cities. Venice, with its Byzantine features, might have created some special problems, but it is altogether remarkable how little Venice—Sarpi notwithstanding—is present in Gibbon's history.

It was Byzantium, of course, not Italy that took up most of the space in Gibbon's *Decline and Fall*. He felt he had more to discover about Byzantium, and through Byzantium he satisfied his curiosity about the Arabs and other Oriental nations. In their turn the Arabs, or rather the Turks, gave him an opportunity to introduce the subject of the Crusades, on which he had so much of interest to say. The Italian Middle Ages are described far more briefly and less impressively. But it is significant that Gibbon should choose Italy—rather than Germany or France—to represent the western side of the medieval world. The alternatives were very real. Germany was the successor to imperial Rome. France was the most impressive political and social organization born out of the ruins of the old Rome—Dubos and Boulainvilliers, as Gibbon knew only too well, had shown what interesting problems the birth of medieval France presented. By choosing Italy, Gibbon both followed his instincts as a classicist and made the interpretation of the Middle Ages offered by Muratori and Giannone his own.

Whatever the differences.may be between Muratori and Giannone, both had said loudly that the struggles against feudal lords and ecclesiastical interference were the line of progress for Italy. Both had emphasized the lack of continuity between ancient Rome and modern Italy. Both had tried hard to keep the spiritual and the political sides of the Catholic Church separate. Both had claimed a special place for Italy as the most civilized territory of Western Christendom in the Middle Ages. Both had recognized the part played by Goths and Lombards and Normans in shaping post-Roman Italy. Gibbon reflects the feelings of both Muratori and Giannone in giving such a positive evaluation of the foreign rulers, under whom the Italians enjoyed a better government than that of any other kingdom formed upon the ruins of the Western Empire. He follows his Italian mentors even in paying comparatively little attention to the development of the Italian *comuni*. His line is the "anti-curial" line of Giannone and Muratori: what interests him is the struggle of the individual Italian states against the church and the institutions (monastic and feudal) supported by the church. The distinction between monarchies and republics became almost irrelevant in this context, except that medieval monarchies were nearer to modern states.

I am not sure that even Muratori would have been pleased to read in Gibbon that the communal republics, by asserting their liberties, vindicated the rights of human nature.[6] It was probably more a question of language than of substance, for Gibbon does not develop this point of view; but, so far as I know, such a language was unknown in Italy in the first part of the eighteenth century. There is also a difference between Gibbon's idealization of the Antonine age and the eighteenth-century Italians' basic mistrust of ancient Rome. One must go back to Biondo, Machiavelli, and Sigonio to find real affection for Rome among Italian historians. But here again it was a question of nuances. Both Muratori and Giannone appreciated the role of Roman law as an obstacle to the political ambitions of the Roman popes and to the anarchy of feudal and ecclesiastical privileges. After all, Muratori, as a good subject of the imperial Duchy of Modena, defended the rights of the (Holy) Roman Empire against the church in the Comacchio affair. Giannone vainly tried to put himself under the protection of this Empire in Vienna. It was precisely the realization that the Roman Empire was still a reality and that Roman law still created difficulties that prevented the reformers of the eighteenth century from idealizing any one stage of the old Roman Empire. Even Giannone had to admit that there was less cause for confusion in the simplicity of Lombard law. Muratori saw the impossibility of keeping Justinian's *Corpus* as the basic law of a modern state and said so in the book *Dei difetti della giurisprudenza* (1741). To explain the need for a modern codification (with or without the help of the church) Muratori was not afraid to present Lombard and Frankish law as preferable to the mass of contradictory interpretations of Roman law which had been piling up since the reintroduction of the *Pandectae* after 1100. Incidentally, a careful reader of Gibbon's chapter on Roman law—which circulated as a separate publication in the German universities—will notice increasing reservations about the usefulness of the Roman legal tradition as he approaches Justinian: Gibbon was not unaware of what had been said against the *Corpus Juris*.

The main point is that Gibbon took over the Italian thesis that papal Rome was not the heir of ancient Rome and that the temporal power of the church, the unruliness of the monastic orders, and the feudalization of the Italian states had been the causes of the decline of Italy. Germanic kingdoms, city republics, and, finally, modern territorial states were the bright spots, the hopes for the future. French as the roots of Gibbon's culture were, his particular brand of Enlightenment was a mixture of Swiss and Scottish traits—not Calvinistic, but, as H. Trevor-Roper has reminded us, the result of the local reaction to Calvinism. This implied a sensitivity to municipal and regional situations, in which feudal lords and the Catholic (or the Calvinist!) Church had been the enemies of reason. Lausanne, Geneva, and Edinburgh were ideal places for appreciating the efforts of emancipation from feudal and ecclesiastical controls. They were therefore good places for understanding the message of Giannone and Muratori.

III

The model adopted by Gibbon failed, however, to account for many features of Italian history. It did not explain the development of the papal state, and it was rather insensitive to the part played by the Holy See in absorbing and even promoting humanistic culture. Gibbon was not only unappreciative of the monastic culture of the Middle Ages from Cassiodorus to St. Thomas, he also found it difficult to reconcile his contempt for the papal government with the beauty and the splendor he recognized in modern Rome. In this position he was of course nearer to Giannone than to Muratori. Pious Muratori could not underrate the weight of the ecclesiastical contribution to Italian arts and letters. Like Giannone, Gibbon allowed his anti-curial prejudices to interfere with an objective assessment of what past and present Italian intellectual life owed to the monastic orders and to the regular clergy both within Rome and outside it.

Here Spoleto comes in—Spoleto or any other Italian city (it might be Bergamo or Siena or Fermo or L'Aquila) which by the eighteenth century had long lost any political initiative and may even never have had any. These cities depended for the relatively high level of their spiritual and social life on their religious orders, on their churches and educational foundations, and on their local saints and "venerables." If there was a contribution from the laity, it came from the aristocracy, whose connections with the church were structural. Italy was a country where the vitality of feudal and pseudo-feudal orders was baffling even to contemporaries. The southern barons were at least a real power, a subject for true historians such as Porzio. But that Tuscan joke—the Cavalieri di Santo Stefano who prospered in the very bourgeois Grand Duchy of the Medici—had acquired respectability and influence. I contemplate it retrospectively every time I walk into the building of the Scuola Normale Superiore of Pisa, their previous official residence. The story of the Constantinian Order, a perfectly bogus institution which nearly ruined Scipione Maffei about 1712, is the most telling confirmation, on the comic side, of the power of such groups. To Gibbon the later proliferations of Italian feudalism are no problem.

Since 1725, there had been a book unknown to Gibbon in which these aspects of Italy were taken into consideration in a peculiar way: Vico's *Scienza Nuova*. To treat the *Scienza Nuova* as an alternative model of Italian history to that offered by Gibbon (and his Italian predecessors) means laying oneself open to the double reproach of unilateralism and of paradox. The double reproach is indeed legitimate, but irrelevant. Long before Gibbon, Vico had presented his version of the decline and fall. He had done so without any recognizable influence, though Montesquieu's *Considérations* (1734) show how much the problem was in the air. With the final edition of the *Scienza Nuova* (1744) the previous generalities on the theory of the *corsi e ricorsi* were developed and formalized in a study of the Middle Ages which now occupied the fifth (and final) section of the work.

The basic difference between Vico and Gibbon was, of course, that Vico was interested in barbarism as the root of civilization itself and studied barbarism not as a problem of degeneration but as the matrix of language, poetry, law, and ultimately of reason. Conversely he realized—the first to do so—that too much reason could lead back to barbarism: there was such a thing for him as the "barbarie della riflessione." He had arrived at these conclusions by drastically separating sacred from profane history. Leaving revelation and truth to the Jews, he set himself the task of exploring the mind of the pagan "bestioni" who had forgotten or never known the revealed Truth. This was not in conflict with Catholic dogmas as he knew them. Whoever wishes to accuse Vico of disguised free-thinking or heresy or deism has to take into account that his *Scienza Nuova* was sent to the printers in three Neapolitan editions during his lifetime with the *imprimatur* of the ecclesiastical authorities. We can trust them to know what they were doing. All the same, Vico's Providence was certainly not conventional in its operations. Stimulated by their appetites which were their secret providence, men had traversed the age of the gods and the age of the heroes to emerge into that great age of reason which had been the Roman Empire. They were no longer expressing themselves by gestures, as in the first age, or by epic poems, as in the second age. They had left behind the stage in which (witness the Twelve Tables) even law was a "serioso poema." In the Roman Empire, jurists formulated model laws for enlightened subjects. Vico did not dream of preferring barbaric law to Roman law. But reason was insufficient to keep control beyond a certain point. Barbaric laws had come as an unavoidable *ricorso*: they reminded Vico of the poetic crudity of the Twelve Tables.

The medieval *ricorso* inspired some of Vico's best pages. They indicate what the *ricorso* brought back of the heroic forms of primitive barbarism: not only archaic law, but the language of symbols and gestures, the old clientship under the new name of feudalism ("ritornarono le antiche clientele romane che furono delle commende") and, finally, the new "primitive" poetry. Vico knew nothing of the *Chanson de Roland* and of the *Nibelungenlied*, but he had some knowledge of French and Spanish *romans* and was delighted to report that "in Silesia nazione di contadini nascono tutti poeti."

As the decline of the Roman Empire coincided with the rise and victory of Christianity, this implied that sacred history had overtaken profane history. Vico was not embarrassed by that. The very totality of the *ricorso* implied a new birth, an explosion of new creative energies: Vico just took it for granted that the new development was in a Christian context. It may surprise us that Vico felt no difficulty, indeed no problem, in joining barbarism with Christianity. But for Vico the *ricorso* was the first stage of the new civilization, of the new Europe, in which the Christian religion went together with the "grandi monarchie nei loro costumi umanissime." Europe had become young again in the Middle Ages. Its new language of gestures and symbols was Christian. Monks and Germans, feudal lords and crusaders, churches and universities were all parts of this unitary process, the great Christian *ricorso*. There are some sentences in the final pages of the 1744 edition of the *Scienza Nuova* which, taken in isolation, seem to imply that the new mature civilization resulting from the combination of good laws and true religion may escape a third *ricorso* in the future. I doubt, however, whether Vico ever put this problem to himself as clearly as Gibbon did. What his exposition conveys, in an entirely unsophisticated manner, is the sense of a positive start with the fall of the Roman Empire: the *ricorso* made modern Europe, and modern Europe was Christian.

Vico saw no conflict between church and state. Giannone's hatred for the Roman Curia was alien to him. Giannone sensed the difference and expressed contempt for his countryman.[7] But Muratori's much more subtle and qualified evaluation of the relations between state and church in medieval and modern Italy was also very different from Vico's unquestioning acceptance of the whole Catholic past of Italy. Vico took no serious interest in Muratori's medieval studies and was inevitably repaid by a corresponding lack of attention from Muratori, though they were on cordial terms, and Muratori took some trouble in procuring the election of Vico to an academy at Urbino. By ignoring the religious conflicts of his age and of previous ages, Vico found himself free to admire Protestant thinkers such as Grotius and Pufendorf and to be altogether more concerned with the great systematic thinkers of the previous century than with the historians and controversialists of his own time. To read him one would assume, on the one hand, that modern Europe emerged providentially from the Middle Ages without any laceration in the texture of its Christian faith. But, on the other hand, the elements of the unity of the Western Middle Ages were not underrated, as they were even in Muratori.

Consequently Vico could not be popular in his own century. His research methods were below the standards of contemporary critical erudition, and he left to Providence—not to reason, or to common sense, or to more enlightened piety—the task of transferring mankind from barbarism to civilization. In the depth of his heart he liked his "bestioni." He became a recognizable alternative to Gibbon only in the following century.

IV

Gibbon's model of the Italian Middle Ages, just because it was derived from Italian sources, was far less anti-Christian than were his chapters on the spreading of Christianity and the decline of the Roman Empire. It emphasized the encroachments of the church on the state and played down the cultural achievements of the monastic orders and of the clergy, but it did not question, as chapters 15 and 16 did, the right of Christianity even to exist. The discrepancy represents, to my mind, a serious structural weakness of the *Decline and Fall* and, as we shall see, explains the role of Gibbon in Italian historical thought of the nineteenth century. But it is not surprising that, immediately after their appearance, chapters 15 and 16 caused as much alarm in Italy as in England. The Italian criticisms came, of course, not from the few and discredited followers of Vico, but from the Catholic theologians.

The success of the *Decline and Fall* in Italy was indeed rapid and conspicuous. The first sixteen chapters were published in an Italian translation based on the French translation by Leclerc de Septchênes in 1779; the place of publication was given as Lausanne, but was in fact Florence. This translation was placed on the *Index Librorum Prohibitorum* in 1783; the translator was F. Zacchiroli. A direct translation from English of chapters 1 through 38 immediately followed in Pisa between 1779 and 1785, under the supervision of the Jansenist fellow-traveler Monsignor Angelo Fabroni, "provveditore agli studi" at the university. Three further chapters were published in 1792; this translation went into a second edition between 1789 and 1794. Unlike the translator from the French, Monsignor Fabroni thought it necessary (or expedient) to include an antidote for the scandalous chapters 15 and 16, and he obtained the cooperation of Nicola Spedalieri, a Sicilian theologian who in 1779 had established his reputation in Rome by publishing a long book against Fréret (or what was considered to be authentic Fréret) on the subject of the proofs of Christianity.

Spedalieri was obviously specializing in polemics against the Enlightenment. To help Spedalieri, Fabroni, who was in touch with English Catholics living in Italy, produced translations for him of some of the pamphlets against Gibbon which provoked his devastating *Vindication*. But Spedalieri took his task so seriously that his refutation of the two chapters grew into two handsome quartos which were published as an independent work in 1784 (a second edition was published in 1798). Fabroni had to content himself with a summary of about a hundred and fifty pages of Spedalieri's work. Other criticisms of the religious opinions of the *Decline and Fall* were added in later sections with the help of the same Anglo-Italian Catholics, but apparently without the intervention of Spedalieri. Gibbon himself was aware, as his *Memoirs* show, of the connection between his Italian and his English critics. But since he did not read—or at least pretended not to have read—Spedalieri's volumes ("Shall I be excused for not having read them?"), he was not in a position to appreciate the difference between Spedalieri and the English critics. The former did not make any secret of the fact that he did not care for the Anglican criticisms against Gibbon transmitted to him by English Catholics. He had no intention of being involved in a discussion about evidence. He did not try to catch Gibbon out in factual mistakes, though he was not above insinuating that Gibbon worked at second hand. His task was to make clear the incompatibility between Gibbon's premises and any Catholic thinking about history. He made explicit what Gibbon had only implied, and he opposed to it the teaching of the church. As Gibbon had banked on ambiguity and delighted in insinuation, Spedalieri had a point.

The point became even more evident when Gibbon refused to accept what Spedalieri, for one, considered the natural consequence of the Enlightenment, namely, the French Revolution. In 1791 (while his book on Fréret was being republished), Spedalieri produced his last and most important work, *I Diritti dell'Uomo*, in which he submitted the Rights of Man to the same theological analysis which he had previously applied to Fréret and Gibbon. He fittingly dedicated his book to Monsignor Fabrizio Ruffo, who as Cardinal Ruffo was to become the symbolic figure of the ferocious reactionary in Italian history. But by that time Spedalieri was no longer giving any new thought to Gibbon, and Gibbon never knew of Spedalieri's *Diritti dell'Uomo*, in which he was not even mentioned. I can easily imagine what Spedalieri would have told Gibbon if they had met on the common ground of their hostility to the French Revolution—but I would have some difficulty in supplying the other side of the conversation.[8]

In any case, Napoleon's army soon made Italy permanently safe for Gibbon. Even during the Restoration, between 1820 and 1830, the Italian translation of his *Decline and Fall* could be reprinted and completed. The Italians have never stopped reading Gibbon since that time. But the significant aspect of the fortunes of Gibbon in the Italian culture of the nineteenth and the early twentieth centuries is that chapters 15 and 16 no longer aroused any controversy; nor was his theory prominent in any of the discussions about the decline of the Roman Empire. I do not know of any Italian who could note in his diary, as Benjamin Constant did, that if he were to write on Christianity he would only be repeating Gibbon.

If anything characterizes Italian historical thought in the nineteenth century it is the coexistence of two features: one is the absence of any serious research on the origins of Christianity, the other is the recognition of the positive contribution of Christianity to the civilization of the Middle Ages. Whether Catholic or anti-clerical, the Italians did not take the trouble to master the new problems of New Testamentary and patristic research which had been formulated outside Italy. More particularly, the Italian Hegelians never derived from their Hegelian premises the consequences for Bible criticism which became so obvious in Germany. At the same time anticlericalism, though it gave prominence to such medieval victims of the Roman church as Arnaldo da Brescia, who figures largely in Gibbon, never questioned the credentials of the church as a civilizing factor.

Even a writer as distant from the church as Carlo Cattaneo emphatically recognizes the work done by the church in shaping the fabric of society as soon as he settles down (in 1844) to describe the social situation of Lombardy in the Middle Ages. When, in the second part of the century, Malfatti wrote his unfinished masterpiece on church and empire in the early Middle Ages, his guiding question was that of the limits of the two authorities, not the legitimacy of either.[9] What may seem the real exception, Amedeo Crivellucci's two-volume *Storia delle Relazioni tra lo Stato e la Chiesa* published in 1885-86, becomes on closer inspection an apparent exception. A free-thinker, intensely aware of the contemporary conflict between Italy and the Vatican, Crivellucci, however, refuses to be influenced by this situation in describing the medieval past. The problem of origins, consequences, and value of Christianity remained basically outside the historical thinking of Italy during the nineteenth century—which is, of course, not to say that it remained extraneous to other, perhaps more important, aspects of the individual and collective life of the Italians.

In this generic sense, Vico's positive evaluation of Christianity as the providential driving force of the barbarians permeated the thinking of the Italian historians of the nineteenth century, whether they were Catholic or not. Benedetto Croce was right in saying that Cattaneo's essay on Lombardy was more Vichean in spirit than any of the dissertations of those who considered themselves Vico's followers. Giuseppe Ferrari represented more than himself when he wrote in his *Histoire des révolutions d'Italie* (1858): "Le génie de Vico nous donne la pensée qui triomphe de l'anarchie italienne."

Gibbon is present in all this thinking and research by what he tells about the dissolution of the Roman state, the contribution of the barbarians to law and order in Italy, the renaissance of Roman ideals with Petrarch and Cola di Rienzo, and even (with the reservation soon to be made) the poverty of Byzantine intellectual and political life. But what is most original in his work—the evaluation of Christianity—is left out. It follows that what the Italian historians of the nineteenth century took from Gibbon was to a great extent, though in a refurbished and more artistic form, what Gibbon had taken from his Italian mentors. The Italian historians established continuity with their predecessors of the eighteenth century through Gibbon.

This is true to the point that, though they were alerted by Gibbon to the value of Byzantium, they were far less interested in it than we would expect. While one of the historiographical masterpieces of nineteenth-century Italy is Michele Amari's history of the Muslim occupation of Sicily, there was no corresponding attempt to assess the more profound impact of Byzantine rule in Sicily, Southern Italy, and the Exarchate of Ravenna. Indeed it is characteristic that perhaps the most obvious follower of Gibbon in Italy is a historian of Islam, Giovanni Battista Rampoldi, whose *Annali musulmani*, published in Milan from 1822 to 1826, continuously betray the influence of the *Decline and Fall*.[10] Even from a merely linguistic point of view, one had to wait for twentieth-century foreign scholars such as G. Rohlfs to have the remains of spoken Greek in Southern Italy systematically collected. The more remote Byzantine Empire studied by Gibbon attracted even less attention. The great Byzantinists of the seventeenth and the early eighteenth centuries had no successors in Italy.

The new element added to the picture of the Italian Middle Ages in the nineteenth century were the *comuni*, the medieval city republics. This element (as we have seen) was adumbrated in Gibbon, but it was Simonde de Sismondi who from Geneva persuaded the Italians to treat the city republics of the Middle Ages as their greatest glory. Neither the man nor his native city was unrelated to Gibbon. Sismondi had studied his Gibbon and belonged to that circle which had Gibbon as one of its spiritual fathers. But what Sismondi gave, no Gibbon—indeed no Giannone or

Muratori—could give: the new enthusiasm for individual liberty, popular (albeit moderately popular) government, mercantile enterprise, and local patriotism. Sismondi had Italianized his own name, found spurious ancestors in an aristocratic (*sic*) family of Pisa, and procured for himself—with his father's money—a foothold as a landowner in Pescia. He persuaded himself and the Italians that he had recaptured the communal spirit by right of descent. In sixteen volumes he gave the Italians many facts they did not know—and some myths out of which Carducci was still making poetry seventy or eighty years later.

As the admiration of Cesare Balbo for Sismondi implies, the Catholics were the first to derive satisfaction from his interpretation of Italian history. Sismondi helped to bury deeply the anti-Christian sentiments of Gibbon. When in his old age he put together his ideas on the decline of Rome and the foundation of the medieval nations, his ideas turned out to be a rather inoffensive combination of moral and political considerations with some digressions on religious toleration. They were first made public in an English translation and were soon communicated to the Italians in a translation by Cesare Cantù, who in his long career as a popularizer never erred on the side of audacity.[11] Gibbon and Sismondi lived side by side in the libraries of every educated Italian of the nineteenth century without any sense of incompatibility. They were reconciled with Vico without any apparent effort.

Sismondi takes us in a direct line to the juvenile works on medieval Florence and Lucca by Salvemini and Volpe, the leading medievalists of twentieth-century Italy. How strongly the Sismondi tradition lived on and how little it was modified are shown by one of the major works of Italian juridical historiography, *La città italiana nell'alto Medioevo* published by Guido Mengozzi in 1914. The historians of law were in fact the main supporters of the Sismondi line.

Mengozzi, who in practice confined himself to northern Italy and to Tuscany, argued powerfully for the survival of the *civitates* and *pagi* of pre-Roman Italy in the Middle Ages. He underlined the important fact that each city had its *suburbium*, that is, a piece of land attached to it which made survival easier in an age of disruption. Mengozzi was almost emotional in pointing out that Roman Italy, not Rome, was the cradle of the medieval cities: "Roma non è, non è mai stata l'Italia." Mengozzi went on to show that ecclesiastical organization played an essential part in helping the Italian communities to survive after the Lombards had dissolved the last remains of the Roman municipal system. According to him, the ecclesiastical "pievi" (= *plebes*) with their markets, local assemblies, administrative offices, and taxes became the backbone of both civic and rural communities. This was not Catholic, or more precisely neo-Guelph, revivalism. The more strongly Mengozzi emphasized (with undoubted correctness) the role of the local ecclesiastical congregations in preserving communal life during the early Middle Ages, the more determined he was to keep the Roman church out of the picture. Northern Italy, he reminds us, never became a "stato della Chiesa."

V

Much of the Italian historical literature of the nineteenth and early twentieth centuries has never been read with the questions in mind that I have tried to formulate in this paper. I myself know too little of it. Croce who had a unique command of this literature—and such a sound judgment about it—did not mention Gibbon once in his two volumes on the *Storia della storiografia italiana nel secolo decimonono*. Nor does Piero Treves, a great connoisseur of Italian classical studies of this period, ever seem to have found Gibbon in his path.[12] What is even more indicative, when, in 1933, G. Falco assessed the position of Gibbon as a student of the Middle Ages, he entirely misunderstood his religious stance.[13] Falco remained true to that nineteenth-century Italian tradition for which Spedalieri meant nothing. It was my essay on the historiography about the Roman Empire that reintroduced a more authentic interpretation of Gibbon's *Decline and Fall* into Italian—and perhaps not only Italian—historical studies.[14] But in 1936 the Italians had more urgent problems to think about.

Gibbon's fortunes in Italy (I do not want to go beyond what can reasonably be called past history) are therefore part of one of the most significant aspects of Italian culture: the persistent refusal to examine critically the problems of the origins and value of Christianity. There was one exception which confirms the rule. At the beginning of this century the modernists—that is, a reform group within the Catholic Church—tried hard to open a critical discussion on the sources and development of the early church. The majority of the Italian Hegelians, including Croce and Gentile, was hostile to this movement and added its denunciations to those of the official church. One of these modernists, Giorgio La Piana, ended as a professor at Harvard. The others—except the indomitable Buonaiuti—were effectively silenced in 1929, if not before, when the *Conciliazione* between the Fascist state and the Catholic Church ensured state support for church excommunication. The persecution of the critical students of church history finally involved the one Hegelian, Adolfo Omodeo, who, while attacking the modernists, had in fact continued their work, especially that of Loisy.

In this perspective the usefulness of Vico was evident. He could support the Catholic thesis of the providential work of the church and at the same time encourage the Hegelian intellectual aristocracy to enjoy privately the post-Christian kingdom of *Vernunft*. Whether Vico deserved this ambiguous role is another question. In fact he helped the Italians to avoid a proper examination of the dilemma posed by Gibbon in chapters 15 and 16—either Enlightenment or Christianity.

REFERENCES

[1]*Ammianus Marcellinus* 14.6.24.

[2]*Codex Theodosianus* 16.5.2.

[3]*Codex Theodosianus* 13.3.5.

[4]Hermann Dessau, *Inscriptiones Latinae Selectae*, 4911.

[5]I do not know of any precise study of this influence, though G. Giarrizzo, *Edward Gibbon e la cultura europea del settecento* (Naples, 1954), has much to offer: The standard monographs on Muratori and Giannone are S. Bertelli, *Erudizione e storia in Ludovico Antonio Muratori* (Naples, 1960); G. Ricuperati, *L'esperienza civile e religiosa di Pietro Giannone* (Milan-Naples, 1970). We owe to S. Bertelli and G. Ricuperati an instructive selection from Giannone's writings, *Illuministi Italiani*, I: *Opere di Pietro Giannone* (Milan-Naples, 1971). In the same series of *Illuministi*, there is an excellent selection from Muratori made by G. Falco and F. Forti in two volumes (1964). On Gibbon's Italian journey, cf. S. Rotta, *Rivista Storica Italiana*, 74 (1962), pp. 324-55.

[6]*The Decline and Fall of the Roman Empire*, chap. 69.

[7]*Opere di Pietro Giannone*, quoted on p. 1161, note 1: "le fantastiche e impercettibili idee del Vico."

[8]On Spedalieri, cf. A. Prandi, *Il Cristianesimo offeso e difeso* (Bologna, 1975); it does not discuss the book on Gibbon. I cannot here go into the Italian reviews of Gibbon. But one at least must be mentioned, given the name and the attitude of the reviewer, the Piedmontese aristocrat G. F. Galeani Napione. In 1773, he had published a *Saggio sopra l'arte storica* to prepare himself for one of the usual histories of pre-Roman Italy, but in 1789 he recognized the importance of Gibbon and defended him against the Abbé de Mably in a review reprinted in *Estratti ragionati di varie opere di grido* (Pisa, 1816), II, pp. 1-58. As is well known, Mably

had blamed Gibbon in *De la Manière d'écrire l'histoire* (1784), p. 184 (for the circumstances, cf. *Supplément à la Manière d'écrire l'histoire* [1784], pp. 125-35). It is also worth mentioning the open letter to Gibbon published in *Giornale Fiorentino Istorico-Politico-Letterario* (1779), pp. 230-33 by "C." (i.e., Francesco Saverio Catani) to defend the Florence translation from the French against the Pisa translation from the English. The *Giornale Fiorentino* was clearly in sympathy with Gibbon's ideas about Christianity, see *ibid.*, p. 290. I owe the last reference to my friend S. Rotta.

[9]C. Cattaneo, *Notizie naturali e civili su la Lombardia*, now in *Scritti storici e geografici*, ed. G. Salvemini and E. Sestan (Florence, 1957), I, pp. 331-432; B. Malfatti, *Imperatori e papi ai tempi della signoria dei Franchi in Italia*, 2 volumes (Milan, 1876).

[10]G. Gabrieli, *Aegyptus*, 3 (1922), pp. 168-90; 321-40.

[11]S. de Sismondi, *Storia della caduta dell'impero romano* (Milan, 1836). For a contemporary discussion, see, for instance, A. Bianchi-Giovini, *Idee sulle cause della decadenza dell'impero romano* (Milan, 1842). Silent repudiation of Gibbon, as might be expected, is to be found in Manzoni. Cf. M. Pavan, *Rivista Storica Italiana*, 70 (1958), pp. 169-87.

[12]P. Treves, *L'idea di Roma e la cultura italiana del secolo XIX* (Milan-Naples, 1962). Gibbon plays no part in the classic chapter on "L'idea di Roma" by F. Chabod, *Storia della politica estera italiana dal 1870 al 1896* (Bari, 1951), I, pp. 179-323.

[13]G. Falco, *La polemica sul Medio Evo*, I (Turin, 1933; the second volume has never appeared).

[14]Now in *Contributo alla storia degli studi classici* (Rome, 1955), 136-43; in the same volume, pp. 195-211, my essay "Gibbon's Contribution to Historical Method," written in 1950.

PETER BURKE

Tradition and Experience: The Idea of Decline from Bruni to Gibbon

I

THIS PAPER OFFERS A BRIEF SKETCH of a vast subject. It is concerned with the various ways in which European historians and other intellectuals conceptualized change for the worse, with traditions of thought about decline and the gradual modification of those traditions by new experiences. The period to be considered will run from the early fifteenth century to the end of the eighteenth, from Leonardo Bruni's reflections on the decline of Rome to Gibbon's. It may be useful to begin with an attempt to place "decline" within the repertoire of concepts or schemata available in this period for discussing various kinds of change—good, bad, and indifferent.

To begin with the indifferent. There was the term *translatio*, which might be translated as "shift" or "transfer" and was used in two traditional contexts—one political and one cultural: the transfer of empire from the Romans to Charlemagne and the *translatio studii*, the shift in cultural predominance from Greece and Rome to Italy or France. Thus Louis Le Roy wrote that "knowledge came from the barbarians to the Greeks and from the Greeks to the Italians."[1] There were several other terms that were used in this period to refer to changes which were neither good nor bad, although the words acquired favorable overtones later: "progress," "development," and "revolution."[2] In the box marked "neutral," we can also place *corso* and *ricorso*, terms which recur in the private language of Vico to describe sequences of change.[3]

Change for the better tends to be described as some kind of "renaissance" or "reformation." Among the terms referring to revival which were current in the fifteenth and sixteenth centuries were *renovatio*, *restitutio*, *regeneratio*, *reparatio*, *revocatio*, *rinascita* (which occurs in a famous passage of Vasari), and *reformatio*, a term which had already been used by the fathers of the church before it became popular in the age of Luther.[4]

In spite of the existence of all these terms, it seems fair to say that throughout this four-hundred-year period, change was usually considered to be change for the worse. The very word "new" seems often (though not always) to have carried pejorative overtones, as it clearly does in Francesco Guicciardini's history of Italy when he refers to the people of Naples and their love of novelties (*cupidità di cose nuove*). "Modern" might be used as a term of abuse, as it was in Filarete's discussion of ancient and modern styles in architecture, and (probably) in the description of the Nominalist school of philosophy as the *via moderna*. On the other hand, terms meaning "old" (*antiquus*, *priscus*, *primitivus*) often carried favorable overtones, as in the case of the "ancient theology" (*prisca theologia*).[5] That pessimism came more naturally in this period than optimism is also suggested by the rich variety of words, images, and formulae then current to describe change for the worse.

We ought not to imagine the thinkers of this period as confined by rigid schemata in their meditations on the past. Schemata there certainly were, but their sheer variety deserves emphasis. A long series of traditional metaphors was available to describe change for the worse. It might be seen as the coming of autumn, or as the cooling of heat or "fervor," as the approach of darkness, the setting of the sun, the waning of the moon, the ebbing of the sea, or, conversely, as the coming of a "flood" of misfortunes. Change for the worse might also be visualized in architectural terms, as the "decay" or "ruin" of a building, or in agricultural terms, as the exhaustion of a once-fertile soil. Particularly popular were the medical metaphors: change for the worse might be described in terms of sickness, "degeneration," exhaustion, old age, and death. Jan Hus described the church as "afflicted with leprosy" from head to foot. Lord Clarendon described the "corruption" of the English nation after the death of the Duke of Buckingham in terms of the spread of "venom" through a body. William Robertson described the Roman Empire as "a vast body, languid and almost unanimated."[6]

Most common of all were the images of downward movement, so common indeed as to produce a series of nouns which were scarcely considered as images at all. There was the Latin *declinatio* or *inclinatio*, with its root meaning of "bend" or "slope," and its equivalents, such as the Spanish *declinación* or the German *Untergang*. There was *decadentia* ("falling"), *lapsus* ("sliding"), *vacillatio* ("swaying"), and their equivalents in modern languages: *Verfall*, "backsliding," "collapse," "decadence," and so on.[7] Then there was *eversio* (or *conversio*, or *perversio*, or *subversio*) with its root meaning of "turning" and its equivalents such as "overturn" or *Verkehrung*. This image might be elaborated into the turning of Fortune's wheel, or into the theme of the topsy-turvy world in which the quarry pursued the hunter, the cart went before the horse, the poor gave alms to the rich, and so on. Social, political, or cultural change was often perceived as a turning of the world upside down. Agrippa d'Aubigné commented on the wars of religion in France:

> . . . l'injustice
> Est principe de droit; comme au monde à l'envers,
> Le vieil père est fouëtté de son enfant pervers.[8]

In other words, a large repertoire of metaphors or schemata existed in this period to characterize change, in particular change for the worse. What the modern reader is likely to take to be an expression of personal experience may be no more than a topos. On the other hand, the repetition of topoi was not necessarily mechanical; traditional elements were frequently arranged into new combinations. The repertoire was used to make sense of a wide variety of experiences, which it may be useful to divide into six major areas.

1) Cosmic decline, the decay of the universe, the old age of the world: The belief in the imminent end of the world was a traditional one which the world's persistent failure to end had done little to weaken. Hence, it was an obvious move to describe the world as an old man, "laches, chetis et molz/Vieulx, convoiteux et mal parlant," as Eustache Deschamps did in a striking variation on the ancient theme.[9] This metaphor

was more than a metaphor for many people, since (in the Renaissance at least) the world was widely regarded as an "animal" (one might translate this term as "organism"), with a body and a soul. The macrocosm, like the microcosm, must endure old age and death.

For an explicit discussion of cosmic decline, we may turn to Godfrey Goodman's book, *The Fall of Man* (1616). Goodman's message is that "nature now beginning to decay, seems to hasten Christ's coming." For example, "the very elements themselves are much decayed in their wonted perfection." The earth has grown barren; the seas do not offer as many fish as they once did; even the heavens are subject to corruption, for "we have lately discovered spots and shadows on the moon." Here the traditional notion of cosmic decline is stretched to accommodate new facts, such as the recent discoveries of Galileo and the rise of prices in England (which modern historians interpret in terms of rising demand, but Goodman sees as the result of declining supply, the scarcity of commodities).[10]

2) Moral decline, or the decay of "manners": Here we find not so much one idea as several which overlap or shade into one another. One is the idea of the "fall" of man, which may be understood as a sudden catastrophe following the disobedience of Adam and Eve, but may also be interpreted in more gradualist terms—man, having been created immediately by God, was most perfect when nearest the creation, and has grown worse ever since, just as a child, who is fresh from the hands of its Creator, is more innocent and more perfect than an adult.[11]

Moral decline may also be seen in more secular terms. The transition from an age of simplicity and virtue to an age of luxury and corruption is often lamented; there is less agreement about its date. The poet Francisco de Quevedo, in his *Epístola satírica y censoria* (1624), describes with distaste the manners of the Spaniards of his day and contrasts them with the time when "robust virtue was in command" (*la robusta virtud era señora*). It was a rough age then, but one of valor, poverty, and simplicity. The riches of the Indies along with the luxuries they buy and the replacement of the joust by the bullfight are among the symptoms of modern decline. In a similar vein, Goodman (who is nothing if not topical) includes "the pampering of ourselves" with luxuries such as tobacco among the evidences of decline.[12]

The examples taken by Quevedo and Goodman suggest that both men are particularly concerned with moral decline over the previous century. The more radical the social critic, the earlier he would date the beginning of moral decline. Some writers dated the transition from virtue to corruption to the period when money first came into use and private property was established—the change from the "golden age" to the "age of gold." This nostalgia for primitive communism is not always very serious; the fact that Winstanley and Rousseau really *did* disapprove of private property turns their views into slightly eccentric variations on this theme.[13]

3) The decline or "fall" of the church: Religious reformers throughout the period contrast the poverty, simplicity, and holiness of the past with the wealth, power, and corruption of the present. An example from the end of the fourteenth century is a treatise by Nicholas de Clamanges, who describes the "golden age" of the church as the time when chalices were made of tin or earthenware, not of gold or silver. "Little by little . . . affluence, luxury and pride conquered the church, piety gradually began to grow cool, virtue to grow faint, discipline to be dissolved, charity to lessen,

humility to disappear. . . ."[14] The sixteenth-century reformers took over this schema, placing rather more emphasis on the rise of papal "tyranny" as a symptom or cause of the other evils; the appeal to the standards of the "primitive" church is one of their basic arguments. As in the case of moral decline, the more radical the reformer, the earlier he dates the decline. For Luther, it began in the time of Pope Gregory the Great, and it grew worse in the time of Pope Gregory VII. The Anabaptists, on the other hand, dated the beginnings of decline as early as the conversion of Constantine and the consequent establishment of the church as an official institution.[15] The idea of the decline of the primitive church is the organizing principle of two important seventeenth-century historical works: Paolo Sarpi's *Treatise on Benefices* and Gottfried Arnold's *Unpartisan History of the Church and Heretics*. The schema could of course be applied to the Lutherans (Arnold did this), or to the Jews, or to Islam.[16]

4) Political decline, or the fall of republics, kingdoms, and empires: Once again we have to deal with several different schemata which merge into one another. The first schema is centered on constitutional changes, on the three basic forms of government and their "corruptions" (monarchy into tyranny, aristocracy into oligarchy, democracy into anarchy), producing the cycle of changes described in one of the best-known passages of Machiavelli. Some writers, such as Leonardo Bruni, Machiavelli, Le Roy, and Harrington, see "corruption" in terms of the loss of liberty, which implies that the transition from democracy to monarchy is as corrupt as is the transition from democracy to mob rule. "I would date the decline of the Roman Empire," wrote Bruni, "to the time when Rome lost her liberty and began to be subject to the emperors."[17]

A second schema is centered on the expansion and contraction of empires (*summa imperia, Hauptmonarchiën*, etc.) that include a number of peoples. The most common form of this paradigm of change is that of a succession of four empires (usually but not always the Babylonian, Persian, Greek, and Roman) and the most popular exposition of the theme in this period was probably Johann Sleidan's book *On the Four Chief Empires*.[18] In a sense, this theme is a variation on that of the *translatio imperii*. Decline in one part of the world is balanced by rise somewhere else. Some authors emphasize the fact that the movement is always westward: Berkeley's famous line about the "course of empire" taking its way toward America was a new application of an old idea.[19] However, in the case of the last world empire, Rome, which is usually discussed in more detail than its predecessors, the focus is less on transfer than on decline and its causes.

Political decline is seen in terms of loss of power, whereas moral and ecclesiastical decline are seen in terms of the corruption of power. Nevertheless, similar language is used for all three. The rise of luxury is invoked yet again: it is said to lead to the loss of liberty in republics and to vulnerability to invasion in the case of empires. As Bacon put it: "When a warlike state grows soft and effeminate, they may be sure of a war. For commonly such states are grown rich in the time of their degenerating; and so the prey inviteth, and their decay in valour encourageth a war." Adam Smith wrote of "the irresistible superiority which the militia of a barbarous has over that of a civilized nation."[20]

5) Cultural decline, or the decadence of language, arts, and sciences: Renaissance humanists emphasize language. In the preface to his *Elegances of the Latin Tongue* (ca.

1444), Lorenzo Valla lamented the corruption of Latin which had followed the fall of the Roman Empire, adding that the arts had also "degenerated" but were now "reviving." His point was taken up and generalized by Antonio de Lebrija in the preface to his Castilian grammar (1492), in which he declared that "language was always the companion of empire, and followed it in such a manner that they began, increased and flourished together, and were afterwards united in their fall." Thus, Hebrew flourished with the kingdom of Solomon, Greek with the empire of Alexander, Latin rose and fell with the Roman Empire, and now (Lebrija tells Queen Isabella) it is the turn of Spanish. Louis Le Roy is another writer with a great deal to say about the "vicissitudes" of languages: "Ont les langues comme toutes choses humaines commencement, progres, perfection, corruption, fin."[21]

Other thinkers are concerned with culture in a broader sense—with literature and learning, with the visual arts, with taste, with talent. They offer a considerable variety of explanations for decline. Jean Bodin suggested that "the same process occurs in human talent as in the fields, which are wont to repay with greater abundance the privilege of lying fallow." Bacon remarked that "learning hath his infancy . . . his youth . . . his strength of years . . . and lastly his old age, when it waxeth dry and exhaust."[22] Leonardo Bruni linked the decline of Latin literature to the decline of Roman liberty: "After the Republic had been subjected to the power of one man, those brilliant minds vanished." Shaftesbury made a more general point about the relation of rhetoric to liberty: In "a despotick power," he wrote, the "pathetick sciences, and arts of speech were little cultivated, since they were of little use," whereas in free nations they reached perfection.[23] An exceptionally systematic, if not exhaustive, discussion of the causes of the decline of poetry and painting can be found in the *Critical Reflexions* (1719) of the Abbé Dubos. He considers the influence of both "moral" and "physical" causes: poverty and wealth, peace and war, patronage, national character, and even climate.[24]

6) Economic decline, or the decline of wealth, trade, industry, and population: Unlike the other types of decline mentioned so far, references to this theme are sporadic and scrappy for the first half of the period. An example of the way in which economic decline was referred to in the fifteenth century can be found in a pageant mounted for Henry VII's visit to Bristol in 1487. In it, Bremmius, the town's reputed founder, declared: ". . . I have been so long away/That Bristow is fallen into decay," and he suggested that the remedy lay in royal help for local shipping and clothmaking.[25] From about the year 1600 onwards, the discussion of economic decline becomes more frequent, more extensive, and more concerned with larger-scale trends than before. The most obvious seventeenth-century examples to take come from the writings of the Spanish *arbitristas* or "projectors," with their various schemes for the "remedy," "restoration," or "conservation" of the "sick" state: González de Cellorigo (1600), Sanchez de Moncada (1619), Caxa de Leruela (1631), Alcazar Arriaza (1646), and a number of others. In these writers the same themes recur: the rise in prices, the increasing poverty of the government and the nation, the decay of agriculture and manufactures, and the decline in the population.[26]

It was not only the Spaniards who were worried about a declining population. Seventeenth- and eighteenth-century writers often expressed the belief that the population of the West had decreased since the time of the Greeks and Romans. For Goodman, fewer people (like shorter people) was a symptom of the old age of the world. Montesquieu was concerned with the "dépopulation de l'univers," as he called it, and so was David Hume.[27]

These types of decline were explained by contemporaries in terms of three kinds of causes: divine, natural, and human. Divine causes were theological explanations in terms of the providence of God. The decline of an empire may be explained in terms of divine punishment for the sins of its rulers or its people. Biondo, for instance, says that the Roman Empire declined because the emperors had persecuted the Christians. How directly God intervened in the affairs of this world was a matter of controversy, but it was often said that God's providence was a relatively remote first cause which did not replace, but rather worked through, secondary causes. The classic providentialist discussion of world history in this period—Bossuet's—is expressed in these terms. Some Renaissance writers refer not so much to God as to the "instability of fortune" when they try to account for decline. The function of the concept "fortune" is much like that of "God"; both are invoked when natural explanations seem inadequate.[28]

Explanations in terms of nature related any given case of decline to universal decline, to the old age of the world. Among more specific natural explanations, the most important by far was astrological. As Giovanni Botero put it, "Human affairs wax and wane as if by a law of nature, like the moon to which they are subject." Empires were believed to rise and fall according to the influence of the stars, and so were churches and sects, according to the doctrine of the "horoscope of religions." Thus Pomponazzi suggested, to the scandal of some of his contemporaries, that the law of Moses, the law of Christ, and the law of "Mahomet" were all subject to the influence of the heavenly bodies.[29] There was ample opportunity for controversy here, and the opportunity was certainly taken. Did the stars incline or compel? What was the relative importance of the horoscopes of princes, eclipses of the sun and moon, and the revolutions of the planets? What about the last star in the tail of the Great Bear? Were comets a cause of disaster or merely a sign? These different astronomical theories were hotly debated until they went into decline themselves at the end of the seventeenth century.[30]

We have, finally, explanations of decline in human terms, and, following the practice of contemporaries, we may divide these human causes into external or internal ones. An obvious extrinsic explanation for the decline and fall of the Roman Empire was the invasion of barbarians from outside: "Rome fut détruite parce que toutes les nations l'attaquèrent à la fois, et pénètrent partout." In the case of Spain, Sanchez de Moncada and other *arbitristas* did their best to explain her decline by the harm done to her by foreigners such as the Genoese merchants and the "Egyptians," or gypsies.[31]

There is rather more to say about internal factors. As Botero remarked, "It rarely happens that external forces ruin a state which has not first been corrupted by internal ones"; large states in particular, he suggested, were subject to this process of decay from within.[32] One more distinction may be in order (and this time, one which was not made by contemporaries): the internal causes of decline may be psychological or social.

The psychological or moral causes of decline are sequences much like those discussed above under the heading of "moral decline"; it is impossible to separate description completely from explanation. Guicciardini explained the decline of Rome primarily by the corruption of manners, *la mutazione degli antichi costumi*. For Machiavelli, the decline of republican liberty was due to a loss of virtue in the people. Milton made the same point unforgettably:

> For what more oft, in peoples grown corrupt
> Than to love bondage more than liberty,
> Bondage with ease than strenuous liberty?[33]

Writing in 1410, Dietrich of Niem explained the decline of the church in moral terms and saw it as occurring when "intolerable pomp, avarice and ambition increased among the pope and cardinals."[34] Botero explained the decline of great empires in terms of "confidence" leading to "negligence" (in other words, hubris to nemesis). Winstanley gave a moral explanation for the rise of private property: "Selfish imagination, taking possession of the five senses and ruling as king in the room of reason therein, and working with covetousness, did set up one man to teach and rule over another."[35] Montesquieu gave a psychological explanation of the contribution of Christianity to the decline of Rome: "Une bigotterie universelle abbattit les courages et engourdit tout l'empire." The decline of the arts is interpreted in psychological terms by Marmontel as "the sickness of surfeit." "L'art s'épuise en raffinements pour ranimer des goûts éteints."[36]

Many writers are not satisfied with explanations of decline in terms of the loss of virtue and want to know how virtue came to be lost; this leads them to offer what we would call economic and social explanations. "Peace creates wealth," wrote Luigi da Porto, "wealth creates pride, pride anger, anger war, war poverty, poverty humility, humility peace, and peace wealth. This is the way the world goes round [*Così girano le cose del mondo*]."[37] Botero made a similar point: "With greatness, riches increase, and with riches, vices increase, luxury, arrogance, lust, . . . kingdoms which have been brought to the top by frugality, have been ruined by opulence."[38] A common theory is that wealth leads to "softness" and the decline of valor, which explains how empires are defeated by less civilized barbarian invaders with a lower standard of living.

It was not only political decline which was analyzed in these terms. Wesley's remarks on the "continual decay of pure religion" are structured in the same way. "Religion must necessarily produce both industry and frugality, and these cannot but produce riches. But as riches increase, so will pride, anger and love of the world in all its branches."[39] This is not so far from da Porto. Rousseau believed that moral corruption had an economic basis, the establishment of agriculture and private property, which led to the enslavement of men by luxuries, so many steps toward what he called "la décrépitude de l'espèce."[40]

Other theories of decline were structural without being economic. Hume explained the decline of the arts and sciences by their very perfection, which discouraged the next generation and also made the public less interested in their work.[41] The most widespread structural theory of decline was surely the idea that the three simple forms of government are all liable to decay, so that they need to be mixed in order to be proof against the ravages of time. Decline is diagnosed as the result of a lack of harmony or balance. The long life of the Republic of Venice was explained by sixteenth-century writers in terms of her mixed or balanced constitution, and the same argument was applied to eighteenth-century England.[42]

A few comments on these theories of decline may be in order. The first is to emphasize that decline is seen as natural, more natural in fact than stability, and that consequently it scarcely needs explanation at all. Are not all human affairs essentially transitory? Thus Machiavelli remarks that, "since nature has not allowed worldly things to remain still, when they arrive at their final perfection, they have no further to climb and so they have to descend [*non avendo più da salire, conviene che scendino*]."[43] The wheel has to keep turning. The same lesson is drawn from the common comparison between the life of a man and the life of a state. Thus Sanchez de Moncada remarks that "monarchies are as mortal as men," and d'Alembert that "les empires, ainsi que les hommes, doivent croître, dépérir et s'éteindre."[44]

If decline is natural, why worry about it? Why give statesmen advice on how to arrest it? One needs to remember that writers of the period distinguished between universal decline and local decline, between a long-term irreversible trend and shorter movements in which a fall is followed by another rise. In the case of specific decline—of the church, of Spanish agriculture, of Italian painting—there was always the possibility of some kind of revival, reform, or regeneration. Some thinkers of the early seventeenth century even believed in the possibility of a "universal reform," as they called it.[45]

A final comment concerns the rich and various imagery employed to discuss the various kinds of decline. What did this imagery mean for the men who used it? Were they the masters or the servants of their metaphors? Did they see the wheel of fortune as metaphorical description or as literal explanation? Did they see the cycles in human affairs as analogous to the revolutions of the planets or as the effects of those revolutions? The decline of empires was often explained in terms of their old age, or, according to Claude Duret, by their "caducité."[46] This is like saying that opium puts you to sleep because it has a *virtus dormitiva*: did this group of highly intelligent men not see that they were arguing in a circle?

A possible rough general answer to all these questions might be to say that the metaphors *were* more than metaphors, at least until the middle of the seventeenth century. Before then, it was intellectually respectable to take them as "correspondences," in other words, to believe that God had so organized the cosmos that what was analogous was also connected, so that (for example) the course of empire was westward like the sun, but also affected by the sun. Yet it might also be suggested that the correspondence theory was a rationalization of a universal human need to think in metaphors and analogies. It is actually very hard to do without the traditional analogy between the "life" of a state and that of a man. It is still tempting to historians—and undergraduates—to describe the Ottoman Empire as "the sick man of Europe," or to describe the "death agony" of Byzantium (the classic riposte to this description was given by Norman Baynes).[47] Our analogies are dignified by the name of "models" (another metaphor); but is there any difference in kind between an input-output model of human behavior and fortune's turning wheel?

II

The first part of this paper has presented an inventory—necessarily incomplete—of European ideas of decline between 1400 and 1800. Its purpose is to make comparisons a little easier to draw and changes over time a little easier to see. The comparisons will not be drawn here. Ideas of decline were not, of course, peculiar to Europeans in this period. There is much to be said about concepts of decline in the Islamic world (Ibn Khaldūn, Lûtfi Pasha, Kochu Bey, Kâtib Chelebi) and about the importance of cycles in classical Chinese historiography, but, for linguistic reasons, I am not the person to say it. When we are dealing with thinking along the edge between the literal and the metaphorical, recourse to translations is even less advisable than it usually is in intellectual history.[48]

The problem of change over time cannot be avoided so easily. Nor can it be usefully considered as if concepts of decline began in the early fifteenth century or thereabouts. The writers of that time—Leonardo Bruni, Lorenzo Valla, Jan Hus, Dietrich of Niem, Nicholas of Clamanges—owed a great deal to their predecessors. They stood in a tradition—or rather in two traditions which had long been influencing one another: the classical and the Christian. The repertoire of concepts, images, schemata for discussing change for the worse was assembled over many centuries. Poets and philosophers, theologians and historians all made their contributions to the common stock.[49]

Within the classical tradition, the golden-age schema goes back to Hesiod, who describes four "races," each worse than the one before, and contributes the arresting image of babies "being born with greying temples" in the old age of the world.[50] The idea of a simple way of life being corrupted by luxury is prominent in Sallust, whose comparison of moral decline to a disease (*contagio quasi pestilentia*), was taken over by many later writers; so was his phrase about the people as "desirous of novelties" (*novarum rerum cupidam*).[51] The description of the symptoms of corruption is elaborated in the satires of Juvenal and the history of Ammianus Marcellinus. Luxury is associated with "softness" or effeminacy, with indolence, with ostentation, with social mobility, with the city.[52] The decline-of-liberty theme is, of course, prominent in Tacitus, who is concerned with its cultural as well as its political consequences—for example, the decay of rhetoric.[53] The analogy between the state and the human body, from infancy to old age, goes back to Seneca and Florus.[54] Later analysis of the internal and external causes of political decline owes a great deal to Aristotle and to Polybius.[55] The decline of the arts was discussed by Cicero, Longinus, and Velleius Paterculus (among others), and all these writers added elements to the common stock of ideas.[56] Late-classical writers had an important contribution to make to discussions of decline, since what was happening to the Roman Empire was all the more obvious in their day. An anonymous Roman reformer (should one call him an *arbitrista?*) of the fourth century after Christ explains decline in terms of imperial extravagance; the Byzantine official Zosimus makes decline and fall the concepts around which to organize his history of the Roman Empire.[57]

As for the Christian (or rather the Jewish-Christian) tradition, the Bible provided at least three influential schemata for later treatments of decline. There is the idea of the "Fall" (Genesis 3:14-24); Daniel's prophecy of the four empires (Daniel 2:38-44), and the vivid description of the fall of Babylon, the coming of Antichrist, and the last days of mankind in the Revelation of Saint John the Divine. Later Christian writers added to the repertoire. St. Cyprian described the decline of the cosmos in terms reminiscent of both the Bible and the classical tradition. St. Jerome discussed the decline of the church (already) and contributed the often repeated phrase about *nostri temporis faeces*.[58] Orosius compared the rising and falling of Rome to the ebb and flow of the sea; suggested that the ruin of the empire was the result of its overextension (*hanc nunc amplissimam dilatationem vastissima ruina consequitur*); and puns on "decline" and "West," an association of ideas which has been influential for some fifteen hundred years (*Orientis occidit et ortum est Occidentis imperium*).[59]

It should be clear that the writers of early-modern Europe who wanted to discuss decline had a substantial stock of concepts and images on which to draw. As late as the eighteenth century, thinkers as original as d'Alembert and Hume sometimes express themselves on this subject in traditional terms. D'Alembert declared that "empires, like men, have their growth, decline, and death"; Hume remarked that "this fabric of the world," like the individuals in it, "must . . . have its infancy, youth, manhood and old age."[60] The thesis of E. R. Curtius about the persistence of traditional topoi in European literature receives yet another confirmation.

However, it is all too easy for historians to exaggerate the influence of tradition and to present the thinkers of one century as mere passive recipients of the "influence" of their predecessors. I would much regret having written this essay if it contributed to a misunderstanding of this kind. On this question, three comments.

The first one is that the later writers in this tradition adapted and transformed the stock of concepts which they inherited from the past, rather than living in idleness off their intellectual capital. As in the case of any living intellectual tradition, the central concepts were not merely repeated; they "migrated" or were "displaced" from one context to another.[61] Reformation writers on the decline of the church, for example, apply to it the idea of the fall of man, or they use the schema of the rise of luxury and avarice which was created to describe the Roman Republic, or they describe the tyrannical rule of the pope in terms reminiscent of Roman emperors. Conversely, Rousseau describes political decline in terms that are borrowed from discussions of the decline of the church. He sometimes sounds like his fellow-citizen Calvin, for example, when he refers to "la mesure dont chaque Peuple s'est éloigné de son institution primitive."[62] Again, the decline of culture may be analyzed by means of concepts borrowed from the political repertoire. Fréron suggests that "the arts and sciences have their beginnings, their progress, their revolutions, their decadence and their final fall just as do the empires of the world."[63] Dubos and Voltaire both describe the four great ages of the arts, applying to culture (whether consciously or unconsciously) the schema of the four world empires.[64]

A second point is that concepts that do not migrate may nevertheless develop. The method employed in this essay, that of juxtaposing relatively short quotations, sometimes risks giving the reader a false impression in this respect. Orosius and Botero, Montesquieu and Gibbon all attribute the decline of empires to over-extension, but the first pair of writers do little more than make the point in passing, whereas the second pair develop it and make it central to their interpretations of the decline of Rome.

A third qualification to any interpretation of intellectual history in terms of traditions is to say that it omits an absolutely crucial factor: experience, both individual and collective. It would surely be an error to explain the persistence of certain commonplaces about decline simply in terms of the force of inertia; this would be too simple, too mechanical an explanation. Ideas surely persist—as they arise—in response to situations, to experience.[65] In a number of the examples discussed so far, it is not difficult to see why a particular individual or group should have been concerned with that particular kind of decline at that time. The concern with the decline of the church which is visible about the year 1400 (Nicholas of Clamanges, Dietrich of Niem, Jan Hus, etc.) was surely provoked by the Great Schism. It may not be coincidence that Sleidan was writing his book on world empires, ending with the Germans, at the time that the Emperor Charles V was preparing to retire. The interest of Lucinge in how states decline centers on the question whether the dreaded Ottoman Empire was now past its peak (a question discussed by the Venetian ambassador to the Porte at much the same time, in 1592).[66] Interest in economic decline increased in the seventeenth century, when the European economy was ceasing to expand. Interest in the decline of the arts and of literature was strong in eighteenth-century France, when people were unhappily aware that the work produced in their day was not up to the standards of the age of Louis XIV. Most obviously of all, Spanish preoccupation with decline was a response to the decline of Spain.[67]

That experience is as relevant as tradition to the arguments of our writers is suggested by the fact that theories of decline do change during the period in a number of respects. Whether or not the concern with cosmic decline was (as has been argued) at its "peak" between 1570 and 1630, it certainly grows "weaker" in the eighteenth century.[68] In its place, economic decline and cultural decline are discussed much more frequently and in far greater detail from the late seventeenth century onward. The explanations offered for decline also change between Bruni and Gibbon. Less emphasis is placed on divine intervention, and the stars also fade away. Comets could hardly be seen in the same way again by anyone who had read Bayle on the subject. An emphasis on moral factors in decline is gradually replaced by an emphasis on social factors. Instead of the rise of avarice, the rise of commerce is invoked by Adam Smith as the main reason for the decline of the church.[69]

From the later sixteenth century, a number of traditional schemata are challenged and rejected. Jean Bodin questioned the value of the four-empires schema and had doubts about the idea of the golden age.[70] Marmontel makes his Belisarius question the inevitability of imperial decline and deny the analogy between the lives of individuals and states: "Tout périt, les Etats eux-mêmes, je le sais; mais je ne crois point que la nature leur ait tracé le cercle de leur existence. . . . Leur décadence n'est donc pas marquée, comme l'est pour nous le déclin des ans; leur vieillesse est une chimère." Turgot also denied the analogy between states and organisms.[71] Hume refused to explain the supposed "superior populousness of antiquity" by "the imaginary youth or vigor of the world," and he also attacked the traditional view that the rise of luxury necessarily leads to the decline of liberty.[72] Most important of all, the idea of a general decline in human affairs was challenged more and more frequently from the time of Hakewill and Lancelloti in the early seventeenth century.[73] Some thinkers continued to believe in universal decline, but, as Joseph Levenson has suggested, to reaffirm a traditional idea after it has been challenged is really to affirm something new.[74]

Perhaps the most vivid illustration of the impact of experience on traditional ideas of decline is the Spanish, and for this reason I have chosen it as a case study. Between 1600 and 1800, between Cellorigo and Campomanes, interest in the decline of Spain persists, but the interpretation of this decline changes. Appropriately enough in this context of vicissitudes, a circular movement of ideas is visible.

In the early seventeenth century, the decline of Spain was generally perceived and analyzed in terms of the decline of Rome. González de Cellorigo quotes ancient writers far more often than modern ones and makes frequent reference to the decline of Rome.[75] In 1619, the *Junta de reformación* comments that the Emperor Justinian had problems like its own—and solved them, for example, by his reform of taxation.[76] Caxa de Leruela has more to say about conditions in ancient Rome than about those in contemporary Spain, his actual subject.[77] Juan de Palafox compares the problems of the King of Spain with those of Augustus and Tiberius.[78] Alcazar Arriaza looks at the later history of the Roman Empire for parallels with the Spanish situation and quotes Salvian on the destruction of Rome by the barbarians.[79] These *arbitristas* do more than simply reiterate the commonplaces of Roman history; they also have a good deal to say about the economic problems of their own day, such as overtaxation, depopulation, and the decay of agriculture. Yet there seems a gap between their perception of immediate problems and their general reflections about the reasons for Spanish decline. Thomas Kuhn's phrase about "ad hoc adjustments" to an old paradigm seems a useful way to describe their analyses.[80] The same point might be made of Tommaso Campanella, whose *Political Aphorisms* (1635) might be described as the work of an anti-*arbitrista*, concerned with the destruction, not the conservation, of the Spanish monarchy. Once again we find some penetrating observations of specific weaknesses, such as the demographic decline of Spain, inserted into a general schema of decline derived from the Roman example.[81]

However, an important change occurs in the later seventeenth century. Experiences render the tradition more and more obviously irrelevant, and the paradigm cracks under the strain. The new paradigm is one in which economic factors are paramount. For example, Andrew Fletcher suggested that it was the discovery of American gold and silver that led to the ruin of Spain because princes and ministers conceived overambitious enterprises, Spaniards went into the army or to the Indies instead of cultivating the land, and so resources of men and money were dissipated. This suggestion takes up points made by the *arbitristas*, and it follows the traditional schema of hubris-nemesis, overextension leading to collapse. However, it fills that schema with new economic content and offers an explanation of Spanish problems which diverges from the Roman model.[82] In a similar way, Paolo Mattia Doria, in a political treatise which might be described as "Machiavelli plus political economy," suggests that the discovery of America has done great harm to Europe in general and Spain in particular; depopulating Spain, encouraging luxury, distracting people from agriculture.[83] The eighteenth-century economist Uztáriz was concerned above all with the decline of Spanish commerce, which he explained, in mercantilist terms, by an unfavorable balance of payments which bled Spain of her treasure. Neither he nor his contemporary Ulloa, who wrote on the way to revive Spanish industry and trade, mentions ancient Rome.[84]

By the eighteenth century, it was ancient Rome which was being perceived in terms of modern Spain, rather than the other way around. Historians, as they often do, were providing a new past on the model of the new present. Montesquieu wrote his *Considerations on the Wealth of Spain* before he discussed the "decadence" of the Romans, and in the later study he compares the East Roman Empire to modern Spain.[85] Campomanes, whose main concern was with Spanish decline, gave, in 1764, what is perhaps the first interpretation of the decline of Rome in terms of her economic policies.[86] Emphasis had shifted from the fall of an empire to the contraction of an economy.

III

The *Decline and Fall* has its place in the tradition of thought we have attempted to discuss here. Gibbon was the direct or indirect heir to this treasury of schemata of decline. He had in fact studied a number of the authors mentioned above. That he knew the Greek and Roman literature on the subject goes without saying.[87] Although he did not take much interest in Renaissance interpretations of history, he praised Machiavelli and Guicciardini in the footnotes to the *Decline and Fall*.[88] He described Sarpi's *History of Benefices* with still more enthusiasm as "a philosphical history" and a "golden volume."[89] He owned Harrington's *Oceana* and Clarendon's *History of the Rebellion*, and he twice refers to Walter Moyle.[90] As for the writers of his own century, Gibbon cited not only Montesquieu but Hume's essay on population, Robertson's *Charles V*, Adam Smith's *Wealth of Nations*, and the *Critical Reflexions* of Dubos.[91]

What did Gibbon make of his inheritance? The language in which he discusses "decay" and "corruption" is often traditional enough, like the image of a collapsing building ("the stupendous fabric yielded to the pressure of its own weight") and that of a "slow and secret poison" which was "introduced into the vitals of the empire."[92] As we have seen, his contrast between the luxury, despotism, effeminacy, and military weakness of declining Rome and the austerity, freedom, manliness, and military strength of the barbarians was nothing if not commonplace. Gibbon's remarks on the decline of the church, which he defined in terms of the growing wealth and power of the clergy and introduction of the worship of saints and relics, follow reformation tradition. Even the relationship between the fall of the Roman Empire and the rise of Christianity had already been explored by Machiavelli and Montesquieu.

Yet Gibbon does very much more than repeat commonplaces. Making decline the central theme of a long work, he had necessarily to be more subtle and complex than his predecessors—or being more subtle and complex, he was able to think of making decline his theme. In the course of his volumes, he distinguished many sorts of decline. He wrote about the decline of the city of Rome, of the Western Empire, and of Byzantium, and he mentioned the decline of "the monarchy of the Huns" and the empire of the caliphs.[93] In the thirty-eight chapters devoted to the decline of the Western Empire, Gibbon discussed various kinds of decline, each proceeding at different speeds. There was the loss of liberty, which had begun as early as Augustus; the decline of learning in the age of the Antonines, described in chapter 2; the corruption of military discipline in the age of Constantine, treated most fully in chapter 17, but hinted at earlier; the decay of agriculture, discussed in chapter 36, but taken back to the reign of Tiberius; and so on.

Gibbon's awareness of the complexity of the process of decline and fall makes his analysis much more satisfying to a modern reader than that of any of his predecessors. But this subtlety has its price—inconsistency. On the one hand, he has much sympathy for the Romans' own analysis of their decline, with its emphasis on moral factors such as the corruption of manners and the rise of luxury, and he frequently repeats their judgments. On the other hand, Gibbon's friendship with Adam Smith may not have been useless to the historian of the Roman Empire; in the later chapters of the *Decline and Fall* he shows increasing awareness of the importance of economic and social factors, and chapter 2 even offers a defense of luxury from an economic point of view.[94] Gibbon would not, or could not, make a synthesis of the two approaches. He suggests many causes for Roman decline, but refuses to arrange them in a hierarchy or relate them to one another. In his "General Observations on the Fall of the Roman Empire in the West," he suggested that the story of the ruin of the

Western Empire was "simple and obvious." Yet, on his own showing, it was neither.[95]

REFERENCES

[1]L. Le Roy, *De la Vicissitude des choses* (1575), (Paris, 1584), fol. 181; cf. E. R. Curtius, *European Literature and the Latin Middle Ages* (New York, 1953), p. 29.

[2]For "progress," see J.-J. Rousseau, *Discours sur l'origine et les fondements de l'inégalité* (1754), (Paris, 1965), p. 97; for "development," *ibid.*, p. 47, and Warton (cited in *OED*); on concepts of "revolution," see K. Griewank, *Der neuzeitliche Revolutionsbegriff* (Weimar, 1955), esp. chaps. 3-7.

[3]G. B. Vico, *La scienza nuova* (1744), books 4 and 5. (Similar terms previously had an astrological meaning, as *cursus* and *reditus* had, for example, in the works of Campanella.)

[4]K. Burdach, *Renaissance, Reformation, Humanismus* (Berlin, 1918); G. Ladner, *The Idea of Reform* (Cambridge, Mass., 1959).

[5]F. Guicciardini, *Storia d'Italia* (Bari, 1929), book 2, chapter 4; A. Filarete, quoted in E. G. Holt, ed., *A Documentary History of Art*, I (New York, n.d.), p. 248; D. P. Walker, *The Ancient Theology* (London, 1972), esp. the Introduction.

[6]J. Hus, *On Simony* (1413), tr. in M. Spinka, ed., *Advocates of Reform from Wyclif to Erasmus* (London, 1953), p. 211; Lord Clarendon, *History of the Rebellion*, ed. W. D. Macray (Oxford, 1888), Vol. I, book 1, section 88; W. Robertson, *The History of the Reign of Charles V* (London, 1769), I, p. 7.

[7]For details, R. Starn, "Meaning-Levels in the Theme of Historical Decline," *History and Theory* (1975), p. 14.

[8]A. D'Aubigné, *Les Tragiques* (1616), in *Oeuvres*, ed. H. Weber (Paris, 1969), p. 26.

[9]Quoted by J. Huizinga, *The Waning of the Middle Ages*, abbreviated Eng. trans. (Harmondsworth, 1965), p. 34.

[10]G. Goodman, *The Fall of Man* (London, 1616), esp. pp. 348f.; on him and other contemporary writers on this theme, see V. Harris, *All Coherence Gone* (Chicago, 1949).

[11]Goodman, p. 349.

[12]F. de Quevedo, *Obras en verso*, ed. L. Astrana Marín (Madrid, 1943), pp. 132f.; Goodman (above, note 10), p. 352.

[13]H. Levin, *The Myth of the Golden Age in the Renaissance* (London, 1970); G. Winstanley, *The True Levellers' Standard Advanced* (1649), in C. Hill, ed., *Winstanley: The Law of Freedom and Other Writings* (Harmondsworth, 1973), p. 77; see also Rousseau, *Discours* (above, note 2).

[14]N. de Clamanges, *De corrupto ecclesiae status* (Schlettstadt, ca. 1519).

[15]J. M. Headley, *Luther's View of Church History* (New Haven, 1963), pp. 156f.; F. H. Littell, *The Anabaptist View of the Church* (New York, 1964), pp. 46f.; for medieval parallels, P. Meinhold, *Geschichte der kirchlichen Historiographie* (Freiburg-Munich, 1967), I, pp. 206, 211f.

[16]P. Sarpi, *Trattato delle materie beneficiarie* (written ca. 1609), in his *Opere*, ed. G. and L. Cozzi (Milan-Naples, 1969), pp. 330f.; G. Arnold, *Unparteyische Kirchen- und Ketzer-Historie*, 2 vols. (Frankfurt, 1699-1700), I, pp. 216, 220; II, pp. 150f.; on Arnold, see E. Seeberg, *G. Arnold* (Meerane, 1923), esp. pp. 94f.

[17]N. Machiavelli, *Discorsi*, book 1, chap. 2; L. Bruni, *Historiarum Florentini populi libri* XII, ed. E. Santini (Città di Castello, 1926), pp. 14f., 98f.; Le Roy, *De la Vicissitude des choses* (cited in note 1), pp. 31f.; J. Harrington, *Works* (London, 1700), pp. 38f.; for a Harringtonian analysis of Roman decline, see W. Moyle, *An Essay upon the Constitution of the Roman Government* (ca. 1699), in C. Robbins, ed., *Two English Republican Tracts* (Cambridge, 1969).

[18]J. Sleidan, *De quatuor summis imperiis* (1556).

[19]G. Berkeley, "On the Prospect of Planting Arts and Learning in America"; cf. K. Peucer, "vires occidentis consumptae sunt," and J. Lipsius, "res et vigor ab oriente . . . in occasum eunt," quoted in C. Curcio, *Europa: Storia di un'idea* (Florence, 1958), pp. 226, 296. The idea goes back at least as far as Orosius.

[20]F. Bacon, "Of the Vicissitude of Things," in *Essays* (London, 1625); Adam Smith, *The Wealth of Nations* (1776), book 5, chap. 1.

[21]L. Valla, *Elegantiae* (Rome, 1475), Preface; A. de Lebrija, *Gramática de la Lengua Castellana*, ed. I. Gonzalez-Llubera (Oxford, 1926); Le Roy, *De la Vicissitude des choses* (above note 1), pp. 32f.

[22]J. Bodin, *Methodus* (1566), trans., B. Reynolds (repr., New York, 1966), p. 301; Bacon, "Of the Vicissitude of Things."

[23]L. Bruni (cited in note 17); A. A. Cooper, Third Earl of Shaftesbury, "Advice to an Author," part 2, section 2, in his *Characteristicks* (London, 1733), I, p. 238.

[24]C. Dubos, *Réfléxions critiques sur la poésie et la peinture* (1719), (Utrecht, 1732). On eighteenth-century French views of cultural decline, see H. Vyverberg, *Historical Pessimism in the French Enlightenment* (Cambridge, Mass., 1958).

[25]S. Anglo, *Spectacle Pageantry and Tudor Policy* (Oxford, 1969), pp. 33f.

[26]M. González de Cellorigo, *Memorial* (Valladolid, 1600; available in microfilm in the Manchester

University Library); Sanchez de Moncada, *Restauración Política de España* (Madrid, 1619); Miguel Caxa de Leruela, *Restauración de la antigua abundancia de España* (Naples, 1631); Jacinto de Alcazar Arriaza, *Medios políticos para el remedio unico y universal de España* (Madrid, 1646). One might regard Quevedo as an *arbitrista*; his poem, cited in note 13 above, was addressed to Olivares.

[27]Goodman (above, note 10), p. 370; Montesquieu, *Esprit des lois* (1748), book 23, chap. 19 and ff.; D. Hume, *Essays* (London, 1742; repr. Darmstadt, 1964), II, essay 10, "Of the Populousness of Ancient Nations." Cf. D. B. Young, "Montesquieu on Depopulation," *Journal of the History of Ideas*, 1975.

[28]F. Biondo, *Historiae ab inclinatione Romanorum imperii* (Venice, 1483); J.-B. Bossuet, *Discours sur l'histoire universelle* (1681), esp. book 3, chap. 8.

[29]G. Botero, *Ragion di stato* (Venice, 1589), p. 5; P. Pomponazzi, *De incantationibus* (posthumous; Basel, 1556), pp. 293f.

[30]On all this, G. Duret, *Discours des causes et effets des décadences . . . des monarchies* (Lyons, 1595), chaps. 5-13.

[31]Montesquieu, *Considérations sur les causes de la grandeur et la décadence des Romains* (1734), chap. 19; Moncada, *Restauración* (above, note 26).

[32]Botero, as cited in note 29.

[33]Guicciardini (above, note 5), book 4, chap. 12; Milton, *Samson Agonistes* (1671), lines 268f.

[34]Dietrich of Niem, *De modis uniendi ac reformandi ecclesiae*, trans. in M. Spinka (above, note 6), p. 170.

[35]Botero (above, note 29), p. 8; Winstanley (above, note 13), p. 77.

[36]Montesquieu, *Considérations*, chap. 22; Marmontel, *Belisaire* (Paris, 1767), p. 88.

[37]L. da Porto, *Lettere Storiche* (ca. 1508), (Florence, 1857), p. 26.

[38]Botero (above, note 29), p. 8.

[39]Wesley, quoted by Max Weber, *The Protestant Ethic and the Spirit of Capitalism* (1904-5; Eng. tr., London, 1930), p. 175.

[40]Rousseau, *Discours*, p. 121.

[41]Hume, *Essays* (above, note 27), I, essay 14, "The Rise of the Arts and Sciences."

[42]G. Contarini, *De magistratibus et republica venetorum* (1543); on England, cf. Z. S. Fink, *The Classical Republicans* (Evanston, 1945).

[43]Machiavelli, *Istorie fiorentine* (completed ca. 1525), book 5, chap. 1.

[44]Moncada (above, note 26), first discourse, fol. 2a; d'Alembert, "Eloge de Montesquieu," prefixed to the London 1757 ed. of the *Esprit des lois*, p. xxii.

[45]F. Yates, *The Rosicrucian Enlightenment* (London-Boston, 1972), pp. 57f., 134f.

[46]Duret (above, note 30), p. 67.

[47]N. Baynes, *The Byzantine Empire* (London, 1925), p. 7: "An empire, to endure a death-agony of a thousand years, must possess considerable powers of recuperation."

[48]Ibn Khaldūn, *Muqadimmah* (written ca. 1377), trans. F. Rosenthal, 3 vols. (New York, 1958), esp. chap. 3, sections 12-15; on the Turks, see B. Lewis, "Ottoman Observers of Ottoman Decline," repr. in his *Islam in History* (London, 1973); on China, see A. Wright, "On the Uses of Generalization in the Writing of Chinese History," in L. Gottschalk, ed., *Generalization in the Writing of History* (Chicago, 1963).

[49]On the history of schemata or commonplaces, see the classic work of E. R. Curtius (above, note 1). W. Rehm, *Der Untergang Roms* (1930) and H. Werner, *Der Untergang Roms* (1939) discuss the idea of the decline of Rome.

[50]Hesiod, *Erga kai Hēmerai*, lines 109f.

[51]Sallust, *Catilinae Coniuratio* (ca. 40 B.C.) 5.10.28.

[52]Juvenal, *Satirae* (second century A.D.), esp. the first, second, and eleventh. Ammianus Marcellinus, *Historiae* (fourth century A.D.), e.g., 22.4.

[53]Tacitus, *Annales* (ca. A.D. 100) 14.14 (on Nero); *Dialogus de oratoribus* 36.41.

[54]S. Mazzarino, *The End of the Ancient World* (London, 1966), p. 33.

[55]Aristotle, *Politica* 5; Polybius, *Historia* 6.

[56]Cicero, *Brutus* (46 B.C.) 70; Longinus, *Peri Hypsous* (first century A.D.) 35; M. Velleius Paterculus, *Historiae Romanae* 1 (conclusion); cf. E. H. Gombrich, "The Debate on Primitivism in Ancient Rhetoric," *Journal of the Warburg and Courtauld Institutes*, 1966.

[57]E. A. Thompson, *A Roman Reformer and Inventor* (Oxford, 1952); Zosimus, *Historia Nea* (fifth century); on him, W. Goffart, "Zosimus," *American Historical Review*, 1971.

[58]Cyprian, *Ad Demetrianum* (third century) 3-4, in Migne, *Patrologia Latina*, 4; on him, E. Tuveson, *Millennium and Utopia* (1964), pp. 13f.; Jerome, *Vita Malchi Monachi* (fourth century) in Migne, *Patrologia Latina*, 23, p. 55; on him, Seeberg (above, note 16), p. 276.

[59]Orosius, *Historiarum adversus paganos libri VII* (fifth century), in Migne, *Patrologia Latina*, 31, esp. book 6, chap. 14, and book 2, chap. 2.

[60]D'Alembert, as cited in note 44; Hume (above, note 27), II, essay 10.

[61]D. Schon, *Displacement of Concepts* (London, 1963).

[62]Rousseau, *Discours*, p. 121.

[63]E. C. Fréron, quoted in Vyverberg (above, note 24), p. 120.

[64]Dubos (above, note 24), II, p. 12; Voltaire, *Siècle de Louis XIV* (1751), ed. R. Groos (Paris, 1930), p. 1.

[65]Cf. B. Schwarz, "The Intellectual History of China," J. K. Fairbank, ed., *Chinese Thought and Institutions* (Chicago, 1957).

[66]L. Bernardo's report in E. Albèri, ed., *Relazioni degli ambasciatori veneti*, 15 vols. (Florence, 1839), series 3, vol. 2.

[67]On Spanish theories about their decline, see V. Palacio Atard, *Derrota, Agotamiento, Decadencia en la España del siglo XVII* (3rd ed., Madrid, 1966).

[68]Harris (above, note 10), p. 87; he offers no precise evidence for his dating of this "peak."

[69]Smith (above, note 20), book 5, chap. 1.

[70]Bodin (above, note 22), chap. 7.

[71]Marmontel (above, note 36), pp. 130-31; on Turgot, Vyverberg (above, note 24), p. 140 (without a reference).

[72]Hume (above, note 27), I, essay 14, and II, essay 10.

[73]Cf. J. B. Bury, *The Idea of Progress* (London, 1920), esp. pp. 88f. Curious that Bury should also have edited Gibbon's *Decline and Fall*.

[74]J. R. Levenson, *Confucian China and Its Modern Fate* (Berkeley, 1958), Introduction.

[75]Cellorigo (above, note 26), quotes Aristotle, Plato, Xenophon, Plutarch, Livy, Sallust, Cicero, Pliny, Tacitus, Suetonius, and Valerius Maximus, all in a few pages.

[76]A. González Palencia, ed., *La junta de reformación* (Valladolid, 1932), Document no. 4 (1619), p. 14.

[77]Caxa (above, note 26) quotes Varro and Tacitus and discusses Alexander Severus in some detail.

[78]Juan de Palafox, *Juicio interior y secreto de la monarquía* (ca. 1640), in *Cuadernos de Historia de España*, XIII (1950), pp. 138f.

[79]Alcazar Arriaza (above, note 26), fol. 17a; the reference is to Salvian's *De Gubernatione Dei* (fifth century).

[80]T. S. Kuhn, *The Structure of Scientific Revolutions* (Chicago, 1964), p. 83.

[81]T. Campanella, *Aforismi Politici* (1635), in L. Amabile, *Fra Tommaso Campanella nel Castello di Napoli*, II (Naples, 1887), pp. 291f.

[82]A. Fletcher, *Discorso delle cose di Spagna* ("Naples," Edinburgh?, 1698), pp. 10f.

[83]P. M. Doria, *La Vita Civile* (3rd ed., enlarged, Naples, 1729), pp. 334f.; on him R. Shackleton, "Montesquieu et Doria," in *Revue de littérature comparée*, 29 (1955), esp. p. 182.

[84]G. de Uztáriz, *Theorica y practica de comercio y de marina* (2nd ed., Madrid, 1742); B. de Ulloa, *Restablecimiento de las fabricas y comercio español* (Madrid, 1740); on these men, see A. Wirminghaus, *Zwei Spanische Merkantilisten* (Halle, 1886).

[85]Montesquieu's essay on the wealth of Spain is reprinted in his *Oeuvres*, ed. R. Caillosi, II (Paris, 1951), and discussed in R. Shackleton, *Montesquieu* (London, 1961), pp. 146f.

[86]Campomanes, *Respuesta Fiscal* (1764), p. 36, on Rome; *Discurso sobre el fomento de la industria popular* (Madrid, 1774), esp. p. clxx, on Spanish decline; cf. R. Krebs Wilckens, *El pensamiento histórico político y económico del conde de Campomanes* (Santiago, 1960), pp. 42f.

[87]He had high praise for Polybius and Tacitus, quoted Longinus and Ammianus Marcellinus on decline, owned Velleius Paterculus and Orosius; G. Keynes, *The Library of Edward Gibbon* (London, 1940).

[88]As reconstructed by Keynes, his library lacked Bruni and Biondo, Botero, Bodin, Le Roy, Duret, and Lucinge. On "great" Guicciardini and "noble" Machiavelli, see the *Decline and Fall of the Roman Empire* (*DF*), ed. J. B. Bury, 7 vols. (London, 1899-1901), chap. 31, p. 329, note 120, and chap. 70, p. 296, note 101.

[89]*DF*, chap. 66, p. 99, note 38.

[90]*DF*, chap. 8, p. 197, note 10; chap. 28, p. 189, note 4.

[91]*DF*, chap. 31, p. 307, note 67 (Hume); chap. 31, p. 329, note 120 (Robertson); chap. 70, p. 298, note 104 (Smith); chap. 69, p. 210, note 2 (Dubos). He also owned copies of Shaftesbury's *Characteristicks* and Marmontel's *Belisaire*.

[92]*DF*, chap. 2, pp. 53f.

[93]On the city, chap. 31, pp. 306f.; on the Huns, chap. 26, pp. 84f.; on the caliphs, chap. 52, pp. 51f.

[94]On luxury, chap. 2, p. 53; on economic factors, chap. 35, pp. 479f.; chap. 36, pp. 53f.; on social factors, chap. 44, p. 471; and chap. 45, pp. 31f. On Gibbon's interest in economics and sociology, see G. Giarrizzo, *E. Gibbon e la cultura europea del 1700* (Naples, 1954), esp. part 2, chap. 1.

[95]*DF*, chap. 38, pp. 160f.

J. G. A. POCOCK

Between Machiavelli and Hume:
Gibbon as Civic Humanist and Philosophical Historian

I

"I HAVE NEVER ASPIRED," wrote Gibbon rather insincerely,[1] "to a place in the triumvirate of British historians." The word "British" here, as so often in the eighteenth century, is very little more than a synonym for "Scottish." David Hume and William Robertson were undoubtedly the first and second members of Gibbon's triumvirate—"le Tacite et le Tite-Live de l'Ecosse," as he once put it[2]—and if the third place had been filled by any other, it must have been by Adam Ferguson or Adam Smith. Gibbon knew all these men well and held their works in high and unfeigned esteem;[3] he corresponded with them regularly, even if, like a true southern English-man, he never went to visit them—Edinburgh was too remote for the man who thought nothing of the journey to Lausanne.[4] But if he was geographically isolated from the society of his northern peers, Gibbon must have felt an intellectual isolation in an England where he had no peers at all. The only other Englishman who could possibly have been nominated for a place in the triumvirate was the formidable Bishop Warburton, and Gibbon looked upon him as an adversary rather than a rival. His early conversion to Catholicism and the subsequent growth of his irreligious skepticism separated Gibbon from the traditions of Anglican scholarship, which might well have claimed him otherwise; and he attached himself instead to the unfolding patterns of Enlightenment historiography, an international style in many respects, to which nevertheless the Scottish school was imparting a development both local and universal, and of great intellectual power. Gibbon was not, as Ferguson—or even Robertson—was, a theoretical sociologist working in the field of history, nor should he be thought of as applying the science which the Scotsmen worked out in its theoretical purity. He went his own way as a historian, and he sailed under a full spread of canvas into seas they had not attempted to chart; but it will be the aim of this essay to disentangle the elements of philosophic history which are latent in Gibbon's thought and to consider how far they provide guiding ideas in the *Decline and Fall*.

Philosophic history in the eighteenth century may be thought of as a tradition of continuous debate about certain questions; as regards the history of civil society and of man as part of it, these may be referred back to the legacy of civic humanism as mediated by Machiavelli and his successors,[5] while, as regards the history of religion and civil society, they possessed a different, complicated, and on the whole more recent pedigree. Since the revival of the ideal of active citizenship by Florentine civic humanists, there had been a gathering reemphasis on the ancient belief that the fulfillment of man's life was to be found in political association, coupled with an increasing awareness of the historical fragility of the political forms in which this fulfillment must be sought. *Virtue* could only be found in a *republic* of equal, active, and independent citizens, and it was a term applied both to the relations between these citizens and to the healthful condition of the personality of each one of them; but the republic was peculiarly exposed to *corruption*—a state of affairs often identified with the dependence of citizens upon the powerful, instead of upon the public authority—and the corruption of the republic must entail the corruption of the individual personality, which could only flourish when the republic was healthy. Machiavelli had seen the relations between virtue and corruption as so intimate and unstable that he had been prepared to use *virtù* in a non-moral and non-civic sense as well as in its more normal meanings. This ambiguity does not directly appear in Gibbon's employment of the word "virtue," but his theory of corruption is profoundly Machiavellian in the sense that it stands in a tradition of debate inherited from the Florentines.

Machiavelli—himself inheriting through Leonardo Bruni and others a tradition of concern with the civic militia—had believed it essential to the citizen's personality and virtue that he should bear arms of his own in the public cause and at the command of public authority. Consequently, a true republic must arm its citizens, and a republic which armed its citizenry must admit them to a share in a government to that extent popular. A republic (such as Rome) must use its arms for conquest and must therefore expand and acquire empire; a "commonwealth for preservation" (such as Venice), which eschewed empire and the armed people, must be content to be ruled by an oligarchy and defended by mercenaries. But the last feature was in itself a sign of corruption; equality among citizens was an equality in arms, and to give up one's arms to another was to give up a vital part of one's capacity for equality, citizenship, and virtue and to become the dependent of those who controlled arms and power. Retainers in a feudal society, *condottieri* in a civic society alike displayed the arms-bearer in a state of social clientage, and both were incompatible with republican virtue. But as the armed popular republic—of which Livian Rome was the paradigm case—expanded its empire and destroyed virtue in others, it might be tempted by wealth and luxury to allow its arms to be exercised by mercenaries or professionals and might be corrupted by the excess of its own virtue. Through Polybius, Machiavelli, Harrington, and Montesquieu can be traced the development of this interpretation of Roman decline.

Harrington, at a turning-point in later Machiavellian theory, anchored the citizen's independence in his arms and his arms in the independence of his property. Land, inherited rather than purchased, furnished the paradigm case of property which guaranteed the independence, virtue, and personality of the individual; and the armies of Livian Rome had been armies of yeoman citizens. The Republic had declined when its institutions failed to guarantee the distribution of conquered lands, and the legionaries had lapsed, first into client dependence on their *imperatores*, whom they had followed in factions and civil wars to obtain their share of land, then into professional service performed for the Caesarian *principes* who had substituted their rule for the Republic. The principate therefore reflected the decline of republican virtue, and neither corrupt citizens nor corrupt soldiers had been able to prevent the growth of civil conflict or the progress of barbarian invasion and the employment of barbarian mercenaries. Feudal society had represented the culminating phase of the social dependence of the warrior and proprietor, but, from about 1500, vassalage had declined, the independence of the proprietor had been restored, and citizenship had become once more possible.

To Harrington's successors, however, the emancipation of the freeholder from tenure began to appear as a profoundly ambivalent process. It had been brought about by the revival of trade, the growth of arts, leisure, and enlightenment—in themselves excellent things, but tending to encourage the citizen to pay mercenaries to defend him while he enjoyed a polite existence. To be defended by professional soldiers was ultimately incompatible with citizenship, and the growth of standing armies[6] had been the growth of corruption and absolute monarchy—a decay only held off, even in the free societies of Atlantic Britain, by the deliberate maintenance of a militia of proprietors. This is one reason why the captain of the Hampshire militia was not useless to the historian of the Roman Empire;[7] why—in the equally subtle thought of Adam Ferguson—the chaplain of a Highland regiment was not useless to the historian of the Roman Republic and of civil society; and why the Second Amendment to the Constitution of the United States maintains the old language of the militia ideal with such paradoxical results to this day.

But the growth of refinement was the corruption of personality. At this point Machiavelli's unintended legacy to Western thought is seen to have been a paradoxical view of the history of civilization, in which the forces that built up human personality were identical with the forces that undermined it, in ways that point toward the thought of Rousseau. In a commercial society, men became more refined, more enlightened, and more specialized—women aiding them in this to the limits of the capacity that social theory assigned them—but they moved away from the single-minded devotion to the city which characterized the warrior, the citizen, the patriot, and (as Machiavelli had stressed) the pre-Christian pagan. Conversely, if (especially in the intellectual company of Ferguson) the historical sociologist worked his way back into the prehistory of citizenship, he encountered a warrior so devoid of the reflective capacity which only the progress of the arts, the circulation of goods, and the division of labor could bring, as to be altogether incapable of citizenship. There was no refuge to be found in primitivism, and none in progress either; for that which made civilization possible was that which ultimately undermined it. In so paradoxical a vision of history, there were no golden ages, but only golden moments at which the creative had not yet begun to destroy. Gibbon's age of the Antonines is a silver moment of this kind, a moment of relaxation in the downward swing of a civilization.

It could be argued—as it was in varying ways by Montesquieu and (with less assurance) by Hume[8]—that a society making economic progress into an indefinite future could contain its own corruptive and degenerative tendencies and even overcome them; more optimistically still, it could be held that the progress of society offered human personality not merely the prospect of further polishing and refining the passions and appetites, but the more utopian vision of a future ("glorious and paradisaical," in the language of Gibbon's *bête noire* Joseph Priestley[9]) in which new human capacities would be created, developed, and satisfied. Yet—perhaps because its conception of human nature remained essentially static—the mind of the Enlightenment remained, so far as the future of humanity was concerned, heavily committed to the skepticism and pessimism latent in the civic-humanist tradition as shaped by the Machiavellian lineage. Neither Montesquieu nor Hume, Smith nor Jefferson was fully able to overcome the proto-Rousseauan vision of a future in which commerce, progress, and specialization corrupted civilization even as they advanced it. Gibbon was no exception to this rule. The *Decline and Fall* recounts the "corruption" of Roman virtue and "the triumph of barbarism and religion,"[10] and this essay will analyze his employment of the first two of these concepts and show him as anchored in the civic-humanist tradition as it had developed from Machiavelli to Hume. If it were possible to turn to the third—to Gibbon's presentation of the civil history of religion—the scene would change, and the civic-humanist analysis, while remaining valid, would be transcended. Gibbon would appear as a *philosophe* rather than a humanist, with a different concern for the history of the human mind; and Hume would appear as his mentor in a new role. That, however, would necessitate another study of at least equal length.

II

There is a sense in which Gibbon presents the decline and fall of the Empire as no more than the working out of forces implicit in the decline and fall of the Republic, the triumph of barbarism and religion as the consequence of the corruption of civic and military virtue. Yet the choice of the Antonine era as the "happy period" from which decline is to be reckoned indicates that there are positive as well as negative aspects to the history of the principate, and our initial problem is to understand the latent paradox in observations such as the following:

> Whatever evils either reason or declamation have imputed to extensive empire, the power of Rome was attended with some beneficial consequences to mankind; and the same freedom of intercourse which extended the vices, diffused likewise the improvements of social life.[11]

The Antonine era is thus defined as a moment at which the forces of degeneration had not yet triumphed over those of progress; but the equation of "improvements" with "vices" is nonetheless clearly established. There is evidence that Gibbon's choice of the Antonine moment was in some respects artificial. The memorable sentence, "If a man were called to fix the period in the history of the world, during which the condition of the human race was most happy and prosperous, he would, without hesitation, name that which elapsed from the death of Domitian to the accession of Commodus,"[12] forms a deliberate antithesis with that from Robertson's *View of the Progress of Society in Europe*, published seven years before the first volume of the *Decline and Fall*: "If a man were called to fix upon the period in the history of the world during which the condition of the human race was most calamitous and afflicted, he would, without hesitation, name that which elapsed from the death of Theodosius the Great, to the establishment of the Lombards in Italy."[13]

It seems likely that Gibbon worked backwards in time, seeking a period which could be set in Plutarchian opposition to that chosen by Robertson, until he hit upon the eighty years of the "five good emperors." Surveying the *Decline and Fall* after its completion, we know, he regretted this choice and felt that he should have begun from A.D. 69 (the "year of the four emperors"), or earlier, instead of 98-180;[14] but had he done so, the only effect would have been a de-emphasis of the Antonine "silver moment," and a greater stress on forces making for disruption about which he was never less than explicit. Volume I of the *Decline and Fall* as we have it holds the positive and negative aspects of empire in careful balance:

> The frontiers of that extensive monarchy were guarded by ancient renown and disciplined valour. The gentle but powerful influence of laws and manners had gradually cemented the union of the provinces. Their peaceful inhabitants enjoyed and abused the advantages of wealth and luxury. The image of a free constitution was preserved with decent reverence; the Roman senate appeared to possess the sovereign authority, and devolved on the emperors all the executive powers of government.[15]

Once we are acquainted with the patterns of eighteenth-century historical thinking, we can read this passage correctly. Military virtue (which was part of civic virtue in its original form) is now to be found only among the legions on the frontiers; in the provinces and cities is to be found something else, the refinement of manners which can develop only where there is peace and wealth, but is liable to "abuse" where there is "luxury." There is a relation between "abuse" and the loss of liberty; the "free constitution" of the Republic is now only an "image," preserved in appearance by the circumstance that emperors and senators are capable—as in the era recorded by Tacitus they were not—of "decent reverence." There is even a hint that something has gone wrong with the separation of powers: since "all" executive power has "devolved on the emperors," the senate does not in reality "possess the sovereign authority."

Gibbon continues to reveal to us how this state of affairs came about:

> The principal conquests of the Romans were achieved under the republic; and the emperors, for the most part, were satisfied with preserving those dominions which had been acquired by the policy of the senate, the active emulation of the consuls, and the martial enthusiasm of the people.[16]

The triad in the second part of the sentence furnished a clear description of Roman *virtus* as it had been manifested in the "mixed constitution" of Polybius—when, as Machiavelli and Montesquieu had made clear, it had been inseparable from conquest and the acquisition of dominion. Gibbon praises—though never unequivocally—the decision of the *principes* to halt expansion at the existing frontiers—"Happily for the repose of mankind, the moderate system recommended by the wisdom of Augustus, was adopted by the fears and vices of his immediate successors"[17]—but makes it clear that, in this decision, Rome has passed, in Machiavellian terminology, from being "a commonwealth for expansion" to becoming instead "a commonwealth for preservation." The latter, in Machiavelli's view, were oligarchical and employed mercenaries; but the end of the Republic and the rise of the principate meant more than the conversion of Rome into a Venice. Conquest and liberty had been inseparable while they both depended upon the free and martial emulation of the senate and the people; with the abandonment of conquest, liberty began to be withdrawn from each.

> In the purer ages of the commonwealth, the use of arms was reserved for those ranks of citizens who had a country to love, a property to defend, and some share in enacting those laws, which it was their interest, as well as duty, to maintain. But in proportion as the public freedom was lost in extent of conquest, war was gradually improved into an art, and degraded into a trade.[18]

This passage is purely Machiavellian, and the closing words even echo the pun implicit in his *"arte* della guerra."[19] It should be observed that conquest, the effect of freedom, is now fatal to it: it was the extension of the Republic that professionalized the legionaries and made them the clients of Marius or Sulla, Pompey or Caesar. Augustus is not to be blamed for this development, but his decision to halt expansion froze, instead of reversing, it and made the professional army the foundation of the principate. In much detail, in his third chapter, Gibbon recounted how Augustus exploited constitutional forms to invest himself and his successors with permanent control over the armies and a permanent monopoly of the essential prerogatives of executive power. This both was and was not a military despotism; or rather, it was, but masqueraded as something else; and insincerity was of its essence and could never be altogether eliminated. It is true that the luridly Tacitean portrait of Augustus as hypocrite, given in chapter 3,[20] is mitigated by the observation that the effects of rule actually transformed him from a ferocious tyrant into a *pater patriae*;[21] and it is true that the long and carefully written encomia on the five good emperors leave us in no doubt that their virtue was real and not assumed. But it is nonetheless made clear that virtue was that which made them observe a restraint which nothing in the constitution obliged them to observe, and was therefore in the last analysis a private, not a public, virtue. The benevolent despot has nothing but his benevolence to rely on.

> The vast extent of the Roman empire was governed by absolute power, under the guidance of virtue and wisdom. The armies were restrained by the firm but gentle hand of four successive emperors, whose character and authority commanded involuntary respect. The forms of the civil administration were carefully preserved by Nerva, Trajan, Hadrian, and the Antonines, who delighted in the image of liberty, and were pleased with considering themselves as the accountable ministers of the laws. Such princes deserved the honour of restoring the republic had the Romans of their days been capable of enjoying a rational freedom.
>   . . . The ideal restraints of the senate and the laws might serve to display the virtues, but could never correct the vices, of the emperor. The military force was a blind and irresistible instrument of oppression; and the corruption of Roman manners would always supply flatterers eager to applaud, and ministers prepared to serve the fear or the avarice, the lust or the cruelty, of their masters.[22]

The principate was therefore corrupt, even where it was most virtuous, and there was an inevitability about the forces which ensured that a Marcus Aurelius would be followed by a Commodus sooner or later. But the root of corruption lay not just in the operations of unchecked despotism, but in the separation of military from civic virtue which had ensured it. The Republic had abandoned the armies to the Caesars because the soldiers had ceased to be citizens. After the sentence in which we learn—the equation of progress with degeneration appearing once more—that war had been "improved into an art, and degraded into a trade," we hear that as the cities became more luxurious, the legions were increasingly recruited from the countryside,[23] and it soon follows that:

> That public virtue which among the ancients was denominated patriotism, is derived from a strong sense of our own interest in the preservation and prosperity of the free government of which we are members. Such a sentiment, which had rendered the legions of the republic almost invincible, could make but a very feeble impression on the mercenary servants of a despotic prince; and it became necessary to supply that defect by other motives, of a different, but not less forcible nature; honour and religion.[24]

With the mention of "honour" we encounter a new element in Gibbon's eight-eenth-century sociology: the quality which Montesquieu had identified as the *principe* of monarchy, but which, in Gibbon's hands, will emerge as the self-love that forms the only social passion of which barbarians are capable. The rustic and half-barbarous soldiers of the Empire—Gibbon will insist repeatedly on their "barbarian," "Illyri-an," and "peasant" character,[25] but here calls them simply "peasant or mechanic"[26]—learn an ethos of ambition and emulation in which their actions confer "glory or disgrace on the company, the legion, or even the army" to which they belong. Gibbon is careful not to use the term "virtue" of what is merely "honour," but leaves us in no doubt that discipline and military spirit are a civilized, not a primitive, characteristic. "From such laudable arts did the valour of the Imperial troops receive a degree of firmness and docility, unattainable by the impetuous and irregular passions of barbarians."[27] This antithesis is many times repeated. As for the "religion" which is associated with "honour," it is the worship of the eagles by the legions which carry them, and it is consequently as remote as can be from the "religion" that will be joined with "barbarism" in characterizing post-Roman society. More than anything else, it resembles the religion of auguries and auspices which Machiavelli had seen as maintaining the military virtue of the legions of the early Republic; and yet the difference between the two is profound. The legions of the Republic were composed of citizens, those of the Empire of mercenaries; the latter, and their religion, were therefore capable only of honor in the room of virtue. The divorce of military and civic principle leads to the degeneration of each. Gibbon starts his history at a moment when senatorial virtue, shown in its decay by Tacitus, is already all but extinct, and the virtue of the principate, raised to philosophical but insecure heights by Marcus Aurelius, is about to receive a fatal blow at the hands of Commodus. He proceeds to show how the legions are first led, by the fatal flaw in the Augustan institution, to tear the fabric of civil government apart, and then, rallying what is left of their honor and discipline in the era of the first Gothic invasions, are led under the great Illyrian soldier-emperors[28] to attempt the reform of the Empire, but succeed only in militarizing it and rendering it more despotic. Later volumes will recount the slow process by which the legions lose even the capacity to defend the Empire; but Gibbon insists upon it even when displaying Roman power at its height. A footnote to his account of military engines in chapter 1 remarks, in language itself thoroughly Machiavellian, "The use of them in the field gradually became more prevalent, in proportion as personal valour and military skill declined with the Roman empire. When men were no longer found, their place was supplied by machines."[29]

III

The cessation of conquest led to a world at peace, in which commerce and the arts might flourish and refine men's manners even as they corrupted men's virtue. The legions "preserved a military spirit, at a time when every other virtue was oppressed by luxury and despotism,"[30] and we might look upon them as the guardians of a world of whose corruption they were the cause, and which would finally corrupt even them. But Gibbon's account of the relations between progress and decay is never simple; it is complicated first by the ambiguities of his attitude toward commerce and luxury, and second by the mounting importance of the theme of religion. At the end of chapter 7 he pauses, at the celebration of the secular games by Philip the Arab, to review the degeneration of virtue since the time of Romulus,[31] and to insert two chapters on the Persians and the Germans respectively, aimed at introducing the external forces which will bring the Empire down. That on the Persians is largely concerned with Zoroastrianism and belongs properly to Gibbon's history of religion; that on the Germans is a systematic sociology of barbarism. It is grounded in eighteenth-century theory about the successive stages of human history, and upon the perception that the history of economic production may be connected with the history of the human psyche.[32] It has therefore as much to do with commerce as with barbarism, and is linked in this way with the older humanist theme of the corruption of virtue.

Gibbon tells us that the Germans of the age before the invasions—who are, throughout this chapter, identified with the Germans described by Tacitus—

> were unacquainted with the use of letters; and the use of letters is the principal circumstance that distinguishes a civilised people from a herd of savages incapable of knowledge or reflection. Without that artificial help, the human memory soon dissipates or corrupts the ideas intrusted to her charge; and the nobler faculties of the mind, no longer supplied with models or with materials, gradually forget their powers; the judgment becomes feeble and lethargic, the imagination languid or irregular.[33]

They were also unacquainted with the use of money as a medium of exchange:

> The value of money has been settled by general consent to express our wants and our property, as letters were invented to express our ideas; and both these institutions, by giving a more active energy to the powers and passions of human nature, have contributed to multiply the objects they were designed to represent. . . . In a civilised state, every faculty of man is expanded and exercised; and the great chain of mutual dependence connects and embraces the several members of society. The most numerous portion of it is employed in constant and useful labour. The select few, placed by fortune above that necessity, can, however, fill up their time by the pursuits of interest or glory, by the improvement of their estate or of their understanding, by the duties, the pleasures, and even the follies of social life. The Germans were not possessed of these varied resources.[34]

Gibbon—whose social outlook, throughout his life, was that of a *rentier*, rather than a proprietor or an entrepreneur[35]—is plainly not much interested in the development of a Protestant ethic; the function of a commercial society, in his view, is to permit the growth of a leisured and civilized ruling class. In these passages he joins a tradition, stemming in a number of ways from Locke, but developed by the Scottish school to a point where it is hard to tell whether Hume, or Ferguson, or Smith is chiefly in Gibbon's mind at this moment; it was a tradition that found the key to history in the growth of means of production, stimulating in turn the growth of social intercourse, exchange, and interdependence, the objects before the human mind and its powers of perception, the passions which focused themselves upon these objects, and the powers of rational understanding which grew through reflection upon the objects and the passions alike. It is perhaps the secret of this process that the passions were moderated as they were developed; as they increased in number and diversity they became increasingly the subject of reflection and refinement, and the growth of a commercial society was the growth of a polished society.

Because the primitive Germans lacked letters and money, they could not control their passions; but it also followed that these passions were few, and by a strange paradox that it was their weakness as much as their strength which made them hard to control. Gibbon quotes Tacitus—whom he regarded as a "philosophical" historian in the eighteenth-century sense of "sociological"[36]—to the effect that the Germans

> delight in sloth, they detest tranquility. The languid soul, oppressed with its own weight, anxiously required some new and powerful sensation; and war and danger were the only amusements adequate to its fierce temper. The sound that summoned the German to arms was grateful to his ear. It roused him from his uncomfortable lethargy, gave him an active pursuit, and, by strong exercise of the body, and violent emotions of the mind, restored him to a more lively sense of his existence.[37]

A medieval moralist would have said that the Germans were employing *ira* as the remedy for *accidia*; to a modern it may appear that Gibbon has discovered *Angst*—appropriately enough, in its homeland. But we should rather emphasize the essentially materialist nature of his social theory; the psychology of the primitive Germans is deduced directly from their means of production. Because they were hardly even agriculturalists—Gibbon is specific on this point[38]—the Germans were proprietors of neither land nor goods; and the warrior's unstable lethargy springs from the fact that he had neither labor to occupy his body nor property to occupy his mind—still less to give him leisure to reflect on his social existence. Gibbon quotes Tacitus, again, as saying that the tribal authorities could order the redistribution of land-holdings every year, but could not order the physical punishment of any freeman; and he comments: "A people thus jealous of their persons, and careless of their possessions, must have been totally destitute of industry and the arts, but animated with a high sense of honour and independence."[39]

The concept of honor that now appears is primitivist in the extreme, and very far removed—though perhaps along a sequence still cyclical rather than stadial—from the military ethos which is all that is left to the legions when virtue has been withdrawn. Germanic honor precedes virtue because it precedes property and productive labor; it is the only mode of social consciousness possible to the warrior who has no productive function and can socialize his own passions only by seeking glory in the eyes of his fellows. Pre-feudal and pre-chivalric values appear at this point, and the ethos of the German war-band is not altogether unlike the legion's worship of its eagle;[40] its social and psychic foundations are, however, entirely different. In a passage of interest to the history of intersexual perception, Gibbon applies his theory of primitive honor to explain why German women were equal and respected, but as savagely warlike as the men and ferociously chaste into the bargain: "Conscious pride taught the German females to suppress every tender emotion that stood in competition with honour, and the first honour of the sex has ever been that of chastity."[41] In a more productive society, women are more feminine and more refined; they contribute significantly to the growth of refinement; but they are also less chaste, since that virtue's "most dangerous enemy is the softness of the mind. The refinements of life corrupt while they polish the intercourse of the sexes."[42]

The paradox of progress has reappeared, and it runs all through Gibbon's analysis of barbarism in this chapter. Honor precedes virtue because it precedes property; virtue is possible only when we perceive what connects us with society; property gives that connection a tangible shape, and as commercial progress multiplies the shapes it can take, the social passions are themselves both multiplied and refined. But virtue is pursued by the terrible paradox that property simultaneously gives government power over us, and corrupts while it confers the independence of mind which alone enables us to resist government:

> A warlike nation like the Germans, without either cities, letters, arts, or money, found some compensation for this savage state in the enjoyment of liberty. Their poverty secured their freedom, since our desires and our possessions are the strongest fetters of despotism. "Among the Suiones (says Tacitus), riches are held in honour. They are *therefore*[43] subject to an absolute monarch, who, instead of intrusting his people with the free use of arms, as is practised in the rest of Germany, commits them to the safe custody not of a citizen, or even of a freedman, but of a slave. The neighbours of the Suiones, the Sitones, are sunk even below servitude; they obey a woman." In the mention of these exceptions, the great historian sufficiently acknowledges the general theory of govern-ment.[44]

In passages such as this, Gibbon draws close to the romantic pessimism ascendant, if never quite dominant, in Ferguson and Rousseau: to a theory of history based on a perceived paradox that what moves society away from savagery and toward virtue and civilization simultaneously undermines its foundations with corruption, so that even virtue and freedom never quite coincide—the latter tending toward savagery, the former toward corruption. We might expect him at this point to present Roman civilization as a society destroyed by its own success and to admit that the growth of commerce which refines civilization renders it incapable of resisting its enemies within or without. But Gibbon avoids formulating this paradox—present as it is in the structure of his thought—as a general law applicable either to Roman society or to his own; and the means by which he avoids doing so throw light both on his ideological predispositions and on—what is not the same thing—his perception and planning of the structure of the *Decline and Fall*.

To begin with, while he is prepared to admit with all his authors that luxury was among the chief causes of the corruption of Rome, he is at some pains to deny either that luxury is a simple consequence of the growth of commerce, or that its corruptive effects have necessarily an economic explanation. In chapter 2, while describing the Antonine world at its height, he remarks that the industry of the people was largely taken up with producing consumer goods for a conspicuously consuming rich:

> Such refinements, under the odious name of luxury, have been severely arraigned by the moralists of every age; and it might perhaps be more conducive to the virtue, as well as happiness, of mankind, if all possessed the necessaries, and none the superfluities, of life. But in the present imperfect condition of society, luxury, though it may proceed from vice or folly, seems to be the only means that can correct the unequal distribution of property. The diligent mechanic, and the skilful artist, who have obtained no share in the division of the earth, receive a voluntary tax from the possessors of land; and the latter are prompted, by a sense of interest, to improve those estates, with whose produce they may purchase additional pleasures.[45]

Gibbon has returned to the defense of a polite society, in which the function of labor is to support a refined and leisured class; and he proceeds to deny that, in the Roman case, such a society impoverished itself even by the export of silver to purchase luxury goods from India[46]—a perennial topic of debate in eighteenth-century Britain. But to deny that the Roman Empire impoverished itself is not to deny that it corrupted itself; and when Gibbon says, a page or two later, that "it was scarcely possible that the eyes of contemporaries should discover in the public felicity the latent causes of decay and corruption,"[47] he is conceding that Antonine peace and prosperity had been bought at the price of a despotism which separated military from civic virtue, and so corrupted both. In the last analysis, a virtuous society had something other to do than to ensure the public felicity; it was concerned with harder matters—with discipline, conquest, and the assertion and preservation of freedom— and Gibbon knew that the contradiction had not been fully overcome. Yet it could be affirmed that not commerce, but despotism, was the cause of luxury; and we find him doing this in those climactic chapters of the second and third volumes (published in 1781) which conduct the narrative from the death of Theodosius to the sack of the city by Alaric. In chapter 27, for example, we find this:

> If it can be affirmed, with any degree of truth, that the luxury of the Romans was more shameless and dissolute in the reign of Theodosius than in the age of Constantine, perhaps, or of Augustus, the alteration cannot be ascribed to any beneficial improvements which had gradually increased the stock of national riches. A long period of calamity or decay must have checked the industry and diminished the wealth of the people; and their profuse luxury must have been the result of that indolent despair which enjoys the present hour and declines the thoughts of futurity. The uncertain condition of their property discouraged the subjects of Theodosius from engaging in those useful and laborious undertakings which require an immediate expense, and promise a slow and distant advantage.[48]

If the Romans were luxurious, it was because they were not laborious and did not practice the virtues of industry, prudence, and frugality; and this is the context in which Gibbon remarks that "the effeminate luxury, which infected the manners of courts and cities, had instilled a secret and destructive poison into the camps of the legions"[49] and recounts the last stages in the disappearance of military virtue, of which luxury is as much the effect as the cause. In chapter 31, that in which the sleeping inhabitants of Rome are "awakened by the tremendous sound of the Gothic trumpet,"[50] Gibbon introduces a long passage from Ammianus Marcellinus describing the luxury, corruption, and superstition of the senatorial class. But he prefaces it with the following passage:

> The opulent nobles of an immense capital, who were never excited by the pursuit of military glory, and seldom engaged in the occupations of civil government, naturally resigned their leisure to the business and amusements of private life. At Rome commerce was always held in contempt; but the senators, from the first age of the republic, increased their patrimony and multiplied their clients by the lucrative practice of usury. . . . The greater part of the nobles, who dissipated their fortunes in profuse luxury, found themselves poor in the midst of wealth, and idle in a constant round of dissipation. Their desires were constantly gratified by the labour of a thousand hands; of the numerous train of their domestic slaves, who were actuated by the fear of punishment; and of the various professions of artificers and merchants, who were more powerfully impelled by the hopes of gain.[51]

And immediately after the passage from Ammianus, Gibbon observes:

> In populous cities, which are the seats of commerce and manufactures, the middle ranks of inhabitants, who derive their subsistence from the dexterity or labour of their hands, are commonly the most prolific, the most useful, and, in that sense, the most respectable part of the community. But the plebeians of Rome, who disdained such sedentary and servile arts, had been oppressed from the earliest times by the weight of

debt and usury, and the husbandman, during the term of his military service, was obliged to abandon the cultivation of his farm. The lands of Italy, which had been originally divided among the families of free and indigent proprietors, were insensibly purchased or usurped by the avarice of the nobles; and in the age which preceded the fall of the republic, it was computed that only two thousand citizens were possessed of any independent substance. Yet as long as the people bestowed by their suffrages the honours of the state . . . their conscious pride alleviated in some measure the hardships of poverty; and their wants were seasonably supplied by the ambitious liberality of the candidates. . . .[52]

It was only when they gave up their political rights that poverty and venality made them into a degenerate and polyglot mob of dependents. In both these passages, Gibbon is projecting his image of an unproductive society plagued by debt into the heroic age of the early Republic—a footnote at this point refers to "those primitive times, which have been so undeservedly praised"[53]—and has indicated that the plebeians brought it on themselves by their contempt for useful industry. In thus apparently undercutting the conventional image of agrarian virtue, of which he has made such extensive use elsewhere, he is substituting a "modern" for an "ancient" account of how Roman virtue prepared the way for its own corruption. To thinkers in the "ancient" tradition that stemmed from Polybius, it seemed that the influx of wealth gained from conquest and empire had been too much for the institutions of the agrarian Republic, so that yeoman land had been absorbed by *latifundia* and yeomen warriors had become clients and mercenaries. Gibbon appears to be indicating that the yeoman warrior, who preferred serving in the legions for the conquest of new lands to the productive cultivation of his own farm for the market, had only himself to thank if neither he nor the nobleman could join in a productive market relationship and were compelled instead to play the mutually destructive roles of debtor and creditor, from which all evils followed. In such a society, political freedom would maintain personal virtue and the freedom of the personality, while economic virtues had not developed to the point of doing so.

Montesquieu and Hume had examined the idea that the economic base of ancient society and its virtue had been too narrow, while offering the image of a modern economy in which productive energy, refinement of manners, and civil liberty of a non-participatory kind took virtue's place. But there was still no really satisfactory account of how civil liberty could flourish for long without classical virtue, of how commercial society might generate its own form of political virtue, or—even though Adam Smith published the *Wealth of Nations* in the same year as the first volume of the *Decline and Fall*—of how the workings of economic society might themselves furnish satisfactory foundations for the human social personality. Gibbon was a philosophical historian, but his business was not to construct a general theory of the progress of human society; he had undertaken the sufficiently gigantic task of narrating and explaining the decline of the ancient world, and had resolved before his first volume appeared that he would not confine himself to the fall of the Western Empire. But in an age of philosophical history, he did not dream of denying that "this awful revolution may be usefully applied to the instruction of the present age";[54] and as one who was, disclaim it though he might, one of a triumvirate with Robertson and Hume, he did not deny that ancient and modern history were to be linked by an account of the progress—which might also be the corruption—of civil society. His handling of the themes of barbarism, luxury, and commerce shows that he had in his mind the makings of such an account; yet we are going to have to look for reasons why he never quite supplied it.

IV

At the end of chapter 38, in his third volume and in that part of the *Decline and Fall* published in 1781, Gibbon appended his "General Observations on the Fall of the Roman Empire in the West," which is both a review of the causes of that part of the decline and an inquiry into the prospects of such a calamity recurring to afflict the civilization of modern Europe. Though it contains many of his more striking pronouncements, this essay is generally considered to be unsatisfactory, for the reason that it appears thin and simplistic when considered as a review of the themes Gibbon has been treating. This thinness is apparent in several ways. The "General Observations" have only three things to say: that the nomad invaders will not return; that modern Europe is not a despotism; and that discoveries in the arts and sciences, once made, can never be entirely lost.[55] We should consider the second of these dicta—the third is really an appendage to it—before returning to examine the first. It has been apparent from the present inquiry that Gibbon ranked the leveling and depersonalizing effects of despotism well above the consequences of luxury and leisure as causes of the corruption of Rome; the principate, and the monarchy erected by Diocletian and Constantine which succeeded it, deprived its subjects of both civil and military virtue, and so of the ability to defend themselves. What he most strongly emphasizes in the "General Observations" is that:

> Europe is now divided into twelve powerful, though unequal kingdoms, three respectable commonwealths, and a variety of smaller, though independent states: the chances of royal and ministerial talents are multiplied, at least, with the number of its rulers. . . . The abuses of tyranny are restrained by the mutual influence of fear and shame; republics have acquired order and stability; monarchies have imbibed the principles of freedom, or, at least, of moderation; and some sense of honour and justice is introduced into the most defective constitutions by the general manners of the times. In peace, the progress of knowledge and industry is accelerated by the emulation of so many active rivals: in war, the European forces are exercised by temperate and undecisive contests.[56]

"If a savage conqueror," Gibbon continues, "should issue from the deserts of Tartary," he will not encounter a society robbed of all virtue by the empire of a single domination. The cycle described by Machiavelli and the theorists of *translatio imperii* has been broken; Europe is not an empire, but "a great republic,"[57] a *république des patries* which preserve one another's virtue and industry by challenging them. This, incidentally, shows that the loss of America by Britain was not a decline and fall in the Roman sense.

Gibbon in 1781 did not know that he would live to see this republic destroyed by forces exploding from within; he did not consider the American Revolution as in any way lessening America's capacity to act as a reinforcement of Europe.[58] But there was, and long had been, a widespread and vocally expressed fear that the progress of commerce, luxury, and the arts was rendering it ever harder to safeguard liberty against corruption; whatever Gibbon's American contemporaries felt about commerce,[59] they certainly saw their revolution as a last-ditch stand against globe-encircling corruption; and though we can see pretty clearly why Gibbon did not share this fear, it is less easy to see why he did not take the trouble to refute it. We know, that is, that he thought despotism, not commerce, the main cause of corruption and luxury; we have uncovered an argument which he could have used to contend that, while the corruption of ancient and agrarian virtue was the correct explanation of the Roman decline, both virtue and its corruption were phenomena of the ancient economy and need not recur in the modern. But it cannot be maintained that this argument controls the explanations given in the first three volumes of the *Decline and Fall*, or that it recurs in the "General Observations" as a reason why modern commercial society should not fear corruption.

The "General Observations" disappoint us in another way. The emphasis given to the reflection that the Russians have conquered the steppe and begun to plough it, that Attila and Genghis Khan will not return, seems abstract and unreal. There are two reasons why we should feel as we do. The way in which Gibbon has initially laid the scene for the *Decline and Fall*, our own knowledge of the thinking of eighteenth-century philosophical historians, our foreknowledge that he will declare that he has recounted "the triumph of barbarism and religion" dispose us to expect, first, a study of whether the processes of Roman decay are likely to recur, and, second, an inquiry into how the interactions between the barbarian invaders and the Christian religion have affected and continue to affect the history of post-Roman Europe. But we receive neither. We are not told whether Europe will become corrupt like Rome, or how it is coping in its enlightened age with the relics of barbarism and superstition; and to be told instead that nomadism is nearly extinct in Central Asia seems a singularly barren approach to both ancient and modern history. But if we consider how it is that we are offered this fare, we shall learn something about the *Decline and Fall* which may still be worth remembering.

Gibbon never returned to the analysis of barbarian society with the depth of sociological and psychological penetration displayed in the chapter on the Germans. When he next considered the phenomena of barbarism, it was in chapter 26 (the last of Volume II in the 1781 printing), which is devoted to "the manners of the pastoral nations," the Huns, Scythians, and Central Asian nomads in general. Concerning these, Gibbon has to say that, as they are shepherds, they are savages,

> and the savage tribes of mankind, as they approach nearer to the condition of animals, preserve a stronger resemblance to themselves and to each other. The uniform stability of their manners is the natural consequence of the imperfection of their faculties. Reduced to a similar situation, their wants, their desires, their enjoyments still continue the same; and the influence of food or climate, which, in a more improved state of society, is suspended or subdued by so many moral causes, most powerfully contributes to form and to maintain the national character of barbarians.[60]

The discovery of a "shepherd," pastoral and pre-agrarian, stage in social evolution was one of the most recent and exciting discoveries in conjectural history;[61] but to Adam Smith it had appeared that this was the stage in which the specialization of function and the beginnings of political power first took effect.[62] To Gibbon, however, it was altogether barren and static. He could visualize world history from A.D. 400 to 1400 as the interactions of the Desert with the Sown, of the nomads of the steppe with the settled agricultural empires from China to Rome.[63] He was not Occidentocentric at all; but he never allowed to the nomads any epithet above that of "savages," or—with one great but partial exception—any social capacity beyond that of mobilizing destructive power.

And the analysis of German society in chapter 9 had clearly shown it to have been a society of herdsmen rather than of farmers. As we follow Gibbon's account of the settlement of the Goths and Franks in the western provinces, it is noteworthy that the barbarians are referred to as "shepherds,"[64] and excluded by implication from any capacity for that agriculture which Gibbon knew to be "the parent of manufactures,"[65] of arts, and of letters. To call the German a "shepherd" could hardly equate him with a pastoral nomad from the steppe, but it did have the effect of de-emphasizing his participation either in that myth of agrarian, pre-commercial, and very often "Gothic" virtue, on which European and American thinking still largely relied, or in the more serious histories of the progress of society from barbarism through agriculture to commerce, which were being written by Gibbon's peers of the Scottish school. That history was generally located in the former Western Empire, in the interactions between Gallo-Roman agriculture, Gothic warrior feudalism, and the reviving imperial, urban, and ecclesiastical institutions of the later Empire. It would be a wild exaggeration to say that Gibbon denied that this progress of society had taken place; what can be affirmed quite certainly, and demonstrated from his projection and execution, is that he had decided not to write its history, and that we should not read the *Decline and Fall* as if he had intended to do so.

Montesquieu and Mably, Robertson and Hume—he knew all but the first of these personally—had been before him in studying or writing the history of the *respublica christiana* which had succeeded the *respublica romana* in the West, and had been transformed into the *république européenne* of his own times. In the last three volumes of his history, Gibbon carried out the plan he had announced when introducing the first in 1776; he carried the narrative from the fall of the Western Empire to the fall of Constantinople in 1453, keeping Byzantine history as the central theme, developing an extended treatment of Arab and Turkish Islam as the true adversary of Byzantium, and treating medieval Western history only as it contributed to the great theme of the decline of the Eastern Empire, and the lesser, if enormously moving, theme of the decay of the city of Rome through the medieval period to the sack of 1527.[66] In short, while we may read Gibbon's later chapters for many important observations on the familiar subject matter of Latin and post-medieval history as seen through eighteenth-century eyes, we have to remember that there is a fundamental sense in which the Roman-Germanic theme has been relegated to the margins of the later *Decline and Fall*.

It is not only our own Occidentalism which makes it difficult for us to accept this. All that we know of eighteenth-century philosophical history encourages us to believe that when Gibbon writes in chapter 2: "The fierce giants of the north broke in, and mended the puny breed. They restored a manly spirit of freedom; and after the revolution of ten centuries, freedom became the happy parent of taste and science,"[67] or in chapter 16: "During the ages of ignorance which followed the subversion of the Roman empire in the West, the bishops of the Imperial city extended their dominion over the laity as well as clergy of the Latin church. The fabric of superstition which they had erected . . . was at length assaulted by a crowd of daring fanatics, who, from the twelfth to the sixteenth century, assumed the popular character of reformers,"[68] he intends to give us the history of these processes; we ignore his very explicit declarations that he has another purpose. We know, what is quite true, that Gibbon had no sympathy for Byzantine civilization and no belief that it had any inner dynamic of its own; we do not inquire into the extraordinary resolution that kept him for seven years writing its history and that of an Islam he liked only a little better.

When we hear the famous phrase "the triumph of barbarism and religion," we think instinctively of the Gothic invaders and the bishops of the Western churches; we do not consider that—whatever resonance Gibbon intended the phrase to have[69]—a reader of all six volumes would have a very good case for applying it to the Arabs rather than the Germans, and to Islam rather than Christianity.

What differentiates the Arabs from all other pastoral nomads is that a prophet-legislator arose among them and founded a new religion and a new civil order; what differentiates Islam from Christianity is that the former arose among heroic and superstitious barbarians, hardly (though sufficiently) touched by city life,[70] whereas the latter arose in the decay of an ancient civic order and an ancient civic religion. These are the themes that interest Gibbon as a philosopher. The heirs of primitive Islam—themselves much corrupted by empire—succeeded in overthrowing the bureaucratic and ecclesiastical hierarchy founded by Constantine, and very little changed after eleven centuries. These are the themes around which Gibbon organized the later volumes of the *Decline and Fall*. As a philosophic historian of Western society, he laid down the pen—except for a limited series of specific purposes—where Robertson had earlier taken it up. He then found new, gigantic, if philosophically recalcitrant, themes, moving into the history of Asia as Robertson moved into that of America; and this had been his intention as early as 1776. If we need to reexamine the *Decline and Fall* with the later volumes at the center of our perception, we need to read the work as its author planned and executed it.

REFERENCES

Note: All references to the *History of the Decline and Fall of the Roman Empire (DF)* are to the chapter and page number of the seven-volume edition of J. B. Bury (2nd ed., London, 1902).

[1]*Memoirs of My Life*, ed. Georges A. Bonnard (New York, 1966), p. 159. Compare the letters to Robertson in *The Letters of Edward Gibbon*, ed. J. E. Norton (London, 1956), II, p. 361, and III, p. 100, in which "a place in the triumvirate," even in the role of "Lepidus," is positively asserted.

[2]*Letters*, II, p. 107. Cf. the references to the low standing of English as compared to Scots historians.

[3]The Index to the *Letters* may be consulted for references to, and correspondence with, both Ferguson and Smith. Gibbon praised *The Wealth of Nations*, but is said to have thought less well of the *Essay on the History of Civil Society*.

[4]*Letters*, II, pp. 359-60 and III, pp. 99-100.

[5]See J. G. A. Pocock, *The Machiavellian Moment: Florentine Political Thought and the Atlantic Republican Tradition* (Princeton, 1975). The next few paragraphs abridge this work's argument.

[6]Lois G. Schwoerer, *"No Standing Armies!" The Anti-Army Ideology in Seventeenth-Century England* (Baltimore, 1974).

[7]*Memoirs of My Life*, p. 117.

[8]Montesquieu, *Esprit des lois*, XIX. 27; Hume, *Essays*, II, 1 and 2; *Machiavellian Moment*, pp. 488-98.

[9]Priestley, *Essay on the First Principles of Government* (2nd ed., London, 1771), p. 5. For Gibbon's opinion of Priestley, see *Letters*, II, pp. 320-23; *DF*, chap. 54, the concluding footnote; *Memoirs*, pp. 171-72.

[10]*DF*, chap. 71, p. 308. See also n. 69, below.

[11]*DF*, chap. 2. p. 51.

[12]*DF*, chap. 3, p. 78.

[13]William Robertson, "View of the Progress of Society in Europe . . .," *History of the Reign of Charles V*, Section I (originally published in 1769; see *Works* [London, 1851], III, p. 9).

[14]*The English Essays of Edward Gibbon*, ed. Patricia B. Craddock (Oxford, 1972): ". . . from the civil wars, that ensued after the fall of Nero, or even from the tyranny that succeeded the reign of Augustus."

[15]*DF*, chap. 1, p. 1.

[16]*Ibid*.

[17]*Ibid.*, p. 2.

[18]*Ibid.*, p. 9.

[19]*Arte* could mean both "art" and "guild" or "trade."

[20]*DF*, chap. 3, pp. 60-61; 70-72.

[21]*Ibid.*, p. 60; cf. chap. 18, p. 204.

[22]*DF*, chap. 3, pp. 78-79.

[23]*DF*, chap. 1. p. 9.

[24]*Ibid.*, p. 10.

[25]E.g., *DF*, chap. 5, pp. 111, 118; chap. 6, pp. 166, 168; chap. 7, p. 194; chap. 11, pp. 283, 292, 313, 315; chap. 12, pp. 376-77. In chaps. 11-13 the emphasis lies on the Illyrian peasant origins of the emperors between Claudius Gothicus and Diocletian.

[26]*DF*, chap. 1, p. 10.

[27]*Ibid.*, p. 11.

[28]See n. 25, above.

[29]*DF*, chap. 1, p. 15, n. 61. Cf. "General Observations on the Fall of the Roman Empire in the West," following chap. 38, pp. 166-67, where it is remarked that modern armies have transformed warfare by "arts which survive and supply the decay of military virtue" and must "be accompanied . . . with a proportionable improvement in the arts of peace and civil policy," rendering virtue in the antique sense no longer necessary.

[30]*DF*, chap. 1. p. 16.

[31]*DF*, chap. 7, pp. 193-94.

[32]The most recent study is that of R. L. Meek, *Social Science and the Ignoble Savage* (Cambridge, 1975).

[33]*DF*, chap. 9, p. 218.

[34]*Ibid.*, p. 220.

[35]His correspondence with Sheffield and others, especially while he lived at Lausanne, is concerned with the income to be derived either from his estates or from their sale.

[36]*DF*, chap. 9, p. 213: "the first of historians who applied the science of philosophy to the study of facts."

[37]*Ibid.*, p. 221.

[38]*Ibid.*, pp. 219-20.

[39]*Ibid.*, pp. 225-26.

[40]*Ibid.*, p. 226.

[41]*Ibid.*, p. 228.

[42]*Ibid.*, p. 227.

[43]Gibbon's italics.

[44]*DF*, chap. 9, p. 223.

[45]*DF*, chap. 2, p. 53.

[46]*Ibid.*, pp. 54-56.

[47]*Ibid.*, p. 56.

[48]*DF*, chap. 27, p. 186.

[49]*Ibid.*, p. 187.

[50]*DF*, chap. 31, p. 321.

[51]*Ibid.*, p. 294.

[52]*Ibid.*, p. 302.

[53]*Ibid.*, n. 51.

[54]*DF*, "General Observations," p. 163.

[55]*Ibid.*, pp. 163-67.

[56]*Ibid.*, pp. 165-66.

[57]*Ibid.*, p. 163.

[58]*Ibid.*, p. 166 and n. 8.

[59]See J. F. Crowley, *That Sheba Self: The Conceptualization of Commercial Life in the American Colonies* (Baltimore, 1972).

[60]*DF*, chap. 26, p. 71.

[61]Meek, cited in n. 32.

[62]See, e.g., *Lectures on Justice, Police, Revenue and Arms*, I, chap. 1, pt. 2.

[63]*DF*, chap. 26, pp. 74-75, 79-81, 84-91; chap. 34, pp. 416-23; chap. 38, pp. 164-67; chap. 42, pp. 349-52, 354-57; chap. 48, pp. 172-73; chap. 57, pp. 224-27, 229-33; chap. 64, pp. 1-22; chap. 65, pp. 42-70. De Guignes's *Histoire des Huns* was a major resource, and Gibbon's references to Chinese history would repay study

[64]*DF*, chap. 38, pp. 129, 132, 164.

[65]*DF*, chap. 2, p. 53.

[66]See the Preface to the first volume, dated February 1, 1776, p. v-vii in the Bury edition.

[67]*DF*, chap. 2, p. 58.

[68]*DF*, chap. 16, pp. 138-39.

[69]*DF*, chap. 71, pp. 308-9. The context is that of the destruction of Roman monuments: "In the preceding volumes of this history, I have described the triumph of barbarism and religion; and I can only resume, in a few words, their real or imaginary connexion with the ruin of ancient Rome" (i.e., the city).

[70]*DF*, chap. 50, p. 316.

STEPHEN R. GRAUBARD

Edward Gibbon: Contraria Sunt Complementa

A MODERN INTELLECTUAL PORTRAIT of Gibbon that emphasized his boldness, bias, and irony would offend no one; it is fully consonant with what many today conceive to be the character of England's greatest eighteenth-century historian. There would be no comparable enthusiasm for a portrait that dwelled on Gibbon's timidity, impartiality, and more than occasional lapses into an uncritical, stolid, almost complacent literal-mindedness; such a representation would seem ungenerous and hostile, and it would also be false.

Gibbon himself would have found neither portrait very satisfactory: the first, while superficially friendly, repeats a charge that he consistently denied; the second, while seemingly hostile, accepts at least his own claim to impartiality. Gibbon would not have known what to make of the vague references to an "uncritical, stolid, almost complacent literal-mindedness." How could he have understood what none of his contemporaries accused him of—that, having written a great tragic history and revealed the significance of that history for his own age, he was too much the prisoner of his own time to transcend it? Was this not the condition that prevented him from knowing what message to bring to a generation increasingly beset by revolutionary troubles? Would Gibbon have understood that those very talents that made him "*the* historian of Rome" precluded his being also "*the* historian of the eighteenth century," except as his work gave incidental testimony to certain of the major intellectual predispositions of his time?

To ask these questions, and others like them, is also to ask whether the conventional explanations of Gibbon's genius may not be too narrow and whether they would not profit from substantial revision. Would our understanding of his character and his great opus not be increased by considering the possibility that he was bold but timid, partisan certainly, but aspiring also to an impartiality that he achieved rather more frequently than is sometimes alleged, a master of irony without peer, but also one who succumbed to forms of analogical literal-mindedness that seemed at times almost to mock his intellectual and literary capabilities? If these several qualities had revealed themselves sequentially in Gibbon, where he showed himself sometimes brave, sometimes meek, sometimes biased, sometimes unprejudiced, sometimes ironic, sometimes complacent, one might say that they simply expressed and reflected those unresolved contradictions in the man, those personal and physical idiosyncracies that others noted in him. What makes these attributes significant, however, is not that they are contradictory, which of course they are, but that they appear to have been complementary, in some way joined. They worked

121

together to produce what is most distinctive in Gibbon both as a historian and as a man of letters.

Gibbon was bold but timid; his boldness was shaped by his timidity, and both influenced his passion, his willingness to distribute praise and blame, but also his capacity to avoid the exaggerated hero-worship that was already common in the Enlightenment and was to become even more virulent with the advent of romanticism. Gibbon's irony was not incidental to his purpose; it was an integral part of his work, but it touched only those matters not affected by his almost excessive caution and prudence; in short, it rarely touched on those eighteenth-century issues that he felt keenly about and could not leave alone.

If Gibbon's prejudices were evident, so was his unremitting concern with fairness and precision; these qualities showed themselves simultaneously, sometimes within a single phrase or sentence. One cannot explain Gibbon's constant use of his favorite conjunction "but," which served to advance his narrative and almost always contained some element of surprise, except as a literary device for achieving purposes that might range from moderating or softening a particularly severe judgment to making an already bold statement even more original and emphatic. Where Gibbon's impartiality would lead him and how it related to his bias—where one started and the other ended—were often mysteries. Nor was it at all obvious why Gibbon felt so constantly impelled to intrude some reference to the modern world in his consideration of Roman, Christian, and Byzantine history. What Gibbon felt at liberty to say about a historically remote age, he did not necessarily feel free to say about his own times.

Whether in his portrayal of the struggle between despotism and liberty, his consideration of the differences between the East and the West—done with so much greater panache than his more feeble efforts to describe the differences between the North and the South—his analysis of Roman military and moral decline, attendant on an unstable imperial succession and an enfeebled senate, his reflections on the adverse effects stemming from the imposition of unjust and oppressive taxes, his inquiry into the lives of particular individuals, religious and secular, his theories about the disastrous consequences that followed on the advent of Christianity and the barbarian invasions, Gibbon gave a form, weight, and importance to each that was meaningful to other eighteenth-century European intellectuals of a rationalist persuasion. They were themselves prepared to view the past and the present in a perspective not too different from his, at least in its essential features. Still, the individuality of Gibbon's judgment needs to be insisted on. In comparing his work with that of other Enlightenment figures, particularly on the Continent, one cannot fail to be struck by both the similarities and the differences.

No other Enlightenment historian traversed Gibbon's territory in the way that Gibbon did; Montesquieu's *Considérations sur les causes de la grandeur des Romains et de leur décadence* did not provide even an outline for what Gibbon eventually chose to do. Had Montesquieu turned to history in the way that Hume did, and had he chosen to make the Roman Empire his subject, he would have written a book very different from Gibbon's. One says this with confidence, not only about the overall plan of such a work, but also about any number of its details. Could the author of the *Esprit des lois* have treated slavery, for example, in the way that Gibbon did? For Gibbon, slaves were the human residue of centuries of war, who, under Rome, had at least some small distant prospect of freedom.[1] Slavery was not, for Gibbon, the moral blight that it was for Montesquieu. But then Montesquieu did not see the problems of war and peace as Gibbon did. Montesquieu was not much given to expatiating on the glories of war; in the end, he was more bold than Gibbon.

The concept of Gibbon as a timid man calls for explanation. The charge is too serious to be bandied about lightly. The evidence, indeed, is striking in Gibbon's *Memoirs*, on a personal and psychological level; it is also apparent in his history, on an intellectual level. Whatever one may conjecture about the reasons that led Gibbon to prohibit publication of his *Memoirs* during his lifetime, we know that his friend and literary executor, Lord Sheffield, thought it perfectly proper to publish them within two years of Gibbon's death.[2] Why had Gibbon rejected the idea of publication during his lifetime? Why, indeed, had he written that, though the manuscript might be shown to "some discreet and indulgent friends," it was to be "secreted from the public eye till the author shall be removed beyond the reach of criticism or ridicule."[3] How is one to explain Gibbon's reticence, particularly when placed in the context of a public reputation for boldness? Did he wish simply to avoid giving pain to his step-mother, knowing how unflattering was his portrayal of his father? Or, was he afraid that his strictures on certain institutions—Magdalen College and the House of Commons, to name only two—would give offense? There is no way of knowing, nor can one hazard a guess about why, sitting in Parliament from 1774 to 1783, a time of unprecedented internal and international disorder, Gibbon never once rose to speak. Would timidity alone explain such extraordinary behavior? Or, does it simply indicate remarkable self-restraint? The evidence is, at best, inconclusive.

The same, however, cannot be said about why or how Gibbon came to write his Roman history. The choice of subject was not a courageous act; the execution of the work showed him to be at once venturesome and conventional. In his *Memoirs*, Gibbon, quoting from a journal that he kept while serving in the militia in 1761 and 1762, suggested that he had known from an early age that he wanted to be a historian; the study of the past preoccupied him, and the problem was simply to find a theme that would engage his interests. For a time, he thought seriously about writing on Sir Walter Raleigh; in the end, however, he rejected the idea. A biography of Raleigh already existed; though it was not very good and might indeed be thought pedantic, Gibbon knew that it contained much of the essential material on Raleigh's life. The prospect of discovering a substantial store of new material was slight. Gibbon, of course, could have written about the period in which Raleigh lived, "the circumjacent history of the times," but that prospect did not much intrigue him. His reasons for avoiding that possibility are revealing. Gibbon wrote:

> But the reigns of Elizabeth and James I are the periods of English history which have been the most variously illustrated: and what new lights could I reflect on a subject which has exercised the accurate industry of *Birch*, the lively and curious acuteness of *Walpole*, the critical spirit of *Hurd*, the vigorous sense of *Mallet* and *Robertson*, and, the impartial philosophy of *Hume*. Could I even surmount these obstacles, I should shrink with terror from the modern history of England, where every character is a problem and every reader a friend or an enemy: where a writer is supposed to hoist a flag of party, and is devoted to damnation by the adverse faction. Such would be *my* reception at home: and abroad the historian of Raleigh must encounter an indifference far more bitter than censure or reproach. The events of his life are interesting but his character is ambiguous, his actions are obscure, his writings are English, and his fame is confined to the narrow limits of our language and our island. I must embrace a safer and more extensive theme.[4]

As a young man of twenty-five, Gibbon was already preoccupied with finding a theme that would have resonance abroad, that would have meaning for men of letters whose first language was not English. He was determined to avoid the study of sixteenth- and seventeenth-century England; that was a field full of danger; it would compel him to choose sides, inevitably winning the applause of some, while provoking the wrath of others. Gibbon had no taste for that kind of battle.

What, then, did he consider doing? The idea of writing "The History of the Liberty of the Swiss" appealed to him. It was "full of public spirit, of military glory, of examples of virtue, of lessons of government the dullest stranger would catch fire. . . ."[5] But, in the end, that theme also seemed unpromising; as Gibbon explained: "The materials of this history are inaccessible to me, fast locked in the obscurity of an old barbarous German dialect of which I am totally ignorant, and which I cannot resolve to learn for this sole and peculiar purpose."[6] Some years later, Gibbon would write about the Arab world, acknowledging his "total ignorance of the Oriental tongues,"[7] but it was one thing to write a few chapters in a greater work, openly admitting one's linguistic handicap, and quite another to write a whole book, where access to even the most basic documents would be difficult.

In any case, Gibbon was already considering another possibility, "The History of the Republic of Florence under the House of Medicis." Gibbon saw Florentine history as the obverse of the Swiss: Switzerland [is] a poor, warlike, virtuous Republic . . . [emerging] into glory and freedom," while Florence "[is] a Commonwealth, soft, opulent and corrupt, . . . precipitated from the abuse, to the loss of her liberty."[8] Gibbon found both histories "perhaps equally instructive," but he wrote neither.

The story of how, in Rome, on October 15, 1764, he decided on the subject that would consume him for the greater part of his adult life needs no repeating. What ought to be emphasized, however, is that though Gibbon began with the intention of writing only about the decay of Rome as a city, much as he might have written about the corruption of Florence, he came in the end to write about the decline of the Empire as a whole. He had taken his Florentine plan, expanded it, related it to Rome, and given it an importance that made it significant for every European intellectual of his generation. Had he written about Florence, he would have had ample materials for discoursing on virtue and vice, and on human folly and institutional decay; however, Florence's history was the history of a single "province" of Europe, as England's history would have been. Gibbon aspired to something greater. He was writing the "ancient history of Europe," a subject calculated to interest all Europeans, whether they lived in Great Britain, France, Spain, Switzerland, or the states of Germany and Italy.

So much for the story of how Gibbon came to make his choice of Rome. It reveals a mind perfectly attuned to many of the opinions of his age; in England, where liberty and despotism were generally made to appear polar opposites, there was no need to develop a conceptual scheme that would show greater discrimination in distinguishing between the incontestably complex societies that Gibbon was required to treat. Showing neither Hume's skepticism about the ultimate worth of certain martial and violent virtues nor Rousseau's deep anguish about their extinction, Gibbon wrote in a way that suggested these virtues survived, at least in the England of his own day.

The *Decline and Fall of the Roman Empire* was in part a moral tale; virtue was made to reside largely offstage in an age occasionally alluded to, but antecedent to the one that excited and preoccupied Gibbon. Using chronology as his organizing principle, much as the other great Enlightenment historians had done, Gibbon painted a canvas infinitely more populated and more detailed than any that men even as bold and venturesome as Voltaire and Hume had attempted. The vastness of Gibbon's subject, his willingness to concern himself with geography and political economy, manners and customs, law and religion, war and politics, all this extending over a millennium and a half, and involving numerous peoples spread over three continents, made all national histories (however grandly perceived) seem suddenly parochial by comparison. Gibbon's themes were impressive: he wrote of politics polluted, bureaucracies corrupted, armies enfeebled, institutions distorted. It was not the Roman intelligence that had failed, though there were instances enough of this failure; it was Roman valor that had declined. Roman character was fatally corrupted; under these circumstances, the challenges of war, revolution, and barbarian invasion were literally too overwhelming. Roman institutions were incapable of coping with disasters of such a magnitude. Gibbon's history was not of a single decline, but of many, some involving peoples recently virile and self-reliant, who succumbed to the hazards of civilization. Independence, valor, trust—these might exist in the forests of Germany, the deserts of Arabia, or the forum at Rome—their vulnerability, in whatever place, was Gibbon's special province.

Did he realize from the beginning how perfectly suited he was to writing such a history? Perhaps not. In any case, the coincidence of interest, ambition, and personality could not have been more perfect. Gibbon chose a subject that was certain to appeal to an international audience; he deliberately avoided the thickets of parochial (English) politics. His education and training were precisely right for the task; while his Greek was not equal to his Latin, he commanded both, claiming also great learning in philosophy and history, both ancient and modern. He knew superbly his classical sources, but was equally at home with the thought of his own time, whether north of the English border or across the Channel. Hume, Smith, Robertson, Montesquieu, Voltaire, Rousseau—all were familiar to him. Also, and happily, his subject did not require him to choose from among these men. He could afford to be eclectic, borrowing from all and showing some measure of indebtedness to all. His history, however different from theirs, did not in any fundamental way challenge theories that they espoused. As between those among this contemporaries who preferred the martial virtues and those who opted for the civilian, Gibbon remained neutral.

This is not to say that Gibbon simply wrote as others did, borrowing indiscriminately from them. There were subtle and sometimes important differences between Gibbon and others of the Enlightenment figures. If Voltaire, for example, in describing the "four happy ages" that the world had known, chose to dwell on the period of Caesar and Augustus,[9] and if Gibbon chose to see the period between the death of Domitian and the accession of Commodus as "the most happy and prosperous" the human race had ever known,[10] the difference was not accidental. Voltaire gave purely intellectual accomplishment an importance that Gibbon probably thought excessive; political stability interested Gibbon more. Beyond all such differences, however—and they might be multiplied many times—lay a fundamental agreement. Voltaire, explicitly, and Gibbon, implicitly, appeared to recognize four great ages in human history: that of Greece, late republican and early imperial Rome, Renaissance Italy, seventeenth- and eighteenth-century Europe. The two might differ in estimating the significance and character of each, but Gibbon would never have been tempted to challenge the basic chronology of "great ages" established by Voltaire in 1751. It would have been as inconceivable for Gibbon to include the medieval period or the Reformation among the "happy ages" of mankind as it would have been for either Gibbon or Voltaire to cite some particular era in the history of China or India. To have done that, Gibbon would have had to transcend the moral values of his day. This, he was incapable of doing.

So, also, with Hume—a man whom Gibbon intensely admired and whose praise for his first volume of the *Decline and Fall* he greatly prized—there were small, sometimes even significant, differences but none that could have led to a major quarrel. Each was gifted in his delineation of character; each recognized the necessity of introducing complexity in his portrayal of individuals of whatever eminence or distinction. If Gibbon is biased in favor of certain men—and who can deny that he is—it is significant that he avoided uncritical praise; it would be difficult to find in Gibbon a portrait comparable to the one that Hume permitted himself when he said of Newton: "This island may boast of having produced the greatest and rarest genius that ever rose for the ornament and instruction of the species."[11] Such praise, even for the few that Gibbon clearly admired (men like Julian and Stilicho, for example), was almost unthinkable in the author of the *Decline and Fall of the Roman Empire*. Gibbon, like Hume, had the great virtue of never mistaking men's words for their thoughts; he looked with a critical eye on men's actions, and while capable of distributing credit and blame, knew instinctively that Rome's ultimate fate was not the result of any one man's failures. If Gibbon deplored the decline of virtue in the senate, it was in part because he recognized the limitations of individual action; whether Gibbon would have demonstrated the same equanimity had he made contemporary England his subject is, to say the least, doubtful. It is good that his timidity led him to a bolder prospect.

Since almost every discussion of Gibbon's bias must begin with some reference to his treatment of the Christian Church—the *locus classicus* for all this being the celebrated chapters 15 and 16, which so much exercised critics in the eighteenth century—it is well to be reminded of what Gibbon said on these matters in his *Memoirs*. The references are illuminating; before the first volume of the history appeared, Gibbon represents himself as having thought "that an age of light and liberty would receive without scandal, an enquiry into the *human* causes of the progress and establishment of Christianity."[12] Clearly, Gibbon had anticipated the possibility of mild criticism, but he had not anticipated the storm that broke. He believed that he could safely represent complexity, making it palatable to his age. This certainly is the implication of a journal entry of February 3, 1779, where Gibbon wrote:

> Had I believed that the majority of English readers were so fondly attached even to the name and shadow of Christianity; had I foreseen that the pious, the timid and the prudent would feel or affect to feel with such exquisite sensibility; I might, perhaps have softened the two invidious Chapters, which would create many enemies, and conciliate few friends. But the shaft was shot, the alarm was sounded, and I could only rejoyce, that if the voice of our priests was clamorous and bitter, their hands were disarmed of the powers of persecution.[13]

The irony of the passage makes one wonder whether, forewarned of adverse reaction, Gibbon would indeed have "softened" certain of the offensive passages. One cannot know. What one does know, however, is that he was delighted by the public reception of this first volume and particularly pleased by the generous tributes paid by Hume and Robertson. Buoyed by the reception of the work, he could write, without self-consciousness, "I have never presumed to accept a place in the triumvirate of British historians."[14]

In November, 1776, Gibbon wrote to J. B. Antoine Suard, Robertson's translator, whom he had met earlier in the year. Gibbon wanted Suard to undertake the translation of the *Decline and Fall of the Roman Empire* into French. To an almost perfect stranger, Gibbon expressed his deep disappointment with his close friend, Deyverdun, who had earlier indicated a willingness to undertake the task of translation and had now reneged on his promise. Gibbon wrote:

> Me voici donc à present libre mais isolé. J'ai toujours meprisé la triste philosophie qui veut nous rendre insensibles à la gloire. J'ambitionne celle d'être lu en France et dans le Continent; et je me verrois au comble de mes désirs, si la même plume qui a si bien rendu l'eloquence historique de Robertson vouloit se preter à un ecrivain son inférieur à tous égards, mais qui a reçu de l'indulgence de ses Compatriotes un accueil presqu'aussi favorable.[15]

Having revealed unmistakably his interest in being published in a French translation, Gibbon wrote also about chapters 15 and 16 and the problems they posed:

> Je sens cependant qu'un homme d'Esprit rompu comme vous dans l'art d'écrire seroit souvent en état d'adoucir l'expression sans affoiblir la pensée. Je ne craindrois pas de vous confier les droits les plus étendus pour changer et même pour supprimer tout ce qui vous paroitroit le plus propre à blesser la delicatesse de votre Eglise et de votre police.[16]

For Gibbon, publication was the essential thing; if particular phrases offended, they might be omitted. He was prepared to defer to what he conceived to be the "prejudices" of others. Rather than fight for every paragraph, least of all for those that others might deem offensive, Gibbon accepted the wisdom of compromise. The letter is significant if only because it indicates how much the criticism of Gibbon in the eighteenth century attached almost entirely to his treatment of Christianity.[17]

What Gibbon thought about other matters seemed scarcely sensational. Who in France, or in England for that matter, cared to take issue with other parts of the work, indicating where and how Gibbon had been unjust in his portrayal of a particular individual or institution? Who, for example, in the eighteenth century cared what Gibbon had said even about a major figure like Augustus? For us, chapters 15 and 16 are infinitely less salient than they were for Gibbon's contemporaries. Our interest, inevitably, is in the bias revealed in the work as a whole. In this connection, it is well to be reminded of R. G. Collingwood's comment on Gibbon's method. Collingwood, impatient with J. B. Bury for trying to "correct" Gibbon, wrote with some asperity:

> Thus he [Bury] was able to accomplish the very strange feat of bringing Gibbon up to date by means of footnotes, adding to the aggregate of knowledge already contained in his pages the numerous facts that had been ascertained in the meantime, without suspecting that the very discovery of these facts resulted from an historical mentality so different from Gibbon's own that the result was not unlike adding a saxophone obligato to an Elizabethan madrigal.[18]

Whatever Collingwood's exaggeration may have been—there was, in fact, a greater utility in Bury's enterprise than he acknowledged—Collingwood was right in seeing that the fundamental unity and worth of Gibbon's work could not be enhanced by citing the findings of more recent historical scholarship. Gibbon's history was a unique, almost personal perception of the Roman world.

Gibbon did not write about Augustus in the way that Voltaire had done; the fact that Rome, in the time of Caesar and Augustus, had been graced by the presence of Lucretius, Cicero, Livy, Virgil, Horace, Ovid, Varro, and Vitruvius was immensely important to Voltaire; Gibbon was less impressed. His interest was largely in the political system established by Augustus, a system that he did not greatly admire. How is one to estimate the bias in an interpretation that shows full appreciation for the historical significance of Augustus, but reveals unmistakable contempt for his policies, together with an unconcealed disdain for those who cooperated with him in imposing and sustaining the new imperial system? Can such a judgment be termed impartial, biased, or both? Gibbon, in this instance, as in so many others, showed the full range of his analytical powers. He did not simply repeat the opinions of his sources; he knew what the contemporaries of Augustus had written; he went beyond them in giving his own opinions:

> . . . the Imperial government, as it was instituted by Augustus, and maintained by those princes who understood their own interest and that of the people . . . may be defined as an absolute monarchy disguised by the forms of a commonwealth. The masters of the Roman world surrounded their throne with darkness, concealed their irresistible strength, and humbly professed themselves the accountable ministers of the senate, whose supreme decrees they dictated and obeyed.[19]

Is it possible to imagine a more complex judgment, where fact and opinion are joined and where the illusion of distance is given, even as evidences of the historian's own deep feelings intrude and where the emperor is made responsible for a historic turning, even as his ultimate importance is subtly diminished? Gibbon, on occasion, gave substantial credit to an individual or a group for a specific development; he could, for example, refer to the Illyrian emperors—Claudius, Aurelian, Probus, and Diocletian—as the "Restorers of the Roman world," recognizing all that they had done,[20] and might even imply that, with Theodosius, "the public safety seemed to depend on the life and abilities of a single man," [21] but he used such expressions rarely. Reality was different from what it was commonly thought to be; most conventional explanations for great events in history concentrated overwhelmingly on purposive action, making it appear that individual leaders were indeed principally responsible for specific events. Gibbon knew this to be much too simple.

Steeped in the history and philosophy of his Scottish contemporaries, Gibbon accepted entirely the idea that many social outcomes were unintended and did not depend on the volition of individuals, however eminent. Gibbon, living in an aristocratic age, recognized the importance and necessity of leadership; he did not, however, exaggerate its ultimate influence. Other forces also needed to be considered. The idea of "unintended consequences" was entirely congenial to Gibbon. Thus, for example, while he was eloquent about what the Antonines had been able to achieve, he insisted on drawing attention also to the price that Rome paid for its "long peace." In Gibbon's view, the peace was itself one of the "latent causes of decay and corruption." Gibbon wrote:

> This long peace, and the uniform government of the Romans, introduced a slow and secret poison into the vitals of the empire. The minds of men were gradually reduced to

the same level, the fire of genius was extinguished, and even the military spirit evaporated. . . . The most aspiring spirits resorted to the court or·standard of the emperors; and the deserted provinces, deprived of political strength or union, insensibly sunk into the languid indifference of private life.[22]

When one recovers from the initial surprise of finding Gibbon's explanation of Rome's decline being in some way related to the "long peace," no other part of his analysis seems outrageous. The idea that a "levelling" and "decline of genius" should have had adverse effects on society was fully consonant with Enlightenment principles. In the preference Gibbon showed for "public life," contrasted with the "indifference of private life," he expressed a view that most English intellectuals of his class and age would have shared.

Gibbon, as a student of the political philosophers of Greece and Rome, was necessarily preoccupied with the degeneration of states, with the process that led free governments to become despotic. If the seeds of Roman despotism were laid by Augustus, who disguised his absolute monarchy with the trappings of a common-wealth, the full extent of the imperial power and the decline of those who still styled themselves senator became apparent only gradually. Augustus, the arch-hypocrite according to Gibbon, understood "that the senate and people would submit to slavery, provided they were respectfully assured that they still enjoyed their ancient freedom."[23] Augustus, recognizing the potential power of the army, feared and dominated it. So, for well over two centuries, did a number of his successors until the death of Commodus. In Gibbon's words: "The soldiers were seldom roused to that fatal sense of their own strength, and of the weakness of the civil authority . . . ."[24] In an elective monarchy, the moment of the transition of power was always dangerous; emperors sought to minimize that danger by investing "their designed successor with so large a share of present power, as should enable him, after their decease, to assume the remainder without suffering the empire to perceive the change of masters."[25] For some time, this system worked. When it fell apart, it was partly because of the blunder of Marcus Aurelius Antoninus, a man who detested war, seeing it "as the disgrace and calamity of human nature," and who showed acuity·in many things but not in the choice of his successor, his young and impetuous son Commodus.

Where is the bias in all this and where is the impartial judgment? Where does one begin and the other leave off? The idea that Gibbon willfully neglected (or distorted) evidence would be difficult to establish, though many have tried to do so. In any case, such a view ignores Gibbon's major contribution, which was to see the relation between seemingly discrete and unconnected events and judge how they ought to be related. Facts were interlaced with opinion, and it was impossible to disengage one from the other. In his analysis of Neoplatonism, for example, Gibbon paid homage to the Illyrian princes who restored the Empire without restoring the sciences, and then went on to represent this world as one where poetry, history, and rhetoric were dead, and where even law and medicine had lost much of their former intellectual distinction. It was in this intellectual desert that the "new Platonists" appeared; though a number of them, like Plotinus, "were men of profound thought and intense application," they invariably asked the wrong questions. Instead of concerning themselves with the sciences—moral, natural, and mathematical—they chose to argue about metaphysical matters. Gibbon refused them any place in the history of science, but acknowledged that they had a certain importance in the history of the church; he promised to treat them in that context.[26]

It would be difficult to fault Gibbon's reasoning. Without distorting the essential facts, he had managed to intrude his own judgments, thereby influencing the reader. Whether reflecting on major schools of thought, whole races and peoples, or specific individuals, Gibbon showed a respect for the facts as he found them in his readings of ancient and modern texts, but this never deterred him from introducing his own opinions. It is difficult not to be impressed by his magisterial approach; individuals followed each other in rapid succession in his history—Gibbon seemed almost to delight in the mere enumeration of their names—but where he stopped to delineate character and action, he showed his characteristic analytic power. With major figures, he was never satisfied simply to define a personality; his interest was generally to relate the individual's accomplishments to what others achieved, to consider this within a political and military context, and to draw some moral lesson. Thus, for example, with Constantine, Gibbon's chief concerns were to describe the changes he wrought in public policy and to estimate their ultimate effects on the Empire. Looking at the divided administration, Gibbon said that "it relaxed the vigour of the state, while it secured the tranquillity of the monarch."[27] Having made an original and subtle judgment about the man, Gibbon quickly followed this with a more sweeping indictment. He saw Constantine's policy as essentially timid; it involved "dividing whatever is united," "reducing whatever is eminent," "dreading every active power," and "expecting that the most feeble will prove the most obedient."[28] Other princes, of course, had pursued the same policy. While Constantine had not invented it, he, more than any other, exemplified it—hence Gibbon's criticisms, based only in part on testimony provided by Constantine's subjects, who "could feel and lament the rage of tyranny, the relaxation of discipline, and the increase of taxes."[29] Such evidence, while important, was at best inconclusive. Constantine's subjects were "incapable of discerning the decline of genius and manly virtue, which so far degraded them below the dignity of their ancestors."[30] Such understanding it was impossible for them to have; it was the historian's duty to intervene, to provide that insight. Gibbon also insisted on another of the historian's obligations, to weigh evidence carefully and not be unduly swayed by certain recorded grievances. As Gibbon explained:

> The impartial historian, who acknowledges the justice of their [the citizens'] complaints, will observe some favourable circumstances which tended to alleviate the misery of their condition. The threatening tempest of Barbarians, which so soon subverted the foundations of Roman greatness, was still repelled, or suspended on the frontiers. The arts of luxury and literature were cultivated, the elegant pleasures of society were enjoyed, by the inhabitants of a considerable portion of the globe. The forms, the pomp, and the expense of the civil administration contributed to restrain the irregular licence of the soldiers; and, although the laws were violated by power or perverted by subtlety, the sage principles of the Roman jurisprudence preserved a sense of order and equity, unknown to the despotic governments of the east. The rights of mankind might derive some protection from religion and philosophy, and the name of freedom, which could no longer alarm, might sometimes admonish, the successors of Augustus that they did not reign over a nation of slaves or barbarians.[31]

Those who have emphasized the extent of Gibbon's antipathy to Christianity as conclusive evidence of his bias have not been wrong to do so. What they have ignored, however, is the relative unimportance of the Christian theme in the work as a whole. For Gibbon, there were other circumstances that seemed equally, or more, compelling and that engaged his attention more consistently. The decline in civic virtue, for example, which was not attributable simply to the triumph of Christanity, was of paramount importance for Gibbon. If he wrote disparagingly of the ignorance, weakness, and passion of ecclesiastical synods, his criticism of the senate was even more severe:

> The fathers of the capitol and those of the church had alike degenerated from the virtues of their founders; but, as the bishops were more deeply rooted in the public opinion, they sustained their dignity with more decent pride, and sometimes opposed, with a manly spirit, the wishes of their sovereign.[32]

This may not seem a very substantial praise of church officials, but it does suggest that what was most preoccupying for Gibbon was the decline in Roman civic virtue.

Gibbon's antipathy to the Church was as nothing compared with his disdain for, and distrust of, despotism, a subject that roused him as few others did. Whether his analysis is deemed biased or impartial, universal or insular, it is impossible to ignore the passion that it provoked in him. If Julian emerged as one of Gibbon's more admirable figures—virtually losing the Apostate designation given him by Christian writers—it was not because Gibbon exulted in Julian's anti-Christian policies. Gibbon's admiration derived from a belief that Julian managed, even in his very brief reign, to achieve something of the character of sage and hero, redolent of an earlier Roman preoccupation with virtue. In recounting Julian's last hours, when the Emperor lay dying of wounds suffered in battle, Gibbon accepted the accuracy of the account given by Ammianus Marcellinus, who was present on the occasion. According to Ammianus, Julian said:

> Detesting the corrupt and destructive maxims of depotism, I have considered the happiness of the people as the end of government. Submitting my actions to the laws of prudence, of justice, and of moderation, I have trusted the event to the care of Providence. Peace was the object of my counsels, as long as peace was consistent with the public welfare, but, when the imperious voice of my country summoned me to arms, I exposed my person to the dangers of war, with the clear foreknowledge (which I have acquired from the art of divination) that I was destined to fall by the sword.[33]

Julian was an "extraordinary man" for Gibbon, but not so extraordinary as to exempt himself from all criticism: "In his last moments he displayed, perhaps with some ostentation, the love of virtue and of fame which had been the ruling passions of his life."[34] If Gibbon placed a great deal of emphasis on the distinctions between freedom and despotism, he was equally interested in distinguishing between the West and the East. The distinction might appear trite, but not in Gibbon's hands. While he came close at times to caricaturing both East and West, his purpose was never to indicate how the East had "conquered" the West, but only to show how its manners and values had insinuated themselves into Roman society and government. Had Rome remained vigorous, loyal to its traditional values, it would never have fallen prey to Eastern ostentation. Gibbon's arguments are complex, though they may at first appear to be simple:

> The manly pride of the Romans, content with substantial power, had left to the vanity of the east the forms and ceremonies of ostentatious greatness. But when they lost even the semblance of those virtues which were derived from their ancient freedom, the simplicity of Roman manners was insensibly corrupted by the stately affectation of the courts of

Asia. The distinctions of personal merit and influence, so conspicuous in a republic, so feeble and obscure under a monarchy, were abolished by the despotism of the emperors, who substituted in their room a severe subordination of rank and office, from the titled slaves, who were seated on the steps of the throne, to the meanest instruments of arbitrary power.[35]

None of this happened because the Empire was divided, with one capital established at Constantinople and the other at Rome; Gibbon was determined that this particular error should be laid to rest. What was significant for him was the decline in Roman virtue. To express his feelings, he used language that was colorful and passionate. To speak of "titled slaves . . . seated on the steps of the throne" was to show bias; yet, for Gibbon, such "bias" was also the highest form of impartiality. He could not conceive that any unprejudiced observer would view the matter differently.

Rome gave Gibbon a perfect stage for the display of the kinds of impartiality that he esteemed. What Gibbon was able to do in describing Rome, he was quite incapable of doing when he approached his own times. His gift for irony, which he used to such effect when writing about emperors and senators, bishops and barbarian kings, seemed to desert him when he came to write about his own age. Gibbon could not restrain himself from bringing his story into the present, but when he did, the results were generally disappointing. Humor deserted him; he became didactic.

He was more convincing (and more combative) when he stayed away from his own time. Thus, for example, in the concluding paragraph of chapter 16, Gibbon argued that "Christians, in the course of their intestine dissensions, have inflicted far greater severities on each other than they had experienced from the zeal of infidels."[36] Whatever one may think of the proposition, which, incidentally, is almost certainly true, Gibbon's method of proving it is surprisingly lame. In the end, he depended on statistics provided by Grotius, "a man of genius and learning," who put the number of Protestants executed in the Netherlands alone during the reign of Charles V as more than a hundred thousand. Clearly, there had never been any such carnage of Christians by infidels.

Gibbon made the same sort of comparison when he contrasted Rome's experience at the hands of Alaric, the barbarian, with what the city suffered after the invasion of Charles V, the Catholic prince.[37] Whatever significance such a comparison may have, one is disappointed that Gibbon could do no better than to recall that the Goths left the city in six days while the armies of Charles V remained more than nine months, inflicting infinitely more damage and showing far greater avarice and cruelty. Such comparisons, however accurate, are intended principally to communicate moral outrage about Christian behavior. It is less clear why, in condemning Constantine for the murder of Crispus, Gibbon felt any necessity to contrast Constantine's behavior with that of Peter the Great.[38] In those observations, Gibbon seemed to be praising modern, civilized behavior (even in Russia) over the cruelties of Byzantium and Rome. Gibbon rarely thought of criticizing his own society in analogous terms. Why, then, did he insist on delivering his homilies? In part, because all the other historians of his day did the same. Why did he do it so blandly when he came to consider his own country? Because he was too comfortable in his own time and place; sitting in George III's library, he could not see the disasters that George III was hatching.

What better proof of Gibbon's failure than his least successful chapter, the addendum to chapter 38 entitled "General Observations on the Fall of the Roman Empire in the West." Gibbon wrote the "Observations" to instruct his contemporaries in the significance of the Roman example for themselves. We know that Gibbon was revising and correcting the pages of this volume in June, 1780, during the Gordon riots[39] and when the loss of the American colonies was a near certainty. One would have expected that one or another of these events might have figured in Gibbon's analysis. Not even the most cursory attention is given to either; instead, the chapter abounds in pompous inanities, many of which are almost wholly beside the point. It would be gratifying to believe that Gibbon was mocking his readers, reminding them that irony is "saying one and gyving to understand the contrarye."[40] The final footnote in chapter 38 almost begs to be read in that way:

> The merit of discovery has too often been stained with avarice, cruelty, and fanaticism; and the intercourse of nations has produced the communication of disease and prejudice. A singular exception is due to the virtue of our own times and country. The five great voyages successively undertaken by the command of his present majesty were inspired by the pure and generous love of science and mankind. The same prince, adapting his benefactions to the different stages of society, has founded a school in his capital, and has introduced into the islands of the South Sea the vegetables and animals most useful to human life.[41]

Gibbon, one would like to believe, must be saying this with tongue in cheek; it is impossible that he has become so uncritical. But, as one reads other parts of Gibbon's "General Observations," there is no escaping the conclusion that no irony is intended. Gibbon was being serious; he meant his words to be taken literally. One's disappointment, obviously, is not so much with a footnote as with the larger conceptions that inform the "Observations."

Gibbon was trying to reassure his age. How did he do so? By suggesting that there was no threat of barbarians from outside. What about *les classes dangereuses* within? There was not even an allusion to that subject. What did Gibbon say about the loss of an overseas empire? Again, not even the vaguest hint of that possibility; instead, there is the suggestion that if the barbarians were to invade (from wherever), carrying "slavery and desolation as far as the Atlantic Ocean . . . ten thousand vessels would transport beyond their pursuit the remains of civilized society; and Europe would revive and flourish in the American world, which is already filled with her colonies and institutions."[42] Because such a prospect seemed quite real even as late as the Second World War, when the Nazis appeared as the New Barbarians, Gibbon could be credited with greater prescience than those in the eighteenth century who imagined that American independence was *the* significant event of their age—the argument might be made that Gibbon saw further than any of his contemporaries. Such an argument would, however, not be sustained by Gibbon's opinions given in this chapter. The "historian of Rome" showed little insight when he reflected about his own society. He had not used his Roman studies to consider what had happened to great European empires more recently. It did not occur to him to reflect on the recent history of Spain. The American experience had taught him nothing; he did not even anticipate the kinds of arguments about imperial obligations that Edmund Burke would soon use in the impeachment proceedings against Warren Hastings. Gibbon was lost in a pedantic exercise, searching for literal analogies and finding none.

Gibbon suggested that the "decline of Rome was the natural and inevitable effect of immoderate greatness"; Rome's geographic extensiveness was a source of its weakness. Was Gibbon drawing an analogy with the expansion of England, in effect minimizing the adverse effects of a loss of overseas possessions? While some may argue that this was Gibbon's intention, the evidence suggests otherwise. For, instead of pursuing the theme, Gibbon moved quickly to insist that Rome's decline was caused, not by the removal of the seat of government to Constantinople—"the powers of government were divided rather than removed"[43]—but by other factors. It was not an administrative decision that led to the decline in Roman virtue, nor, for that matter, was it Christianity that had *caused* Rome's decline, though its influence had to be weighed. Gibbon, following Montesquieu, explained: "If the decline of the Roman empire was hastened by the conversion of Constantine, his victorious religion broke the violence of the fall, and mollified the ferocious temper of the conquerors."[44]

What, then, was *the* significant cause of Rome's fall? Clearly, the invasion of the barbarians. Gibbon found himself reflecting on whether Europe—that "great republic" which Voltaire had defined in *The Age of Louis XIV*—was still endangered by barbarians outside. While he expected that the balance of power between the several European states would continue to fluctuate and that "the prosperity of our own or the neighbouring kingdoms may be alternately exalted or depressed," he did not expect that European civilization as a whole would soon be threatened by barbarians. On this, Gibbon was entirely sanguine. There was no real danger from the North; in the East, the situation was somewhat less clear, but even here "the reign of independent Barbarism is now contracted to a narrow span." It was impossible to feel absolutely secure—"new enemies and unknown dangers, may *possibly* arise from some obscure people, scarcely visible in the map of the world," but Gibbon recognized this to be a remote possibility.[45]

In any case, the kingdoms of Europe were not as vulnerable as the provinces of Rome had been; they were not dependent "on the personal merit of one or two men, perhaps children, whose minds were corrupted by education, luxury, and despotic power."[46] Europe, in Gibbon's day, was a society of twelve kingdoms, three commonwealths, and numerous independent states. In Gibbon's words, "the chances of royal and ministerial talents are multiplied" by this situation; besides, "republics have acquired order and stability; monarchies have imbibed the principles of freedom, or, at least, of moderation; and some sense of honour and justice is introduced into the most defective constitutions by the general manners of the times."[47]

If Europe's security was not sufficiently guaranteed by these obviously favorable conditions, yet another cause was adduced to reassure the anxious reader. Gibbon spoke of the power of European arms; to fight against these new weapons, the barbarians would have to adopt the same arms; in short, they would be compelled to adopt Europe's science and this would then become the first step in their becoming civilized. Gibbon was totally sanguine:

> Their [the barbarians'] gradual advances in the science of war would always be accompanied, as we may learn from the example of Russia, with a proportionable improvement in the arts of peace and civil policy; and they themselves must deserve a place among the polished nations whom they subdue.[48]

If this was not enough to calm all anxieties, Gibbon provided a final solace; man, he said, arising from the brutish state of nature, had learned imperishable things; these things could never be lost:

> The splendid days of Augustus and Trajan were eclipsed by a cloud of ignorance; and the Barbarians subverted the laws and palaces of Rome. But the scythe, the invention or

emblem of Saturn, still continued annually to mow the harvests of Italy; and the human feasts of the Laestrygons have never been renewed on the coast of Campania.[49]

Gibbon, having concluded that man's ascent was always upward, could only end with a statement that gave full expression to this idea of permanent progress. He did so, saying: "We may therefore acquiesce in the pleasing conclusion that every age of the world has increased, and still increases, the real wealth, the happiness, the knowledge, and perhaps the virtue, of the human race."[50] Macaulay was to echo similar sentiments, without even the reservation of a "perhaps" in expressing his high hopes for mankind in his essay on Southey. From Gibbon's day until the time of Victoria, nothing that happened in the world dimmed the optimism of most English men of letters who imagined that their own country would, for one reason or other, be spared the tragedies that must inevitably accompany empire. The evidence is overwhelming that when Gibbon came to consider his own age, his critical capacities deserted him; he was no longer capable of irony; he was simply complacent.

Just before his death, Gibbon was at work on "An Address" that he never completed; it perfectly represented Gibbon's appreciation of his age and country:

> That history is a liberal and useful study, and that the history of our own country is best deserving of our attention, are propositions too clear for argument and too simple for illustration. . . . We contemplate the gradual progress of society from the lowest ebb of primitive barbarism, to the full tide of modern civilization. We contrast the naked Briton who might have mistaken the sphere of Archimedes for a rational creature, and the contemporary of Newton, in whose school Archimedes himself would have been an humble disciple. . . . Without indulging the fond prejudices of patriotic vanity, we may assume a conspicuous place among the inhabitants of the earth. The English will be ranked among the few nations who have cultivated with equal success the arts of war, of learning, and of commerce: and Britain perhaps is the only powerful and wealthy state which has ever possessed the inestimable secret of uniting the benefits of order with the blessings of freedom.[51]

Believing this, how could Gibbon have used his Roman history to instruct his British contemporaries? What possible lessons could his history have for a people of such good fortune and such virtue? The conjunction "but" disappeared when Gibbon came to consider his own age; there was no longer any room for nuance, irony, qualification, or surprise. In comments about his own society, Gibbon was as conventional as the most ordinary squire who came to Westminster, or the most run-of-the mill *philosophe*. He was infinitely less critical than Montesquieu, infinitely less passionate than Rousseau, and much less prescient than Hume.

It was fortunate for Gibbon (and for us) that he chose the subject that he did. It permitted him to be bold, painting on a vast canvas in chiaroscuro, although his natural inclinations were to be timid. The subject evoked all his passion—giving room for his bias but also for his fierce ambition to be fair and impartial—and, most importantly, it permitted his imagination to roam and provided room for his irony— these were closed out only when he came to discuss his own age, where an unreflecting patriotism and a deplorable tendency to use the popular intellectual clichés of his time made him seem suddenly innocent.

We know how partial Gibbon came to be to the views of Edmund Burke after the French Revolution, when both looked with horror at what was happening in France. Would Gibbon have gone as far as Burke in believing that "the glories of Europe are extinguished forever," or did he have a deeper understanding of history, which told him that the scythe had indeed permanently won out, and that it could never be destroyed? Did Gibbon not have a sense of time different from Burke's? Did he not realize that events were rarely so cataclysmic and that change did not happen suddenly? Did his rather undramatic and balanced view of the past not lead him ultimately to a wisdom that those on both sides of the barricades lacked?

Was this not the ultimate reason for his being so confident almost to the end, and for his feeling of being so much at ease in the Zion of his day? Is the realization that even the scythe may not be saved from the holocaust that threatens us today not the ultimate source of our own very different kind of anxiety? Do we not read Gibbon in part because he reminds us of another state of mind—his own—and of another century? But the paradox remains: how could a man write a great tragic history when he himself lacked a sense of tragedy.

REFERENCES

Note: References to Gibbon's *History of the Decline and Fall of the Roman Empire (DF)* are to chapter and page of the seven-volume World's Classics edition (London, 1903-4).

[1]*DF*, chap. 2, pp. 44-45.

[2]Edward Gibbon, *Memoirs of My Life*, ed. Georges A. Bonnard (London, 1966), p. vii.

[3]*Ibid.*, p. 1.

[4]*Ibid.*, pp. 121-22.

[5]*Ibid.*, p. 122.

[6]*Ibid.*

[7]*DF*, chap. 50, p. 364.

[8]Gibbon, *Memoirs*, p. 122.

[9]Voltaire, *The Age of Louis XIV* (Everyman ed., London, 1926), p. 1.

[10]*DF*, chap. 3, p. 89.

[11]David Hume, *The History of England* (London, 1830), VI, p. 341.

[12]Gibbon, *Memoirs*, p. 157.

[13]*Ibid.*, pp. 159-60.

[14]*Ibid.*, p. 158.

[15]*The Letters of Edward Gibbon*, ed. J. E. Norton (London, 1956), II, p. 122.

[16]*Ibid.*

[17]See J. E. Norton, *A Bibliography of the Works of Edward Gibbon* (Oxford, 1940), pp. 64-93; also, Shelby McCloy, *Gibbon's Antagonism to Christianity* (London, 1933).

[18]R. G. Collingwood, *The Idea of History* (Oxford, 1946), p. 147.

[19]*DF*, chap. 3, p. 76.

[20]*DF*, chap. 11, p. 322.

[21]*DF*, chap. 26, p. 157.

[22]*DF*, chap. 2, pp. 63-64.

[23]*DF*, chap. 3, p. 80.

[24]*Ibid.*, p. 82.

[25]*Ibid.*, p. 83.

[26]*DF*, chap. 13, pp. 441-42.

[27]*DF*, chap. 17, p. 200.

[28]*Ibid.*, p. 202.

[29]*Ibid.*, p. 227.

[30]*Ibid.*

[31]*Ibid.*, pp. 227-28.

[32]*DF*, chap. 20, p. 373.

[33]*DF*, chap. 24, p. 580.

[34]*Ibid.*, p. 581.

[35]*DF*, chap. 17, p. 181.

[36]*DF*, chap. 16, p. 159.

[37]*DF*, chap. 31, p. 388.

[38]*DF*, chap. 18, p. 237.

[39]Gibbon, *Letters*, II, p. 245.

[40]G. G. Sedgewick, *Of Irony* (Toronto, 1935), pp. 8-12.

[41]*DF*, chap. 38, p. 202.

[42]*Ibid.*, p. 198.
[43]*Ibid.*, p. 193.
[44]*Ibid.*, p. 195.
[45]*Ibid.*, p. 197.
[46]*Ibid.*
[47]*Ibid.*, p. 198.
[48]*Ibid.*, p. 199.
[49]*Ibid.*, p. 201.
[50]*Ibid.*, pp. 201-2.
[51]Edward Gibbon, *Miscellaneous Works*, ed. John, Lord Sheffield (London, 1796), pp. 707-8.

JEAN STAROBINSKI

From the Decline of Erudition to the Decline of Nations: Gibbon's Response to French Thought

GIBBON INCLUDED in his *Memoirs of My Life* a critique of his own first work, the *Essai sur l'étude de la littérature*. Among the things he singled out for disapproval was his imprecise use of the word *littérature*: "Instead of a precise and proper definition [of] the title itself, the sense of the word *Littérature* is loosely and variously applied. . . ."[1] He is, however, being rather hard on himself, for when he wrote his *Essai* the meaning of the term *littérature* in French had in fact been somewhat ambiguous. The preoccupation of French lexicographers and philosophers of the time with introducing a clear and precise definition and distinguishing among its various meanings was symptomatic of a more general feeling that revisions in concepts were needed, and the imprecision of which Gibbon a posteriori accused himself reflected that situation: the young author of the *Essai* by deciding to adopt the French language had necessarily also to submit to the ambiguities attached to its vocabulary.

In the seventeenth century, belles-lettres was a scholarly discipline defined as the "knowledge of the orators, poets, and historians."[2] It was in that sense that the term was included into the name of the Académie des Inscriptions et Belles-Lettres, which was founded in 1663. But when d'Alembert refers to *belles-lettres* in the *Discours préliminaire de l'Encyclopédie*, he does so in order to use it as a pendant for *beaux-arts*, thus making it a generic term for any original creation of the "beautiful" in the three fields of eloquence, poetry, and history. A more specific word was consequently required for designating knowledge of the works of the distant or more recent past, and this was how the concept of *érudition* acquired new significance: it came to refer to the detailed knowledge that was brought to bear on all documents from past times. By restricting belles-lettres to products of the "imagination," d'Alembert had found himself obliged to find parallel names for the other two branches of the encyclopedic tree corresponding to the other two faculties of the mind—"memory" and "reason"; he chose "erudition" and "science." The resulting triad was presented as part of a "contrasting" definition at the very beginning of the entry for "Erudition":

> This word [*erudition*], which comes from the Latin *erudire* ["to teach"], originally and literally meant "knowledge," both systematic and in terms of a body of facts: but it has more aptly been applied to the latter, that is, to the acquisition of facts that results from much reading. The term *science* has been reserved for that knowledge which more immediately relies upon reasoning and reflection, such as physics, mathematics, etc., and that of *belles-lettres* for the pleasant productions of the mind, in which imagination plays the important part, such as eloquence, poetry, etc.[3]

139

Erudition is thus clearly distinguished from letters, for it involves a totally different faculty. To the degree that, according to d'Alembert, the discipline of erudition results from knowledge of books, it has to take letters into account; but erudition encompasses more, for it also includes non-literary documents from the past and other languages.[4] In other words, the objects of erudite study are not limited to the repertory of eloquence, poetry, and history alone. To define the knowledge that applies only to them, another term was needed. The *Encyclopédie*—here under the authorship of Marmontel—uses the word "literature" to define the corpus of knowledge applied to what d'Alembert called belles-lettres, and to establish the distinction between it and erudition.

> There is a difference between erudition and literature. . . . Literature is the knowledge of letters; erudition is the knowledge of facts, places, times, and the monuments of antiquity, and it is the work of the erudite to clarify factual questions, define periods, and explain the monuments and writings of the ancients.
>
> The man who cultivates letters profits from the work of the erudite. Thus enlightened, he has acquired the knowledge of great models in poetry, eloquence, history, moral and political philosophy—either of past centuries or more modern times—he is very much the littérateur. He may not know what the scholiasts have said of Homer, but he knows what Homer said. . . . The erudite may or may not be a good littérateur, for exquisite discernment and a good and carefully furnished memory require more than study alone. In the same way, a littérateur may lack erudition. Should both of these qualities be present, the result is a learned and cultivated man. But these two things do not produce a man of letters. The creative gift characterizes the man of letters: with wit, talent, and taste, he can produce ingenious works with no erudition at all and with very little knowledge of letters. Fréret was a profound erudite, Malesieux a great littérateur, and Marivaux a man of letters.[5]

The sense Marmontel conferred upon the word "literature" is closer to the meaning Montaigne gave it than it is to the one in use today.[6] According to Marmontel's conception, literature was more than the simple knowledge of facts, but it did not include the capacity to "produce ingenious works." Between the erudite and the man of letters, using the littérateur as intermediary, Marmontel proposes a gradation which runs from passive storage to active production. Set in an intermediate position, literature profits from erudition, but it does so in order to understand and enjoy what is essential, that is, a fuller comprehension of the "great models." Today, we would define Marmontel's littérateur as an enlightened amateur, a cultivated man (the term is used by Marmontel)—a literate man. In the text we have just quoted, erudition is the necessary, if insufficient, condition for literature; but neither erudition nor even literature is required for the activity of the true writer. At best, erudition has a preliminary function, a preparatory role.

This also holds true for d'Alembert. Placing the development of arts and letters in a historical perspective that begins with "the renaissance of letters," he sees the various disciplines succeeding one another in a chronological order that at the same time corresponds to a hierarchy of values:

> When we consider the progress of the mind since that memorable epoch, we find that this progress was made in the sequence it should naturally have followed. It was begun with erudition, continued with belles-lettres, and completed with philosophy.[7]

The principal justification for erudition was that it "was necessary to bring us to letters."[8] Of course erudition deserved to be defended from those who disparage it, and who, like certain great men, "are quite happy to be learned, so long as they need take no pains at it."[9] But d'Alembert does not spare the irony:

> The realm of erudition and of facts is inexhaustible; the effortless acquisitions made in it lead one to think that one's substance is continually growing, so to speak. But the realm of reason and of discoveries is, on the contrary, rather small. Through study in that realm, men often succeed only in unlearning what they thought they knew, instead of learning what they did not know. That is why a scholar of most unequal merit must be much more vain than a philosopher or even perhaps a poet. For the inventive mind is always dissatisfied with its progress because it sees beyond, and for the greatest geniuses, even their self-esteem may harbor a secret but severe judge whom flattery may momentarily silence but can never corrupt. Thus we should not be surprised that the scholars of whom we speak gloried so proudly in practicing a science that was thorny, often ridiculous, and sometimes barbarous.[10]

Gibbon's entire *Essai* is, of course, a reply to these lines and to others like them. He does not follow the definitions proposed by the Encyclopedists. He uses the term *belles-lettres* in its early sense of "knowledge of eloquence, poetry, and history," not in the later sense of "pleasant productions of the mind." To him, *littérature* was synonymous with *belles-lettres*; he preferred the term *littérateur* to that of *érudit*—in a note he tells us that in 1721 the Abbé Massieu complained that *érudit* was a neologism. He willingly sacrificed what he called "a pedantic erudition"—one that compiles without reason.[11] But if he is ready to leave the activities of the imagination to others, he does not see why erudite memory and philosophical reflection cannot work together, contrary to the dichotomy formulated by d'Alembert. His ideal, expressed at the very beginning of the *Essai*, is erudite research "guided by the flame of philosophy."[12] Far from conceding that an opposition existed between philosophy and erudition, Gibbon associated them with each other, and he saw in this association one of the characters of a true critic's activity: criticism is "a good species of logic."[13] He is convinced that literature can contribute to form a philosophical mind, through the habit of identifying with men of the past. "I conceive, however, that the study of literature, the habit of becoming by turns a Greek, a Roman, the disciple of Zeno and of Epicurus, is extremely proper to exercise [the] powers and display [the] merit [of the philosophical mind]."[14]

D'Alembert and Marmontel made the attempt to give erudition its due, to acknowledge its role as informant; but they soon left it behind as they came more and more to rely on those activities stemming from the reflective or the imaginative faculties of the mind. Gibbon, however, insisted upon thinking in terms of facts first accumulated through erudition, and he well understood that such fact-collecting is a process of intelligent selection. Chapter 49 of the *Essai*, in particular, emphasizes that facts cannot be blindly gathered: vigilance and thought must preside over the entire process from the beginnings of the historical inquiry to the presentation as evidence of those facts that are finally judged to be relevant. Facts must be neither over- nor underestimated. From the start, reflection must temper the collection of data. The notion that it would be possible to abandon "literature" to devote oneself entirely to "reason" was therefore manifestly absurd.

If one examines d'Alembert's theory a bit more closely, moreover, one soon discovers that even with him the separation between erudition and letters is not so radical as we first supposed. If the erudite is a historian who is familiar with languages, and books, and if, according to traditional nomenclature, history, eloquence, and poetry constitute the field of letters, it becomes immediately apparent that there is contact—perhaps even a direct continuity—between historical erudition and history seen as a "pleasant product of the mind."[15] At the very least, nothing prevents the incorporation of solid erudition into works to be read by a large, "cultivated" public. Indeed, nothing does prevent it, even if, in practice, d'Alembert's theory equally justifies "philosophical" history of the kind produced by many Franch writers (first and foremost, by Voltaire)—history whose rather skimpy erudite baggage and documentary preparation allow it to rise too quickly and easily to the most sweeping generalizations.[16]

But if Gibbon rejects the validity of the idea that a distinction must be made between erudite activity and philosophical thought, he still agrees, in the *Essai*, with the general conclusion of d'Alembert and most of his contemporaries that all the evidence points to a decline in belles-lettres (in the sense of knowledge of the corpus of poets, orators, and historians), literature (cultivated comprehension of the great models), and erudition. Their practitioners are fewer, less brilliant, less honored; interest has turned elsewhere.[17]

So the diagnosis is the same. But while d'Alembert saw in the decline of erudition a phenomenon that conformed to the logic of the mind's development, Gibbon found in it only a manifestation of a new vogue—there was no justification for the present hegemony of physics and mathematics. Although they were latecomers, their modernity did not imply superiority. The picture he painted at the beginning of the *Essai* was one of a "hardly reasonable," erratic favoring of one or another of the disciplines at one or another time. This succession of preferences was not guided by any inherent logic, nor was the temporary triumph of a particular discipline any indication of its greater legitimacy: "Natural philosophy and mathematics are not in possession of the throne: their sisters fall prostrate before them; are ignominiously chained to their car, or otherwise servilely employed to adorn their triumph. Perhaps their reign too is short, and their fall is approaching."[18]

Those who complained about the loss of erudition placed its origins somewhere around the end of the seventeenth century: "It is from this era," Gibbon wrote, that letters "may date the commencement of their decline."[19] Then he calls his first witness, Jean Le Clerc, to support this claim; although he does not cite it directly, he refers to the *Parrhasiana*, a work published in two volumes in Amsterdam in 1699. A collection of miscellaneous remarks and thoughts, it is subtitled *Random Thoughts on Matters of Criticism, History, Morality, and Politics* and is signed with the pseudonym Théodore Parrhase. Following three sections dealing respectively with poetry, eloquence, and history, Le Clerc adds another entitled "On the Decadence of Letters"; it begins as follows:

> Doubtless, there is decay in the republic of letters, and in several respects, although I wish to speak only of the decay of belles-lettres. It is certain that for more than a generation it has been impossible to find, in all of Europe, anyone to equal the illustrious critics of the last century or the beginning of this one. No one, for example, could equal, either in knowledge or application, or in the greatness or the quantity of their works the likes of Joseph Scaliger, Juste Lipse, Isaac Casaubon, Claude de Saumaise, Hugo Grotius, Jean Meursius, John Selden, and so many more whom I hardly need to mention.[20]

Many of the famous names cited here by Le Clerc are also cited by Gibbon, who does attempt, however, to discriminate between the greater and lesser minds among them (Saumaise, for example, is "a pedant swollen by useless erudition").[21] For Le Clerc, the causes of decline are many and varied, and the learned must bear some of the responsibility. They have not facilitated access to knowledge: "The clever men in this branch of learning have not shown the slightest effort to make it accessible to others."[22] Good critical editions are lacking, commentary is often inappropriate. Excessive praise of the ancients has ultimately done a disservice to the humanities. The vainglory of the scholars has made them ridiculous. And, what is even more serious, letters have lost protectors from among the great and are now suspect, especially in the Catholic countries, for political reasons:

> The supporters of the sovereign authority of the ecclesiastical monarchy, on the one hand, and those of the arbitrary power of the secular princes, on the other, have decided that, rather than heeding the works of pagan or Christian antiquity which have for so long been believed, it would be better if the republican ideas of the Greeks and Romans were forgotten and if the thoughts of ancient Christians of both East and West were to remain hidden by the veil of an unknown language. Men were sought who would obey without questioning, who would reason only to uphold and increase authority, both spiritual and temporal, without regard for the ideas of the past; soldiers without principle and without virtue and churchmen who are the blind slaves of authority, examine nothing, and execute any order given them now pass for the unshakable pillars of Church and State. No one will any longer listen to those who quote antiquity and who have principles independent of the will of the sovereign.[23]

But Le Clerc does not stop at these discouraging conclusions. There are "reasons for once again cultivating letters," and these reasons also have to do with politics:

> But in places where people take pride in having no laws other than those founded upon natural equity, there is no reason to fear anything contrary in republican Antiquity; and so those who try to make it known to others, who try to profit from its lights, must be favored.[24]

In Le Clerc's view, the teachings of republican antiquity fully agree with those of the scriptures. "The exact search for truth" cannot but reveal them, and the results will also be beneficial to politics: "The better it [truth] is known, the greater the authority of the laws and the more justice will flourish."[25]

In the next chapter, entitled "Of Decadence in Several States," Le Clerc touches upon a closely allied problem, although he establishes no direct link between the decline of letters and the decline of states: nations decline as their populations dwindle; they waste away as their industries and revenues shrink and from the effects of intolerance. A state can flourish only if "its members and those who govern it" are in agreement and seek "only the public good."[26] It is harmful if the clergy and the nobility are too numerous and too privileged; those non-productive classes constitute a burden to the state. He directs some of his comments particularly toward Spain and France:

> It cannot be denied, politically speaking, that a large number of secular and regular ecclesiastics, who have no industry to help their country flourish and who enjoy considerable revenue without paying any taxes, are a public burden; this is so because they greatly diminish the state's revenue, they prevent the state from being populated by those who would increase it, and they have no skill which might attract foreign money. . . .[27]

The large numbers of nobles and of others who possess privileged positions have the

same effect on the diminution of the state's income and on the industry that could
increase it. . . .[28]

Hence, we can conclude that wherever dignity is in the hands of the clergy or the
nobility, wherever they hold the wealth of the country, it follows necessarily that the
people are trod upon by those two parties, that they are disgusted by the state in which
they live, and that those who are talented among them, or who have money, try to buy a
noble title or to push their way to ecclesiastical dignity. All the while, the arts and
industries which cause the state to flourish are neglected, public revenues diminish, and
the state is weakened.[29]

This remarkable text deserves a detailed commentary, but it must suffice here to
emphasize the "economic" analysis of the dangers that a too numerous clergy
represents for the state. The theme was to be found later in Montesquieu, Voltaire,
and Gibbon, to mention only the more important. Thus we see that the decline of
letters and the decline of states are treated side by side in one of the authors that
young Gibbon most admired. There he found described that situation in scholarly
studies with which he was to concern himself in the *Essai*. He also made note of those
somewhat incidental reflections on the fall on the Eastern Empire in which Le Clerc
made a comparison between the number of monks and the number of soldiers:

The great number of these people who did not feel obligated to help the state
either with their wealth, or their industry, or their persons is a clear source of its
decline. . . . It was without doubt . . . one of the causes of the ruin of the Eastern
Empire, which would otherwise have cut the Saracens and Turks to pieces had it been
able to muster half as many soldiers as it had monks and nuns, not counting other
ecclesiastics.[30]

We will find this argument repeated in the *Decline and Fall*—in chapter 20, for
example: "The whole body of the Catholic clergy, more numerous perhaps than the
legions, was exempted by the emperors from all service, private or public. . . ." And
in chapter 68, before recounting the religious debates which distracted Constantinople's defenders from its imminent danger, Gibbon does not fail to mention the
monks as being among those individuals unable to fight against the Turkish assault:

In her last decay, Constantinople was still peopled with more than a hundred
thousand inhabitants; but those numbers are found in the account, not of war, but of
captivity; and they mostly consisted of mechanics, of priests, of women, and of men
devoid of that spirit which even women have sometimes exerted for the common
safety.[31]

In the pages that Jean Le Clerc devoted to the decline of letters, he does not
suggest that erudition was supplanted by other tastes or preoccupations; poorly
served by pedants and arrogant fools, repressed by tyrannical powers, it simply
faded: nothing had taken its place, it was not forced out. On several occasions, Pierre
Bayle also treated this subject, but he suggested that erudition had been supplanted
by other interests. In one of the famous notes of his *Dictionnaire*, he relates "what
happened in a conversation between several men of letters in the year 1697" on the
subject of the "decadence of erudition"; an anonymous character, no doubt of Bayle's
invention, speaks at some length: To those who heap abuse on the Jesuits by saying
that there are scarcely "any clever people among their numbers today," he responds
that the Protestant side is no better off, and he continues:

A change in taste is all that is involved in what you call the decline of erudition. The study of criticism has fallen off; people have turned to the accuracy of reasoning. The mind is cultivated more than the memory. The desire now is to think with delicacy and to express oneself politely. Such occupations do not produce those huge volumes which are so imposing to the public and build such great reputations; but in reality, they result in greater enlightenment and in a skill more estimable than the vast learning of the grammarians or the philologists.[32]

Bayle then refers to a preceding note which reads:

While the reign of criticism and erudition lasted, several prodigies of erudition were seen throughout Europe. Now that the study of the new philosophy and that of living languages have introduced a new taste, this vast and profound literature has ceased to appear; but, in return, a certain finer wit has spread throughout the republic of letters, and it is accompanied by a more exquisite discernment. People today are less learned and more skilled.[33]

These remarks seem to be totally in favor of philosophy and wit—in short of the new taste. But Bayle discerned the abuse that certain "superficial and lazy minds" could make of it; he undoubtedly foresaw that his own critical activity could be subjected to the same scorn that the "wits" were heaping upon erudition by identifying it with pedantry:

Times have changed. No account is made of an author who thoroughly knows mythology, the Greek poets, and their scholiasts and who uses his knowledge to interpret or correct difficult passages, chronological points, questions of geography or grammar, variants in narration, and the like. It is not enough to prefer new writings in which there is nothing which resembles the work of such authors; this kind of erudition is also treated as pedantry, and there is no better way to rebuff all those young men who would otherwise have the gifts necessary to succeed in the study of the humanities. . . . There can be no doubt whatsoever that one of the major reasons for the decline of letters is that certain so-called (or authentic) wits have made it a custom to condemn quotations from Greek authors and erudite observations as sophomoric and crassly pedantic. They have been so unjust as to include in their ridicule writers who display civility and a knowledge of the world. . . . After witnessing such treatment, who would think of displaying his reading and critical remarks if he aspired to the glory of wit?[34]

Having designated philosophy, mental acuity, and accuracy of reasoning as the legitimate successors of erudition, Bayle denounced "wit" as a usurper. And if, in one respect, he anticipated Voltaire, he was not so far, in other respects, from the theses that the defenders of erudition would uphold in the first half of the eighteenth century.[35]

The "new philosophy" Bayle spoke of was Cartesianism. As we know, Cartesianism advocated a geometric, mathematical approach to the natural world. For the erudite men of the eighteenth century, the favored rivals were philosophy, mathematics, and wit. At the Académie des Inscriptions et Belles-Lettres (with which Gibbon felt some solidarity), a defensive attitude prevailed, and the counterattack adopted was aimed at two very different targets: the outrageous pretentions of the "calculators" and the frivolous superficiality of the wit.[36] The partisans of belles-lettres and erudition declared themselves to be closer to the true philosophical spirit. As an example, we might mention the discourse presented to the Académie des Inscriptions in 1741 by the Abbé Du Resnel,[37] an analysis and summary of which appeared at the beginning of the sixteenth volume of the *Histoire de l'Académie*. Its title is already significant: "General Reflections on the Disadvantages Caused by the Exclusive Taste Which Seems to Be Established in Favor of Mathematics and Physics."[38] The Abbé Du Resnel's "complaint is not so much that the exact sciences should have become so flourishing among us, but that letters should have ceased to be so; not so much that a new empire should have risen, but that it should have risen upon the ruins of another."[39] Du Resnel approves of the philosophic mind. A new term must then be made available to designate the attitude of those who wish to extend immoderately the sway of the exact sciences:

> We must be careful not to confuse the philosophical mind with the calculating mind, which by its very nature is enclosed in a circle and should not be allowed a greater radius. We will not hide the fact that our century is beginning to lose sight of this distinction; that in taking pride in geometry—or rather, in its desire to reduce everything to calculation, to apply that method everywhere, or to erect it as a universal instrument— our century has practically ceased to be philosophical.[40]

In the Abbé Du Resnel's remarks, "false wit" is added to the calculating mind, and a conceptual and terminological pair is formed whose persistent presence in texts of the period can be found through careful reading. In his conclusion, Du Resnel offers the model for this association.

> Letters are the only barrier capable of stopping the progress of false wit, of limiting the conquests of the calculating mind: the first tries to seduce us, the second to subjugate us. By maintaining the taste for truth which the Ancients gave us, letters will teach us not to mistake the tinsel of the first for gold: in the same way, they will teach us to contain the second within its limits.[41]

Occasionally, Du Resnel's "calculating mind" is replaced by the term "sophistic philosophy," but in either case the object is to save the honor of "true philosophy," which cannot be attacked and which no one wishes to regard as the enemy. In this way, the anti-philosophers are able to make common cause with the erudites, by taking on a combined adversary, "false" wit (or frivolity) and "false" philosophy (the calculating mind, geometry as usurper). Bishop Georges de Pompignan (the brother of the poet), in a book with the revealing title *La Devotion réconciliée avec l'Esprit*, writes about grammar as follows:

> If this study . . . seems to have slowed down for some time now, at least as it concerns the classical tongues, and if it is to be feared that in future it will slow down even more and ultimately stop altogether, it is hardly to devotion that this decadence must be imputed. It can perhaps be ascribed to the modern taste, which is as opposed to devotion as it is to good literature. This is a taste for two things which appear contradictory, but which our century has secretly found a way of uniting: the frivolous, which is too excessively loved to permit the serious study of language, and a sophistic philosophy, which scorns the science of words (even though it prepares one for the science of things) as well as the knowledge of things written and thought during the most illustrious centuries and in the most enlightened nations.[42]

In 1787, Rigoley de Juvigny, a resolute adversary of the Enlightenment and the *philosophes*, once more incriminates the geometry-wit pair by designating it as responsible for the ill-fated evolution of letters and mores. The metaphor he uses is that of an "epidemic," an illness:

Geometry was attacked by Wit's disease. The sickness lasted so long that Geometry began to stray. It started, in fact, to imagine that it could set the laws for poetry and eloquence, that it could subject the happy transports of the Muses to Euclid's rules. Women, who set the tone in every trifle, left off their fans for Uranie's compass. But since they possess the power to transform everything, Galantry became Geometry's major attribute; and the dryest, most exact, most serious of sciences, no longer spoke anything but small talk."[43]

Who are the targets here? D'Alembert, without question, and Madame du Châtelet. But the main culprit—and Rigoley de Juvigny mentions him by name—is Fontenelle, with whom wit began its reign. A Cartesian (Rigoley refers to his attachment to the "chimerical hypothesis" of whirlwinds), a perpetual secretary of the Académie des Sciences, an author of operas, madrigals, and eclogues, Fontenelle was the embodiment of the "new taste" that the defender of erudition and letters considered so pernicious. Here is the rest of Rigoley's indictment: "Once wit, with its mincing graces, its trinkets, its pompoms became the idol of the multitude, it thought of nothing but establishing its empire by carrying Fontenelle to the throne of literature."[44] The final tabulation for the century is distressing:

Ever since intrigue, spiteful gossip, and greed were introduced to letters, sciences, and arts by the ignorance of false wit and haughty philosophizing, we have had little choice but to put up with the flaws of our times. But an essential observation must be made: the more the positive sciences, geometry, algebra, and mathematics, and the rest, rise and become perfected, the more we lose in sentiment, the more taste will be lost, the more letters will waste away, and the more genius for the fine arts will flicker and die.[45]

We could cite many such passages. They help us understand why "philosophers" and "wits" can be found in each other's company in chapter 6 of Gibbon's *Essai*. They allow us to observe the degree to which, in 1761, Gibbon espoused the modes of thinking and writing common to the Frenchmen he had read or met. The possessive "our" (*nos*) he used applies exclusively to the French intellectual universe:

Since that time [i.e., of the quarrel of the ancients and the moderns] our philosophers have been surprised that men could spend a lifetime compiling facts and words, in loading the memory instead of enlightening the mind. Our wits have felt the advantages the ignorance of their readers afforded them. They scorn the ancients and those who study them.[46]

The paragraph quoted above is a rather good example, in the style of its construction, of Gibbon's imitations of Montesquieu: the sentences grow shorter as the paragraph goes on; parallel subjects are used in the first two sentences ("our philosophers" . . . "our wits"); a short last sentence seeks an epigrammatic effect. There is no obscurity here: Gibbon is thinking of other parts of his *Essai* when he deplores the "fatal" effect of his imitation of Montesquieu.[47] Nor was he the only young writer who succumbed to that influence in the years following the publication of the *Esprit des lois*. In his *Essai de psychologie* (1754), Charles Bonnet also adopted a choppy, disjointed style, for which the critics had reproached him, and he also recognized its source in his memoirs, which he wrote much later (1778): "I was too full of Montesquieu's manner for it not to have influenced my own."[48]

By the time he wrote his *Memoirs*, Gibbon no longer approved of the "sententious and oracular brevity" he sometimes used to dress up a "common idea." These very criticisms had been aimed at the *Essai* at the time of its publication by the *Journal Encyclopédique* and the *Critical Review*.[49] Rousseau had said much the same thing in a letter to Moultou: "I have reviewed his book—he chases wit and puts on airs."[50] Could the young Gibbon—who attacked "wits"—have been contaminated by wit? And did he not owe this contamination to the man he had taken as a model? We need only recall Voltaire's opinion: "Let us agree with Madame du Deffand that *The Spirit of the Laws* is often spirited wit about the laws,"[51] and, elsewhere:

> I sought a guide for a difficult road: I found a traveling companion hardly more knowledgeable than myself; I found an author of spirit and much wit, but rarely the spirit of the laws; he hops more than he walks, shines more than he enlightens; sometimes he satirizes more than he judges; and he makes one wish that so handsome a genius had more diligently sought to instruct rather than surprise.[52]

It would be easy to attribute the following observations, presented by the Abbé Massieu in his preface to the works of Tourreil, to a surly, conservative, and even retrograde mind:

> It seems that a conspiracy has been joined to overthrow our language and totally corrupt our taste. Pray, . . . what excesses are not committed these days? Not only do they want to tear from our hands the great models Antiquity has left us, but, worse, they would turn us away from the safe roads that excellent writers have traced out for fifty years. The works of such writers are now found to be too simple, too uniform, too careless. The natural beauties which were the main object of their attention are abandoned, and only elaborate ornament is sought. Their periodic and varied phrases are replaced by a choppy style devoid of harmony. For the happy irregularities our writers were careful to leave in their works and which contributed much to the energy and vivacity of their discourse, they substituted a depressing exactitude which only exasperates diction and makes it less fluent. Our prose and poetry today are filled only with quips and antitheses, affectations and refinements. No one wishes to say anything except with wit. So many words, so many witticisms. . . . Everything sparkles, everything bubbles. Instead of being tossed in small handfuls, as the masters of the art command, flowers are dumped by the bucketful. Words are made up by private authority; the ones that already exist are abused and so monstrously combined that readers are quite astonished to find them side by side. These are the same freedoms that destroyed one of the most beautiful languages that ever was—I refer to the one the Romans spoke. We fear that the times in which we live will be seen in the future as a period of the decadence of our language and that, just as the great men who preceded us were Ciceros and Virgils, in the eyes of posterity, we shall be Senecas and Lucians. One thing is certain and this is that in the peril which threatens French letters, those who love it and are concerned with the glory of our nation cannot make too great an effort to hold on to the good taste that is escaping us and to reject the bad taste which gains on us, in order at least to conserve our language at that level of perfection to which our fathers brought it.[53]

These lines, written in the same year as the *Lettres Persanes* (1721),[54] very aptly describe the style that Montesquieu had so perfectly captured and offer quite a good description of the rococo in literature: wit seeks to reign, to increase its impact, to bedazzle. Gibbon's youthful fascination has led him to imitate it; but, according to those with whom Gibbon sympathized, it only hastened the decay of language and with it that of the nation. The obvious parallel that immediately came to mind was that of Rome.

Was Massieu's a rear-guard action? He was a partisan of the ancients and foresaw no good from the recent triumph of the moderns. But it was not simply a question of the fate of erudition or the fall into oblivion of the ancient models: the very life of the French language was at stake. And the decline of French, like that of Latin, forbode the decline of the nation generally. In Massieu, an author Gibbon knew and quoted, this theme is formulated, and it is the theme that would also serve as a point of departure for the *Essai* and would subsequently appear throughout the *Decline and Fall*.

But fears about the corruption of the language and obsessions about a future that could be likened to Roman decline were not restricted solely to the writings of the conservatives. As we know, the partisans of the moderns were also fond of organic metaphors—flowering, maturity, and the like. Although they held that modern writers were in no way inferior to the ancients, they stopped short of proclaiming an indefinite progress.[55] After the perfection attained by the moderns, there would necessarily be a decline.

We need only recall Voltaire's declarations: "By the time of Louis XIV's death, nature seemed to be taking a rest. . . . And the multitude of masterpieces has resulted in a feeling of surfeit. . . . It would be wrong to imagine that one can go on indefinitely creating new and striking forms of great tragic passions and sentiments. There are limits to everything. . . . So genius can only belong to a single age, and after that it is bound to degenerate."[56] As to what happens next, Voltaire proposes two theses, sometimes successively, sometimes simultaneously: The first, the optimistic one, emphasizes the rise of the philosophy and enlightenment that follow the great products of poetic genius: It invites the reader to console himself for his losses (which included—almost as an afterthought—erudition) with his gains. The second, the pessimistic one, emphasizes literary decline and, albeit jocularly, announces the approach of barbarism—as in the last verses of his *Epistle to Mademoiselle Clairon*:

> From the age in which we live, what can we expect?
> Enlightenment, it's true, grows in respect;
> With fewer talents, one is more informed:
> But taste has been lost, and the mind's gone astray.
> This ridiculous century is one of brochures,
> Of songs, of excerpts, but mostly of boors.
> Barbarism approaches and Apollo outraged
> Leaves the happy shores where his laws held sway.[57]

Voltaire, as he so frequently did, combined these two theses: the rise of reason and the fall of letters in fact go hand in hand. As for the French language, although it is threatened by corruption—as any widely spoken language would be—Voltaire does not seem concerned about its fate: "It contributes, throughout Europe, to one of the greatest pleasures of life."[58]

D'Alembert, however, cries out in alarm:[59] "Our language is denatured and degraded." By allowing themselves to be won over by "an ephemeral branch of society," "our authors" have moved away from the "true" and the "simple." Are they still able to come back to them? "Perhaps . . . the happy times will never return. It appears that similar circumstances irrevocably corrupted the language of Augustus's century." Like the Abbé Massieu in 1721, d'Alembert detects the signs of a serious alteration in the French tongue, and he sees the coming of a decline on the very model of the Roman one. For him, the cause is not simply a change in taste. In the very title of his essay, he indicts the "society of men of letters and of the powerful." He incriminates the dependency of writers on aristocratic and rich protectors. D'Alembert is no more indulgent of frivolity than are the champions of erudition, but he seeks for it a social origin, and he finds it in the salons of the rich and powerful. It is there that "our authors" go to seek a "twisted, impure, and barbaric language." This argument is based on a social criticism which has an undeniably prerevolutionary tone. But one can also detect in it traces of the ideas set forth in Tacitus's *Dialogus de oratoribus* and in chapter 15 of the Pseudo-Longinus: Eloquence degenerates and vanishes when political liberty disappears. It was with Diderot, in chapter 10 of his *Vie de Sénèque* (1778), a true autobiography by "projection," that the link between political and linguistic decadence was most clearly affirmed in terms that are at once very "Roman" and very prerevolutionary:

> Tryanny stamps a base character on productions of all kinds. Language itself is not protected from its influence: Can it be a matter of indifference whether a child hears around its cradle the timorous murmurs of servitude or the noble and proud strains of freedom? . . . Oratorical art could not survive even among a great people if it were not concerned with lofty affairs and did not ultimately lead to the dignity of the State. Seek true eloquence only among the Republicans.[60]

Diderot is more reassuring about contemporary French: "The French we speak is not corrupt."[61] How could he despair of his own language after having worked for so long to enrich it with his many terms for the "arts and professions"? But Diderot also assures us that "there is a point in the sciences beyond which they will not be able to go," and he even comes to imagine "some great revolution" that will interrupt "the progress of science, the work of art," and cast back "into the shadows a portion of our hemisphere."[62]

It is in Rousseau—specifically in the last chapter of the *Essai sur l'origine des langues* (composed for the most part between 1755 and 1762)—that we must seek a radical expression of a triple decline affecting public freedom, language, and eloquence in contemporary France:

> Societies have reached their final form; nothing can change any longer except by arms or wealth. And since the only thing that is said to the people is "Give money," it can be said by placards on the corners of the streets or by soldiers going from house to house. No one need be assembled for that—on the contrary, people must be kept apart: that is the first maxim of modern politics.
> There are languages favorable to liberty. They are sonorous, harmonious languages, rich in prosody, whose discourse can be heard from afar. Our own languages are made for buzzing at each other on divans. . . . Now I say that any language with which one cannot make oneself understood by the assembled people is a servile language. It is impossible for a people to remain free and to speak such a language.[63]

The weakening of language and the disappearance of eloquence are closely connected with the loss of political freedom. Such a loss would be the most important of all; the alteration of language is only symptomatic of it. For Diderot and Rousseau, it is not knowledge that is at stake (Rousseau actually considers its accumulation harmful) nor is it the creation of oratorical masterpieces; at issue is civil freedom, conceived as the exercise of democracy. Thus, for Diderot and particularly for Rousseau, the diagnosis of the present state of things is so serious that the prognosis for the immediate future becomes one of two alternatives: either bloody disorder and irrevocable catastrophe or regeneration. For only something like a resurrection can bring civil society back to its true principles[64] and restore its lost freedom.

In the revival of the body social (if Rousseau is to be believed), the legislator's words have a role to play. Called upon for so solemn an occasion, as if a choice had to be made between death and rebirth, language must recover the strength it has dissipated. By force of will, an end can be made to decadence and dissolution. The basic word, soon supported in its use by all individuals who had become citizens again, imposes a completely new beginning. Among those writers who sympathize with what will later be called the "first revolution"—I am thinking of André Chénier here—this myth of a new beginning is joined with the fervor of Winckelmann's neoclassicism: the arts are born of freedom alone. The Greek world possessed simultaneously a profound intimacy with nature and a free democracy. Chénier entrusted to French poetry the task of bringing freedom back to life. To make this possible, the writer would have to infuse or transfuse new life into French verse. For this, the will alone was not enough—one must find in the past the "flame" and its warming strength, and Greek poetry, itself the fruit of liberty, would be its major source. In the program Chénier sets forth (scattered unsystematically throughout many texts),[65] a renaissance of erudition was sought, but erudition that would contribute to the renaissance of great poetry, which in its turn would inaugurate the reign of a new freedom where all the arts that flowered under the ancient freedom would be reborn.

As we can see, this system of thought is governed by a taste for dichotomy: it starkly opposes servitude and freedom. It uses themes set forth by Tacitus and Longinus to reach a verdict that could not be appealed. The decline of eloquence was a gauge for the extent of the nation's servility, and only radical change—a revolution—could bring back both eloquence and freedom.[66] The present state of society, painted in the most somber hues, was the very opposite of what reason dictated; consequently the institutions that were responsible for man's unhappiness had to be overthrown. Perceived in terms of this extreme dichotomy, the future could only hold either absolute disorder or a return to order. The writer, the philosopher, the poet could only oppose, so that their efforts could prepare the advent of the contrary of what was.

Faced with such appeals for regeneration, Gibbon was more reserved; although he deplored the decline of erudition in his *Essai* and although the present fate of England might have inspired his interest in the decline and fall of Rome, he nonetheless rejected these melodramatic interpretations of the present. He was not the sort to think in terms of all-or-nothing, nor to see the future played out in terms of salvation or perdition. He remained too removed from the religious spirit to allow himself to be seduced by a historiosophy that brought the promise of redemption to human history. He seems to have decided in favor of the superiority of the ancients, both in poetry and in the products of the imagination more generally, but this superiority, far from representing the flourishing of an admirable state of liberty, was the result of imperfect political institutions, less advanced than his own, that allowed violence and passion to prevail:

> The manners of the ancients were more favourable to poetry than ours; which is a strong presumption they surpassed us in that sublime art. . . .

The ancient republics of Greece were ignorant of the first principles of good policy. The people met in tumultuous assemblies rather to determine than to deliberate. Their factions were impetuous and lasting; their insurrections frequent and terrible; their most peaceful hours full of distrust, envy, and confusion: The citizens were indeed unhappy; but their writers, whose imaginations were warmed by such dreadful objects, described them naturally as they felt. A peaceable administration of the laws, those salutary institutions, which, projected in the cabinet of a sovereign or his council, diffuse happiness over a whole nation, excite only the poet's admiration, the coldest of all the passions.[67]

In these lines, which clearly echo the thesis openly defended by Maternus in the *Dialogus de oratoribus*, Gibbon, to say the least, does not invite us to regret the passing of the Greek world. It was not a good place to live, even if its poetry had risen to unsurpassed heights. Gibbon preferred the periods during which efficient and orderly institutions prevailed, and his political model for them was the Empire under the Antonines: he did not allow himself to be dazzled by golden ages; he was not inclined to embellish the image of the democracies of antiquity,[68] nor did he believe in the joys of the pastoral life[69] any more than he believed in the golden age that he thought the French revolutionaries wanted to establish.[70] Rousseau was able to bring his indictment down upon the arts and sciences by opposing them to a world of frugality and virtue, "a happy shore toward which the eyes turn constantly, which one regrets to leave."[71] If this was the lost past, the "earliest time," then our society with all its luxuries had to be seen as "degenerate." The young Gibbon replied by rejecting the antithesis and by refusing the condemnation:

The sciences, it is said, take their rise from luxury, an enlightened must be always a vicious people. For my part, I cannot be of this opinion. The sciences are not the daughters of luxury, but both the one and the other owe their birth to industry. The arts, in their rudest state, satisfied the primitive wants of men. In their state of perfection they suggest new ones, even from Vitellius's shield of Pallas, to the philosophical entertainments of Cicero. But in proportion as luxury corrupts the manners, the sciences soften them; like to those prayers in Homer, which constantly pursue injustice, to appease the fury of that cruel deity.[72]

Rousseau's historical logic was based on antithesis, and it required an almost immediate decision, a conversion, a regeneration. Gibbon, by disarming the antithesis, had no need to require urgent action. He de-dramatized what Rousseau and his revolutionary disciples tended to overdramatize. By conferring upon history a span of very long duration, Gibbon provided himself with the possibility of determining the slow process of civilization as it made its way through all its ruptures, disasters, and collapses.[73] Nothing is more revealing than the commentaries on a quotation from the last chapter of *De Sublimitate* with which Gibbon concludes chapter 2 of the *Decline and Fall*:

"In the same manner," says he [Longinus], "as some children always remain pigmies, whose infant limbs have been too closely confined; thus our tender minds, fettered by the prejudices and habits of a just servitude, are unable to expand themselves, or to attain that well proportioned greatness which we admire in the ancients; who, living under a popular government, wrote with the same freedom as they acted." This diminutive stature of mankind, if we pursue the metaphor, was daily sinking below the old standard, and the Roman world was indeed peopled by a race of pigmies, when the fierce giants of the north broke in, and mended the puny breed. They restored a manly spirit of freedom; and after the revolution of ten centuries, freedom became the happy parent of taste and science.[74]

In the expanded perspective which Gibbon unfolds before our eyes, the dramatic opposition between republican freedom and the servitude of the imperial age is surmounted and overwhelmed by the vision of a new freedom, reappearing, with beneficial consequences for culture, after a long interval. For Gibbon, who invites us to consider the entire chain of history, freedom had already returned after a long eclipse; and it happened that its worst defeat was at the same time the necessary condition for its rebirth; for those, especially in France, who were attempting to set up parallels between present and Roman times, freedom had again been lost, though no one had concerned himself very much with how it had been able to return in the interval.[75] So Longinus's accusation was gladly repeated in order to cast an anathema upon the present. *"De te fabula narratur,"* shouted Diderot (about an aesthetic point, it is true), in evoking "Longinus's pigmies."[76]

In the last decades of the eighteenth century, the desire to return to first principles, which had already animated geometric and mathematical thought and were then seen as applicable everywhere, turned to a less abstract domain and became an even more emphatic desire to return to historical origins, to primitive revelations, to vital forces irreducible to the laws of mechanics.[77] Much has been said, and rightly so, about the "crisis of the geometrization of the universe"[78] that took place around 1750. At that time, the "erudite" study of documents had its revenge. In an aesthetic climate of "anticomania" and with the help of some novelistic touches, the Abbé Barthélemy, a member of the Académie des Inscriptions et Belles-Lettres, had one of the most stunning literary successes of the century with his *Voyage du jeune Anacharsis* (1788): an erudite avenged his confreres for all the affronts about which Massieu, Du Resnel, and Gibbon had complained. And the writer whose *Essai sur l'étude de la littérature* might have seemed completely misdirected in 1761 came to be seen as the precursor of a movement that was later to be represented in France by Sismondi, Augustin Thierry, Michelet, and, especially, Renan, whose *Avenir de la science* (1848) recognized philology as the key science.

Assuredly, in the judgment he brought against Christianity and the priests and in his accusation of the Empire's excessive extent, Gibbon was close to Montesquieu, Voltaire, and the *philosophes*. But his way of thinking, which excluded antithetical formulations, dichotomies, pressing summations in the name of collective salvation, and idealizations of the past or future, was as foreign as it could be to the more or less systematic statements that formed the language of the Revolution in France. In September, 1789, when the revolutionary process began to accelerate, Gibbon saw France as being in a state of "dissolution."[79] The loudest speakers then were those whose purpose it was to put an end to decadence and degeneration and to restore the fundamental pact of the nation. But seeing that the effort to restore the primitive liberties had culminated in precisely the contrary of what had been sought, Gibbon could only feel justified by the definition of the "philosophical genius" he had provided in his youth:

> A philosophical genius consists in the capacity of recurring to the most simple ideas; in discovering and combining the first principles of things. The possessor of this distinguishing faculty has a view as piercing as extensive. Situated on an eminence, he

takes in a wide extensive field, of which he forms a precise and exact idea; while a genius of an inferiour cast, tho' what he sees he distinguishes with equal precision, is more contracted in his views, and discovers only a part of the whole. . . .

What a retrospect is it to a genius truly philosophical, to see the most absurd opinions received among the most enlightened peoples; to see barbarians, on the other hand, arrive at the knowledge of the most sublime truths; to find true consequences falsely deduced from the most erroneous principles; admirable principles, bordering on the verge of truth, without ever conducting thither. . . .[80]

Gibbon was too perceptive—at once too ironic and too skeptical—to be unaware of the metaphoric[81] character of the terms (so frequently borrowed from the organic scale) which he used in his great history. They "are ideas justified by language." These terms were the tools he used to explain the changes that had taken place in the world since the Antonine era: Does the historian have any other language available to him? But we would do well to remember that he mistrusted any political action that was inspired by the prestige of antithesis or metaphor. It is this mistrust, as much as his mildly Tory opinions, that, it seems to me, determined his attitude toward the French Revolution. He knew that, at best, the outcome would be "a Richelieu or a Cromwell, arising, either to restore the Monarchy, or to lead the Commonwealth."[82]

REFERENCES

[1]*Memoirs of My Life*, ed. Georges A. Bonnard (London, 1966), p. 103.

[2]As set forth in Richelet's *Dictionnaire* (1680).

[3]*Encyclopédie*, under the entry for "Erudition."

[4]D'Alembert continues: "Erudition, considered in relation to the current state of letters, is comprised of three main branches: knowledge of history, of languages, and of books. The knowledge of history can be divided into several sub-branches: ancient and modern history; the history of our own country and of foreign countries; the history of arts and sciences; chronology; geography; medals and antiques." Clearly, the traditional classing of history in company with eloquence and poetry troubles d'Alembert; it is hard for him to see it as a product of the imagination. This is why, at the end of the first paragraph of the entry for "Erudition" cited above, a simple "etc." marks the henceforth vacant place of history among "the pleasant products of the mind." According to the figurative "system of human knowledge" and the ramifications of the encyclopedic tree, history and erudition will draw closer as products of memory. This is not at all to exclude history from the system of letters. The system of letters simply ceases to belong to one branch alone; it cuts across several branches of the encylopedic tree. Consequently, a considerable distance separates history, a product of memory, from poetry, a product of the imagination. Philosophy, a product of reason, occupies an intermediate position between the two, while eloquence tends to fade as a specific genre and is soon reduced to a natural talent which can do without rules.

[5]Marmontel's text is an addition to the main entry for "Littérature," written by Jaucourt. It is a significant addition, for it responds to a need for terminological preciseness. The *Eléments de littérature*, presented in dictionary form, uses all Marmontel's contributions to the *Encyclopédie*.

[6]Cf. the *Essais*, Book II, chap. 19, on the subject of Julian the Apostate: "Among other rare qualities, he excelled in all kinds of literature."

[7]"Discours préliminaire de l'Encyclopédie," in *Encyclopédie* (Lausanne, 1778), I, p. xxxiii. English text taken from Richard N. Schwab, *Preliminary Discourse to the Encyclopedia of Diderot* (New York, 1963), p. 60.

[8]*Ibid.*, p. xxxvi.

[9]*Ibid.*, p. xxxvii.

[10]*Ibid.*, p. xxxv, Schwab, p. 63-64.

[11]As a result of so many distinctions, the positions ultimately drew closer. Those whom Gibbon treats as adversaries were openly critical of "wit."

[12]In no way did d'Alembert exclude such a collaboration: "To the advantage of the exact sciences, much is made of the philosophical spirit which they have certainly contributed to spread among us. But can we not think that the philosophical mind finds frequent exercise in matters of erudition?," *Encyclopédie*, "Erudition."

[13]*Essai sur l'étude de la littérature*, chap. 26, in *Miscellaneous Works*, II (London, 1796), p. 463 (henceforth cited as *Essai*).

[14]*Essai*, chap. 47, p. 475. This and subsequent passages were taken from the translation, *An Essay on the Study of Literature*, published in London in 1764.

[15]Cf. note 4, above.

[16]What Gibbon said about Voltaire's superficiality has been quoted many times—and rightly so. See "Extraits raisonnés de mes lectures," *Miscellaneous Works*, II (1796), p. 69.

[17]Contemporary views are in agreement. D'Alembert: "A taste for witty, brilliant works and for the study of exact sciences has taken the place of our fathers' taste for erudite subjects. Those of our contemporaries who still cultivate such study complain of the exclusive and invidious preference we give to other objects" (in "Erudition"). Jaucourt: "It is time to seek and point out the reasons for the decline of literature, which falls more out of favor each day, at least in our nation; assuredly, we cannot flatter ourselves for having sought a remedy. The time has come in this country when no account is made of a learned man who uses his erudition to interpret or correct difficult passages from the authors of antiquity, or to explain a chronological point or an interesting question concerning geography or grammar. Erudition is considered pedantry. . . ." The *Encyclopédie* entry for "Littérature."

[18]*Essai*, chap. 2, p. 450.

[19]*Essai*, chap. 6, p. 451.

[20]*Parrhasiana*, 2 vols. (Amsterdam, 1699), I, pp. 223-24.

[21]Note for March 14, 1761, in "Extraits raisonnés de mes lectures," *Miscellaneous Works*, II (1796), p. 1.

[22]*Parrhasiana*, I, p. 225.

[23]*Ibid.*, pp. 259-60. Writing in a Protestant country, Le Clerc sees the intervention of other, but less serious, obstacles (pp. 256-57).

[24]*Ibid.*, pp. 260-61.

[25]*Ibid.*, p. 261.

[26]*Ibid.*, p. 289. As a good Arminian, Le Clerc adds that intolerance hastens the decline of the state.

[27]*Ibid.*, p. 276.

[28]*Ibid.*, p. 277.

[29]*Ibid.*, p. 280.

[30]*Ibid.*, p. 277.

[31]*The History of the Decline and Fall of the Roman Empire (DF)*, one volume (London, 1831), chap. 68, p. 1173.

[32]*Dictionnaire historique et critique*, entry "Alegambe," note D. On the scorn of erudition for the sake of "politeness" (generally put forward by the great and by men of standing), see La Bruyère, who takes the defense of erudition (fragments 18 and 19 of the chapter "Des Jugements").

[33]*Dictionnaire historique et critique*, entry "Aconce," note D. Fifty years later, Voltaire says much the same thing in the entry "Gens de lettres," edited for the *Encyclopédie*: "In the past, during the sixteenth century and early in the seventeenth century, the littérateurs were generally occupied by grammatical criticism of the Greek and Latin authors. It is to their work that we owe our dictionaries, our corrected editions, and the commentaries on the masterpieces of antiquity. Today, such criticism is less necessary and has been succeeded by the philosophical mind: it is this philosophical mind which seems to form the character of our lettered people. And when good taste is joined to it, the result is an accomplished littérateur. . . . The thorough and purified reason that some men have helped spread through their conversations has contributed much to the instruction and polish of the nation, their criticism is no longer aimed at Greek and Latin words, but, supported by a healthy philosophy, it has destroyed all the prejudices which infected society." Note the quick and quite natural transition from "textual criticism" to "social criticism."

[34]*Dictionnaire historique et critique*, entry "Meziriac," note C.

[35]On the quarrel in general, see Jean Seznec, "Le Singe antiquaire," in *Essais sur Diderot et l'Antiquité* (Oxford, 1957), pp. 79-96.

[36]Voltaire dodges the accusation by making a distinction between the "man of letters" and the "wit": "A man of letters is not what is called a *wit*: wit alone supposes less culture, less study, and demands no philosophy. It consists, for the most part, in a brilliant imagination, in the pleasures of conversation helped along by common reading. A wit could easily not deserve in any way the title of man of letters; the man of letters might well be unable to claim the brilliance of wit" (entry "Gens de lettres").

[37]Translator of Pope, in 1750 Du Resnel brought the censure of the theological faculty at Paris upon himself. Cf. Robert Shackleton, *Montesquieu* (Oxford, 1961), p. 368.

[38]*Histoire de l'Académie*, XVI (1751), p. 15.

[39]*Ibid.*, p. 23. On the role of philological criticism in the formation of the philosophical mind in the eighteenth century, cf. Reinhart Koselleck, *Kritik und Krise* (1973), especially pp. 81-103.

[40]We might add that Du Resnel strove to demonstrate the usefulness of the knowledge of the ancients to the exact sciences, as Fréret did later, and Gibbon did in chapters 40-48 of his *Essai*.

[41]*Histoire de l'Academie*, XVI, p. 36.

[42]De Pompignan, Bishop of Puy, *La Dévotion réconciliée avec l'esprit* (Montauban, 1755), pp. 38-39. We should note, however, that the Bishop does not take up the defense of erudition. Religious educators, such as the Abbé Fleury, mistrust the "curious sciences" which come close to being "useless sciences." Cf. Claude Fleury, *Traité du choix et de la méthode des études* (Paris, 1753), pp. 247-58, in which the study of Oriental languages is held to be dangerous: "They flatter vanity by their singularity and prodigy.

Moreover, they are the mark of profound erudition, because ordinarily they are only learned *after* the more common tongues."

[43]*De la Décadence des lettres et des moeurs, depuis les Grecs et les Romains jusqu'à nos jours* (Paris, 1787), p. 385.

[44]*Ibid.*, p. 348.

[45]*Ibid.*, p. 476.

[46]Gibbon finds Fontenelle charming in the *Eclogues*, but he judges the *Histoire des Oracles* "somewhat superficial." *Miscellaneous Works*, II (1796), p. 55.

[47]*Memoirs of My Life* (cited above, note 1), p. 103.

[48]Raymond Savioz, *Mémoires autobiographiques de Charles Bonnet de Genève* (Paris, 1948), pp. 168-69.

[49]George A. Bonnard, "Gibbon's *Essai sur l'étude de la littérature* as Judged by Contemporary Reviewers and by Gibbon Himself," *English Studies*, XXXII:4 (August, 1951), pp. 145-53.

[50]J.-J. Rousseau, *Correspondance Générale*, ed. Dufour-Plan, IX, p. 327.

[51]Voltaire, *Commentaire sur l'esprit des lois* (1777), art. 19.

[53]Massieu, *Oeuvres de M. de Tourreil*, I (1721), Preface, pp. xvii-xix.

[54]As Jean Seznec has pointed out, letter 145 contains a precise allusion (and with what wit!) to the conflict between philosophy and erudition: "A philosopher possesses a sovereign scorn for a man whose head is loaded with facts, and, in his turn, he is considered a dreamer by a man with a good memory." It must be added that the *Lettres Persanes* also raises the problem of the decline of nations (in connection with the Ottoman Empire), and, in an essay conducted through a series of letters, proposes some conjectures (which are hardly indulgent toward Christian institutions) about the reasons behind the depopulation of the globe.

[55]Cf. H. R. Jauss, "Aesthetische Normen und geschichtliche Reflexion in der 'Querelle des Anciens et des Moderns,' " in Charles Perrault, *Parallèle des Anciens et des Modernes en ce qui regarde les arts et les sciences* (reprinted, Munich, 1964).

[56]Voltaire, *Siècle de Louis XIV, Oeuvres complètes* (Paris, 1827), I, chap. 32, p. 940; translation taken from J. H. Brumfitt, *The Age of Louis XIV* (New York, 1963), pp. 185-87.

[57]Voltaire, *Epître à Mademoiselle Clairon*.

[58]Voltaire, *Siècle de Louis XIV*, chap. 32; Brumfitt, p. 188.

[59]We quote from the *Essai sur la société des gens de lettres et des grands* (1752), after the text of Volume I of *Mélanges de littérature, d'histoire et de philosophie* (1759).

[60]Diderot, *Essai sur la vie de Sénèque le philosophe* (Paris, 1778; dated 1789 on the title page), pp. 38-39.

[61]*Ibid.*, p. 37.

[62]Entry for the *Encyclopédie* in Diderot, *Oeuvres complètes*, II (Paris, 1969), pp. 379-80.

[63]Rousseau, *Essai sur l'origine des langues*, chap. 20.

[64]Cf. *Du Contrat social*, Book II, chap. 8.

[65]Specifically, I am referring to the text published under the title *Essais sur les causes et les effets de la perfection et de la décadence des lettres et des arts*, to the ode "Jeu de Paume," and especially to "L'Invention."

[66]We have to admit that, from around 1770, French literary production showed an abundance of mediocre works. See Robert Darnton's study on "The High Enlightenment and the Low Life of Literature in Pre-Revolutionary France," in *Past and Present*, 51 (May, 1971), pp. 81-115.

[67]*Essai*, chap. 11 and 12. This is the thesis upheld by Hume in the essay "Of Eloquence," as Gibbon reminds us in a discreet note to chapter 12. Diderot, in one of his "Pensées détachées," discusses the same idea. Cf. *Oeuvres complètes*, X (Paris, 1971), pp. 80-81.

[68]For example: "Every popular government has experienced the effects of rude or artificial eloquence. The coldest nature is animated, the firmest reason is moved by the rapid communication of the prevailing impulse; and each hearer is affected by his own passions, and by those of the surrounding multitude" (*DF*, chap. 22, p. 6). See also, in chapter 50, the remarks about the eloquence of the Arabs.

[69]Or again: "The sober historian is forcibly awakened from a pleasing vision; and is compelled with some reluctance, to confess, that the pastoral manners, which have been adorned with the fairest attributes of peace and innocence, are much better adapted to the fierce and cruel habits of a military life" (*DF*, preamble to chap. 26).

[70]*The Letters of Edward Gibbon*, ed. Prothero (London, 1896), II, p. 210.

[71]*Discours sur les sciences et les arts*, in *Oeuvres complètes*, III (Paris, 1964), p. 22.

[72]*Essai*, chap. 82.

[73]See the famous "Observations" which conclude chapter 38.

[74]*DF*, concluding lines of chap. 2.

[75]Even though Diderot and many others along with him delighted in comparing Louis XV's France to the Rome of Claudius and Nero, they remained rather vague—and with good reason—when it came to defining a preceding French period which would then correspond to Rome's Republican era.

[76]*Pensées détachées sur la peinture*, in *Oeuvres complètes*, XII (Paris, 1971), p. 337.

[77]One example among many: "Unfortunately, literature is becoming a profession and a trade: most authors write without having anything to say; everything is reduced to useful speculation". . .

[78]Yvon Belaval, "La Crise de la géométrisation de l'univers dans la philosophie des Lumières," *Revue Internationale de Philosophie*, XXI:3 (1952).

[79]*The Letters of Edward Gibbon* (above, note 70), II, p. 206.

[80]*Essai*, chaps. 46-47.

[81]Cf. Randolph Starn, "Meaning-Levels in the Theme of Historical Decline," *History and Theory*, 1975, pp. 1-31; cf. also H. Vyverberg, *Historical Pessimism in the French Enlightenment* (Cambridge, Mass., 1958), and R. Mortier, "L'idée de décadence littéraire au XVIIIe siècle," *Studies on Voltaire and the Eighteenth Century*, LVII (1967), pp. 1013-29.

[82]*The Letters of Edward Gibbon* (above, note 70), II, p. 210.

FRANÇOIS FURET

Civilization and Barbarism in Gibbon's History

IN THE PARIS OF THE ENLIGHTENMENT, from which Gibbon drew much of his intellectual inspiration, the century had begun with the so-called quarrel between the ancients and the moderns, a literary controversy that seems to have run its course by Gibbon's time, but that nevertheless went to the heart of his intellectual life. At issue in the quarrel as it began toward the end of Louis XIV's reign was the nature of the cultural identity between the ancient and modern thought that had constituted the common heritage of the European intelligentsia since the Renaissance. The moderns did not deny their ties with antiquity and its heritage, but they rejected the notion that the contribution of philosophy should be limited to the rediscovery of a Greco-Roman model. They declared the "modern" to be superior to the "ancient," especially in regard to the progress of knowledge, the rigor of reasoning, and the quest for truth; in doing so, they broke with the classical conception of history as cyclical and replaced it with a belief in the creative value of time, which would progressively separate truth from error.

This detachment of the concept of "modern" from its ties with antiquity gradually allowed the development in the course of the eighteenth century of an evolutionary history and a theory of progress. After the providential histories of churchmen, after the cyclical histories of the humanists and the Reformation, now history could be opened up infinitely into the future. The fears that were latent in the notion of an infinite and unknown future were conjured away by the spectacle of a continuing advance in the arts and sciences, which seemed to promise a more general progress.

The ideas of the moderns were given their definitive form for the eighteenth century in d'Alembert's *Discours préliminaire* and Condorcet's *Esquisse d'un tableau historique des progrès de l'esprit humain*. In them we find that "civilization" was a process before it was a state; its purpose was to make "civil," "to police" the uncivilized. The word "civilization" itself, which dates from this period in both French and English, was invented to express this drive of enlightened society toward what ought to be, the conviction of being on the right road, the certitude that the future was in fact infinite and that history had a purpose.[1]

But, in many respects, Gibbon wrote a history very different from others of his century; his history was at once more "ancient" and more "modern": more ancient, because Gibbon was a professional antiquarian and lived in the company of the learned and the scholarly societies of Europe in the seventeenth century, into whose proceedings his mastery of French permitted him easy access; more modern, because he integrated this erudition with the art of retelling the past and, in so doing, invented the historical panorama which was to become so important in the romantic era. Gibbon was somewhere between Tillemont and Renan, but this "somewhere" constituted more than simply the philosophical consensus of the Enlightenment; it was also an original vision of the past and present in Europe.

His own biography already reveals some of this vision in the studious, retiring years in Lausanne undertaken by an English gentleman who had tasted the charms of the salons of Paris and London. For, on the banks of Lake Geneva, in those Franco-German confines which were so crucial for the transformations of European culture, Gibbon saw only a retreat where he could continue his work. A place of exile in his youth, Switzerland became a shelter in his maturity. By choosing Switzerland, he avoided belonging to any of the nations of Europe and thus signified that his only loyalties lay with his two universal homelands: historical erudition—that most international of cultures—and Rome, the mother of Europe. The revelation of October 15, 1764, had given a meaning to his life amounting almost to a religious conversion. Freud entered Rome only after he had already become Freud and was ready to confront the classical studies of his youth, which constituted at the same time the world of the gentile. But Gibbon did not become Gibbon until that day in October when he trod "with a proud foot upon the ruins of the Forum." He received from Rome more than his idea of civilization; he received from it his cultural identity.

Between Rome and Gibbon lay the same link that connected the European intellectuals of the Renaissance to antiquity. It was a romance, complete with the same delight in discovery and the same freshness and joy in the recapture of lost secrets. Since the Renaissance, education had put Rome into everyone's store of knowledge: the Latin and history that one learned from Cicero and Tacitus continued to be the basis of the scholarly apprenticeship expected of future gentlemen. Thus, when Gibbon discovered Rome, he was familiar with it already. It was the most classical "topos" of European culture, the basis for its theater, its art, its moral philosophy, its historical reflection. What is strange is that his meeting with a place already so heavily charged with significance should still contain any surprise at all, much less one amounting almost to an existential conversion. In contrast, when Montesquieu had visited Rome in 1729, though he could hardly have been accused of indifference to Roman history—he had written his *Essai* (1716)[2] before his famous *Considérations* (1734)[3]—precisely because ancient Rome was for him a legitimate subject of study, he retained in his reactions to Pontifical Rome something of the attitudes of an intelligent tourist—an observer of customs, politics, and the arts.[4] Thirty-five years later, Gibbon saw only the *urbs* in Rome: "Each memorable spot where Romulus stood, or Tully spoke, or Caesar fell, was at once present to my eye; and several days of intoxication were lost or enjoyed before I could descend to a cool and minute investigation."[5]

This traveler's sentiment, which anticipates the emotional investment the romantic writers were to bring to history, also reflects Gibbon's devotion to the humanities of classical Europe and to the tradition of the sixteenth and seventeenth centuries. According to this tradition, Rome was a model of civilization that had never been surpassed. For Gibbon, however, this was not a philosophical proposition. He did not theorize about man in society, about natural law, about the social contract; he had no interest in that essential question of his time: What is a "savage" and where does one place him in the history of humanity? He was instinctively and totally the historian, that is, he was an empiricist, a narrator, and completely and unquestioningly Europocentric in the midst of a world where only Greco-Roman antiquity, the Judaeo-Christian tradition, and their offspring—Europe—counted.

The superiority of Rome was therefore not something that had to be demonstrated. It was in the order of evidence, a fact. It was a unique experience that had only to be described and had nothing to do with historical laws. Gibbon had read and admired Montesquieu, but in the end the two works had little in common. For Montesquieu, Roman history was merely a "case study" for a general typology of political regimes. The reasons for Rome's greatness were at the same time the reasons for its fall: the expansion of the Empire necessitated a monarchical government that was incompatible with the laws that had nonetheless made it necessary. Gibbon, though he intermittently echoed his predecessor's theory, was not given to rigorous conceptualizations. He was eclectic, and he multiplied not only the possible explanations for Rome's greatness and fall, but even the kinds of explanations. For him, Roman history was not just another collection of human experiences; it was quite simply, in the second century after Christ, the highest point in human history, "the period in the history of the world, during which the condition of the human race was most happy and prosperous."[6] It was a unique moment, which did not fit into any general concept of historical change.

This view of second-century Rome as representing a privileged moment in human history was impossible to integrate into a linear view of humanity's progress, such as the one Condorcet wrote later on (1793). But such a conception was typical of cyclical histories, according to which civilization had no purpose toward which the cumulative progress of mankind was heading, but rather consisted of a series of intermittent "happy and prosperous" periods. In this conception, second-century Rome represented the crowning of history's most splendid cycle—and to such a degree that the hope Gibbon assigned to classical Europe was not to surpass this model and the values it bore, but to constitute a less fragile vessel for them.

It is difficult to determine very precisely or securely the reasons behind Gibbon's worshipful admiration for the Empire. Nowhere does he present a systematic description of Roman civilization. He is so permeated with the idea of its superiority that he feels no need to discuss the reasons for it, nor to take stock of its elements. The famous judgment from chapter 3 of the *Decline and Fall* quoted above, regarding the exceptionally happy state of humanity during the Antonine period, is supported only by some rather brief justifications relating to the virtue and wisdom of the emperors who came after the civil unrest in the first century. The loss of freedoms—those famous Roman freedoms that nourished so many of the century's books—was more than compensated by the exercise of an equally enlightened despotism.

Gibbon was, in fact, indifferent to the political philosophy that so excited many of his contemporaries. He wrote, as did his masters in antiquity—Thucydides, Cicero, and Tacitus—moral history. For a period to be great, it was necessary, but also sufficient, for it to have produced a certain kind of man. The emperors of the second century were his *exempla*; they were at once a culture and a moral.

Nevertheless—and not surprisingly—Gibbon's history of Rome is also a history of Gibbon. The cult of the Antonines reflected the views the historian held toward his own present. In this respect, Gibbon was an entirely original writer. He did not, as did the men of the Renaissance, have to rediscover Rome beneath the medieval sediment, for that work had been done for him. But neither did he believe, as did the artists and men of letters of the seventeenth century, that Rome could truly be imitated. He was already too much of a historian—in the nineteenth-century sense of the word—not to conceive of history as flux, never representing the same situations—or the same successes—twice. The cycles of civilization that history presented were not comparable, and they were transient. The *Decline and Fall of the Roman Empire* is dominated throughout by the romantic notion of the uniqueness and transience of the great periods of history. It is an extraordinary example of that moment when the old cyclical conception of history hung in balance with nineteenth-century historicism.

Gibbon, we must remember, did not write a history of the Roman Empire; he chose to write a history only of its decline and fall. In the very years when impeccably neoclassical ruins contributed their note of controlled sadness to the parks of aristocratic castles, Gibbon joined his powerful voice to the melancholy chorus of European scholars—far from being history's promise, civilization was the historian's nostalgia. The clearest expression of this comes at the end of chapter 38, in the famous "General Observations on the Fall of the Roman Empire in the West," which forms the only genuinely analytic commentary on the problem that gave the *Decline and Fall* its title. As we know, Gibbon, after having summarized the causes of the fall of Rome, proposed to draw from them lessons for his own time. Does this mean that he found a similarity between eighteenth-century Europe and the Roman Empire in its years of fading splendor? Yes and no. Yes, because he points out, at the risk of appearing unpatriotic, that he considers Europe a great republic, united precisely by its participation in the same civilization, for all its inhabitants have attained "almost the same level of politeness and cultivation." By this he means that the European élite of his time, regardless of the vicissitudes in power relations among nations, displays a "state of happiness" and a "system of arts, and laws, and manners" common to all nations, and these are what constitute a civilization. There is nothing in this attitude that cannot be found in Enlightenment thought of the most classic kind. At the same time, however, the comparison with the civilization of the great Roman period was only made with references to external dangers: Roman history no longer constituted the basis of cultural identity, as in the classical period, but a lesson for Europe's defense.

In short, what fascinates Gibbon about Roman civilization is not so much that in it lay the foundations of Europe, but that it was so fragile, as fragile perhaps as Europe's civilization now was. As he looks upon the ruins of Rome, the humanist gentleman asks the future about the chances of survival for the things he loves. Gibbon's feeling of belonging to a special but threatened moment in history does not come from an analysis of the inner contradictions of Euorpean civilization. On the contrary, he says that the fact that the majority of nations carries on this civilization and emulates it is in his view a source of strength, not of weakness. He does not even suspect that, within this community of European culture, nationalism would become an element of disintegration. He reasons only in terms of a possible eventual barbarian (or, more precisely, "savage") menace, as if the invasions had been the sole cause of the dismemberment of the Western Empire (though several pages earlier he expressly blamed its excessive size and the disintegrating influence of Christianity) and as if the multinational Europe of the eighteenth century could be compared to the extended Roman frontiers (though a few pages later he points out that northern Europe, once a stronghold of barbarians, had little by little been civilized).

The comparison, in fact, comes out in favor of eighteenth-century Europe. Gibbon lists the elements militating in favor of a relative stability for the civilization it has attained—its geographic extent, its national diversity, its mastery of the art of war, the undeniable distinction of its inventions and basic technology—and in the end he even advances the idea of a continuous progress of humanity "since the first discovery of the arts." But it was still the case that Europe's civilization, even if it was probably indestructible, remained subject to the challenge of the "savage nations of the globe." It could be seriously threatened, forced to retreat, to become expatriated "in the American world." In a century that had witnessed a rapid acceleration in the Europeanization of the globe, which had characterized history everywhere since the Renaissance, Gibbon discussed the reverse hypothesis drawn from the Roman example. It was not that he thought it likely, but that his concept of civilization already included a threatening reversal, a permanent exterior menace—the savage world.

Savage, or barbarian? Generally speaking, the Enlightenment distinguished between these two terms by defining them as two different steps in the evolution toward civilization. The *Encyclopédie* (1751) still confused them, however, for in it "savages" were described as "barbaric peoples who live without laws, without police, without religion, and who have no fixed habitation." But it then adds: "There is this difference between savages and barbarians, namely, that the first form scattered little nations that have no desire to unite, whereas the barbarians often unite, and this happens when a chief submits to one of the others. Natural liberty is the sole concern of the police among the savages; along with this liberty, nature and climate are almost the sole governing forces among them. Occupied by hunting or agriculture, they do not burden themselves with religious observances and do not make their religion a basis for organizing their lives."

Some time later, the *Dictionnaire* of Trévoux (1771), although it followed the *Encyclopédie* very closely, took pains not to use the term "barbarian" as a synonym for "savage." The latter term "is also used for those people who wander in the forests, without fixed habitation, without laws, without police, and almost without religion." Thus, the two dictionaries agree with Montesquieu in distinguishing between the savage and the barbarian by stating that the first "live scattered about, retreating into the forests and the mountains, without uniting, while the second often unite and sometimes live under a chief to whom they have submitted."[7] Ferguson (1767) writes that the savage, in America, has neither property, nor government, nor judges, while the barbarian, in Europe, had property and obeyed a chief.[8] Pauw (1768) distinguished clearly different stages in history, when, for example, he differentiated between the treatment of prisoners by "the most savage," "ordinary savages," "semi-barbarous peoples," and "the least barbarous" nations.[9]

Thus, the Enlightenment, in France and in England, constructed a three-stage progressive scheme of history: "savage-barbarian-civilized." Just after Démeunier,[10] Robertson, in 1778, defined the same three stages of evolution but this time according to more materialistic criteria: the savages had neither writing, nor metals, nor domesticated animals (America); the barbarians had metals and domesticated animals (Europe, Mexico, and Peru); the civilized nations had industry and the arts.[11] To this materialistic classification, destined for a great future in the following century, the eighteenth-century thinkers usually added philosophico-political criteria: the savage belonged to the natural order. He was without fixed habitat, without religion, without laws, without customs, the embodiment of human origins. Yet he was capable of acceding to history and to a policed society so long as his natural character was not corrupted by contact with Europeans. The barbarian, however, already belonged to history: he formed nations, he established states, but he did not enjoy the protection of regular laws and his knowledge and customs remained, or reverted to being, crude. For barbarism was what preceded, threatened, or came after civilization. "Nations have all oscillated," wrote Diderot, "from barbarism to the policed state, from the policed state to barbarism, until unforeseen causes have brought them to an equilibrium which they never perfectly maintain."[12]

Gibbon, however, did not distinguish between the savage and the barbarian. In this respect, he was behind the times, still fixed on the historical dichotomy of the beginning of the century. For he was not really interested in man in nature, the concept of the savage that so engaged the philosophers of the Enlightenment. His perception was more historical than philosophical; it was perhaps entirely historical. The fall of the Roman Empire is played out between a civilized society, on the one hand, and those outside this society, on the other. Ultimately this former reader of Thucydides and Tacitus adopts the classical distinction between Greek and barbarian, or Roman and barbarian: the barbarian is the one who is on the other side of the frontier. But Gibbon also calls him "savage," in part at least because the word was so commonly used in the eighteenth century, but also to emphasize the gap that separated him from civilized man.

One has only to read chapter 9 of Gibbon's history, which is devoted to the Germanic tribes, to become convinced of this. Here Gibbon closely follows Tacitus, his master and model. He wants to understand what has made those "wild barbarians of Germany" Rome's most formidable enemy. No cities, no letters, no arts, no monetary system—such are the negative traits which define what he calls a "savage state." When he comes to the famous theme of the Germanic freedoms, so important in the historiography of the period, especially in Montesquieu and Mably whom Gibbon had read attentively, the description of the system of assemblies and the independence of the soldiers do not arouse any "democratic" sympathy in him. The backward state of German customs, letters, and arts carries its own condemnation to his way of thinking; on several occasions he refers to the Germanic tribes as "savages," until he arrived at the following perception which more precisely defined his thought: "Modern nations are fixed and permanent societies, connected among themselves by laws and government, bound to their native soil by arts and agriculture. The German tribes were voluntary and fluctuating associations of soldiers, almost of savages."

An extraordinary judgment for a writer so passionate about the historiography of his time, a witness of the central controversy of French historiography over the origins of the nation: were they Roman or Frankish? At no time did Gibbon seem interested in what had constituted in Europe since the sixteenth century one of the *raisons d'être* of history and the fundamental impetus for it: the quest for origins, the original contract from which a nation arose. Of the two questions that the eighteenth century posed for history—what is a nation? what is civilization?—Gibbon was only interested in the second. He had read Boulainvilliers, Montesquieu, Dubos, and Mably, not as their heir, but purely as an erudite, as an ethnologist of the Franks. As a result, he deprived the Germanic peoples of their basic dignity; they existed only as "near-savages."

The same sort of judgment can easily be found when Gibbon deals with other peoples whose movements threatened Rome. In chapter 26, for example, Gibbon describes the nomadic tribes of the Far East, whose growth would ultimately affect the Empire by driving the Goths to the West, along with "so many [other] hostile tribes more savage than themselves." In discussing those populations of nomadic shepherds, Gibbon says that what makes the study of them so simple is their proximity to animality:

> . . . it is much easier to ascertain the appetites of a quadruped than the speculations of a philosopher; and the savage tribes of mankind, as they approach nearer to the conditions of animals, preserve a stronger resemblance to themselves and to each other. The uniform stability of their manners is the natural consequence of the imperfection of their faculties. Reduced to a similar situation, their wants, their desires, their enjoyments, still continue the same; and the influence of food or climate, which in a more improved state of society, is suspended or subdued by so many moral causes, most powerfully contributes to form and to maintain the national character of Barbarians.

Consequently, barbarians are savages. Gibbon recognizes neither natural man nor the "noble savage." There is only historical man, and certain of his manifestations, unchecked by reason, remain bogged down in a dependency predicated upon natural conditions, stagnation, and the absence of a policed state. At the other end is civilized man, who is not necessarily the conqueror: the fall of the Empire proves that point. The paradox is that Gibbon was so interested in the victory of barbarism over civilization.

This paradox is resolved when one realizes that Gibbon wrote a second history alongside the first, but distinct nonetheless; this second history is that of Christianity. Gibbon was the first historian to treat the history of Rome and the history of religion together. This innovation lies behind the chronological distortion to which he subjected Roman history: he was trying to comprehend not just the secrets of the greatness of Rome, not just the collapse of that greatness, but beyond that the passage from imperial Rome to papal Rome. If the fall of the Empire encompassed all the Middle Ages, it was because the historian sought to describe more than the fall of a civilization invaded by barbarians. Ultimately he says so, with a disarming directness: "I have described the triumph of barbarism and religion" (chapter 71).

"Barbarism and religion"—the phrase clearly indicates that if, in the dramatic history of Rome's fall, the two phenomena contributed to the same result, they nevertheless remained distinct. Religion helped barbarism to win, but it was not itself barbaric. For the religious phenomenon was multiform because it was rooted in that fear and ignorance which were inseparable from human society. Gibbon was an enthusiastic disciple of Bayle, who perfectly reflected Enlightenment thinking on the subject. But he goes further than Bayle. He was the first historian systematically to place religion in a relative position in human events, which hardly means that he reduced its importance—on the contrary, he paid particular attention to it—but that he integrated it in all its many forms into the societies and empires whose history he outlined. There is thus in Gibbon a historian of paganism, a historian of the cults of the ancient Germans, a historian of Islam, and a historian of Christianity. Religion is a cultural phenomenon which he examines with great care, even to details of its refinements, as the chapters devoted to the theological controversies of the first centuries of Christianity demonstrate.

Religion thus becomes a part of the great social and historical drama of the fall of the Roman Empire. But when Gibbon writes that he has described "the triumph of barbarism and religion," he means only one religion: Christianity. The analysis of the religious phenomenon, of the generic, becomes specific. In the same way that, in the

eyes of this gentleman-scholar, there have been several societies in history which have
attained the status of, and embodied, civilization, though none so perfectly as the
Roman Empire, so too, inversely, have there been many religions in human history,
though probably none of them quite so noxious as Christianity. Here we reach the
second major theme in the *Decline and Fall*. The first revolved around the external
confrontation between Rome and the barbarians, the second around the internal
disintegration of the Empire at the hands of the Christians. It is a Rome weakened by
"the spirit of Christianity," we might say, borrowing from Montesquieu, that is
finally conquered by the barbarian invasions. And the real victor, as the history of
both the Eastern and Western Middle Ages shows, was Christianity.

This is perhaps the reason—or the existential impulse—that led Gibbon to write,
not a panorama of Roman civilization, but an account only of its fall. Of course, like
his contemporaries, Gibbon was sensitive to the transience of history's great successes, but this feeling hardly justified his having extended his account as far as the
fifteenth century! If he wished to encompass the entire Middle Ages into the fall of
Rome and under what was, in that context, a very strange title, it was because
Christianity's history fascinated him as much as, perhaps even more than, that of
Rome. He invested his account with his hatred, not of the Christian faith, but of the
church, the priests, and monks; he committed to it his struggle against intolerance and
fanaticism; he deployed for the purpose the whole anticlerical tradition of the French
Enlightenment.

He was too good a historian, however, to say—and he never did say—that the
Christianity of the established churches for which he professed no love was a form of
"barbarism." On the contrary, he seized every opportunity to show how Christianity
was in fact the important reconstructive principle of his historical world—the Europe
built upon the debris of the Roman Empire. On the one hand, he wanted to express,
through the three-dimensional historical space in which civilization, barbarism, and
Christianity evolved, his preference for a pre-Christian civilization rather than a
Christianized barbarism. But, on the other hand, he constantly—and more radically—showed that what motivated his worship of Rome, its values, its "spirit," and its
moral figures was the existence of a civilization in its chemically pure state—and that
meant without the church.

REFERENCES
    [1]E. Benveniste, "Civilisation, contribution à l'histoire du mot," in *Hommage à Lucien Febvre* (Paris,
1954).
    [2]*Politique des Romains dans la religion* (1716).
    [3]*Considérations sur les causes de la grandeur des Romains et de leur décadence* (1734).
    [4]*Voyage de Graz à La Haye* (Ed. de La Pléiade), I, pp. 663 and 69.
    [5]*Memoirs of My Life*, ed. Georges A. Bonnard (London, 1966), p. 134.
    [6]*The History of the Decline and Fall of the Roman Empire*, chap. 3.
    [7]*Esprit des lois* XVIII.2.
    [8]*History of Civil Society* (1767), pp. 124, 185.
    [9]*Recherches philosophiques sur les Américains* (1768), I, p. 218.
    [10]*L'Esprit des usages et des coutumes*. The development of these ideas owes a great deal to the attention that
Edna Lemay has devoted to that book in her recent study "Naissance de l'anthropologie sociale en
France au XVIIIe siècle: Jean Nicholas Démeunier et l'Esprit des usages et des coutumes" (unpublished
· dissertation, Paris, 1972).
    [11]*Histoire de l'Amérique*, *passim*.
    [12]*Histoire des Indes*, cited in M. Duchet, *Anthropologie et histoire au siècle des Lumières* (Paris, 1971).

FRANK E. MANUEL

Edward Gibbon: Historien-Philosophe

WRITING HIS AUTOBIOGRAPHY at the height of his eminence, Gibbon could look down patronizingly, yet fondly, on the fledgling author of the *Essai sur l'étude de la littérature* (1761): "I shall presume to say that the Essay does credit to a young writer of two and twenty years of age, who had read with taste, who thinks with freedom, and who writes in a foreign language with spirit and elegance."[1] This mixed bag of reflections on the worth and uses of the study of ancient literature contained more penetrating revelations about his image of himself as a man with the vocation of a historian than he later recognized. Doubtless the mature Gibbon would have retracted some of the grandiloquent generalities and surrounded others with cautions; but his practice as a historian never departed far from the model of the perfect *historien-philosophe* delineated in this youthful exercise.

The term *philosoph-historicus* is an old one going back to Jean Bodin, though I doubt whether Gibbon had read the *Methodus, ad Facilem Historiarum Cognitionem* (1566) at this point in his career, and it appears in none of the catalogues of his libraries. Voltaire had not yet made popular the phrase *philosophie de l'histoire*, which he first adopted as the title of a pseudonymous work in 1765, and to my knowledge Gibbon at no time employed it. When in the *Essai* he set forth the considerations that should govern the philosophical historian (a word combination reasonably current by then), he was acting independently, as though oblivious of predecessors, with the confidence of a bold young innovator breaking new ground in the conceptualization of history-writing.

Gibbon made a vital distinction between the creative genius in a field of human endeavor and the plodder: the former was always a philosopher. Granted that the purpose of any historian was to collect facts and deal with causes and effects, the truly philosophical historian had to be endowed with a unique capacity: to single out those facts that dominated a whole system of interrelationships. He used the word "system" loosely to connote a nexus of relations within a spatio-temporal parameter, not a rigid philosophical theory. Gibbon had imbibed the prejudice of the age against the *esprit de système*, and, while he would write history *en philosophe*, he was no builder of philosophical structures. Certain critical facts, few in number, were the springs of action (*ressorts*) that put everything in the system into motion. Philosophical historians of genius who were "capable of distinguishing these types of fact in the vast chaos of events and drawing them forth pure and unalloyed" were rare creatures. The facts they focused upon were not necessarily the sonorous formal pronouncements of historical figures or the most dramatic events of history. On the contrary, *petits traits* and apparently insignificant customs and manners might hold within them the great secrets that propelled nations and ages into movement.

From the outset Gibbon conceived of the historian as a man charged with unveiling, with probing the innermost recesses, of past societies. This sense of mission might be related psychologically to a longing for primal knowledge and a metaphysical anguish about where he came from, to fantasies about his ancestry, to boyhood images of an *Ile de la félicité*, and to the womb-like libraries in which he enclosed himself in London and Lausanne—but I shall forgo the attempt. Gibbon himself preferred facts not deliberately reported by the actors as more likely to convey essential information than public decisions of historical protagonists. It would be grossly anachronistic to say that he had a theory of unconscious acts, but he was creeping up on the idea. "There is no façade in the performance of trivial actions. One undresses when one expects not to be seen. But the curious inquirer tries to penetrate the most secret hiding-places."[2] Clinicians have found that voyeurism and the fear of being seen, passions not uncommon among some of greatest historians and archaeologists, are often combined in the same person. Professor Bowersock points out that Tacitus, Gibbon's ideal philosophical historian, was the model for his search into the *arcanum* of the Empire—such a probing may also have had deeper roots.

While Gibbon pleaded for the importance of small details, he categorically rejected the Pascalian Cleopatra's nose thesis; there were no great effects from minor causes. Details, however, far from being devoid of significance, were crucial to the philosophical historian who could interpret them as revelatory of the profound springs of a nation's action. Young Gibbon dared to challenge the great d'Alembert, who in one of his essays had casually proposed a radical way of dealing with the fast-growing accumulation of unassimilated data in all branches of science that threatened to engulf society: at the end of each century, d'Alembert counseled, mankind should select those that added to positive knowledge and throw the rest away. On the contrary, Gibbon argued, no fact however trivial should be destroyed because one could not know what a Montesquieu would make of it. Montesquieu had discovered the spirit of the laws, not in the declamations of popes and kings, but in the multiple minor characteristics of nations. This esteem for an exhaustive knowledge of all things in the past, without discrimination, which went along with a vindication of erudition, had a limited number of enthusiastic proponents in the eighteenth century, Vico among them; but their voices were feebler than the dogmatic Cartesian condemnation of history as an obfuscatory burden on the human mind in its search for truth.

Gibbon's ideal philosophical historian had some attributes that were later associated with the romantics. He had to be capable of penetrating the mentality of every nation and people, even of following an Iroquois's mode of reasoning. Gibbon may not have had a Vichian conception of the *mente* of successive ages as embodying different modes of perception, and he never hypostasized *tre spezie di natura*. Whatever distinctions he recognized among different ages and nations, there was only one human nature, modifiable under varying conditions. But the idea that a historian, by entering into an alien mentality that reasoned falsely, could nevertheless discover a signal truth about human nature was already prominent in the *Essai* and underlay Gibbon's attempt to grapple with the theological disputations of the early church.

By implication, Gibbon made apparent his own views on the potency of both systematic rational purposiveness and caprice in human behavior. While other historians had portrayed men as either *trop systématiques* or *trop capricieux*, he saw them as an amalgam of reason and caprice. Demonstrating the rational purposiveness of great personages, perhaps the major historiographical preoccupation of the time, was not his exclusive concern, because he had observed that expressed intent usually concealed men's real passions and penchants. People were driven to vicious conduct by passion, and they then justified their actions by subtle rationalizing. The dominant forces in history were emotive, not reasonable. In an even more striking passage (unconnected with his description of the philosophical historian), Gibbon naughtily confessed: "I like to see the judgments of men take a tincture from their prejudices. . . ."[3] Reviewing the parade of emperors and churchmen in the six volumes of the *Decline and Fall*, he rarely missed an opportunity to savor his malice by showing up the hypocrites who covered their desires with legal or theological mouthings. But he played holier-than-thou only in extreme cases. For the most part, he recognized the fickle superficiality of his own reasonings in the face of desire. On one occasion he flippantly wrote his friend Holroyd (later Lord Sheffield): "As I used to reason against riding, so I can now argue for it; and indeed the principal use, I know in human reason is, when called upon, to furnish arguments for what we have an inclination to do."[4]

While history was the science of cause and effect, it was the part of the philosophical historian to look for general and determinate, not particular, causes. Gibbon excluded the providential as a primary cause beyond his ken and, at least in later utterances, the presumed absolute laws of history or universal historical systems, the most common of which was still the worn-out formula of the four monarchies derived from the Book of Daniel. The Bossuet whose writings had been instrumental in Gibbon's brief conversion to Catholicism had lost his sway over the apostate. With youthful abandon Gibbon proposed a "philosophical history of man" that would yield a knowledge of general, though finite, causes. He called for a new Montesquieu to carry out this project; and who was this Montesquieu but Gibbon himself? "He would reveal for us [these general causes] controlling the rise and fall of empires; successively assuming the features of fortune, prudence, courage, weakness, acting without the concurrence of particular causes, and sometimes even triumphing over them."[5] This paragon among philosophical historians would follow the operation of profound causes in long-term trends, whose slow but certain influence changed imperceptibly the face of the earth. The idea that events happen "insensibly," which became a tick in the later volumes of the *Decline and Fall*, had made its appearance in the phrase *sans qu'on puisse s'appercevoir*.[6] Manners, religion, and whatever depended on opinion were the primary fields in which these secret causes left their mark, without anyone's being consciously aware of the fundamental changes society was experiencing.

The key word in Gibbon's philosophico-historical reflections in the *Essai* is *ressort*, one of the widely current, baffling terms of eighteenth-century Anglo-French thought that are so difficult to understand precisely. It has obvious, mechanistic overtones, but it was commonly applied to individual and social action by writers who by no means subscribed to the conception of an *homme-machine*. Since Montaigne, *ressort*, by analogy to a clock or an automaton, had come to mean a moving cause, an energizing force, generally hidden, that created movement.[7] In the mid-eighteenth century, medical terminology was beginning to mingle vitalistic with mechanical ideas in explaining the life-giving force in animal bodies, and such notions were adapted to the study of history and society. Gibbon's "spring" is eclectic and fuses mechanistic and vitalistic connotations without his having had much contact with contemporary medical controversies.

Gibbon's remarks about *ressorts* in the *Essai* can be illustrated from the *Decline and Fall*, though he did not repeat the sweeping theoretical imperatives of the earlier work. His magnificent choice of 1,300 years of the history of the physical entity that was the Roman Empire was at once extensive and finite, a universe of discourse that allowed him to avoid both the teleology of the theologian's universal history and the amorphousness of the contemporary academic scholarship with its disparate minutiae. Within this world of the Roman Empire, we can now discern in the *Decline and Fall* three subordinate and relatively autonomous systems of relationships—to resurrect the terminology of the *Essai*—that have definable inner springs of action: the Roman, the Christian, and the barbarian. And we can watch Gibbon shift his spotlight from one system to another with consummate skill as he unfolded the drama of Rome's decline—the theatrical analogy is eminently appropriate for this inveterate playgoer.

Gibbon was specific about the pervasive forces that drove each of these determinate systems. The Roman ruling passions—their "springs"—were military glory and civic virtue, which impelled them to extend the Empire to the uttermost frontiers of barbarism, a stock eighteenth-century explanation of Roman hegemony. The exercise of military prowess was in the end a major element in the breakdown of the Roman system. Gibbon is the grand historian of the working out of the ultimate consequences of these *ressorts* in the physical and moral realms: imperial overextension led to the loss of a sense of liberty among nations in the Roman world, the breakdown of civil and military administration, and the corruption of morals. The springs of the Christian system were of a different character. Zeal and fanaticism in the propagation of faith, passions derived from the Jews, and a promise of life after death brought about Christianity's spiritual triumph throughout the Roman Empire and at the same time undermined the civic virtue of the Romans. Religious disputation and persecution that further weakened the cohesion of the body politic were inherent in the fanatical nature of Christianity itself, so different from the tolerant spirit of Roman paganism. And finally there was the system of the barbarians, whose *ressorts* were the most elementary and primitive. They were driven by fear of starvation, their natural cruelty, and an innate need to wander. The interplay of the three systems, presented as if they were characters in a tragedy, became the "greatest, perhaps, and most awful scene, in the history of mankind."[8]

I doubt whether Gibbon sat down and deliberately sketched any such total pattern in advance—we know that his history grew like Topsy and that the three stages in the publication of the six volumes, 1776, 1781, and 1788, mark disjunctures in his thinking—but the achievement of this type of configuration involving the discovery of a few concealed springs and an exposition in detail of how they persistently operated over a long period of time were already goals of the young historian-in-the-making back in 1761.

Gibbon described other overlapping or derivative systems of relationships, the separate universe of the thousand-year history of Byzantium, for example. Here a system was formed that had no original motive drive of its own. Its lifeless hands held on to a portion of the territories of the Romans and its voice parroted the ideas of the Greeks. It was dominated by no other passion than the mere maintenance and preservation of its inheritance. This was a closed system in a state of stagnation.

But what were the origins of the particular "springs" themselves in any system of relationships? Except for a few remarks about geography, Gibbon was not very enlightening on this score: remote and primary causes were not his field of investigation. Sometimes the springs of action appear to resemble innate components of national character; at other times they seem to be extensions onto the body politic of the prevalent psychology of the ruling passion in individuals.

Gibbon was familiar with the long catalogue of forces and active agents that in Montesquieu's theory fashioned the *esprit* of a nation, an idea not alien to his own concept of *ressort*. For the neophyte in search of a historical model, the narrative had to demonstrate the interpenetration of these elements and their mutual reinforcement, creating a unity. In entries of his journal in the sixties, he explicitly rejected the work plan of the French Historiographer-Royal, Voltaire, exemplified in *The Age of Louis XIV*, where each type of human activity had been isolated and boxed in a separate chapter. To write history *en philosphe* would mean establishing interconnections and tracing their operation through time. Montesquieu's structuralist tendencies, which our own contemporaries appreciate, were flaws in Gibbon's eyes, and he violated chronological order only in the last books of the history, where the barbarians become the major protagonists, for aesthetic and literary reasons.

A philosophico-historical problem that preoccupied Gibbon in the *Decline and Fall* is only touched upon in the *Essai*, the phenomenon of progression and decline in the arts and sciences and in the dominion of empires. Gibbon did not entertain the abstraction of the idea of progress or perfectibility, but he dwelt upon one aspect of the concept, as he tried to define his position in the literary quarrel of the ancients and the moderns, a hangover from the seventeenth-century disputation. Wrestling with the preferences in 1761, he came out nowhere in particular. While modern Europeans might surpass the ancients in the politics of domestic tranquility, the present peaceful situation of society was not favorable to the genius of poetry, in which the ancients excelled. There is a dilution of Rousseau's pessimism in Gibbon's confidence that sciences will make manners more gentle and act as a countervailing force to the tendency of luxury to make men languid. The analogy he drew from the *Iliad*, however, hardly turns him into a progressionist: the sciences (and he means knowledge, not merely the physical sciences) are likened to prayers that fly over the earth in the wake of injustice to mollify the fury of this cruel divinity. Gibbon did not yet accept anything remotely resembling the proposition of Turgot's *Sorboniques* of 1750—the inevitable continuation of progression somewhere on the globe despite local setbacks. His analysis was often painfully shallow, as he attributed the flourishing or decay of one or another art or branch of knowledge to a mere change of fashion.

The *Encyclopédie* had underplayed historical and literary subjects in favor of mechanics and positive science, and in adopting the Baconian schema had depressed history to the low estate of the art of memory. At this period of his life, when he was trying mightily to justify the study of ancient literature and combat the denigration of history among many of the reigning Encyclopedists, Gibbon refused to be impressed by the much-vaunted triumphs of physical science. There is an undercurrent of hostility on the part of this defender of literary culture against the physical scientists with their pretensions to extending over all forms of human knowledge the spirit of geometry, "that imperious queen who, not content with ruling, proscribes her sister sciences, and declares all reasoning hardly worthy of the name that is not concerned with lines and numbers."[9] Young Gibbon went so far as to contest the idea that the scientific improvements of the moderns necessarily represented an advance over the ancients, and his vindication of the study of ancient literature was intended to preserve it by proving that its utility was at least as great as that of the new physical sciences. Only rather late in life did Gibbon take to auditing lectures on astronomy and chemistry, and whenever there was occasion for mentioning mathematics he promptly shied away from it. His appreciation of technology probably grew with time, as we shall see; but a certain ambivalence about it persisted. Young Gibbon was a man of one culture and his concept of civilization did not necessarily require scientific and technological triumphs. When he wrote of civilization he surely implied a widespread use of the mechanical arts and the observance of legal norms and civility in social intercourse among members of his class; but high civilization still meant, first and foremost, literary-philosophical culture. Only three of the one hundred and thirty-nine pages in the 1785 subject catalogue of his Lausanne library are devoted to physical sciences.[10]

Though the mature Gibbon was in touch with the major currents of thought on both sides of the Channel—his Anglo-French education was comprehensive in most branches of history, literature, theology, and philosophy—two writers, one French and one English, who viewed history philosophically played the principal roles in his intellectual life and help to locate him in the spectrum of prevailing ideas, Montesquieu and Hume. Adam Ferguson, with whom he was personally acquainted, is less of a direct influence than an interesting parallel, though Gibbon reviewed the *Essay on Civil Society*, and the *Decline and Fall* echoes some of Ferguson's apprehensions about the loss of virtue among over-polished peoples. Voltaire, who had received Gibbon without being particularly impressed by the young Englishman, left his imprint on the style and wit with which the theological controversies of the early church were treated. Both, of course, had drunk deeply of the patristic sources and reveled in turning their pious traditions upside down. Gibbon's chapter 15, "On the Progress of the Christian Religion," which aroused the orthodox, bears more than passing resemblance to Voltaire's *Dieu et les hommes* (1769), with its chapter headings on "Des causes des progrès du christianisme" and "De la fin du monde et de la resurrection annoncée de son temps" as well as its statistical digressions on *barbaries chrétiennes*.

In the *Essai*, Montesquieu was the modern constantly cited with favor. Gibbon even applied to himself the closing phrase of the preface to the *Esprit des lois*: "Ed io anche son pittore." Such reservations to Montesquieu's thesis as Gibbon had arose from his own commitment to the chronological method of exposition and from occasional misgivings about Montesquieu's promulgation of historical generalities as if they were laws of nature rather than "determinate" generalities limited in time and space—though it would not require too diligent a research to compile from the history observations on human conduct and the motivations of men that appear to be universal, after the manner of Montesquieu. Contemporary critics were quick to recognize that some of the underlying conceptions in the *Decline and Fall*, the explanations for the decline, were not very different from Montesquieu's two causes for the decadence of the Romans. Montesquieu, however, had concentrated primarily on the evil consequences of extension, whereas Gibbon introduced Christianity as a principal, an open affront to religion that Montesquieu would have been reluctant to risk. While there are obvious similarities between Montesquieu's theory of the different ruling passions of nations and Gibbon's idea of the profound, deep-rooted causes that were the springs of action in a society, the scale of Gibbon's six volumes was of an entirely different order from Montesquieu's elegant little treatise. And if Gibbon adopted a number of Montesquieu's generalities, they were almost commonplaces by the latter part of the century. The *Encyclopédie* had summarized them in an article on the Roman Empire, and the basic formula, "it sank under the weight of its own greatness and power," would re-echo in Gibbon's text.

In my judgment, it was Hume's influence that was the more pervasive in the formation of the philosophical historian. Hume, too, was of the older generation, but he did not die until after the publication of the first volume of Gibbon's history and the bestowal of his accolade upon the new literary knight. Gibbon treasured praise from the dying Hume above all other appreciations, and he kept quoting the words of approval to all his correspondents. Though there is no evidence that the tightly reasoned *Treatise on Human Nature* meant much to him, we know from his journal that he read the *History of the Stuarts* in the early sixties, and arguments from the *Natural History of Religion* and other essays were cited a number of times in the footnotes of the first volume of the *Decline and Fall*. But it was no single work of Hume that dominated Gibbon; it was the man and his writings in their totality that were congenial to him and set Hume above all other contemporary philosphical writers. We know of the personal acquaintance of the two men, of Hume's securing a clerk's job in the government for Gibbon's lifelong friend Georges Deyverdun, of Hume's brief contribution to the abortive venture of Gibbon and Deyverdun into literary journalism, the *Mémoires littéraires de la Grande Bretagne*, which ran for two issues, of Gibbon's combing Hume's essays for information as well as spiritual guidance. But beyond all this, close affinities can be found in what these two corpulent bachelors considered to be moral and civilized. Moreover, neither Hume nor Gibbon had any doubt that it was the responsibility of the historian to act as a moral judge. The ideal values in Hume's *Enquiry Concerning the Principles of Morals*, the combination of the *utile* and the *dolce*, were also Gibbon's. There is not a virtue Hume extolled that Gibbon would have failed to embrace. If one ransacked the writings of Hume and Gibbon and drew up a list of positive and pejorative characteristics cited by each, one record would mirror the other. Gibbon constantly measured historical personages by these standards and then established history as the world court of judgment. "Whatever subject he has chosen," Gibbon wrote of the important office of the historian, "whatever person he introduces, he owes to himself, to the present age, and to posterity, a just and perfect delineation of all that may be praised, of all that may be excused, and of all that must be censured."[11] One of his more pompous utterances.

To win Gibbon's plaudits, men of the past had to exhibit the same kind of civilized behavior as contemporary gentlemen. They could not be addicted to anything—women, the hunt, wine, honors, godliness. They had to favor a policy of peace and reconciliation. They were obliged not to act dishonorably, break their word, deceive, be hypocrites, delude themselves. His heroes were men who promulgated codes of law, established order, fostered the arts and sciences, extended mercy to the vanquished. In the end, his estimates of private individuals and his descriptions of historical persons became interchangeable counters. He was always playing with chiaroscuro effects. He juxtaposed virtues and vices to present a credible human being. But to meet with the approval of the philosophical historian sitting as the Great Judge the balance of a man had to be weighted in the direction of the eighteenth-century virtues Hume had identified in the *Enquiry*.

The civilized way as Gibbon recognized it had been embodied in two societies, the Roman (with side glances at the Greek) and his own Britain (with side glances at the pre-1789 French). For both Hume and Gibbon, civilization was a fragile thing. It was forever being assailed by the forces of darkness—religious fanaticism and mass barbarism. Gibbon had no more admiration than Hume for the pretensions of the religious to a sublime experience or for the grandeur of the heroic virtues. Both were content to rest with what Hume, with a touch of self-mockery, called the aldermanic virtues. This does not mean that Gibbon never approached the fire—occasional passions flicker briefly and two friendships lasting for decades bordered on love; but once he was free from his father, his overt equilibrium was only. rarely upset by onslaughts of emotion. Deep anxieties existed, but his biographers have thus far failed to probe beneath the mask of complacency.

Like his master, David Hume, Gibbon stood for civilization defined in terms of the class and culture in which he was born and bred. Though he was the grandson of a director of the South Sea Company, he identified himself with the style of the aristocracy of Britain and France and the "bourgeoisie" who were the nobility of the Swiss republics. If the report is true that Gibbon and Deyverdun were Freemasons walking in the footsteps of the Huguenot aristocrat who was Deyverdun's uncle, a known Freemason, the values of aristocratic Freemasonry that had abandoned the sword for the virtues of benevolence and peace were those of Gibbon. (There was a list of regular lodges of Freemasons in his library.[12]) He could be accused of inconstancy in love, in religion, and in political party allegiance—and he was sensitive to the charges of being a turncoat in all three areas—but he would have been profoundly dismayed if he had been found wanting in the virtues that both he and Hume associated with civility. If civility is set at the heart of his intellectual and emotional existence, his work and his life show a remarkable degree of harmony, despite the "contradictions" in the man Gibbon, of which he was conscious and which he sometimes flaunted.

The destruction of Roman culture on the part of the Christian ecclesiastics could not be forgiven. Compared to the religious fanatics, the barbarians had virtues or at least the seeds of virtue, especially a love of liberty, which when tamed by the revived law of the Romans again restored civility. Mankind had paid dearly for the hegemony of the churchmen, and never again should it countenance their rule over society: that was one of the morals of the story. Gibbon was not the implacable enemy of religion; he would merely keep it in its place, the civil place it had occupied in the Roman world before the advent of Jewish and Christian zealots. After his conversion back to the Church of England, Gibbon would defend the institution as necessary to civilized existence—a utilitarian argument, already present in Montesquieu, that was in consonance with Gibbon's reputed Freemasonic affiliation. Hume's chronicle of the evil contagion of enthusiasm in his history of the Stuarts had a profound influence on Gibbon's world-historical view. The seventeenth-century "enthusiasts" had made an assault on the recovered civilization of antiquity, and it was fortunate for mankind that they had been worsted so that eighteenth-century Britain might exist.

Though Gibbon still considered himself an *historien-philosophe*, in 1776, on the eve of a century that witnessed the appearance of the major European systematic philosophies of history (old style), he was untouched by this kind of theorizing. Vico's *Scienza Nuova*, whose last version appeared seven years after Gibbon's birth, was no more within his sphere than it was within that of the overwhelming number of European intellectuals. The German thinkers Herder and Kant and the Swiss Isaak Iselin, who published philosophies of history during Gibbon's lifetime, did not come to his notice (he knew no German and at most was acquainted with German thought through his friend Deyverdun, who had translated *Werther*). Suzanne Curchod's daughter, the redoubtable Madame de Staël, had not yet invaded Germany, returning with her Teutonic trophies. The currents of intellectual influence generally moved from west to east in the eighteenth century, rarely the other way. Gibbon did know of the efforts of Englishmen and Frenchmen who speculated on the origins and growth of civilization, such as Goguet, Court de Gébelin, Boulanger, Monboddo, but the closest Gibbon seriously approached to the early history of mankind was a flirtation with Isaac Newton's new system of world chronology. Gibbon's seal was adorned with Plato's head, but like many literary gentlemen of the age he did not appreciate metaphysics ancient or modern, neither Plato nor Leibniz, whose philosophy he at one point summarized in vulgar clichés.

When he came to maturity, Gibbon at first turned his back on the grand design he had outlined for himself in his youth. It was as if he took fright and swung in the opposite direction, in his first projects seeking refuge in such little worlds as a life of Sir Walter Raleigh, or the history of the liberty of the Swiss, or the history of the republic of Florence under the Medicis. His final settling on a daring subject, the decline of the Roman Empire, represents at least a partial return to philosophical history. As he struggled through the maze, he tried to recapture the general goals he had outlined in his youth. The conclusion of the first volume (he then thought he had come to the end of his project), which raised in a forthright manner the problem of the causes of the decline, harked back to his early quest for general and determinate causes. His presentation was probably spiked with a desire to shock his readers, much as he would entrance the ladies in a salon with his wicked *boutades*.

By 1781, fortune having smiled upon him, Gibbon became more adventuresome, and at the end of Volume III he again picked up philosophico-historical questions that were preoccupying European intellectuals, above all the decline and fall of civilization in general. Many of the illustrious *philosophes* in the later seventeen-seventies had begun to feel that their society was on the brink of a decline; it was not only Diderot's advancing age that led him to identify himself with Seneca, though the plain fact that the rambunctious *philosophes* were getting old and beginning to die off was certainly an element in the formation of this sentiment. In his last years Diderot often expressed the idea that the renascence of the arts and sciences, that flowering of civilization which had reached its zenith with the Encyclopedists, had run its course. The internal difficulties of the French monarchy were patent, and the corruption of morals was widely portrayed in France, often in a new type of literature. Gibbon read the novels of Restif de la Bretonne, the "Rousseau des ruisseaux"—Restif is even mentioned in the autobiography—and Laclos's *Liaisons dangereuses*, along with his normal diet of works of erudition. The chronicler of the moral decadence of the Romans was not impervious to the new emotional tonalities that were being sounded in France.

The insurgency of the American colonists created political anxieties in Britain which, though different from those inspired by French "decadence," affected Gibbon more immediately. The Gibbon who had come to live his history far more profoundly than the gentleman of fashion was prone to admit could not escape the analogy between Rome and Britain. Sitting in Parliament, he fancied himself a Roman senator, and he was conscious of his partiality toward the old paganism. The distance he achieved artistically from the events and characters he portrayed was often a self-consciously Horatian pose. The daily events of the War for American Independence, 1775-1783, during the very period when Gibbon was writing a major part of the history, were constantly raising in his mind a history of the decline of the British Empire. Parallel lives and parallel histories were part of the literary canon. The Abbé Mably, Gibbon's competitor in historiography, had composed a parallel history of the Romans and the French (though he later repudiated the grossness of the analogy). Gibbon never actually wrote a parallel history of the British and the Romans, but the comparison was in the background of his thought. No nineteenth-century positivist, he was untroubled by the reality that when one depicts past ages one draws them, "sans s'en appercevoir," after models that are before one's eyes.[13] His letters during this decade are full of the resemblances between Britain and Rome. Often they were a subject of wit. "As for the man of letters and the statesman," he wrote to Georges Deyverdun, "rest content with the knowledge that the declines of the Two Empires, the Roman and the British, are advancing at an equal pace. I have, to be sure, contributed more effectively to the former. In the 'Senate' I am still just as you left me, *mutus pecus*."[14] But there was genuine concern beneath the jesting.

The apprehensions of many eighteenth-century *philosophes* over the internal decay of their society were reinforced by the haunting fear of another barbarian irruption from the heart of darkness that would overwhelm Western civilization in a repetition of the awful spectacle of the fall of the Roman Empire. Tartary was usually assigned as the point of departure for the invasion, though sometimes it was intentionally left vague or declared to be unknowable. The *Avertissement* to the eighth volume of the *Encyclopédie* is perhaps the *locus classicus* for the expression of this anxiety. "It is possible that a revolution [from the context it is clear that Diderot meant a massive outburst destructive of civilization] whose seed may even now be burgeoning in some remote region of the world or secretly incubating at the very center of civilized countries should break out with time, overthrow cities, again disperse peoples, and bring back ignorance and darkness." After the publication of the *Decline and Fall*, Condorcet, last of the *philosophes*, continuing to grapple with possible negations of *progrès indéfini*, in his prognostication of the future progressions of the human mind, reflected that "only one *combinaison*, a new invasion of the Tartars from Asia, might impede this revolution."[15] (Here the fluid word refers to the diffusion of Enlightenment throughout the globe.)

In the *Encyclopédie*, Diderot's response to his own fear of a recrudescence of barbarism either from within or from without was a magnificent boast uttered in a moment of triumph when his task was nearing completion: "All will not be lost, if a single copy of this work survives." Condorcet's manuscripts are dotted with practical projects for encapsulating all knowledge into an encyclopedia written in a universal, hieroglyph-like language and burying it in a fireproof repository, protection in case of geological cataclysms as well as political upheavals; and in the *Esquisse* (1795) he argues at length the proposition that the eventuality of a barbarian invasion is henceforth impossible. Gibbon prefigured much of Condorcet's reasoning, though he avoided dogmatic terms such as "impossible" and customarily modified bold assertions with adverbs of doubt: "perhaps," "probably," "possibly," "essentially."

At the end of chapter 38 of the *Decline and Fall*, in a section entitled "General Observations on the Fall of the Roman Empire in the West," Gibbon tried to dispel the gloom of Britain's fading prospects by dismissing the question of her decline in favor of the broader problem of chances for survival of European civilization as a whole. And here, putting aside the discomfiture of the patriot, Gibbon offered his fellow-men the consolations of a philosophical historian—though he provided himself amply with loopholes and escape clauses, lest he be one day judged a false prophet. These "Observations" are not an integral part—they are surely not a summary—of the three volumes he had completed by 1781, and his remarks might be viewed as an independent response to the contemporary world. Again, Gibbon thought his task was finished in 1781, and he was making final reflections *en philosophe*.

The argument of an absent adversary was simple: If Rome succumbed, what was there so extraordinary about modern European civilization that it might escape a similar destiny? In making reference to Scipio's confession to Polybius that as he watched Carthage burning he recalled the vicissitudes of human affairs and wept as he envisaged the future calamities that would befall Rome, Gibbon bore witness to the weight of the ancient Greek historian's contention that all states and empires were subject to decay. In the face of the overwhelming experience of the nations, the burden of proof that modern Europe was in some way an exception to the common rule was on the philosophical historian. The arguments are Gibbon at his most Gibbonian.

Gibbon advanced three "probable" reasons why Europe should now feel secure, in contrast with the tragic inevitability of the fall of Rome, a structure crumbling under its own weight.

The first reason was based upon a consideration of human geography. Under the Roman Empire, the territories beyond the Rhine and the Danube had been sparsely populated and occupied by roaming tribesmen; once the impetus of a Chinese attack against the Huns set everything into motion, one tribe of barbarians pushed another through the great vacant spaces—a sort of eighteenth-century version of our domino theory—until the tribesmen overflowed onto the territories of Rome. In Gibbon's day, fortunately, the whole of the northeastern part of the Continent was occupied by the civilized Russian Empire of Catherine II, darling of the *philosophes*—remnants of Calmucks and Uzbeks were no longer to be feared—and this extensive settled territory served as a buffer for the republic of Europe. But Gibbon had no sooner made the argument than he withdrew a few paces: "This apparent security should not tempt us to forget, that new enemies, and unknown dangers, may *possibly* [italics his] arise from some obscure people, scarcely visible in the map of the world."[16] There was, after all, the precedent of the Arab conquests. And in a footnote Gibbon indicates that barbarian movement in the other direction was not excluded: "Nor will I venture to ensure the safety of the Chinese empire."

The second reason was related to the contrast between the imperial constitution of the Roman Empire, which had crushed the freedom and spirit of individual client nations and thereby made them more vulnerable, and the numerous independent kingdoms and republics that constituted modern Europe, where there were restraints on the abuses of tyranny and even the most defective governments had some sense of honor and justice. The Europeans, though an agglomeration of polished nations, had not been allowed to fall into somnolence because of the constant emulation among themselves in the acquisition of knowledge and in the practice of industry. Should barbarians once again invade, Gibbon raised the prospect—in some respects absurd— of a united, energetic Europe, comprised of the most varied elements joined to repulse them: "If a savage conqueror should issue from the deserts of Tartary, he must repeatedly vanquish the robust peasants of Russia, the numerous armies of Germany, the gallant nobles of France, and the intrepid freemen of Britain. . . ." Having made this oratorically optimistic point, he again became circumspect—"who, *perhaps* [italics mine], might confederate for their common defence."[17] But then he bounded back: In case of danger there was always America to which the survivors could flee in "ten thousand vessels"; the Atlantic Ocean would serve as an ultimate bulwark of European civilization-in-America against barbarian aggressors. Though writing when the political separation of the colonies from Britain seemed, at least to Gibbon, a foregone conclusion, he soothed his countrymen with the expectation that the manners of Europe would be preserved and the English language diffused over an immense continent.

The third comfort derived from revolutionary transformations in the military art that had resulted from the invention of gunpowder. To this technological superiority—a mainstay of the debate between the ancients and the moderns at least since Bacon—Gibbon added a few new considerations. He had frequently observed in the *Decline and Fall* that despite Roman excellence in devising new instruments of war, the valor of the soldiers fell off with the progressive decline of laws and manners. But modern science and technology had effected changes in the defensive capacities of Europe of a qualitatively different order: industry could now make European cities impervious to barbarian conquest even if the military virtue of the polished Europeans should be found wanting. Once again Gibbon receded from this blanket assurance, but this time by taking refuge in a paradoxical turn of thought. The barbarian invaders might conceivably be victorious over the fortified European cities, but in order to achieve this triumph they would have to become so skilled in the use of sophisticated European techniques of warfare that in the process they would cease to be barbarians. Though conquest might be its fate, European civilization would not be annihilated. This form of reasoning, which saw civilizing processes deriving dialectically from the war-lust of power-hungry despots, was running through Europe and was even adopted by Kant in distant Königsberg, in his famous essay of 1786 on universal history, to strengthen his confidence in the moral improvement of mankind.

But what if all these speculations on the immediately favorable situation of Europe should somehow prove to be vain? To allay his own uncertainties, Gibbon raised his sights and took an anthropological view of the development of mankind. His broadgauged analysis of the "improvements of society" appeared to break the bounds of the historical in support of the presumption that total collapse was no longer possible. Dimensions were enlarged even beyond the European continent, as he examined the progressions from the condition of the human savage over four thousand years earlier to man's present state of civility. The process had had slow beginnings and then redoubled velocity, a changing tempo that Turgot had remarked upon. It was not rectilinear and had experienced moments of rapid downfall. Though Gibbon inherited the Renaissance belief in the vicissitudes and he was reluctant to prognosticate the height to which the human species might aspire in its advance toward perfection, nevertheless—and this is as far as he would go at this point in the direction of the Turgot-Condorcet convictions—"it may safely be presumed, that no people, unless the face of nature is changed, will relapse into their original barbarism." Even the Romans had not fallen so far as to renew the "human feasts of the Laestrygons on the coast of Campania." To promise his fellow-men freedom from anthropophagy was no resounding affirmation of the certain progress of civilization, but it was further than many thinkers of the older generation of Anglo-French culture were prepared to venture.

Much of the detailed reasoning about the "improvements of society" recalls Turgot's ideas, still in manuscript when Gibbon wrote, and what Condorcet would publish a few years after Gibbon's death. (The only work by Condorcet in Gibbon's library was a hostile consideration of Pascal, *Eloge et pensées de Pascal* [1778], though some far-out progressionist prophecies were available in Mercier's *An 2440*, which Gibbon also possessed.) Direct evidence of "influence" from these French *philosophes* is lacking, but the resemblances are plentiful. Most striking is Gibbon's division of the improvements of society into three different types, along with an estimate of the diverse fortune each was likely to experience in the course of the ages. Turgot had made a similar diagnosis of the varying fortunes of the progressions, intellectual-scientific, artistic, mechanical, and moral. Gibbon lumped together poetic and scientific genius and made both the product of mere chance and spontaneity. Turgot, though he would have agreed as to the rarity and inexplicable character of genius, had a well-nourished theory about the relations of the state of society and the capacity of a genius to fulfill himself that was not approached by Gibbon, who on the whole seemed to feel that nothing much could be done about the marvelous, unaccountable appearances of genius—its incidence was not affected by historical forces. (And yet in the *Decline and Fall* itself he had sometimes maintained a contrary position.) But industrial accomplishments, the cultivation of the arts and sciences, which were common experiences of mankind, and the laws were less independent phenomena and as a consequence were subject to the complex machinery of the social order. They could be destroyed by violence or allowed to fall into gradual decay. Achievements in these realms did not always endure, and Gibbon was silent on the subject of their necessary accumulation. The only improvements of society about which he expressed confidence were the mechanical arts, whose preservation was dependent neither upon genius nor upon the whole fabric of society. Elementary techniques learned in families and villages in the course of time were the most durable acquisitions. Turgot made a similar appraisal of the continuity of mechanical progression even in the darkest ages of mankind, though his emphasis was somewhat different from that of Gibbon, who was concerned primarily with survival. "Private genius and public industry may be extirpated," Gibbon wrote, casting a last dubious look on the great achievements of European civilization, but the "hardy plants"—he was referring to the mechanical arts—"survive the tempest. . . ." Turgot had written on the usefulness of war in spreading the arts; Gibbon held a similar view. "Since the first discovery of the arts [I believe that in this context he referred chiefly to the useful or mechanical arts], war, commerce, and religious zeal have diffused, among the savages of the Old and New World, these inestimable gifts: they have been successively propagated; they can never be lost," he wrote in one of his rare, unqualified affirmations.[18]

I cannot demonstrate that Gibbon was acquainted with Turgot's ideas on progress, though the two men met in Paris. Memoirs on Turgot's life and thought were published by Dupont de Nemours in 1772 and by Condorcet in 1786, but the actual texts of Turgot's reflections on philosophical history remained mere "projects" and did not appear during Gibbon's lifetime. Though David Hume was well aware of his friend Turgot's conceptions, which he rejected in their correspondence, Gibbon's personal ties to Hume were not close enough to suggest oral transmission. Turgot's ideas remain parallels, not documented influences, though often the similarities are arresting. Gibbon's chapter 53 on the stultification of Greek culture during the thousand-year reign of the Christian Byzantines is a good illustration of Turgot's thesis that the archenemy of progress, a sickly tendency toward repetition and sameness, was responsible for sinking whole societies into a rut. Gibbon placed the blame for the stagnation of Byzantium on its isolation and the absence of competition both within the Empire and with other societies. "In all the pursuits of active and speculative life, the emulation of states and individuals is the most powerful spring of the efforts and improvements of mankind."[19] As a consequence of Byzantium's addiction to the mere repetition of what had been received from the ancients, Gibbon issued his famous verdict: "In the revolution of ten centuries, not a single discovery was made to exalt the dignity or promote the happiness of mankind."[20]

Before propositions demonstrating the inevitablity of progress were set forth in Turgot's *Sorboniques* and Condorcet's *Life of Turgot*, it is hard to find members of the Anglo-French philosophical school who staunchly maintained an absolute position. Such a pre-Revolutionary thinker as the Abbé Raynal might be quite radical in his reformist zeal, believe that the mission of the age was to wipe away the debris of the old order, and yet conclude, as he did in the *Histoire philosophique* (which Gibbon knew well) that the changes effected would not be enduring. Raynal likened the rise and fall of nations to turns of the weather vane, Leibniz, to the movement of the tides; and both Voltaire and Diderot, in their casual, unsystematic way, saw the dominion of nations increasing and diminishing without rhyme or reason. The Abbé Galiani perceived the rise and fall of civilization as phases of the moon, a recurrent natural phenomenon from which there was no escape. Such analogies are far less intricate than some of the Renaissance doctrines of the vicissitudes, but they appear to have satisfied the philosophico-historical needs of major thinkers in the early and middle periods of the Enlightenment. When Turgot and Condorcet offered proofs of the *inevitability* of progression in the scientific and the moral realms, not merely an alternativity of progress and decline, they were opening up a very different prospect.

After all his tergiversation, one is prepared to receive Gibbon into the fold of the partial lapsarians, a middling, normative, *philosophe* position, when the concluding sentence of chapter 38 makes a giant leap into the realm of limitless, unbounded progress. "We may therefore acquiesce in the pleasing conclusion, that every age of the world has increased, and still increases, the real wealth, the happiness, and perhaps the virtue, of the human race." The attentive reader, hardly prepared for any such enthusiastic adherence to the idea of progress in its full-blown Turgot-Condorcet version, is left bewildered. He can only be grateful for the introduction of the saving "perhaps," before Gibbon, carried away by his own rhetoric, binds every age of the world to progress in "virtue." Though Gibbon went along with the negative argument of Turgot and Condorcet that declension was not inevitable, to my knowledge he never forthrightly subscribed to the positive one, except in that lone sentence concluding Volume III of the *Decline and Fall*, which seems almost like the attempt of the salon conversationalist to end on an amiable and pleasing note.

A year after the appearance of the last volume of the *Decline and Fall*, revolution broke upon France; for once, Gibbon's Olympian serenity abandoned him, and he exhorted all good Englishmen to resist the French contagion. He announced himself a Burkean in everything; he even forgave Burke for his superstitions. Gibbon was ready to resort to any act of policy that would strengthen the moral fiber of his countrymen, even to the point of helping draft and signing a solemn petition of loyalty that would join men of all parties in support of the British constitution. Before he was shaken by the events of the French Revolution, the *historien-philosophe* who had incisively diagnosed the gradual, insensible forces that brought about the decline and fall of Rome over the centuries would not have given great weight to such verbal prophylaxis.

By the seventeen-nineties, Gibbon was beginning to fear the destruction of France and with it a danger to all of European civilization. He viewed the affairs of France with a crescendo of alarm. On September 25, 1789, he had written to Lord Sheffield: "That country is now in a state of *dissolution*."[21] On December 15, 1789, "the honestest of the Assembly" were characterized as "a set of wild Visionaries."[22] By February 23, 1793, he wrote to Lord Loughborough of the threat to the whole of Europe: "As a friend to government in general I most sincerely rejoice that you are now armed in the common cause against the most dangerous fanatics that have ever invaded the peace of Europe—against the new Barbarians who labour to confound the order and happiness of society, and who, in the opinion of thinking men, are not less the enemies of subjects than of kings."[23] Gibbon in Lausanne was ready to go into mourning over the execution of Louis XVI, but he was "afraid of being singular."[24] When two requirements of appropriate civilized behavior clashed, Gibbon's more enthusiastic resolves always crumbled. The *historien-philosophe* maintained his outward social equipoise to the end.

REFERENCES

[1]Edward Gibbon, *Memoirs of My Life*, ed. Georges A. Bonnard (London, 1966), pp. 103-4.

[2]Gibbon, *Essai sur l'étude de la littérature* (London, 1761), p. 98.

[3]*Ibid.*, p. 91.

[4]Gibbon, *Letters*, ed. J. E. Norton (London, 1956), I, p. 294, Gibbon to Holroyd, October 1, 1771.

[5]Gibbon, *Essai*, p. 108.

[6]*Ibid.*, p. 109.

[7]Paul Robert, *Dictionnaire alphabétique et analogique de la langue française* (Paris, 1964), XVI, p. 153.

[8]Gibbon, *The History of the Decline and Fall of the Roman Empire (DF)*, 6 vols. (London, 1776-88), chap. 71, p. 645.

[9]Gibbon, *Essai*, p. 85.

[10]New York, Pierpont Morgan Library, *Catalogue de la bibliothèque de M. Gibbon; fait à Lausanne le 26 septembre, 1785* (RV 10 B; not in Gibbon's hand).

[11]Gibbon, *Miscellaneous Works*, ed. John, Lord Sheffield (London, 1796), II, p. 619.

[12]General John Meredith Read, Jr., *Historic Studies in Vaud, Berne, and Savoy* (London, 1897), II, p. 297; G. Keynes, *The Library of Edward Gibbon* (London, 1940).

[13]Gibbon, *Letters*, II, p. 127, Gibbon to Suzanne Necker, November 26, 1776.

[14]*Ibid.*, p. 218, Gibbon to Georges Deyverdun, June 4, 1779. Gibbon is probably referring to Horace's *mutum et turpe pecus*.

[15]Condorcet, *Esquisse d'un tableau historique des progrès de l'esprit humain* (4th ed., Genoa, 1798), p. 313.

[16]*DF*, "General Observations" (following chap. 38), p. 635.

[17]*Ibid.*, p. 636.

[18]*Ibid.*, pp. 639-40.

[19]*DF*, chap. 53, p. 517.

[20]*Ibid.*, p. 515.

[21]Gibbon, *Letters*, III, 171, Gibbon to Lord Sheffield, September 25, 1789.

[22]*Ibid.*, p. 184, Gibbon to Lord Sheffield, December 15, 1789.

[23]*Ibid.*, p. 321, Gibbon to Lord Loughborough, February 23, 1793.

[24]*Ibid.*, p. 318, Gibbon to Lord Sheffield, February 18, 1793.

Silhouette of Edward Gibbon by Mrs. Brown.
By courtesy of the Trustees of the British
Museum.

JOHN CLIVE

Gibbon's Humor

OLIPHANT SMEATON, EDITOR of the "Everyman" *Decline and Fall*, speaks of "those silly witticisms as pointless as they are puerile in which Gibbon at times indulges."[1] How would the great historian have dealt with that comment and its author? The latter's name, though the mere act of pronouncing it may even now raise a smile, would not have lent itself to punning—unlike that of the Abbé le Bœuf, "an antiquarian, whose name was happily expressive of his talents."[2] But his censorious remark might have moved Gibbon to credit him with "that naïveté, that unconscious simplicity, which always constitutes genuine humor."[3]

To take issue with Oliphant Smeaton is neither to deny that any historian who admits the comic spirit to his pages puts strict historical truth at risk, nor to maintain that Gibbon's humor demands to be treated with reverence and awe. To be sure, he had learned from Pascal the art of wielding "grave and temperate irony" in a great cause. But it did not require the excesses of the early Christians to set free his sense of farce and his ability to indulge in what, writing of Bayle, he referred to as "wicked wit."[4] Delinquent authors sufficed. For evidence one need look no higher than his footnotes, which in themselves constitute a veritable academy of raillery and humor. Voltaire is a favorite target, casting, as he does, "a keen and lively glance over the surface of history."[5] Thus, "unsupported by either fact or probability, [he] has generously bestowed the Canary Islands on the Roman empire."[6] As a Gibbonian victim, the Patriarch of Ferney duly takes his place alongside Ammianus Marcellinus, whose bad taste is such "that it is not easy to distinguish his facts from his metaphors"; Salmasius, who "too often involves himself in the maze of his disorderly erudition"; St. Augustine, "[whose] learning is too often borrowed, and . . . [whose] arguments are too often his own"; and Corneille, whose tragedy of Heraclius "requires more than one representation to be clearly understood; and . . . after an interval of some years, is said to have puzzled the author himself."[7]

Sex and Christianity are conventionally mentioned as two of the principal arenas in which Gibbon's wit disported itself to the fullest, and there is little reason to dispute that judgment. Like Theodora's murmurs, pleasures, and arts, some of Gibbon's anecdotes involving sexual matters "must be veiled in the obscurity of a learned language."[8] And so we hear of Lycopolis, the modern Siut, or Osiot, which has a very convenient fountain, *cujus potû signa virginitatis eripiuntur*.[9] At other times, a learned language is not required; for instance, when Gibbon describes Claudius as the only one of the first fifteen Roman emperors "whose taste in love was entirely correct"; or when he reports that Arius reckoned among his immediate followers "two bishops of Egypt, seven presbyters, twelve deacons, and (what may appear almost incredible) seven hundred virgins."[10] No essay about Gibbon's humor may omit the younger Gordian: "Twenty-two acknowledged concubines, and a library of sixty-two thousand volumes, attested the variety of his inclinations, and from the productions which he left behind him, it appears that the former as well as the latter were designed for use rather than ostentation." The footnote reads: "By each of his concubines, the younger Gordian left three or four children. His literary productions were by no means contemptible."[11]

The combination of sex and Christianity seems to be particularly effective in triggering Gibbon's risibilities. When he describes those nuns of Constantinople who were torn from the altar by the conquering Turks, "with naked bosoms, outstretched hands, and disheveled hair," he cannot refrain from commenting that "we should piously believe that few could be tempted to prefer the vigils of the harem to those of the monastery."[12] When he recalls that he has somewhere heard or read the frank confession of a Benedictine abbot—"My vow of poverty has given me a hundred thousand crowns a year; my vow of obedience has raised me to the rank of a sovereign prince"—he cannot stop there, but must add: "I forget the consequences of his vow of chastity."[13]

It is, of course, no accident that Gibbon's wit is so frequently directed at Christianity and its adherents. The same "arms of ridicule and *comic* raillery"[14] which Constantine employed against the heretics, Gibbon employed against the Christians. One of his aims in the *Decline and Fall* was to capture the territory of early church history for the secular historian. In order to accomplish that aim, it was not enough— at least it was not enough for Gibbon—to put fact in place of fancy. The miraculous had to be ridiculed as well as questioned. And this he proceeded to do, with a mastery of literary devices designed both to infuriate the orthodox and to delight and titillate his fellow skeptics.

C'est le ton qui fait la musique. By no means the least effective of those devices was the tone of mock seriousness which Gibbon was able to assume at will when he dealt with sacred matters. From the beginning of chapter 15, when he complains about "the melancholy duty" imposed on the historian who "must discover the inevitable mixture of error and corruption which [religion] contracted in a long residence upon earth," to its end, when he records in a matter-of-fact manner that during the age of Christ, his Apostles, and their first disciples, "the lame walked, the blind saw, the sick were healed, the dead were raised, demons were expelled, and the laws of Nature were frequently suspended for the benefit of the Church,"[15] that tone reinforces the secular implications of the five "secondary causes" for the rapid growth of Christianity. The Old Testament is not immune. After quoting from Numbers 14:11—"How long will this people provoke me? and how long will it be ere they *believe* me, for all the *signs* which I have shown among them?"—Gibbon assures his readers that it would be easy, "but it would be unbecoming," to justify the complaint of the Deity from the whole tenor of the Mosaic history. After noting that there exist some objections against the authority of Moses and the prophets which too readily present themselves to the skeptical mind, he feels bound to add that these "can only be derived from our ignorance of remote antiquity, and from our incapacity to form an adequate judgment of the Divine economy."[16]

That tone of voice is not confined to chapter 15. It reappears at the conclusion of the second of the "Christian" chapters, where the observation that the Christians in the course of their intestine dissensions have inflicted far graver severities on each other than they have experienced from the zeal of the infidels is called "a melancholy truth which obtrudes itself on the reluctant mind";[17] and, later, in Gibbon's account of the monastic saints: "They familiarly accosted, or imperiously commanded, the lions and serpents of the desert; infused vegetation into a sapless trunk; suspended iron on the surface of the water; passed the Nile on the back of a crocodile; and refreshed themselves in a fiery furnace."[18] More difficult feats, certainly, than those of the Empress Eudocia. All *she* did was to enjoy the conscious satisfaction of returning to Constantinople "with the chains of St. Peter, the right arm of St. Stephen, and an undoubted picture of the Virgin painted by St. Luke."[19] Hardly ever can a "melancholy duty" have been performed in a more sprightly fashion.

Part of the humor all along resides in the sort of persona that Gibbon presents to his readers, in the disjunction between the skeptical man of the world and the mask of credulity and devotion which he so readily assumes. Throughout the *Decline and Fall*, there is carried on a benevolent conspiracy between the reader and the historian, carefully engineered by the latter, who uses it to entertain his audience as well as to take it into camp. Gibbon is ever present. "Before we enter upon the memorable reign of that prince [Diocletian]," he writes, "it will be proper to punish and dismiss the unworthy brother of Numerian."[20] Later, he confesses that "I have neither power nor inclination to follow the Hungarians beyond the Rhine."[21] Concluding his sketch of Muhammad's life, he admits how difficult it is to decide whether to call him an enthusiast or an impostor: "At the distance of twelve centuries I darkly contemplate his shade through a cloud of religious incense."[22]

As the history draws to a close, the historian increasingly mocks himself. The feudal knight, he tells us, devoted himself to speaking the truth as the champion of God and the ladies—and adds, parenthetically, that "I blush to write such discordant names."[23] Before remarking that even in this world the natural order of events sometimes affords strong appearances of moral retribution, he solemnly announces: "I shall not, I trust, be accused of superstition."[24] And, as he takes leave of the papacy in the sixteenth century, he has some praise even for the temporal government of that institution. "For myself," he movingly declares, "it is my wish to depart in charity with all mankind, nor am I willing, in these last moments, to offend even the Pope and clergy of Rome."[25]

The reader acts throughout as the historian's good-humored accomplice—civilized, impatient of too much detail, and not averse to a little mockery of himself. "In the course of this history," Gibbon writes, "the most voracious appetite for war will be abundantly satiated."[26] But that is not *really* what the reader wants. For after quoting the stern Tertullian on what will happen at the Last Judgment—"so many sage philosophers blushing in red-hot flames with their deluded scholars; so many celebrated poets trembling before the tribunal, not of Minos, but of Christ; so many tragedians, more tuneful in the expression of their own sufferings; so many dancers—" here the historian breaks off in mid-passage, in the belief that "the humanity of the reader will permit me to draw a veil over the rest of this infernal description, which the zealous African pursues in a long variety of affected and unfeeling witticisms."[27] Gibbon's readers are generous as well as humane. If, in his *Anecdotes*, Procopius insinuates that "the fame and even the virtue of Belisarius were polluted by the lust and cruelty of his wife," and that the hero deserved "an appellation which may not drop from the pen of the decent historian," that is something which "the generous reader" will confess only reluctantly, having cast away the libel and been persuaded only by the evidence of the facts.[28] The reader's attention is apt to wander, especially when it comes to the deliberations of Church councils. In the treaty between the Greek and the Latin churches, "it was agreed," so Gibbon writes, "that the Holy Ghost proceeds from the Father *and* the Son, as from one principle and one substance; that he proceeds *by* the Son, being of the same nature and substance; and that he proceeds from the Father *and* the Son, by one *spiration*, and production." After the word "agreed," the historian felt it incumbent upon him to insert the phrase, "I must entreat the attention of the reader."[29] Faced with such an entreaty, few of his readers would be so hardhearted as to withhold their attention, and few would fail to forgive Gibbon for using his appeal to them for his own sly ends.

But where his humor is concerned, one must not make too much of Gibbon's polemical intentions, sly or otherwise. His irony, it has been pointed out, could serve many purposes: it could be used as a weapon; it could provide the requisite distance between himself and his subject matter, and thus lend the appearance of Olympian detachment to his history; it could act as a useful protective device in an age when explicit attacks on the essentials of Christian faith and doctrine still held a certain amount of danger; it could help to mediate an amused and objective view of human nature in all its (sometimes paradoxical) variety; it could also help the historian to evade judgments where he did not wish to make them. Gibbon's sneer was not always good-humored, and has even been seen by some as an outlet for his aggressions. But, granted all that, it is still worth remarking that there is in him a playfulness, a gaiety, a delight in wit for its own sake, that bubbles up time and again, irrepressibly. Like Julian, he "could not always restrain the levity of his temper."[30] Take the Armoricans, for instance. Armorica was the Roman name for the maritime counties of Gaul between the Seine and the Loire; whenever he comes to deal with the inhabitants of that region, Gibbon cannot resist verbal allusions to events taking place in his own time in certain other provinces. And so we hear of the Armoricans "in a state of disorderly independence"; of "the slight foundations of the *Armorican* republic"; of the Bretons of Armorica refusing their customary tribute; and of liberty peopling "the morasses of Armorica."[31]

Other forms of verbal wit abound in the *Decline and Fall*, some taken over from his sources, some of his own making: "A swarm of monks" issues from the desert; Julian's beard, louse-infested, earns the right to be called "populous"; pursuit of religious controversy affords a new occupation to "the busy idleness" of Constantinople; Roman senators complete their ruin "by an expensive effort to disguise their poverty"; Simeon Stylites spends thirty years on his column, "this last and lofty station."[32] Boswell had found spring guns and man-traps in Gibbon's garden of flowery eloquence. How the historian must have enjoyed setting them! Here is one: " 'May those who divide Christ be divided with the sword, may they be hewn in pieces, may they be burned alive!' were the charitable wishes of a Christian synod."[33] Here is another: "He [Justinian] piously labored to establish with fire and sword the unity of the Christian faith."[34] And here is a third: The Syracusans had held out for more than twenty days against the Arab besiegers; "and the place might have been relieved, if the mariners of the Imperial fleet had not been detained at Constantinople in building a church to the Virgin Mary."[35]

It may be argued, of course, that the last three examples combine high spirits with the censure of Christian hypocrisy. That particular form of censure could not be passed by Gibbon, or anyone else, upon the learned Origen, who, eager for perpetual chastity, "judged it the most prudent to disarm the tempter." Here the historian's gloss is sympathetic rather than critical: "As it was his general practice to allegorise Scripture, it seems unfortunate that, in this instance only, he should have adopted the literal sense."[36] Gibbon's wit was not tied to his polemical sallies, even when it accompanied them. When he remarks, "But there *is* a Providence (such at least was the opinion of the historian Procopius) that watches over innocence and folly,"[37] he is less concerned with disabusing his readers of a providential interpretation of history than with making a good joke. And the same sense of mischievous fun impels him to quote Malaterra to the effect that the bite of the tarantula "provokes a windy disposition, quae per anum inhoneste crepitando emergit—a symptom most ridiculously felt by the whole Norman army in their camp near Palermo."[38]

Is that, then, all there is to Gibbon's humor—footnoted reprimands for delinquent authors, sexual innuendo, solemn sneers at religion, amusing games played with his readers, and, throughout, an irrepressible element of playfulness and sheer high spirits? Let us look at a few more examples, and try to establish what, besides possibly exhibiting one or the other of the qualities already adverted to, they may have in common:

Their peaceful inhabitants enjoyed and abused the advantages of wealth and luxury.[39]

Such folly was disdained and indulged by the wisest princes.[40]

Strangers and pilgrims who already felt the strong intoxication of fanaticism, and, perhaps, of wine.[41]

. . . the sacred but licentious crowd of priests, of inferior ministers, and of female dancers.[42]

. . . some resemblance may be found in the situation of two princes who conquered France by their valor, their policy, and the merits of a seasonable conversion.[43]

. . . the Romans invited the Huns to a splendid, or, at least, a plentiful supper.[44]

By the repetition of a sentence and the loss of a foreskin, the subject or the slave, the captive or the criminal, arose in a moment the free and equal companions of the victorious Moslems.[45]

In these examples the humor arises in large part from Gibbon's undercutting the abstract, the spiritual, the unworldly, the formal, the pompous, the pretentious, the merely verbal, with the concrete, the mundane, the down-to-earth, the reality as he sees it. That same attitude characterizes a good many of his epigrams:

It is easier to deplore the fate, than to describe the actual condition, of Corsica.[46]

Corruption, the most infallible symptom of constitutional liberty. . . .[47]

It is much easier to ascertain the appetites of a quadruped than the speculations of a philosopher.[48]

What is involved, of course, is a particular view of human existence—cynical, realistic, disdainful of cant and hypocrisy. It assumes that human beings everywhere and at all times share a desire for power, for material gain, and for pleasure, a desire they might be able to control to a certain extent by exercising a rational prudence, but which resists idealistic or suprarational efforts (however well-intentioned) to extirpate it. One is reminded of La Rochefoucauld's maxim: "Les vertus se perdent dans l'intérêt comme les fleuves se perdent dans la mer." True wisdom resides in those who can rebuff or rid themselves of chimerical dreams and are able to adopt instead an unvarnished view of human character and a utilitarian view of social and political institutions. Those who refuse to do this, who let themselves be misled by the idle speculations of poets or priests, or chastise themselves in the vain hope of denying their natural proclivities, become the object of Gibbon's amusement as well as of his censure.

Thus Julian "gradually acquired for his troops the imaginary protection of the gods, and for himself the firm and effective support of the Roman legions."[49] Thus the attachment of the Roman soldiers to their standards was inspired to some extent by the united influence of religion and honor. But "these motives, which derived their strength from the imagination, were enforced by fears and hopes of a more substantial kind."[50] Two adverse choirs chanted the Trisagion in the cathedral of Constantinople; "and, when their lungs were exhausted, they had recourse to the more solid arguments of sticks and stones."[51] After the failure of the line of Alaric, royal dignity was still limited to the pure and noble blood of the Goths: "The clergy, who anointed their lawful prince, always recommended, and sometimes practised, the duty of allegiance."[52] "The various modes of worship, which prevailed in the Roman world, were all considered by the people as equally true; by the philosopher, as equally false; and by the magistrate, as equally useful."[53]

Gibbon's sympathies clearly lie with the magistrate. He would surely have agreed with Lord Melbourne's complaint that things had come to a pretty pass when religion was allowed to invade private life, though he might have added, "and to evade public life." It was, after all, the withdrawal of the early Christians from civic duty and responsibility that contributed to Rome's fall. This is one serious message of the Christian chapters. As we have observed, their comic effect lies, in part, in the mock solemnity of the author's tone. But only in part. For the same view of human nature which informs the work as a whole informs these chapters as well, and it is there, as elsewhere, integrally related to Gibbon's center of levity:

> Disdaining an ignominious flight, the virgins of the warm climate of Africa encountered the enemy in the closest engagement: they permitted priests and deacons to share their beds, and gloried amidst the flames in their unsullied purity. But insulted Nature sometimes vindicated her rights, and this new species of martyrdom served only to introduce a new scandal into the church.[54]

"Insulted nature" here represents the sexual passion which will not let itself be entirely repressed. Elsewhere, it is the desire for pecuniary gain that resists curbing: "Even the reverses of the Greek and Roman coins were frequently of an idolatrous nature. Here, indeed, the scruples of the Christian were suspended by a stronger passion."[55] Men, in Gibbon's view, crave material rewards, and those who claim to despise these more likely than not are able to make that claim because they cannot, in fact, obtain them: "It is always easy, as well as agreeable, for the inferior ranks of mankind to claim a merit from the contempt of the pomp and pleasure which fortune has placed beyond their reach."[56] Cyprian "had renounced those temporal honors which it is probable he would never have obtained."[57]

In these examples the humor arises from a tacitly assumed agreement between the historian and his reader that there must be something irrational, something almost demented, certainly something comical, about a religion that expected men to renounce carnal desires and worldly success. As for miraculous intervention, one story told by Gibbon and his comment on it can stand for many others of a similar kind:

> The victorious king of the Franks [Clovis] proceeded without delay to the siege of Angoulême. At the sound of his trumpets the walls of the city imitated the example of Jericho, and instantly fell to the ground; a splendid miracle, which may be reduced to the supposition that some clerical engineers had secretly undermined the foundations of the rampart.[58]

Here, as elsewhere, practical common sense triumphs over the miraculous; the engineer (even if, this time, he be a *clerical* engineer) over the priest. And the reader is meant to smile. But what Gibbon has in mind is more than mere entertainment, more, even, than yet another lighthearted blow at the truth or efficacy of Christian miracles. The ground bass of practicality and common sense that resounds in so much of his humor both echoes and sustains one of the major themes of the *Decline and Fall*: that the past and future progress of civilization rest not on the unbridled abstractions of speculators or the vain incantations of priests and poets, but rather on the slow and steady conquests of science and the practical arts.

That theme is to be found throughout the work. But it is in the "General Observations on the Fall of the Roman Empire in the West"[59] that Gibbon proclaims it with the greatest eloquence. Here he ascribes the end of the barbarian incursions, "the long repose," not to a decrease of population, but to the progress of arts and agriculture. From an abject condition of savagery—naked both in mind and body, destitute of laws, arts, ideas, and almost of language, man has gradually arisen to command the animals, to fertilize the earth, to traverse the ocean, and to measure the heavens. It may safely be presumed that no people, unless the face of nature is changed, will relapse into their original barbarism.

Gibbon then proceeds to view the improvements of society under a threefold aspect: Poets and philosophers first—but their superior powers of reason or fancy are rare and spontaneous productions. The benefits of law and policy, trade and manufactures, arts and sciences come second—but that complex machinery may be decayed by time, or injured by violence. But, fortunately for mankind, the more useful, or at least the more necessary, arts are in no such danger.

> Each village, each family, each individual, must always possess both ability and inclination to perpetuate the use of fire and of metals; the propagation and service of domestic animals; the methods of hunting and fishing; the rudiments of navigation; the imperfect cultivation of corn or other nutritive grain; and the simple practice of the mechanic trades. Private genius and public industry may be extirpated; but these hardy plants survive the tempest, and strike an everlasting root into the most unfavorable soil.[60]

It is true, as Gibbon goes on to point out, that since these practical arts were first discovered, religious zeal, as well as war and commerce, has helped to diffuse them among the savages of the Old and the New World. But they are more than the sum of those agents of diffusion. They are nothing less than the bedrock of civilization. Useful and practical, they stand in no need of elaborate speculations and feverish imaginings. They correspond in their steady and constant operation to the happy mean of human nature, free from extremes of virtue and vice, solidly based on a recognition of reality. That is one of the great lessons of the *Decline and Fall*. And when the reader laughs and smiles with the historian at the excesses and absurdities of misguided men and women, be they pagan, Christian, or Muslim, he shows that he has learned his lesson. By his laughter and his smile he is helping to support the foundations of Gibbon's own rampart.

REFERENCES

[1]*Gibbon's Decline and Fall of the Roman Empire (DF)*, Everyman's Library Edition, 6 vols. (London, 1910; reprinted, 1966), chap. 58, p. 48. All subsequent references are to chapter and page of this edition.

[2]*DF*, chap. 19, p. 204.

[3]*DF*, chap. 23, p. 395.

[4]*DF*, chap. 69, p. 471.

[5]*DF*, chap. 51, p. 313.

[6]*DF*, chap. 1, p. 27.

[7]*DF*, chap. 26, p. 1; chap. 51, p. 357; chap. 28, p. 143; chap. 46, p. 503.

[8]*DF*, chap. 40, p. 155.

[9]*DF*, chap. 27, p. 112.

[10]*DF*, chap. 3, p. 76; chap. 21, p. 273.

[11]*DF*, chap. 7, p. 171.

[12]*DF*, chap. 68, pp. 448-49.

[13]*DF*, chap. 37, p. 14.

[14]*DF*, chap. 21, p. 285.

[15]*DF*, chap. 15, pp. 430, 499.

[16]*Ibid.*, pp. 434, 441.

[17]*DF*, chap. 16, p. 68.

[18]*DF*, chap. 37, p. 19.

[19]*DF*, chap. 32, p. 317.

[20]*DF*, chap. 12, p. 339.

[21]*DF*, chap. 55, p. 517.

[22]*DF*, chap. 50, p. 272.

[23]*DF*, chap. 58, p. 56.

[24]*DF*, chap. 62, p. 239.

[25]*DF*, chap. 70, p. 546.

[26]*DF*, chap. 39, pp. 120-1.

[27]*DF*, chap. 15, p. 457.

[28]*DF*, chap. 41, p. 273.

[29]*DF*, chap. 66, p. 374.

[30]*DF*, chap. 22, p. 340.

[31]*DF*, chap. 35, p. 407; chap. 38, pp. 52, 93, 100.

[32]*DF*, chap. 21, p. 310; chap. 22, p. 349; chap. 27, p. 75; chap. 36, p. 437; chap. 37, p. 18.

[33]*DF*, chap. 47, p. 27.

[34]*Ibid.*, p. 41.

[35]*DF*, chap. 52, pp. 421-22.

[36]*DF*, chap. 15, p. 467.

[37]*DF*, chap. 31, p. 249.

[38]*DF*, chap. 56, p. 560.

[39]*DF*, chap. 1, p. 1.

[40]*DF*, chap. 40, p. 161.

[41]*DF*, chap. 28, p. 146.

[42]*DF*, chap. 23, p. 373.

[43]*DF*, chap. 38, p. 53.

[44]*DF*, chap. 34, p. 362.

[45]*DF*, chap. 51, p. 377.

[46]*DF*, chap. 1, p. 27.

[47]*DF*, chap. 21, p. 300.

[48]*DF*, chap. 26, p. 3.

[49]*DF*, chap. 23, p. 379.

[50]*DF*, chap. 1, p. 11.

[51]*DF*, chap. 47, p. 35.

[52]*DF*, chap. 38, p. 86.

[53]*DF*, chap. 2, p. 29.

[54]*DF*, chap. 15, p. 467.

[55]*Ibid.*, p. 446.

[56]*Ibid.*

[57]*Ibid.*, p. 483.

[58]*DF*, chap. 38, p. 60.

[59]*Ibid.*, pp. 103-12.

[60]*Ibid.*, p. 111. See Hugh R. Trevor-Roper, ed., *Gibbon: The Decline and Fall of the Roman Empire and Other Selections* (New York, 1963), p. xxix, for the suggestion that the interplay between the history of empires and the history of the sciences provides the constant theme of the *Decline and Fall*.

FRANCIS HASKELL

Gibbon and the History of Art

AN ART HISTORIAN IS BOUND TO FEEL somewhat out of place among the scholars from so many other fields who have joined to pay homage to Edward Gibbon. The references to the visual arts in Gibbon's published works tend to be few and perfunctory, and, although he counted such considerable artists, *amateurs*, and artistic theorists as Reynolds, Walpole, and Burke among his acquaintances, their enthusiasms hardly seem to have impinged on his own personality. Nor did he participate very actively in the artistic pursuits of his two dearest friends. During the seventeen-seventies, John Holroyd was employing the architect James Wyatt to build Sheffield Place in Sussex, one of the earliest large-scale Gothic Revival country houses in England. Gibbon certainly showed the interest to be expected of a well-wisher, and he tried to help in small practical matters, but he makes only one comment (in a letter to his stepmother of September 25, 1776) on the issue of taste, and even that—"Mr H. wishes for an opportunity of promoting eloquence in Mrs Gibbon on Gothick Architecture"— suggests that he himself was not very concerned with the matter. And when, in September, 1788, he was about to leave London for Switzerland and asked Wilhelm de Sévery to "choisir pour moi ou plutôt pour Deyverdun quelques estampes nouvelles et d'un bon goût jusqu'à la concurrence de quatre ou cinq louis," the casual tone reveals clearly enough his own indifference to such matters. Nevertheless, I have decided somewhat recklessly to try to make out a strong (if, at first sight, rather paradoxical) case for the claim, which grew on me the more I thought about him, that Gibbon did, almost despite himself, play a really significant role in the development of art history and theory.

The recent publication in full of the journal that Gibbon kept during part of his Italian travels (though not, alas, in Rome, Naples, or Venice) shows us how misleading is the brief and almost casual account of that journey which he has given us in his autobiography—an account only memorable for the few famous sentences in which he describes the impact on him of Roman associations and the inspiration for his life's work. In fact, we now know that Gibbon studied works of art, modern as well as ancient, with almost as much concentration as he did books and scholarly publications; consequently, we can assume that he may well have been the most "visually educated" of any historian before—and of the great majority since—his period. He was the man, moreover, who in Parma was to acknowledge that the art of Correggio had quite unexpectedly revealed to him "le pouvoir de la peinture" and, in Florence, to go into quite uncharacteristic raptures over the *Venus de' Medici*.[1] One real and rewarding question that can be asked about him is why he should have put his artistic experiences to such little use.[2]

An enthusiastic admiration for Correggio or the *Venus de' Medici* was certainly not surprising in the middle of the eighteenth century, and in fact Gibbon's artistic tastes were strictly conventional—if anything, slightly *retardataire* and in no way touched by that incipient reaction against the Baroque which we find in some travelers of the period. But his actual approach to art was very distinctive, and it marks him off from most of the cultivated grand tourists of his own and previous generations.[3] We can see the point most clearly if we compare his attitude with that of the three visitors to Italy—an Englishman, a Frenchman, and a German—whose published comments on art meant most to him. Joseph Addison had visited Italy in the first years of the century, and—as will become clear—Gibbon refers to his views almost exclusively for the purpose of refuting them. Johann Georg Keysler had made very exhaustive travels throughout various parts of Europe, including Italy, between 1729 and 1731, and his *Travels* were published some ten years later and translated into English in 1756. Winckelmann was to comment that "les Voyages de Keysler, dans lesquels il traite des Ouvrages de l'Art qui sont à Rome & ailleurs, ne méritent aucune attention; car il a tiré tout ce qu'il dit des Livres les plus misérables."[4] This characteristically ruthless judgment of a highly influential book is not wholly unjust; the English translation (which was used by Gibbon) teems with wild inaccuracies. But the four large volumes do contain a vast amount of information—social, political, and intellectual—and many shrewd observations, though the artistic comments rarely venture beyond such generalized terms as "fine," "celebrated," or "beautiful."

Very different was the case of Charles Nicolas Cochin, whose *Voyage d'Italie*, first published in 1758, has always been looked upon as one of the most significant books of its kind to appear in the eighteenth century. The journey had been undertaken between December, 1749, and September, 1751, at the behest of Madame de Pompadour, who wished to prepare her brother, later to become the Marquis de Marigny, for his post of Directeur général des bâtiments. Cochin, a highly talented illustrator and administrator, the architect Soufflot, and the Abbé Leblanc took their young protegé on a very elaborate tour of almost every public and private building in Italy in order to direct his taste toward the "grand manner" and away from the rococo and genre painting that aroused his more spontaneous sympathies. Cochin's comments on the innumerable pictures which he saw with the eyes of an artist, as well as of a teacher, are fresh and perceptive, and Gibbon carried these three little volumes of encapsulated good taste around with him wherever he went. But his own judgments were very different. Where Cochin looked for beauty, Gibbon—who was clearly familiar with a problem that had been keenly discussed by theorists for many years—was interested primarily in "expression." The very word crops up on every page of his journal, and almost every picture is examined to see how far the expression is suited to the action it is meant to illustrate. Let me give one example among many: Looking at an *Incredulity of St. Thomas* in Genoa, on May 30, 1764, Gibbon commented:

> Il y a beaucoup d'expression dans la bonté du Sauveur qui cherche à vaincre l'infidelité de l'Apôtre et dans cette action de confiance avec laquelle il lui met lui-même la main dans sa côte. Je vois avec plaisir que St Thomas conserve dans sa physionomie cette defiance qui paroit plutôt l'ouvrage de tempérament que de la raison et du moment. Ce n'est que ces habitudes que le peintre puisse exprimer dans les traits. Les passions ne doivent se montrer que dans l'attitude, la couleur et les yeux. . . .[5]

This concentration on the drama of the situation, so typical of Gibbon's general approach to art, is significantly different from the more casual observations of earlier visitors to the Palazzo Brignoletti, but, although already showing an acute insight into the resources at the painter's disposal, it was only three weeks later, in Modena, that Gibbon took the decisive step of appreciating that those "expressions" on which he set such store only had any recognizable meaning if the story they illuminated was already known. The revelation came when he was looking at some medals in the Este collection, and remembering Addison's *Dialogue* on the value that these held for the historian, he suddenly asked himself: "Est-il si commun que l'âme se lise dans les traits? Je voudrais voir d'ailleurs qu'un ignorant à qui l'on montreroit une tête de Néron s'écrit Voila un Scelerat! Cette decision est si facile à un Savant qui sait d'avance qu'il l'a été."[6] It is tempting to speculate whether Gibbon's very skepticism concerning the value of the visual arts in providing psychological evidence for the historian may not have stimulated the extraordinarily dynamic and subtle quality of his own *literary* portraiture. Nor should his friendship with Garrick and his passion for the theater be forgotten in this context. It is, in any case, legitimate to claim that the questions he raised challenged the whole basis on which portraits had been made and judged ever since the Renaissance.

Indeed, it is only very recently and very tentatively that we have, even now, begun to understand that some knowledge of social history, convention, and artistic techniques are just as important for interpreting the psychology of a sitter as is the apparent realism with which his features are rendered.[7] Gibbon himself, when looking at Raphael's *Portrait of Julius II* in the Uffizi, was temporarily unnerved by his own skepticism, but he recovered enough to insist that, though in this case "l'âme de ce pape fier est peinte sur la toile," as a general rule the evidence of portraiture was dangerously misleading.[8] And it was in the Uffizi that the future historian of the Roman emperors was once again put to the test. Confronted by the busts of virtually all the emperors—"peut-être le trésor le plus précieux de la galerie"—he yet confines to a minimum his meditations on the character of each (nor, later, does he make use of his notes when he comes to writing his book), and is struck, rather, by the "plaisir bien vif . . . de suivre le progrès et la décadance des *arts* [my italics]."[9]

To some extent, it is true, Gibbon was to draw on this very decadence as a symptom of the wider historical and spiritual decline which he was to begin to chart so vividly some ten years later, but he did so almost as an afterthought; and, although he sometimes refers to Winckelmann, whose *Geschichte der Kunst des Altertums* was published in the very year of Gibbon's arrival in Rome (but was only read by him in the French translation of two years later), he never followed the German historian in treating art as a sort of thermometer with which to determine the moral health of an age. For this act of self-control, he could also produce very cogent reasons, which he may indeed have derived from Winckelmann, not only through the books but even more directly through the medium of James Byres, the Scotch antiquary who acted as his guide in Rome.[10] Winckelmann was rightly obsessed by the absurd archaeological theories that had again and again been built on foundations of heavily "restored" antiquities, but he was convinced that he at least could see through such falsifications. Gibbon, however, despite a certain show of bravado, lacked self-confidence in his artistic judgment, but was intelligent enough to be just as aware of the dangers:

Si l'homme de goût . . . est frappé de tant d'associations bizarres (car on a souvent suivi une autre manière et employé un marbre différent de la Statue antique), le

Littérateur craint toujours de bâtir des systems sur les caprices d'un Sculpteur moderne. On peut dire hardiment que de tous les ornemens qui paroissent caracteriser les Dieux ou les hommes il y en a très peu qui ne soient modernes. M. Gori a souvent prodigué l'érudition pour expliquer ou pour justifier l'imagination bizarre d'un artisan Florentin.[11]

At heart he knew that he was a "Littérateur" rather than an "homme de goût," but I would claim that it was his very taste and extraordinary insight into the nature of art that encouraged him to reject any systematic reliance on the evidence provided by the arts when planning the *Decline and Fall.*

It was, however, just in the field of art-historical scholarship that the book was to make its first considerable impact. Early in 1777, a few months after the publication of the first volume, a very rich Frenchman—an "homme de goût," if ever there was one—came to London.

Jean-Baptiste-Louis-George Seroux d'Agincourt was born in 1730 (seven years before Gibbon—the importance of this point can hardly be overemphasized); he was an extremely successful *fermier-général* of the widest possible interests and acquaintances. Voltaire himself had written to him, "Je vois, Monsieur, que vous êtes patriote et homme de lettres autant pour le moins que fermier-général,"[12] and he seems to have been on close terms with Buffon, Rousseau, Suard, Morellet, and Marmontel—to name only a few of his more conspicuous friends among the *philosophes* and their circle.[13] His noble origins helped to win him the benevolent patronage of Louis XV—to whose memory he remained devoted to the end of his long life—and the entry to the estates of great families such as the Soubise. He was a habitué of the salon of Madame Geoffrin, who had had his portrait drawn and engraved by Cochin.[14] Even more impressive were his links with the artistic world. Caylus, the most famous of Winckelmann's predecessors, had discussed antiquities with him, and Mariette, possibly the greatest of all connoisseurs, "voulut bien, dans ma jeunesse, servir de guide à mes premiers travaux." His exact contemporary, d'Angiviller, who, in 1774, replaced Marigny as Directeur général des bâtiments—a post which he held with the utmost distinction until the Revolution—was on the most cordial terms with him,[15] and among his personal friends he numbered many of the leading artists of the day, Fragonard and Hubert Robert especially. His fine collection of drawings contained superb works by Boucher.[16]

It is not clear whether Seroux d'Agincourt met Gibbon in London: the historian, in fact, spent part of 1777 in Paris. But I have said enough about the width of Seroux's circle to make it clear that if they ever did come across each other (and as yet I have no evidence pointing in either direction) they could just as easily have done so in the French as in the English capital. It is not possible even to prove (though it seems to me most likely) that it was at this moment that Seroux d'Agincourt read the first volume of the *Decline and Fall*, but whenever it was, it had, I believe, a profound impact on him. The only certain facts that we do know about the journey to England are that during the course of it Seroux d'Agincourt visited the celebrated collection of antiquities which had been assembled by the great collector Charles Townley[17] and was warmly received at Strawberry Hill by Horace Walpole, who encouraged him to look at various Gothic cathedrals. This was evidently the first time he had been brought into touch with an utterly unfamiliar culture, for conspicuously absent from among his French friends seem to have been La Curne de Sainte-Palaye and the medievalists associated with him.[18] The contact with England was to prove of lasting importance.

From England, Seroux d'Agincourt traveled to the Low Countries and northern Germany, carefully examining the Gothic churches wherever he went, and thence, after a brief return to Paris, he left France (forever, as it turned out) and proceeded to Italy. In every city he seems to have met the local rulers and the local scholars—the King of Sardinia, the Abate Morelli, Tiraboschi—and, at the very end of November, 1779, he reached Rome,[19] where he was greeted by the brilliant society gathered round the French ambassador, the Cardinal de Bernis, and by the artists studying at the French Academy. A year or so later, he went for a few months to Naples, Pompeii, and Paestum. But after his return to Rome he never again left the city, and he died there in 1814 at the age of eighty-four.

Somewhere on the road to Rome, Seroux d'Agincourt, the rich, well-connected, amiable, scholarly dilettante, had found the inspiration for the arduous, grinding, and painful task which was to keep him occupied until almost the end of his life.[20] What were the ruins among which he sat musing he never tells us, but certainly by the time he reached Bologna (and possibly before), he had decided to write his *Histoire de l'Art par les Monumens, depuis sa décadence au IVe siècle jusqu'à son renouvellement au XVe*. It is the contention of this paper—indeed its only justification in this context—that both the idea and much of the nature of this massive undertaking were derived from his study of Edward Gibbon, and that without an awareness of this relationship Seroux d'Agincourt's achievement was bound to be (and always has been) misunderstood.

That art *had* declined no one had ever doubted, at least since the Renaissance. No anticipation of Wickhoff or Riegl is to be found in Vasari's masterly preface to the *Vite de' più eccellenti Architetti, Pittori et Scultori Italiani da Cimabue insino a' tempi nostri*, which illustrates the process of decadence with an example that was to be used again and again over the centuries (by Gibbon, among others):

> The triumphal arch made for Constantine by the Roman people at the Colosseum, where we see, that for lack of good masters not only do they make use of marble reliefs carved in the time of Trajan, but also of spoils brought back to Rome from various places. Those who recognise the excellence of these bas-reliefs, statues, the columns, the cornices and other ornaments which belong to another epoch will perceive how rude are the portions done to fill up gaps by sculptors of the day. . . .

Indeed, it would not be too misleading an exaggeration to say that Seroux d'Agincourt's hundreds of pages and thousands of illustrations constitute essentially a vast elaboration of Vasari's succinct account. But why devote huge volumes to the decline and fall of art when others, like Vasari himself, had been content to refer to the matter as briefly as possible before passing on to happier things? Seroux himself had doubts: "J'aurais volontiers détourné mes yeux de ce spectacle, sans toucher au voile qui s'épaissit de plus en plus sur les détails et les preuves de cette décadence déplorable; mais . . . l'Histoire générale et la Philosophie m'ont semblé réclamer contre cet oubli, et vouloir que le vide fut rempli. . . ."[21]

And so, backed up by unlimited wealth and influential contacts, Seroux began his formidable research into "un désert immense, où l'on n'aperçoit que des objets défigurés, des lambeaux épars."[22] The exploration of this unknown territory was too great a task for one man, however industrious, and Seroux naturally relied to some extent on the collaboration of correspondents in different parts of Europe; but his real innovation was to employ a significant number of artists to copy and engrave what I believe today still constitutes the largest number of late antique and medieval artefacts to be illustrated within the pages of a single book.[23] By 1782, much of the preparatory work was done; by 1789, shortly after the appearance of the last volume of the *Decline and Fall*, the whole enterprise seems to have been ready for publication.

The book cannot be considered here, even in outline, but certain points must be stressed. Seroux d'Agincourt believed that it was useless to study the art with which he was concerned without first providing a summary of the political, civic, and religious history of the twelve centuries between the Emperor Constantine and Pope Leo X, because only this would "faire ressortir l'influence des causes générales qui, dans tous les temps et dans tous les lieux, décident du sort des beaux-arts comme de celui de tous les nobles produits de la civilisation."[24] He devoted twenty-eight chapters to this *Tableau historique*, and his guides, as he himself made quite clear, were Montesquieu and Gibbon,[25] for both men had demonstrated that the ruin of Roman power had brought with it the ruin of literature as well and hence, by implication, that of the fine arts. On a number of occasions Seroux goes out of his way to acknowledge Gibbon as his source for some particular episode or argument, but in fact the indebtedness of this section of the book to the *Decline and Fall* is so apparent that the point need be pressed no further.

It is, however, worth giving two instances, one trivial, the other more significant, of Gibbon's impact on Seroux's treatment even of strictly artistic matters. As an ardent worshiper of Winckelmann's achievement, Seroux felt no doubts about the absolute supremacy of Greek art, and honesty compelled him to acknowledge that it was in Constantinople (which neither Winckelmann, nor Gibbon, nor he himself had ever visited) that Greek· influence must have survived longest. Faced with the dilemma of reconciling this assumption with the views on the Eastern Empire which he had absorbed from the *Decline and Fall*, Seroux found himself explaining that the total degradation of art in the East was due more to the pernicious influence of Byzantine civilization than to any inherent weakness of the artists living there. Like the ancient Egyptians, the Byzantine Church stifled true talent, but as soon as Greeks could escape to a more congenial atmosphere they at once demonstrated their superiority to local ability: this explained the particular excellence of the Pisa Cathedral, which Seroux, in common with other scholars of the time, believed to have been designed by a Greek architect.[26]

More interesting are the conclusions that can be drawn from a survey of the changing critical fortunes of Diocletian's palace at Spalato. The extreme importance of these remains had been brought to the attention of scholarly Europe by those enterprising travelers Jacob Spon and George Wheler in 1678.[27] Their relatively complete account of what they had seen was neutral in tone, but they pointed out that the details of the Temple of Jupiter (which had been converted into a cathedral) "n'étoient pas de si bonne manière que du temps des premiers Empereurs." Early in the eighteenth century, the great Austrian Baroque architect Fischer von Erlach made use of Spon and Wheler's description and their very puny illustration (as well as various drawings which were sent to him directly from Spalato) to "reconstruct" Diocletian's palace as it must have been in its heyday for his *Entwurff einer historischen Architektur*, which was first published in 1721 with some ninety plates illustrating the architecture of all civilizations from the Temple of Jerusalem to Von Erlach's own most recent buildings. The text, in French and German, refrained from any comment on the quality of the palace which Fischer von Erlach had, of course, never seen.[28] In 1764, Robert Adam, who had visited the site with the French draftsman Charles-Louis Clérisseau seven years earlier, published his magnificently illustrated volume of the *Ruins of the Palace of the Emperor Diocletian at Spalatro in Dalmatia*, and, as the impressive list of subscribers indicates clearly enough, the book achieved a wide and influential circulation throughout Europe. Its importance to Adam's own practice as an architect is not relevant here, nor are his small technical criticisms of such details as cramped staircases. It is, however, significant that the concept of the decline of late Roman art had already made such headway that Adam found it necessary to emphasize that "Diocletian had revived a taste in Architecture superior to that of his own times and had formed architects capable of imitating, with no inconsiderable success, the stile and manner of a purer age."[29]

The splendor of the book seemed to settle the matter, and Winckelmann was sufficiently impressed by it to agree that Diocletian's palace showed that Roman architecture had, to a large extent, escaped the degeneration that had by then corrupted painting and sculpture.[30] But ten years later the Abate Alberto Fortis, a Venetian polymath whose interests lay above all in geology and botany,[31] published his *Viaggio in Dalmatia*, which attracted attention throughout Europe partly through its rhapsodic account, clearly written under the influence of Rousseau, of the customs of the wild, nomadic Morlachs. Fortis went out of his way to disclaim any specific interest in art, and, when describing Spalato, he did no more than refer to "l'Opera del Signor Adams, che à donato molto a que' superbi vestigj coll'abituale eleganza del suo toccalapis, e del bulino."[32] But he could not refrain from insisting that, although the palace was among the most respectable monuments surviving from antiquity and he did not want in any way to detract from its merits, too close a study of it would nonetheless be damaging to architects and sculptors because "in generale la rozzezza della scalpello, e 'l cattivo gusto del secolo vi gareggiano colla magnificenza del fabbricato."

Gibbon's account of Diocletian—his "sumptous robes . . . of silk and gold," his shoes "studded with the most precious gems," his eunuchs, his theatrical ostentation and Persian magnificence—ranks among his most incisive portraits, and it was not easily reconcilable with Robert Adam's view that the Emperor had "revived . . . the stile and manner of a purer age." How welcome, therefore, must have been the biting comments of the Abate Fortis, eagerly quoted by Gibbon in a footnote, which, however, exaggerated their impact by omitting all the qualifications with which they had been hedged around in the *Viaggio in Dalmatia*.[33] Moreover, Gibbon pursued the issue by slyly observing that the elegance of Adam's "design and engravings has somewhat flattered the objects which it was their purpose to represent." This insinuation was repeated almost without alteration by Seroux d'Agincourt, who writes of Adam's volume that "les planches donnent une belle et peut-être trop belle idée de cette architecture"; and his own comments on the illustrations of the palace indicate so clearly the impact on him of Gibbon, the moralist, at the expense of Adam, the witness, that they deserve to be quoted at some length:

Il est donc évident qu'il faut placer la corruption de l'Art avant Constantin. Les vices que nous venons de remarquer dans les constructions de Spalatro ne laissent aucun doute à cet égard. Cet édifice présente des dissonances de tous genres, un mélange discordant de colonnes en granit, en porphyre et en marbre, des colonnes dont le fût est de ces matières, et la base et le chapiteau d'une autre, des bas-reliefs enfin dont les sujets annoncent un choix fait sans jugement et sans goût. Si l'impéritie des artistes se montre sur l'arc de triomphe de Constantin dans l'exécution des ornemens, elle ne se fait pas moins reconnoître avant le règne de ce prince, dans la surabondance et la lourdeur des parties accéssoires qui surchargent l'architecture. . . .[34]

Seroux expressed the hope that the two French artists, Cassas and Dufourny, who had recently visited Spalato, would give a more faithful account of the palace than Adam had done. In fact, Cassas's beautifully designed and illustrated volume was accompanied by a text of Joseph Lavallé, which, without ever mentioning Adam (visitors to Dalmatia were noticeably ungenerous to their predecessors), provided a purely Gibbonian interpretation of the remains. While acknowledging their splendor, the general conclusion was as follows:

> . . . il est facile de reconnoître que, dès cette époque, l'art de l'architecture avoit déjà fait un grand pas vers la décadence. On peut l'attribuer au mauvais goût que la faste et la richesse, toujours avide d'ornements, forçoient les architectes à contracter; et il est assez simple de penser que les princes qui, comme Dioclétien par exemple, avoient quitté la toge romaine pour le costume et le luxe des monarches asiatiques, avoient du penchant à trouver beau ce qui n'étoit que riche: car si l'on considère la pureté de la porte de ce temple et de la galerie extérieure, il est aisé de se convaincre que ces architectes étoient encore sensibles aux beautés de l'antique, et qu'ils savoient les étudier avec fruit. . . .[35]

It is tempting to believe that Seroux himself may have had a hand in formulating these judgments.

Such instances—and many more could be quoted—hint clearly enough at Seroux d'Agincourt's dependence on Gibbon for specific details, but his real debt is of another order altogether. For he could find no guide to help him in the archaeological or art-historical literature of the time. Winckelmann had ostentatiously neglected any art later than that of the golden age, as he visualized it, while the innumerable local antiquarians, on whose researches Seroux often relied, were, it is true, determined to push the chronological boundaries of conventional study as far back as possible, but only so as to find ever more precocious ancestors for the art of the Renaissance. If a painter of some distinction could be found, in Pisa or Siena for example, who anticipated Cimabue or Giotto in the depiction of the human form, such a discovery would enhance the reputation of either city at the expense of Florence. It is partly for this reason that art historians today, especially in Italy, have been keen to give credit to such local studies, and the undeniably valuable results they achieved, to the detriment of Seroux d'Agincourt.[36] For Seroux, like Gibbon, and like him alone, was interested in the process by which perfection disintegrated. Nothing could make this point more clearly than the first plate with which he illustrated the section of his book devoted to sculpture. The large folio page is divided into thirty-two miniature reproductions to constitute a "choix des plus beaux monumens de la Sculpture antique"—the *Apollo Belvedere* and the *Capitoline Venus*, the *Laocoön*, the *Agrippina*, the *Marcus Aurelius*, the *Daughters of Niobe*, and many more. This absurdly unhistorical presentation, so typical of an "homme de goût," matches in its evocative power the opening chapters of the *Decline and Fall* before the rot set in.

It is true that, as the book progressed, Seroux became increasingly fascinated by some of the oddities he found; he came to scoff, and sometimes he paused to praise. But here, too, he could find occasional precedents in Gibbon for such an attitude, and it is, I believe, falsifying his overall design to pick out for admiration only such sympathetic responses. If, here also resembling Gibbon, Seroux ends his book on an increasingly happy note—indeed, in his case, the note is one of absolute triumph—it should never be forgotten that he was concerned essentially with the process of decline.

It would, however, be wrong to make the relationship between them too schematic. Living in Rome and a favorite of the ecclesiastical society of the city, Seroux shared none of Gibbon's contempt for the development of Christianity—or, if he did, he was remarkably successful at concealing it. He goes out of his way to emphasize that the decadence of art preceded the conversion of Constantine, and he gives what I believe to be the first historical survey of the emotional impact exerted by Gothic architecture throughout the ages. This friend of Voltaire lived to read—and to appreciate—the rhapsodies of Chateaubriand.[37] Nonetheless, I hope that I have produced enough evidence to suggest that, in a very real sense, Seroux d'Agincourt's fundamental book demonstrates the application of Gibbonian interpretations to the study of art.

Fundamental—I use the word with some hesitation. We have seen that Seroux's book was almost exactly contemporary with that of Gibbon, whose influence on it was so strong, and that it was due to be published within a year or two of the *Decline and Fall*. The Revolution put an end to so elaborate and expensive a venture, and in fact it was not until 1810 that the first fascicules began to appear.[38] During the twenty-year interval between completion and publication, Seroux, impoverished now through the abrupt cessation of his income from France, tinkered relentlessly with his manuscripts, making repeated alterations, trying to keep abreast of new research, looking back nostalgically to the past. In the light of our present knowledge, it is impossible to follow the process with any confidence. Had the book indeed appeared at much the same time as the last volumes of Gibbon (the younger man of the two), the affiliation would inevitably have been noted, and the *Histoire de l'Art* would have taken its rightful place in the world of scholarship as a sort of supplement to the *Decline and Fall*. Twenty years later everything had changed.

Seroux's researches had become well known—Goethe, for example, had commented on them during his visit to Rome—and many of his collaborators and friends had in the meantime published brief and valuable monographs on early art. In themselves these need no more have affected the grand design of Seroux's majestic volumes than the continuing flow of treatises on Roman commerce or clothing impinged on the *Decline and Fall*. Much more serious was the fact that the whole approach to the subject had changed by 1810. Two generations earlier, Gibbon himself had been aware that another attitude than his toward the decline of the Roman Empire was at least a possibility to be reckoned with. But he had dismissed it with scathing irony: "They massacred their hostages, as well as their captives," he had written of Attila and his followers: "Two hundred young maidens were tortured with exquisite and unrelenting rage; their bodies were torn asunder by wild horses, or their bones were crushed under the weight of rolling waggons; and their unburied limbs were abandoned on the public roads, as a prey to dogs and vultures. Such were those savage ancestors, whose imaginary virtues have sometimes excited the praise and envy of civilized ages!"[39] And, indeed, to a surprising extent his self-assured sense of values survived relatively intact until long after his death.

Seroux was less fortunate. Where he had picked his way with gingerly determination through centuries of decay, here and there holding up for cautious admiration the occasional Byzantine ivory or Lombard church or medieval fresco, his disciples, who belonged to a civilization very different from that in which he had been brought up, began to reject his evolutionary approach to art and to admire "primitive" artifacts for their own sakes, with no concern for the direction in which they were moving, sometimes, indeed, with actual distaste for that direction. Seroux had written with genuine warmth of Giotto, praising his innovations, his expressive power, and his composition, but the framework in which he had done so was still that evolved by Vasari and taken up by all subsequent writers who viewed the artist as having been great, "considering the times in which he had lived," above all, because he had shown the way that led to still greater things. However, William Young Ottley, one of those who made illustrations for the *Histoire de l'Art*, went so far as to claim that

> . . . in respect of the three great requisites of *invention, composition*, and *expression*, and for the *folding of the draperies*, the best productions of these periods may even now be studied with profit, and those of *Giotto*, especially . . . abound in examples in which, by the employment and ingenious distribution of the figures, the intended subject is developed with a degree of perspicuity seldom equaled, and perhaps never surpassed, by painters of later times.[40]

It is true that a long period was to elapse before late Roman art—the *décadence*, rather than the *renaissance* or the *renouvellement*, in Seroux's schematization—was to be seen as progress, but nonetheless the growing enthusiasm for early sculpture and painting led, even in Seroux's own lifetime, to the whole balance of the book being disturbed. The process has continued ever since, and the author has therefore been praised or blamed according to whether he admired or neglected the art, whose serious "rediscovery" began only when he was in his seventies or eighties. Partly because he lacked Gibbon's supreme literary skill and single-mindedness of vision, the *Histoire de l'Art* has suffered in the eyes of posterity far more seriously than the *Decline and Fall* has for even greater misjudgments, such as—to take a notorious instance—that concerning the nature of Byzantine civilization.

This was, for the most part, still in the future. But even before his book began to be published, Seroux saw with alarm one effect of his researches. In what are for us today surely the most moving pages in the whole *Decline and Fall*, Gibbon had asked "with anxious curiosity whether Europe is still threatened with a repetition of those calamities, which formerly oppressed the arms and institutions of Rome."[41] His answer was fairly reassuring, but Seroux lived to see—partly, as he thought, through his own responsibility—the collapse of an artistic culture which he cherished. As a young amateur, he had loved the art of his rococo contemporaries, Boucher and Fragonard; in middle age, he had been "converted" by the Neoclassical admirers of Winckelmann; as he grew older, he could see artists (and not merely connoisseurs) cultivate with fanatical zeal the "primitive" he had brought to their attention. In his last years he writes with something like remorse. Fortunate Winckelmann to have studied only Greek perfection and to have been able thereby to indicate to artists what they should imitate: "Je leur montrerai ce qu'ils doivent fuire. C'est ainsi qu'à Sparte, l'ivresse mise sous les yeux des enfants, leur en inspirait l'horreur. . . ."[42]

He renewed his warnings by writing, at the very end of his life, a little book on the antiquities of his own private collection.[43] This was a direct return to the practice which had been advocated and carried out by the Comte de Caylus when Seroux was a brilliant young man. Appropriately enough (though without his knowledge), when the book appeared after his death, there was published as a frontispiece the portrait of him that had been drawn by Cochin for Madame Geoffrin, so that even in its physical appearance the book seems to constitute a return to a long-dead past. It was dedicated "aux élèves des beaux arts, mes jeunes amis," and with deep feeling Seroux emphasizes, "Je reviens aujourd'hui à la plus parfait manière d'instruire, aux leçons que présente la belle sculpture antique; je les chercherai dans les divers morceaux dont l'acquisition et la jouissance ont fait, pendant un long espace de temps, toute ma consolation." The illustrations must suffice with commentary reduced to a minimum: "Je ne me piquerai point d'une profonde érudition; ma tête, plus qu'octogénaire, n'en serait plus capable," and he insisted once more, for the last time, on the utility of his life's work, if only it were studied in the right spirit. "Sachez-moi quelque gré du travail que je me suis imposé, pendant trente ans, pour réunir et mettre sous vos yeux un pareil amas d'exemples qu'il vous importe d'éviter."

If Gibbon had survived to see not merely the first stages but the irredeemable breakup of "Europe as one great republic, whose various inhabitants have attracted almost the same level of politeness and cultivation,"[44] and if he found real reasons for believing that the accounts he had given to the world of heresies and fanaticism, barbarian invasions and cruelty had actually been adopted as guides to conduct, he might have shared some of the feeling of his somewhat older French contemporary.

But, despite his qualms and despite many inadequacies of research, Seroux d'Agincourt had produced a work of fundamental importance. A final Gibbonian analogy is apt. Reviewing Milman's *History of Christianity*, Cardinal Newman was forced to observe: "It is notorious that the English Church is destitute of an Ecclesiastical History; Gibbon is almost our sole authority for subjects as near the heart of a Christian as any can well be."[45] For many years after Newman wrote these words, very similar sentiments could have been expressed about Seroux's labors by any student of the arts ranging between the third and the fifteenth centuries.

REFERENCES

[1]*Gibbon's Journey from Geneva to Rome: His Journal from 20 April to 2 October 1764* (hereafter cited as *Journal*), ed. Georges A. Bonnard (London, 1961), pp. 97 and 179. Gibbon's conversion to Correggio was to have a satisfying sequel. One of the few analogies with art which he makes in the *Decline and Fall* comes in the course of an ironical account of miracles in the famous chapter 15: "The recent experience of genuine miracles should have instructed the Christian world in the ways of providence, and habituated their eye (if we may use a very inadequate expression) to the style of the divine artist. Should the most skilful painter of modern Italy presume to decorate his feeble imitations with the name of Raphael or of Correggio, the insolent fraud would be soon discovered and indignantly rejected" (*DF*, p. 571, edition cited in note 33, below). Gibbon had more right to make this bold assertion than he himself could have realized, or than the results of eighteenth-century connoisseurship could have justified. In Reggio Emilia he was shown a *Crucifixion* said to be Correggio; he was evidently not convinced and merely commented in his *Journal* (p. 102): "J'ignore l'auteur de ce tableau." He was right to be skeptical of the attribution, for the picture (now in the Galleria Estense in Modena) is in fact by Guido Reni.

[2]The glib answer would be to say that before Michelet no historian would have thought of drawing on the arts to substantiate his arguments. I hope to show that the issue is much more interesting than that, but would like to point out that I cannot agree with Albert Hoxie who has recently discussed just this problem and appears to suggest that Gibbon did not refer to late Roman or medieval art because he did not like it. See Albert Hoxie, "Mutations in Art," *The Transformation of the Roman World: Gibbon's Problem After Two Centuries*, ed. Lynn White, Jr. (Berkeley and Los Angeles, 1966), pp. 266-90.

[3]For whom, see especially Ludwig Schudt, *Italienreisen im 17. und 18. Jahrhundert* (Vienna-Munich, 1959).

[4]J. Winckelmann, *Histoire de l'art chez les ancients*, 2 vols. (Amsterdam, 1766), "Préface de l'auteur," p. x.

[5]*Journal*, p. 74. Here, as elsewhere, I have silently corrected some of Gibbon's more obvious slips of spelling, etc. The picture was almost certainly a version of a lost composition by Caravaggio.

[6]*Journal*, June, 1764, p. 112-18.

[7]Gibbon's skepticism about the value of ancient portraiture to the historian was taken up again—perhaps consciously—by Norman Douglas in a brilliantly entertaining account of the surviving busts of Tiberius, which includes: "But what type of man these busts figure forth can only be deciphered by those

who have made up their minds on the subjects beforehand. Long years will elapse before serious psychological deductions can be drawn from the data of iconography." *Siren Land* (Penguin Books, 1948), pp. 66-68.

[8]*Journal*, July 5, 1764, p. 138.

[9]*Journal*, July 16, 1764, p. 166.

[10]For Byres and his guiding of English visitors and references to him in the letters of Winckelmann, see Brinsley Ford, "James Byres—Principal Antiquarian for the English Visitors to Rome," *Apollo*, 1974, pp. 446-61.

[11]*Journal*, July 21, 1764, p. 178.

[12]*Voltaire's Correspondence*, ed. Theodore Besterman, 107 vols. (Geneva, 1953-65), Vol. LXXVII, letter 15812, October 17, 1770, pp. 169-70.

[13]As there is no biography of Seroux d'Agincourt except the brief account of his life by Gigaut de La Salle in Michaud's *Biographie Universelle*, most of what we know about him comes from his own books. Except where otherwise indicated, all the information in this and the next few paragraphs is taken from the following pages in his *Histoire de l'Art par les Monumens, depuis sa décadence au IVe siècle jusqu'à son renouvellement au XVIe*, 6 vols. (Paris, [1810]-1823) (hereafter cited as *Histoire de l'Art*), I, "Notice sur la vie et les travaux de J. L. G. Seroux d'Agincourt," and (for the friendship with Buffon), I, "Architecture," p. 48. For Louis XV and the Soubise, I, "Architecture," p. 84, and II, "Sculpture," p. 70. For his relations with Caylus and Mariette, II, "Sculpture," p. 85 and I, "Architecture," p. 103. For his reminiscences of Hubert Robert, "mon très ancien ami," see I, "Architecture," p. 15, and for Horace Walpole, I, "Architecture," p. 69 and p. 80.

[14]The portrait is used as a frontispiece to his (posthumous) *Recueil de fragmens de sculpture antique en terre cuite* (Paris, 1814).

[15]See, for instance, *Correspondance des Directeurs de l'Académie de France à Rome avec les surintendants des bâtiments* (publiée . . . par MM. Anatole de Montaiglon et Jules Guiffrey), 18 vols. (Paris, 1887-1912), XIII, p. 385 and XIV, p. 350.

[16]Jean-Baptiste Le Brun, *Almanach historique et raisonné des architectes, peintres, sculpteurs, graveurs et ciseleurs, Année 1777* (Minkoff Reprint, Geneva, 1972), p. 185.

[17]*Recueil de fragmens*, p. 8. I am grateful to Mr. W. S. Lewis for indicating to me two letters from Seroux d'Agincourt to Horace Walpole which will be published in the forthcoming volumes of the Yale edition of the Walpole correspondence.

[18]See Lionel Gossmann, *Medievalism and the Ideologies of the Enlightenment: The World and Work of La Curne de Sainte-Palaye* (Baltimore, 1968), who discusses Sainte-Palaye's importance for Gibbon, but does not mention Seroux d'Agincourt.

[19]The exact date is given in the "Notice" at the beginning of the *Histoire de l'Art*, and is confirmed in the *Correspondance des Directeurs*, XIII, p. 477. It is odd that it should have aroused such controversy and confusion in recent years.

[20]He himself says that he began his research in 1779, *Histoire de l'Art*, II, "Peinture," p. 129. The "Notice" (p. 5) mentions that he spent several months in Bologna, almost certainly in that year, "car déjà il avoit conçu le vaste plan de l'ouvrage qui devint l'objet de toutes ses recherches, et la principale occupation de sa vie." It is, however, possible that he had begun to think of it some two years earlier, and hence under the immediate impact of Gibbon; see II, "Peinture: Décadence," p. 45: "Occupé depuis longtemps du projet de composer, par les monumens, l'histoire de l'art de peindre, depuis sa décadence . . .," and (in a note), "Je m'étais proposé de faire usage de quelques uns des beaux manuscrits que possédait M. le duc de La Vallière, surtout pour les XVe et XVIe siècles. Cet illustre amateur m'avait promis, en 1777, avant mon départ pour l'Italie, de m'en donner une libre communication . . . ."

[21]*Histoire de l'Art*, I, "Discours Préliminaire," p. v.

[22]*Ibid.*, p. iii.

[23]The essential modern contributions to our understanding of Seroux d'Agincourt are those by Giovanni Previtali, *La fortuna dei primitivi dal Vasari ai Neoclassici* (Turin, 1964); André Chastel, "Le gout des 'Préraphaélites' en France," *De Giotto à Bellini* (an exhibition at the Orangerie), (Paris, 1956); Christopher Lloyd, *Art and Its Images: An Exhibition of Printed Books Containing Engraved Illustrations After Italian Painting* (Oxford, 1975); and Angela Cipriani, "Una proposta per Seroux d'Agincourt: La Storia dell'Architettura," *Storia dell'Arte*, 1971, pp. 211-61.

[24]*Histoire de l'Art*, I, Preface, p. 1.

[25]*Ibid.*, "Tableau Historique," chapter 3, and see also chapters 7 and 14.

[26]See, especially, *Histoire de l'Art*, II, "Sculpture," p. 47 and I, "Architecture," p. 43. It is true that his attitude to Greek *painting* was often very much more hostile.

[27]Jacob Spon and George Wheler, *Voyage d'Italie, de Dalmatie, de Grèce et du Levant, fait aux années 1675 et 1676*, 2 vols. (Amsterdam, 1679), I, pp. 76-81. I am grateful to Mrs. Richard Kindersley for her help concerning travels to Spalato.

[28]Johann Bernhard Fischer von Erlach, *Entwurf einer historischen Architektur* (Vienna, 1721), Book II, tables 10 and 11.

[29]Robert Adam, *Ruins of the Palace of Diocletian at Spalatro in Dalmatia* (London, 1764).

[30]Wickelmann (cited above, note 4), II, pp. 332-33.

[31]For Fortis and his reputation, see Gianfranco Torcellan, "Profilo di Alberto Fortis," reprinted in *Settecento Veneto e Altri Scritti Storici* (Turin, 1969).

[32]Abate Alberto Fortis, *Viaggio in Dalmatia*, 2 vols. (Venice, 1774), p. 2.

[33]Edward Gibbon, *The History of the Decline and Fall of the Roman Empire* (*DF*), 6 vols. (London, 1776-88), chapter 22, notes 121 and 122.

[34]*Histoire de l'Art*, I, "Architecture," p. 119 and p. 11.

[35]Joseph Lavallée, *Voyage pittoresque et historique de l'Istrie et de la Dalmatie, rédigé après l'itinéraire de L. F. Cassas* (Paris, 1802). There is an intriguing sequel. As late as 1887, when the architect and traveler T. G. Jackson wrote his great book on Dalmatia, he found it necessary to refer to Seroux's opinions on Diocletian's palace, but by now he could refute them from a new standpoint: "the . . . irregularities at Spalato are so well executed and artistically managed that it seems mere pedantry to condemn them as barbarisms of men who would have done better if they could. If, as seems likely, the architect of Spalato deliberately forsook the old paths because he found a clue that led him to a new one he should surely be praised for having enriched his art, rather than blamed for degrading it . . . ." T. G. Jackson, *Dalmatia*, 3 vols. (Oxford, 1887), II, pp. 30-31. Thus, at last, after more than a century, was the ghost of Gibbon's *Decline and Fall* exorcised from art history.

[36]See, especially, Previtali whose important book is nonetheless fundamental to most of the issues discussed here.

[37]*Histoire de l'Art*, I, "Architecture," pp. 68-69.

[38]It appeared in 24 *livraisons* between 1810 and 1823.

[39]*DF*, chapter 35.

[40]Quoted in Haskell, *Rediscoveries in Art: Some Aspects of Taste, Fashion and Collecting in England and France* (London, 1976), p. 47. The book contains some further references to Seroux d'Agincourt and his contemporaries.

[41]*DF*, "General Observations on the Fall of the Roman Empire in the West," following chapter 38.

[42]*Histoire de l'Art*, I, "Discours Préliminaire," p. v.

[43]*Recueil de fragmens*, cited above, note 14.

[44]See note 41.

[45]J. H. Newman, "Milman's View of Christianity," reprinted in *Essays and Sketches*, 3 vols. (New York, 1948).

Brandoin del.   lith. de C. Constand

Gibbon.
after the original in the
possession
of Monsr le Prof.^r Saine
de Lausanne.

Portrait of Edward Gibbon by Michel-Vincent
Brandoin. By courtesy of the Trustees of the
British Museum.

ROBERT SHACKLETON

The Impact of French Literature on Gibbon

THE FRENCH PHILOSOPHES OF THE EIGHTEENTH CENTURY were not in all cases men of learning, nor were the learned men of that age always sons of the Enlightenment.[1] Certainly French universities were in decay: they made scarcely more contributions to learning than to *la philosophie*. The Académie des Inscriptions et Belles-Lettres was active and its members were learned, but few of them were closely linked to the *philosophes*. Montesquieu, writing in his *Pensées* around 1736, mocks "ces savants qui ont toute leur science hors de leur âme, et qui annoncent la sagesse des autres sans être sages eux-mêmes."[2] He had already, in the *Lettres persanes*, remarked on the hostility between the *philosophe* and the man of learning: "Un philosophe a un mépris souverain pour un homme qui a la tête chargée de faits, et il est, à son tour, regardé comme un visionnaire par celui qui a une bonne mémoire."[3] Voltaire speaks equally harshly, in the *Lettres philosophiques*, of the Académie des Inscriptions: "On se serait . . . fort bien passé de je ne sais quelle dissertation sur les prérogatives de la main droite sur la main gauche, et de quelques autres recherches qui, sous un titre moins ridicule, n'en sont guère moins frivoles."[4] Nor does he even spare the Académie de Bordeaux, of which he was a member.[5]

This cleavage between *philosophes* and *savants* was not absolute, as is shown by the career of Fréret, by the posthumously published works of Boulainvilliers, and by the historical books of Montesquieu's *Esprit des lois*; but its existence was a tenet of *philosophe* doctrine, and it was consecrated in d'Alembert's *Discours préliminaire* to the *Encyclopédie*, the great profession of faith of the French Enlightenment. Gibbon saw and deplored this gap, and it was his achievement, so far as it was a feature of the European Enlightenment as a whole, to bridge it.

The first French writer known to have been read by Gibbon, however, was Bossuet, two of whose works, the *Exposition de la doctrine de l'Eglise catholique* and the *Histoire des variations des églises protestantes*, he read in English translation as an undergraduate; his conversion to Roman Catholicism was partly a result.[6] The effect of his later readings in French literature was quite different.

It was during the five years of his first stay in Lausanne that Gibbon became well acquainted with French writers. He describes how first, in the uncongenial household of the pastor Pavilliard, he read and wrote an analysis of Le Sueur's *Histoire de l'église et de l'empire*. But wider horizons presented themselves as he became accustomed to the intellectual atmosphere of Lausanne, where the rigor of what had been a narrow Calvinism had latterly been relaxed. D'Alembert, in the famous article "Genève" of the *Encyclopédie*, published in 1757, described the broadness of the religious views of the ministers of Geneva: they had abandoned the belief in eternal torment, they had become selective in their interpretation of the Bible, they rejected mysteries and all irrationality. In short, says the *encyclopédiste*: "Un respect pour Jésus-Christ et pour les écritures sont peut-être la seule chose qui distingue d'un pur déisme le christianisme de Genève."[7] D'Alembert was exaggerating, as Genevan protests made clear, but undoubtedly the Calvinism of Geneva wore a liberal mask. So it was in the Pays de Vaud. Gibbon himself attributes the credit for this to Jean-Pierre de Crousaz by whose writings (he had died in 1750) Gibbon himself was strongly influenced.[8] Crousaz was one of those unfortunate writers, like the Jesuit Garasse a century earlier, whose refutations enhance the fame of their intellectual enemies rather than their own, and it was no misfortune for Bayle or Pope that Crousaz attacked them.[9] Consequently, Gibbon was able to say that Crousaz had a stronger claim on his gratitude than on his admiration, and more specifically:

> The logic of de Crousaz had prepared me to engage with his master Locke and his antagonist Bayle, of whom the former may be used as a bridle and the latter as a spur to the curiosity of a young philosopher.[10]

The contact with Bayle was fruitful: no writer could better help Gibbon to bridge the gap between erudition and philosophy; nor did his "wicked wit"[11] fail to inspire the mocking style of the *Decline and Fall*.

So far as Gibbon's French reading during his first stay in Lausanne is disclosed by his *Memoirs*, he concerned himself both with the *philosophes* and their more immediate predecessors and also (though in smaller degree) with the *érudits*. He studied Grotius and Pufendorf, made French by the versions and commentaries of Barbeyrac; he mentions Vertot and La Bléterie; he read Pascal's *Lettres provinciales*; outside France he mentions particularly Locke and Giannone; but his delight "was in the frequent perusal of Montesquieu whose energy of style and boldness of hypothesis were powerful to awaken and stimulate the Genius of the age."[12]

On March 19, 1755, he began to keep his *Common Place Book* in which he recorded what he found most remarkable in his historical reading.[13] Like many such documents, it did not last long, but it reveals his interests. He read thoroughly the *Mémoires historiques* by Amelot de La Houssaye, from which he made detailed notes on the history of the nobility and on Spanish history. He learned something of historical method from Lenglet du Fresnoy, the abbé who was half-*philosophe* and half-Jansenist and thus had a double claim, fully exploited, to see the inside of the Bastille. La Hontan taught him about the American Indians, Bayle's dictionary is shown to have been a normal work of reference. The *Bibliothèque raisonnée* provided an easy means of access to such authors as Fra Paolo Sarpi. Giannone's *Istoria civile del regno di Napoli* he is seen to have read in the 1742 French translation. Voltaire's *Annales de l'Empire* he read promptly, for it was published only in 1753. He especially noted the vile career of John XXIII. Voltaire's account of this pontiff appears likely to have been the genesis of the famous condemnation in the *Decline and Fall*: "The most scandalous charges were suppressed; the Vicar of Christ was only accused of piracy, murder, rape, sodomy, and incest."[14]

Gibbon's reading at Lausanne was fortified by personal encounters with scholars. When only nineteen he was able to propose to Crevier an emendation to the text of Livy, which the French scholar welcomed, later manuscript evidence confirmed, and posterity accepted. Returning from Switzerland he met the French historian Beaufort at Maestricht. But above all—the climax of his enjoyment in discovering the French Enlightenment—he met Voltaire, "the most extraordinary man of the age."[15] The greatest intellectual result of his first stay in Lausanne, where he was sent in order to be rescued from popery, was the thrill of contact with the advanced French thought of the day.

But in Lausanne he must have read far more widely in the French *érudits* than his journal suggests, for a great part of his *Essai sur l'étude de la littérature* was prepared there. Though he did not regain England until early in May, 1758, a version of the *Essai* was completed and submitted for comment to Matthew Maty in October;[16] and indeed he asserts that the first chapters were written at Lausanne.[17] It was published eventually in 1761, appearing early in July. It is a work of unique interest. Written in French when Gibbon was barely of age, it combines evidence of vigorous intellectual activity with clear signs of immaturity; it shows an uncertain command of the language, but above all, written at a time when Gibbon's exposure to French culture (albeit mediated in Switzerland) had been complete, it shows in gestation the mind which was to produce the *Decline and Fall*.

The first marginal heading is striking: *Idée de l'histoire littéraire*. The word *littéraire* itself was new. The *Dictionnaire de Trévoux* of 1752 proclaimed it a neologism; it was not accepted by the Academy in the 1718 edition of its dictionary, but it appeared there in 1740. Its English equivalent, "literary," was rejected in 1755 by Johnson in his dictionary, though he was later to rejoice over his membership in the Literary Club. Although the Benedictines of Saint-Maur had begun to publish their *Histoire littéraire de la France* in 1733, the notion of literary history as a scholarly concept, without complement, as Gibbon uses it, was new in 1761, and the term was newer still.

His text likewise begins with a striking sentence: "L'histoire des empires est celle de la misère des hommes"—a laicized and democratic echo of Bossuet's "les révolutions des empires sont réglées par la providence et servent à humilier les princes."[18] He considers the evolution of letters and science, insists that each age has its own speciality, and, as if he had been living fifty years earlier, enters the quarrel of the ancients and moderns firmly and clearly on the side of the ancients. Thus in the *Essai* are new and old attitudes, modernity and archaism, linked in a rather uncertain framework. He deplores the decadence, in his own day, of belles-lettres. By this term it is rapidly made clear that he means erudition, and the decline of erudition is attested by the growth of historical Pyrrhonism.

In speaking of *pyrrhonisme historique*, Gibbon was preceding Voltaire and following Bayle, but more precisely, in the context he chose, he had in mind Lévesque de Pouilly and Beaufort, who denied all certainty in the first five centuries of the history of Rome. He deplored their writings, preferring the solid learning of Fréret and Sallier, and he takes the opportunity of emphasizing the difficulties of historical scholarship.

In the discussion which follows of *l'esprit philosophique*, Gibbon was adding his word to a discussion which attracted many in contemporary France. Indeed, the Académie française had proposed for its prize in 1755 the subject "En quoi consiste l'esprit philosophique?," though the limits to the Academy's own commitment are shown by the instruction that the topic was to be treated in relation to the scriptural admonition *nolite sapere plus quam oportet sapere* and by the award of the prize to a Jesuit. Gibbon's thoughts again were set in motion by d'Alembert,[19] who in the *Discours préliminaire* had written in praise of "cet esprit philosophique, si à la mode aujourd'hui, qui veut tout voir et ne rien supposer."[20] Gibbon seeks to analyze *l'esprit philosophique*: it consists of being able to return to simple ideas, of seizing and combining first principles. The man who possesses *l'esprit philosophique* may be a geometrician, an antiquary, or a musician, but he is always a *philosophe*—a contradiction of d'Alembert's claim that *l'esprit philosophique* and belles-lettres cannot be mixed without detriment to the latter. For Gibbon, the philosopher can profitably study false and even absurd opinions. Using a picturesque image, he says that history to an *esprit philosophique* is what gaming was for the inveterate gambler, the Marquis de Dangeau, who died in 1720: "Il voyait un système, des rapports, une suite, là où les autres ne discernaient que les caprices de la fortune. Cette science est pour lui celle des causes et des effets."[21] Not surprisingly, he here invokes Montesquieu, known as the philosopher of second causes, and opposes him to d'Alembert who, with tongue in cheek, had advocated the destruction of the great bulk of historical evidence at the end of each century.

He continues with the mention of the author of the *Esprit des lois*:

> La théorie de ces causes générales serait, entre les mains de Montesquieu, une histoire philosophique de l'homme. Il nous les ferait voir réglant la grandeur et la chute des empires, empruntant successivement les traits de la fortune, de la prudence, du courage, et de la faiblesse, agissant sans le concours des causes particulières, et quelquefois même triomphant d'elles. . . . Pour moi, j'y trouve simplement une occasion de m'essayer à penser.[22]

Here Gibbon, putting on more maturity than elsewhere in the *Essai*, and beginning almost predictively to depict the philosophical historian, was treating a theme which d'Alembert had been considering in the *Encyclopédie*. In the article "Erudition,"[23] filled with disparagement of learning for its own sake, he admits that an infusion of *l'esprit philosophique* could improve erudition, or make it less shallow; but he has no sustained doctrine and no theory of history. Gibbon, building largely on Montesquieu's practice, evolves a clear theoretical base for philosophical history.

He then gives a specific example of its application in the study of the origin of pagan gods: a subject intensely popular in France at the time of his writing,[24] as is evidenced by the almost simultaneous publication of the Président de Brosses, *Du culte des dieux fétiches* (s.l., 1760) and Nicolas-Antoine Boulanger, *Recherches sur l'origine du despotisme oriental* (Geneva, 1761). The savage exteriorizes his own need, for "le sentiment n'est qu'un retour sur nous-mêmes";[25] he is baffled by the world of nature, and from his uncertainty invents the gods: "Cet arbre qui lui prodiguait ses glands, cette eau claire où il se désaltérait, étaient des bienfaiteurs qui rendaient sa vie heureuse."[26] This is a precise development from Fontenelle, who attributes elementary questionings to primitive man confronted with the phenomena of nature. Then, "de cette philosophie grossière, qui régna nécessairement dans les premiers siècles, sont nés les dieux et les déesses."[27] But Gibbon, bolder than Fontenelle, goes on to trace the growth of monotheism out of primitive religion. As nations become enlightened and as general laws are seen to govern the universe, so men approach the idea of a single god. This psychological approach to religion is more refined, and more historical, than the imposture theories also current in eighteenth-century France.

At the end of the *Essai*, Montesquieu and Rousseau are brought into the discussion.

A quotation from the *Considérations sur les Romains* is given in a form so distorted as to deprive it of meaning,[28] and a barb is aimed at Rousseau: "Les sciences, dit-on, naissent du luxe: un peuple éclairé sera toujours vicieux. Je ne le crois pas." Gibbon joins d'Alembert in attacking Rousseau's *Discours sur les sciences et les arts*.[29]

Other French writers also inspired Gibbon in his *Essai*. In footnotes he quotes, of earlier writers, Montaigne, Boileau, and Racine; of the immediate precursors of the Enlightenment, Huet, Fénelon, Bayle; the poet La Motte; of the *philosophes*, Voltaire, Président Hénault; and of scholars, Tillemont, La Bléterie, Beausobre, Fréret, Fleury, d'Herbelot, Banier, Massieu, Fourmont, Vertot, Mallet, Terrasson, and Bougainville.

One who is not mentioned, but whose mark is evident, is Pascal. Both Gibbon's mention of *esprit géomètre*[30] and his use of the antithesis *raison-volonté*[31] suggest that he has in mind Pascal's *De l'esprit géométrique*, first published in 1728. So, too, the opposition of *raison* and *autorité*[32] and that of *raisonnements* and *faits*[33] are Pascalian, and, though the *opuscule* in which they appear (*Préface sur le traité du vide*) was unpublished until 1779, Pascal's words were taken into the *Logique de Port-Royal* which was readily available throughout the eighteenth century. Similar ideas to these last are found, moreover, in the eighteenth of Pascal's *Lettres provinciales*, and of these Gibbon wrote: "From the *Provincial Letters* of Pascal, which almost every year I have perused with new pleasure, I learned to manage the weapon of grave and temperate irony even on subjects of ecclesiastical solemnity."[34] The polemical qualities of Gibbon's style rival the sharpness of Pascal's and owe much to his example.

The extraordinary depth and range of Gibbon's early reading are attested by the *Essai*. When he went to Lausanne, he was little more than a dropout from Oxford. When he returned to England in 1758, he had identified the great flaw in French thought which it was to be his lifework to transcend, the conflict between the *érudits* and the *philosophes*: he had read the works of both camps; he had described the qualities needed in the philosophical historian and had illustrated their application to the study of religion; he had shown himself an inspired textual scholar.

On his return to England he joined the army.

Gibbon's reading at Lausanne had been mainly from borrowed books. In England he had access to his father's library, but he began to buy books himself and "gradually formed a numerous and select library." The joy with which, for £20, he bought twenty volumes of the proceedings of the Académie des Inscriptions he committed to paper.[35]

A sequential account of his reading from August, 1761, to August, 1764, is given in Gibbon's *Extraits raisonnés de mes lectures* and *Extraits de mon journal*.[36] He records extended reading of the newly acquired *Mémoires de l'Académie des Inscriptions*. He read more of d'Alembert, commenting on the second volume of his *Mélanges* that it was "very sensible and well written."[37] He read six volumes of Fontenelle, and began to read right through LeClerc's periodical, the *Bibliothèque universelle*. Of Bayle's great defense of religious toleration, the *Commentaire philosophique*, he said: "the most useful work Bayle ever wrote, and the least sceptical"; he began to doubt the value of the *Dictionnaire historique et critique*: "Upon the whole, I believe Bayle had more of a certain multifarious reading, than real erudition."[38] He expressed a similar but severer criticism of Voltaire's historical writing:

When he treats of a distant period, he is not a man to turn over musty, monkish writers to instruct himself. He follows some compilation, varnishes it over with the magic of his style, and produces a most agreeable, superficial, inaccurate performance. But [in the *Siècle de Louis XIV*] the information, both written and oral, lay within his reach, and he seems to have taken great pains to consult it.[39]

He read La Mettrie, Raynal, Montesquieu, Condillac, Maupertuis, Buffon, Duclos, and La Condamine, but, along with these *philosophes*, he continued to attend to the works of professional scholars.

Now, the list of his reading had largely become the list of his purchases. The catalogue of his library, skillfully drawn up by Sir Geoffrey Keynes,[40] should be supplemented by the twenty-four volumes of tracts, containing 403 pamphlets, that previously belonged to Gibbon, which are now found in the library of the Athenaeum.[41]

The French books in Gibbon's library constitute a rich, but not a splendid, collection. They form a scholar's working library of high quality, with the addition of recent editions of the French classics. They include the first edition of Buffon's *Histoire naturelle*, the first collected edition of Montesquieu, the dictionaries of Morery and of Trévoux, but not, surprisingly, the *Encyclopédie*, save nine volumes of the *Encyclopédie méthodique*. There are present the entire works of Bayle, two complete editions of Fontenelle, Boulainvilliers's *Etat de la France* and *Vie de Mahomed*, the *Annales politiques* of the Abbé de Saint-Pierre, many works of travels—Chardin, Bernier, Tavernier, La Mottraye, La Condamine, La Lande—and many atlases. The collection of tracts contains much material on French eighteenth-century history, including a great deal on the quarrel over the Bull *Unigenitus*, and—most interesting of all—a manuscript copy of the celebrated *Traité des trois imposteurs*, in which it was contended that Moses, Christ, and Muhammad were three impostors who had deceived mankind.[42]

So much for the self-administered education of Gibbon and the knowledge it gave him of French literature. It was inevitable that, speaking and writing French, he should think of making personal contact with the civilization of Paris. His 1763 visit, lasting from January 28 to May 9, is not as well documented as one would wish, but from Gibbon's correspondence, his *Memoirs*, and the fragmentary journal of his visit,[43] it is possible at least to establish the pattern of his acquaintance and the sequence of introductions.

Lady Hervey gave Gibbon introductions to the Comte de Caylus and to the great hostess of Paris, Madame Geoffrin. Maty provided introductions to two *philosophes*, Raynal and La Condamine, and to the great patron of learning the Duc de Nivernais, who in turn gave Gibbon seven introductions. These were to Caylus again, to the *philosophes* d'Alembert and Duclos, and to the savants Caperonnier, Sainte-Palaye, Foncemagne, and the Abbé de La Bléterie. David Mallet gave introductions to Madame Bontems whom, with her lover the Marquis de Mirabeau, Gibbon saw frequently, and to the obscure La Motte, who became his close friend. It was at Madame Geoffrin's house that Gibbon met Helvétius, and through him in turn he met d'Holbach. Others whom Gibbon is known to have met include, on the *philosophe* side, Diderot, La Lande, and Suard, and among the *érudits*, Barthélemy, Bougainville, de Guignes, and the Abbé Hooke, the son of a friend of Pope and not without philosophical leanings. Among the ladies were Madame Du Bocage and the Duchesse d'Aiguillon. Gibbon enjoyed meeting Helvétius, who treated him "not in a polite but in a friendly manner,"[44] but he was unable to approve "the intolerant zeal of the philosophers and the Encyclopaedists."[45]

Scarcely any record survives of the impression made by Gibbon on this visit to Paris, but Madame Verdelin, writing to Rousseau, gives a good report. Several Englishmen who were at d'Holbach's house are on their way to Switzerland to meet Rousseau: "Si M. Gibbon est du nombre, mon voisin [she says], traitez-le bien, il a, dit-on, plein d'esprit et beaucoup de bonnes qualités. Il a beaucoup vu ici M. de Foncemagne, chez qui je l'ai rencontré."[46]

The dichotomy in Gibbon's reading between *philosophes* and *érudits* is matched exactly in his social acquaintance in Paris. It is much to be regretted that so little is known of his own thoughts about the society in which he moved there.

The formation Gibbon had received before that memorable day, October 15, 1764, on which he resolved to write the *Decline and Fall*, equipped him to be a philosophical historian. His reading in the classics (not studied above) was deep and extensive. His knowledge—entirely that of an autodidact—of scholarship, particularly in France, was far-ranging and secure. His acquaintance with the writings of the *philosophes* was likewise profound, though his sympathy was selective. A close sequential examination of his reading in the rest of his life would be less rewarding. His aim was fixed, and his reading was now planned with that aim in view. His attitude to the books he read had matured; it was active rather than passive: he controlled and dominated his reading. A study of his reading then would be less a study of the intellectual influences which shaped him than of the organization of his work.

Some aspects of the *Decline and Fall* can, however, be looked at as illustrating Gibbon's position in relation to his French background and to his use of French sources.

The article "Histoire" in the eighth volume of the *Encyclopédie*, which was from no less a pen than that of Voltaire, draws a distinction between sacred and profane history. The former, says Voltaire, treats the divine and miraculous operations by which God has been pleased, in the past, to guide the Jewish nation and, today, to test our faith. For his part he will not deal with that respectable subject: "Je ne toucherai point à cette matière respectable." Voltaire, of course, was not serious, as is shown by his replacing the last sentence by a facetious quotation from La Fontaine[47] when the same article was used in the *Dictionnaire philosophique*, but in separating the two kinds of history he was expressing a principle widely accepted by French historians.[48] The separation, when effected by Bodin in his *Methodus ad facilem historiarum cognitionem* of 1566, had been intended to set secular history free from the control of scriptural and patristic authority; but it also preserved the history of Christianity from rational investigation. Bossuet's *Discours sur l'histoire universelle* of 1681 preserved the same separation.

Jean Le Sueur, the seventeenth-century Calvinist historian whom Gibbon read at Lausanne, tentatively added to his religious history an abridgment of the history of the Roman Empire, admitting that the one could not be understood without the other, and his work became an *Histoire de l'église et de l'empire*. Though in this respect an innovator, he was a mediocre historian, the reading of whom Gibbon places "in a middle line between my childish and my manly studies."[49]

Of a different order was Le Nain de Tillemont, much admired and much used by

Gibbon and described by him as "that incomparable guide." When preparing his ancient history, Tillemont had proposed to combine sacred and lay history in one narrative, but difficulty with a censor and the ensuing advice of his friends caused him to separate them into two distinct works.[50] This separation Tillemont, as a devout Jansenist, could justify to himself by invoking St. Augustine's discrete contrast between the City of God and the earthly City, and the distinction made, in the *Logique de Port-Royal* as well as in other Jansenist writings, between the differing fields of operation of reason and faith.

No such reticence was, in the long run, going to be acceptable to the philosophical historian as he had been defined by Gibbon in the *Essai*, and in the *Decline and Fall* the historian who is also a *philosophe* is seen applying the whole of his mind, with serious intent, to the history of Rome. The study of Christianity, far from being separable from the study of the Empire, was to be one of Gibbon's major and most famous preoccupations. At the beginning of the celebrated fifteenth chapter, he makes his position clear in a passage curiously reminiscent (as Giarrizzo has pointed out) of certain words of Voltaire in the *Essai sur les moeurs*. Voltaire had written:

> Rien n'est plus digne de notre curiosité que la manière dont Dieu voulut que l'Eglise s'établît, en faisant concourir les causes secondes à ses décrets éternels. Laissons respectueusement ce qui est divin à ceux qui en sont les dépositaires, et attachons-nous uniquement à l'historique.

This is echoed by Gibbon:

> Our curiosity is naturally prompted to inquire by what means the Christian faith obtained so remarkable a victory over the established religions of the earth. To this inquiry an obvious but satisfactory answer may be returned; that it was owing to the convincing evidence of the doctrine itself, and to the ruling providence of the great Author. But . . . we may still be permitted, though with becoming submission, to ask not indeed what were the first, but what were the secondary causes of the rapid growth of the Christian church.[51]

Gibbon's analysis can be compared in its detail with those of Montesquieu and with an article in the *Encyclopédie* whose authors so often produced statements which, in their boldnesses and their reticences, are characteristic of the French Enlightenment: this is the article "Christianisme." Formerly attributed to Diderot but now simply held anonymous, the article begins with the methodological reservation which is characteristic of the *philosophes*: "Le Christianisme peut être considéré dans son rapport, ou avec des vérités sublimes et révélées, ou avec des intérêts politiques." The tone of the article is a curious blend of mockery and respect—to the point, indeed, that one is inclined to attribute it to more than a single author. The enumeration of the reasons which led the Roman Empire to the adoption of Christianity is mild and feeble:

> . . . cet esprit de douceur et de modération qui le caractérise; cette soumission respectueuse envers les souverains (quelle que soit leur religion) qu'il ordonne à tous ses sectateurs; cette patience invincible qu'il opposa aux Néron et aux Dioclétien qui le persécutèrent, quoique assez fort pour leur résister et pour repousser la violence par la violence: toutes ces admirables qualités, jointes à une morale pure et sublime qui en était la source, le firent recevoir dans ce vaste empire.[52]

In his *Considérations sur les Romains*, Montesquieu barely touched the problem. It was not for nothing that he had submitted his manuscript to the scrutiny of the Jesuit

Castel. Though he made the same distinction as Voltaire and Gibbon when he laid on one side the "secret paths which God selected and he only knows" for the establishment of Christianity, the only cause he specified was the introduction by previous emperors of foreign gods, so that the people's mind was habituated to religious innovation.[53] When he wrote the *Esprit des lois*, however, he was emboldened specifically to treat religion. Book 25 contains a chapter of exceptional interest, "Du motif d'attachement pour les diverses religions."[54] Here Montesquieu is concerned with the psychological basis of religious sentiment, and he displays an analysis which is at once bold and subtle and which can be compared with Gibbon's.

The first reason given by Gibbon for the adoption of Christianity is its intolerant zeal, inherited from its Jewish ancestry, which the author of "Christianisme" had himself mentioned earlier in the article. The intolerance of Christianity was a commonplace of *philosophe* thought. It was succinctly expressed in 1760 by the Président de Brosses, who explained the success of Christianity and Islam by the purity with which they maintained the doctrine of the unity of God (already placed in its historical context by Gibbon in the *Essai*) and by the intolerance which they both derived from their begetter, Judaism.[55]

The belief in a future life, which is Gibbon's second cause, is mentioned in passing by the author of "Christianisme" and also by Montesquieu, who asserts that "une religion qui n'aurait ni enfer ni paradis ne saurait . . . plaire [aux hommes]." Gibbon next alludes to the miraculous power ascribed to the primitive church as a factor making for its acceptance, and then to the exemplary quality of Christian ethics, "the pure and austere morals of the Christians," expressly praised in the article "Christianisme" and emphasized by Montesquieu: "pour qu'une religion attache, il faut qu'elle ait une morale pure."

The final cause in Gibbon's list is "the union and discipline of the Christian republic." He sees the specific political character of the Christians, organized in communities, as promoting the growth of their power. Here was a subject of debate. In his *Continuation des pensées diverses*, Bayle had discussed the political qualities of Christians.[56] He evokes their quietness, their otherworldliness, their willingness to turn the other cheek. He asks whether a society wholly composed of true Christians and surrounded either by infidels or by worldly Christians could survive, and he concludes that it could not.

This pronouncement of Bayle, buried in the fairly obscure pages of the *Oeuvres diverses*, was made famous by Montesquieu in the *Esprit des lois*, where he describes it as the second paradox of Bayle—the first, discussed a few pages earlier, being the contention that it is better to be an atheist than an idolater.[57] Montesquieu, firmly imbued with a belief in the social consequences of religion, thinks it better for a man to have a bad religion than none at all, since religion is a means of social discipline.

In this conflict between Montesquieu and Bayle, Gibbon tacitly takes the side of Montesquieu, and he is indeed far removed from Bayle when he writes that the union and discipline of the Christians

> . . . united their courage, directed their aims, and gave their efforts that irresistible weight which even a small band of well-trained and intrepid volunteers has so often possessed over an undisciplined multitude.[58]

Bayle, for all his learning, was not historically minded. His claim that a society of Christians could not exist is purely a priori, as indeed is much of his scholarship. But

Montesquieu's argument here is not much better. Gibbon, a greater historian than either of them, bases his generalization on an express study of the history of the early Christians.

Of all French writers of the eighteenth century it is Montesquieu whose influence on Gibbon is the strongest, although this influence did not extend to his scholarly method. As Camille Jullian has shown,[59] Montesquieu's use of sources in his work on the Romans is naïve: in each chapter he selects one or two authorities and adheres to them through thick and thin. In discussing Augustus he uses Tacitus, Suetonius, and Dion Cassius. In his short chapter on the decline of Rome his authority is Appian. On the corruption of the Romans he follows Sallust. This is not a method to appeal to Gibbon, with his admiration of Tillemont's meticulous mastery and comparative handling of sources. Nor did Gibbon follow Montesquieu very far in his theory of climatic influence.

But the belief that the historian should trace out the causes of the rise and fall of peoples comes directly from Montesquieu. It is a lesson that Gibbon learned as early as the first stay at Lausanne and that is reflected in the *Essai sur l'étude de la littérature*. The mature Gibbon did not disdain to remember that early lesson. This is made clear in the "General Observations on the Fall of the Roman Empire in the West," which is appended to chapter 38 of the *Decline and Fall*.

After a brief discussion of the greatness of Rome, with a direct echo of Montesquieu ("honour, as well as virtue, was the principle of the republic"), Gibbon addresses himself to its decline:

> The decline of Rome was the natural and inevitable effect of immoderate greatness. Prosperity ripened the principle of decay; the causes of destruction multiplied with the extent of conquest; and, as soon as time or accident had removed the artificial supports, the stupendous fabric yielded to the pressure of its own weight. The story of its ruin is simple and obvious; and, instead of inquiring why the Roman empire was destroyed, we should rather be surprised that it had subsisted so long.[60]

Let this be juxtaposed to Montesquieu:

> Si la grandeur de l'Empire perdit la république, la grandeur de la ville ne la perdit pas moins. . . . Il est vrai que les lois de Rome deviennent impuissantes pour gouverner la république; mais c'est une chose qu'on a vue toujours, que de bonnes lois, qui ont fait qu'une petite république devient grande, lui deviennent à charge lorsqu'elle s'est agrandie. . . . Rome était faite pour s'agrandir, et ses lois étaient admirables pour cela. . . . Elle perdit sa liberté parce qu'elle acheva trop tôt son ouvrage.[61]

A direct textual borrowing is not to be alleged here, but Montesquieu's words were known to Gibbon and inspired him.[62] Inferior to Montesquieu as a social philosopher, as a historian Gibbon stood on Montesquieu's shoulders and saw further than he. But the *Decline and Fall* would be barely conceivable, had not Montesquieu gone before.

REFERENCES

[1]All writers on Gibbon owe a great deal to two outstanding papers by A. Momigliano, "La formazione della moderna storiografia sull'Impero romano," *Rivista storica italiana*, 5: I, 1 (1936), pp. 35-60; 5: I, 2, pp. 19-48; and "Gibbon's Contribution to Historical Method," *Historia*, 2 (1951), pp. 450-63, both reprinted in A. Momigliano, *Contributo alla storia degli studi classici* (Rome, 1955), pp. 107-64 and pp. 195-211. The most valuable study of Gibbon's thought is G. Giarrizzo, *Edward Gibbon e la cultura europea del Settecento* (Naples,

1954). A very useful, and the most up-to-date, study is M. Baridon, *Edward Gibbon et le mythe de Rome*, 2 vols. (Paris, 1975). On the relations between *philosophes* and *savants*, see J. Seznec, *Essais sur Diderot et l'antiquité* (Oxford, 1957), pp. 79-96, and L. Gossman, *Medievalism and the Ideologies of the Enlightenment* (Baltimore, 1968), pp. 87-125.

[2]Montesquieu, *Oeuvres complètes*, 3 vols. (Paris, 1950-55), II, p. 275.

[3]Montesquieu, *Lettres persanes*, ed. P. Vernière (Paris, 1975), letter 145 (also in *Oeuvres complètes*, I,C, p. 306).

[4]Voltaire, *Lettres philosophiques*, ed. G. Lanson and A.-M. Rousseau (Paris, 1964), II, p. 175.

[5]Voltaire, *Candide*, ed. A. Morize (Paris, 1931), p. 146.

[6]*Memoirs of My Life*, ed. G. A. Bonnard (London, 1966), p. 59.

[7]*Encyclopédie* (Paris, 1751-80), VII, p. 578.

[8]*Memoirs*, p. 73.

[9]Crousaz, *Commentaire sur la traduction en vers de M. l'abbé du Resnel de l'Essai de M. Pope sur l'homme* (Geneva, 1738); *Examen de l'Essai de M. Pope sur l'homme* (Paris, 1748); *Examen du pyrrhonisme ancien et moderne* (The Hague, 1733).

[10]*Memoirs*, p. 78.

[11]*The History of the Decline and Fall of the Roman Empire (DF)*, ed. J. B. Bury, 7 volumes (London, 1909-14), chap. 69, p. 229.

[12]*Memoirs*, p. 78.

[13]*The English Essays of Edward Gibbon*, ed. P. B. Craddock (Oxford, 1972), pp. 9-24.

[14]*DF*, chap. 70, p. 300.

[15]*Voltaire's British Visitors*, ed. Sir G. de Beer and A.-M. Rousseau (*Studies on Voltaire and the Eighteenth Century*, XLIX), pp. 32-35, 38.

[16]*Letters*, ed. J. E. Norton, 3 volumes (London, 1956), I, p. 104, note 1; p. 113, note 3.

[17]*Memoirs*, p. 105. References to the *Essai* are to the first edition, London, 1761.

[18]Bossuet, *Discours sur l'histoire universelle* (Paris, 1681), p. 430.

[19]Paragraph 44 of the *Essai* is casually written, but the reference is certainly to d'Alembert, and elsewhere he is cited by name.

[20]*Encyclopédie*, I (1751), p. xxxi.

[21]*Essai*, pp. 94-95: Gibbon is inspired by, and refers to, the *éloge* of Dangeau by Fontenelle.

[22]*Essai*, pp. 108-9.

[23]*Encyclopédie*, V (1757), p. 917.

[24]See especially F. Manuel, *The Eighteenth Century Confronts the Gods* (Cambridge, Mass., 1959).

[25]A phrase used by Montesquieu (*Lettres persanes*, letters 59 and 83, also in *Oeuvres complètes*, I, C, pp. 119 and 169).

[26]*Essai*, p. 130.

[27]Fontenelle, *De l'origine des fables*, ed. J.-R. Carré (Paris, 1932), p. 17 (also in *Oeuvres complètes* [Paris, 1818], II, p. 390).

[28]"La corruption de tous les ordres des Romains vint de l'étendue de leur empire, et produisit la grandeur de la république." *Essai*, p. 156.

[29]*Essai*, p. 157. Cf. Rousseau, *Oeuvres complètes*, ed. B. Gagnebin and M. Raymond, II (Paris, 1964), p. 19. Perhaps it was for this reason that Rousseau spoke ill of Gibbon's *Essai*: "J'ai revu son livre, il y court après l'esprit, il s'y guinde," Rousseau to Moultou, June 4, 1763, in *Correspondance complète*, ed. R. A. Leigh (Banbury, 1972), XVI, no. 2742.

[30]*Essai*, p. 86.

[31]*Ibid.*, pp. 137-38.

[32]*Ibid.*, p. 47.

[33]*Ibid.*, p. 74.

[34]*Memoirs*, p. 79.

[35]*Ibid.*, p. 97.

[36]Edward Gibbon, *Miscellaneous Works*, ed. John, Lord Sheffield, 5 volumes (London, 1814), V, pp. 213-485.

[37]*Ibid.*, p. 217.

[38]*Ibid.*, pp. 234-35.

[39]*Ibid.*, pp. 247-48.

[40]*The Library of Edward Gibbon*, with an introduction by Geoffrey Keynes (London, 1950). A manuscript catalogue of Gibbon's library is held by the Pierpont Morgan Library.

[41]These pamphlets are said to have been presented to the Athenaeum by a member of Gibbon's family, but the club has no record either of his name or of the date of the gift.

[42]Vol. XXIII, no. 10.

[43]*Miscellanea Gibboniana*, ed. G. R. de Beer, G. A. Bonnard, and L. Junod (Lausanne, 1952), pp. 85-107.

[44]*Letters*, no. 41, Gibbon to Dorothea Gibbon, February 12, 1763.

[45]*Memoirs*, p. 127.

[46]*Correspondance complète de Rousseau*, ed. Leigh, XVI, no. 2693, Marquise de Verdelin to Rousseau, May 14, 1763.

[47]*Fables*, VIII, 25: "Si j'apprenais l'hébreu, les sciences, l'histoire!/Tout cela, c'est la mer à boire."

[48]See R. Shackleton, *Montesquieu, A Critical Biography* (Oxford, 1961), pp. 159-61.

[49]*Memoirs*, p. 71.

[50]M. Tronchay, *Vie de M. Le Nain de Tillemont* (Cologne, 1711), p. 19.

[51]Voltaire, *Oeuvres*, ed. L. Moland, 52 vols. (Paris, 1877–85), XI, p. 222; *DF*, chap. 15, p. 2; Giarrizzo, *Gibbon e la cultura* (cited above, note 1), p. 312.

[52]*Encyclopédie*, III, p. 386; cf. J. Proust, *Diderot et l'Encyclopédie* (Paris, 1962), p. 532.

[53]Montesquieu, *Considérations*, chapter 16 in *Oeuvres complètes*, I, C, p. 463.

[54]*Lois*, XXV. 2.

[55]C. de Brosses, *Du Culte des dieux fétiches* (s.l., 1760), p. 239.

[56]P. Bayle, *Oeuvres diverses*, 4 vols. (The Hague, 1737), III, p. 360.

[57]Montesquieu, *Lois*, XXIV. 6 and 2.

[58]*DF*, chap. 15, pp. 57-58.

[59]Montesquieu, *Considérations*, ed. C. Jullian (Paris, 1895).

[60]*DF*, chap. 38, pp. 173-74.

[61]Montesquieu, *Considérations*, chapter 9 in *Oeuvres complètes*, I, C, pp. 412-16.

[62]An earlier borrowing from the *Esprit des lois* is found in the "Letter on the Government of Bern," where the terminology of the chapter on the English constitution is used (*Miscellaneous Works* [1814], II, p. 22). I owe this reference to the kindness of G. Giarrizzo.

OWEN CHADWICK

Gibbon and the Church Historians

EDWARD GIBBON WAS SOMETIMES INCLINED to mistrust "ecclesiastical historians," as we can see from phrases such as "the ecclesiastical historians, who are more or less to be suspected."[1] The unwary modern reader might suppose that in doing so he was assailing the traditions of ecclesiastical history since the Reformation, from Baronius to Tillemont on the Catholic side and from Flacius to Mosheim on the Protestant side. But such phrases were conventionally used to mean the primitive historians of the church, especially the fifth-century writers Socrates and Sozomen, to whom custom ascribed the title, and it was in this sense that Gibbon used them as well. The Catholic historians from Baronius to Tillemont and the Protestant historians—if not from Flacius in the age of the Reformation, at least from Basnage in the later seventeenth century—were necessary to Gibbon in weaving the rich texture of the *Decline and Fall*. And his attitude to these authorities, especially the Catholics with whom he was less likely to sympathize, discloses something important about the nature of his history.

When the Reverend Thomas Bowdler produced an edition of the *Decline and Fall* "for the use of families and young persons" and "with the careful omission of all passages of an irreligious or immoral tendency," he omitted an entire chapter on the early councils of the Christian church, to the acts of which Catholicism looked back as to foundation deeds. But Bowdler achieved nearly as much effect merely by omitting footnotes. Throughout the book, but especially in passages touching upon the history of the Catholic Church, the atmosphere of the unadorned text is subtly different from that of the text with each of its footnotes in place. The difference does not in the least result from a desire to exile the salacious to the foot of the page; a large part of it is made up of delicious little thrusts at the authorities Gibbon used, especially the Catholic historians: "At the mention of that injured name [Hypatia], I am pleased to observe a blush even on the cheek of Baronius."[2] Since Baronius was a cardinal and the classic among Catholic historians, the most papal of all historians, the single word *even* changed the nature of the footnote from a reference to a dagger. Look up the *Annals* of Baronius upon the subject of Hypatia:[3] it is hard amid that dry, ungainly Latin to discern a sentence that could be called a blush.

Gibbon wrote at a key point of time in the history of Christianity. The Renaissance, the Reformation, and then the Counter-Reformation gave that impetus to historical studies which begat modern historical writing. The origins of Christianity were in controversy. The nub of the argument between Catholic and Protestant lay in early Christian history. The Magdeburg *Centuries* on the Protestant side and the

219

Annals of Baronius on the Catholic side marked giant strides in the organization of historical evidence. But both sides marshaled their evidence to prove a case, not because they wished to misuse evidence, but because they were incapable of a detached attitude. Never for a moment could they doubt themselves. The Centuriators would not avoid—and had no wish to avoid—pointing the moral, showing how their information proved the Catholic Church corrupt. Baronius could not avoid— and had no wish to avoid—the notes of exclamation (*O summa dementia!*)[4] which registered his shock as he described deviations of bishops who should have known better.

These were men of the sixteenth century and the age of religious war. By Gibbon's day the atmosphere had changed. No one, whether Catholic or Protestant, could write history with the crude bludgeons of the Centuriators and Baronius. Over the intervening century and three-quarters, knowledge increased in depth and range and precision; no one had done more to increase it than Catholic monks, such as Mabillon and the Benedictines of St. Maur, or learned Catholic scholars, such as Tillemont and Muratori. Without them, parts of the *Decline and Fall* would have been impossible to write.

The great folio volumes of the Magdeburg *Centuries* were obsolete. The great folio volumes of Cardinal Baronius were obsolete in their temper. When Gibbon mocked the blushes of Baronius, he mocked a vanished world. But, unlike the *Centuries*, the *Annals* still lived; the Cardinal had the run of the Vatican, and he placed in his *Annals* documents which could only be found in its Library. The Franciscan Pagi, when a young man, discovered mistakes in Baronius and dedicated his life to annotating the *Annals* so that the new edition would remain indispensable as a book of reference. Though a lack of detachment still shrieks from its double columns of print, though the uncritical air of the original might still perplex or irritate even the Catholic reader, men must still refer to it. The volumes were indispensable. Gibbon's penultimate tribute to Tillemont ran, "Once more, and almost for the last time, I appeal to the diligence of Tillemont. The annals of Baronius and Pagi will accompany me much farther on my long and laborious journey."[5] Gibbon could not organize his work without using a book of reference two centuries old, from a different intellectual environment, and therefore mockable. The mockery is sometimes delicious.

In his assaults upon the age of the fathers, a part of the color was imparted by the contrast of light and shade. Gibbon's enemy, Cyril of Alexandria, attended and directed the council held in 431 at Ephesus. As the Third Ecumenical Council it was canonized in Christian tradition. But for behavior by bishops nothing equaled or exceeded it except the meeting, also held at Ephesus only eighteen years later, known to the world as the Robber Synod. Few moments of history gave Gibbon more occasion, perhaps more pleasure. Occasion and pleasure lay in the contrasts—a council holy to posterity and unholy in conduct. The Patriarch of Alexandria was a tyrant. The Patriarch of Constantinople bribed his way. The meetings were accompanied by outrage, insult, and blasphemy. But Gibbon heightened the effect—and the fascination—by lofty descriptions to make contrasts: "the assembly of the saints"; John of Antioch advancing "with a small though respectable train of divines," the holy abbots; "the trembling monarch listened to the prayers and adjurations of the saints," and, meanwhile, "every avenue of the throne was assaulted with gold"; not just "Ephesus defiled," but "Ephesus, city of the Virgin, defiled" with rage and clamor, sedition and blood.

Throughout the book little sallies in the footnotes denounce or poke fun at Cardinal Baronius, most Roman of historians. Baronius was blamed for being credulous about miracles; for relating the transmutation of barrels, "not of honey but of gold"; for defending the pope's right to make war; for championing the discovery of the true cross; for concealing the truth that the early patrimonies of St. Peter consisted of farms and not kingdoms; for defending a pope when he flattered a usurper; for deciding the theological orthodoxy of a Byzantine racing faction; for maintaining the absolute wrong of Easterners in their conflict with popes; for multiplying the numbers of martyrs beyond the sane judgment of history; for seeking the cause of great events in heaven instead of on earth; and, above all, again and again, for defending intolerance, or praising emperors who closed the churches of dissenters. Much of this blame is cast in the form of delicate little stabs of satire.

Gibbon was by no means flogging a corpse, for Baronius, in his various later editions, still survived. Nor should we judge these sallies apart from Gibbon's equally extraordinary utterances regarding other writers. It would be hard to imagine a modern historian of quality characterizing an Italian author who recorded observations in Mesopotamia as a "gentleman and a scholar, but intolerably vain and prolix."[6] One of the delights of the *Decline and Fall* is Gibbon's frankness regarding contemporaries. When we find him calling Baronius a "bigot," we think him to be damning, until we find him also calling Voltaire a bigot, or Dr. Samuel Johnson "a bigoted, though vigorous, mind, greedy of every pretence to hate and persecute those who dissent from his creed,"[7] though we know that Gibbon otherwise thought Johnson "a critic of high renown."[8]

We notice, then, about Gibbon as a church historian that he is (in some manner at least) a Protestant, and a Protestant of the extreme left. On Catholic dogma—monks, nuns, polemical divines, hierarchs, superstitions, unedifying or extraordinary miracles, excessive ritual or ceremony—Gibbon wrote like any Protestant critic, though more amusingly. His attitude often reminds the reader of the book by Conyers Middleton on the miracles of the fathers, the book which acted so explosively in Gibbon's mind when he was a young man at the University of Oxford. If a Protestant of the left wing like Jean Le Clerc had written a decline and fall of the Roman Empire, it might have been less subtle and less satisfying as history, but its attitude would have been similar to Gibbon's history. The new age of Protestant thought was willing to use ridicule as well as argument against certain Catholic positions, and it was the more powerful against Catholicism because, to win the attack, it was willing to risk or jettison positions traditional to Protestantism.

Gibbon listed[9] "the most learned and rational divines" whom he used as guides. The list is illuminating—Basnage, Le Clerc, Beausobre, La Croze, Mosheim, Jablonski—all Protestants. The first three were Huguenots who fled from Louis XIV and had good reason to hate Catholicism. La Croze was a French Benedictine who, threatened with prison by his superior, fled to Basel and became a Protestant. Only the two Germans, Mosheim and Jablonski, had an assured background as Protestants (Mosheim's father was probably a Catholic, but the fact is unimportant to his career).

At the beginning of chapter 47, Gibbon summarized his attitude to these guides, their utility and their defects:

Petavius . . . a work of incredible labour and compass . . . his Latinity is pure, his method clear, his argument profound and well connected; but he is the slave of the fathers, the scourge of heretics, the enemy of truth and candour, as often as they are inimical to the Catholic cause.

Le Clerc . . . free both in his temper and situation; his sense is clear but his thoughts are narrow; he reduces the reason or folly of the ages to the standard of his private judgment, and his impartiality is sometimes quickened, and sometimes tainted, by his opposition to the fathers.

Beausobre . . . a treasure of ancient philosophy and theology. . . . Yet his refinement is sometimes excessive; he betrays an amiable partiality in favour of the weaker side; and while he guards against calumny, he does not allow sufficient scope for superstition and fanaticism.

[Mosheim] Less profound than Petavius, less independent than Le Clerc, less ingenious than de Beausobre, the historian Mosheim is full, rational, correct, and moderate.

If we leave out of account the malice against Petau, the only Catholic of the four, who was a theologian not a historian, these judgments are sensitive and balanced. To the modern mind, Mosheim is the best general writer in the list; he marked a long step between the age of Baronius and the age of Ranke by his fair and moderate synthesis of the existing state of knowledge. Gibbon well understood Mosheim's commanding place in the development of church history. As Gibbon rightly judged, he was not a profound thinker, nor was he an oddity like Le Clerc, nor a clever theorist. But he was the first historian of the early Christian church who can still be read by someone who wants a fair picture of what happened. Gibbon knew it. "The Protestants," he wrote of later iconoclasm,[10] "except Mosheim, are soured with controversy." No one, not even Tillemont, received more compliments from Gibbon; he regarded parts of Mosheim's narrative as "masterly."[11]

Gibbon's attitude toward the Catholic historians—at least toward Dupin, Petau, Fleury, and especially the "brutal bigotry of Baronius"—is so contemptuous that one instinctively places him within the stream of Protestant writing from the Magdeburg *Centuries* to Basnage and Mosheim. Certainly he was far nearer to these works than to the Catholics in his sympathies. Mosheim is a much more "modern" historian when compared with the first controversial historians of the Reformation. But in one important attitude he stood with the Centuriators of Magdeburg: history showed the corruption of the church in the fourth and fifth centuries, the fading of light and the coming of darkness which were dispelled at last by Luther. Gibbon, on the other hand, disapproved of Luther. But his attitude was curiously cousin to that of the Centuriators. They described the corruption and fall of the Roman Church, he the decline and fall of the Roman Empire. Sometimes the reader of Gibbon half fancies that he is reading a reflection of historical theory among the Protestant warriors: "the triumph of barbarism and religion" meaning what the Protestant historians conceived as "the triumph of barbarism and superstition."

In this theory of the Protestant left, the idea of corruption was carried much further back than by the old Protestant historians of the Reformation. Flacius and his Magdeburg Centuriators and the Anglican historians looked to the primitive church of the first five centuries—or at least of the first three centuries—and exempted the fathers from charges of corruption. Conyers Middleton, Daillé, Chillingworth, Le Clerc, or Bayle saw far more clearly an essential Catholicism in the fathers, and they therefore decided that corruption had been present from the time of the New Testament. Gibbon agreed, and in showing the reader how, he also showed that the positive side of Protestant theory—the purity and simplicity of the original faith—

was not foreign to his nature: "a pure and humble religion";[12] "a pure and spiritual worship, equally adapted to all climates as well as to every condition of mankind";[13] "the purity of the Christian religion, the sanctity of its moral precepts, and the innocent as well as austere lives of the greater number of those who, during the first ages, embraced the faith of the gospel";[14] the benevolent temper of the gospel."[15]

To identify Gibbon with the Protestants of the left wing is therefore tempting. He used them among his best sources and guides. His outlook has much in common with theirs. The melancholy business of the historian is the corruption of a religion.[16] But he is distinguished from them in three ways: first, by the assured character of an eighteenth-century "philosopher"; second, by the greater power of his historical analysis; and third, by an attitude toward the Catholic historians that for his day was unique.

To see the subtle links between Gibbon and his predecessors is only to see that no historian can emancipate himself wholly from his environment and that this environment includes the reigning fashions in historical writing. But sometimes he sounds as though he were exempt from that environment, or as though he were disembodied, so independent in mind that he depended upon none. He saw himself at a turning point in historical study: the point where the rival streams of history, Catholic or Protestant, ceased to satisfy and men might at last acquire the detachment of mind which was the *sine qua non* of seeking truth in history.

Gibbon's judgment of Le Clerc is fine criticism: "He reduces the reason or folly of the ages to the standard of his private judgment, and his impartiality is sometimes quickened, and sometimes tainted, by his opposition to the fathers." Since this is an elegant way of stating an accusation that is usually lodged against Gibbon himself— and was lodged by the nineteenth century against most histories written by men of the Enlightenment—it is delightful to find Gibbon aware of the classical problem of enlightened history and recognizing it in a historian who had personal reasons, as Gibbon had not, for hating clergymen, synods, and orthodoxies. Enlightened history, with Protestant history as a father and Catholic history as a mother, detached itself from its parental traditions and then was seldom aware, as Gibbon was aware when he judged Le Clerc, of the peril of "reducing the reason or folly of the ages to the standard of private judgment."

Sometimes Gibbon felt himself a new creature, standing within neither tradition, Protestant or Catholic, able to observe the bias of both sides and to rise above prejudice into clearer air. Sometimes he was inclined to think this feat easier for him than it was in truth. When he came to the dispute over images, he said that Baronius and Pagi and the Catholic historians treated the subject with "learning, passion and credulity," that the Protestant historians stood upon the other side and therefore,[17] "with this mutual aid and opposite tendency, it is easy for *us* to poise the balance with philosophic indifference." The italicizing of the word *us* is one of Gibbon's darts of historical arrogance. "It is easy"—for a moment he shared the crude confidence of the age of Voltaire. He was often aware that philosophic indifference was far from easy.

Unfamiliar with modern discussions over the nature of historical bias, Gibbon occasionally sounds as though he supposed a perfect detachment from environment to be intellectually possible. This impression derives from the circumstance that he was one of the first generation of historians who freed modern history from its roots in particular European controversies. He was detached from the Catholic tradition of history, though less detached than he supposed, for he could not write his own history without using, and coming to admire, one or two of the Catholic historians. He was also detached from the Protestant tradition of history, though less detached than he supposed, for he often needed Mosheim, and in the *Memoirs* he confessed how Beausobre caused a turning point in his own intellectual development in theology.

This sensation of detachment from both traditions could occasionally produce utterances that now sound arrogant. The most pompous of these deserves quotation for this aspect of the historian's mind.[18] When he reached the Vandal conquest of North Africa, and so the person of St. Augustine of Hippo, he mentioned the subsequent controversies over grace, free will, predestination, and original sin and how the Arminians of Holland "stand aloof and deride the mutual perplexity of the disputants"; he then could not resist adding: "Perhaps a reasoner still more independent may smile in *his* turn when he peruses an Arminian commentary on the Epistle to the Romans." Again the italicizing of the personal pronoun. Blaise Pascal in the *Provincial Letters* ridiculed these disputations, and Gibbon once said that, in his handling of the weapon of ridicule in controversy, Pascal was his master. But this particular utterance of Gibbon on the old controversy carries the tone, not of the simple Pascal, but of a pseudo-Pascal grown egoistic.

Still Gibbon was too interested in bias—as we call it—in prejudice—as he called it—to think himself capable of an absolute freedom: occasionally he allowed, half-humorously, that his own detachment might be imperfect. One of the most charming statements about Cardinal Baronius, on a discussion about the authenticity of a document, ends with a double-edged thrust: "The names of Vatican and Cardinal awaken the suspicions of a Protestant, and even of a philosopher."[19] The "even," again, used to jab, but this time also at his own breast.

This detachment is illustrated by Gibbon's care to be propapal, or at least to criticize Protestant historians for their antipapal prejudice. Those who put Gibbon squarely into the Protestant school of history, regarding him merely as a Protestant of the left wing, like Le Clerc or Bayle or Jortin, find themselves jolted from time to time. For example, Gibbon admired the Protestant scholar Basnage for his learning, his impartiality, even his "manly spirit." Yet Basnage, he suddenly tells us, is too firmly resolved to depreciate "the authority and character of the Popes."[20] Gibbon knew that La Croze was an excellent author, but suddenly he turned around and gave a sly dig at the Protestant prejudices of this ex-Benedictine: "The work of a Jesuit must have sterling merit when it is praised by La Croze."[21] He saw how those learned men, for all their new knowledge and their larger air of impartiality, still stood within the tradition of the old controversialists of the Reformation.

One famous passage is remarkable in this light for its restraint. The legend of the female Pope Joan ought to have attracted both of Gibbon's obsessions. No sane historian could any longer believe the legend, and Gibbon professed to be a little shocked with Mosheim for writing about it that there was no smoke without a fire. He reproached various Protestant historians for refusing to abandon "this poor engine of controversy."[22] He made capital, not out of the legend which he knew to be false, but from the situation of Rome in the tenth century, with its "rare genealogy," the descendants of the harlot Marozia. This context of Marozia is often forgotten by those who quote the saying: "To a philosophic eye the vices of the clergy are far less dangerous than their virtues." In its context the celebrated *mot* was Gibbon's way of rebuking the Protestant historians for their cruder antipapal prejudice and of subtly distinguishing his claim to detachment. What is interesting in Gibbon's treatment of Pope Joan is its restraint.

   This historian, then, who is regarded as incapable of overcoming his prejudices in the realm of religious history, began to be much interested in the phenomenon and nature of historical bias. This was amply illustrated by his chapters on ecclesiastical history because here, and here alone, Roman society of the fifth century was still a subject of controversy in European society of the eighteenth. But as Gibbon's history advanced, he began to encounter other forms of bias: national attitudes—different in France and in Germany—to the coronation of Charlemagne,[23] or dynastic attitudes to the early history of the Italian states,[24] or various attitudes hard to categorize, but still attitudes, in the differing accounts of the rise of Islam. This Voltairean among historians came finally to blame Voltaire for saying that man who in God's name makes war on his own country is capable of anything. Though he aligned himself with the "philosophers," and believed that the "philosophers" were detaching history from the crude prejudices of the past, he saw how claims to an enlightened detachment were not necessarily detached, and he once blamed even Voltaire for his "prejudice" against Catholics.[25]

   In this quest for detachment, Gibbon thought that even the most extreme of Catholic historians had his utility. He saw that if a historian was to be independent and yet was forced by the weight of evidence to use predecessors, he must see how various different pairs of eyes saw that evidence. The Protestant historians helped men to emancipate themselves from the prejudices of Catholic history. But Protestant historians, descended to a man from the Magdeburg Centuriators, also had their prejudices. Therefore Cardinal Baronius—even Baronius—was important to Gibbon, not only because he provided evidence that could be found nowhere else, but because he saw the evidence with un-Protestant eyes. Some writers made parts of the evidence prominent, other writers left them in shadow and fastened attention upon other extracts or documents. Baronius might indeed sink "to the lowest degree of credulity, which was compatible with learning." But he at least had learning and a viewpoint. We must collect all opinions from the evidence, weigh, sift, set off one form of bias against another, watch rival passions and prejudices, and even combine them, and so "we may frequently extract knowledge from credulity, moderation from zeal, and impartial truth from the most disingenuous controversy."[26]

   All this church history was no digression to Gibbon; it was necessary to his plan. It was part, perhaps the main part, of the sense of European continuity.

   Contrast Gibbon with the best of his predecessors. For all his modernity, Mosheim was still a man of the old tradition, organizing the history by years instead of by themes, allowing the *Annals* to dominate narrative, and therefore unable to portray complex development and forced to describe events as isolated. Gibbon had not quite departed from such masters; the notion of explaining the complex development of a society had not entered his mind. But, by abandoning the annalist's arrangement, he made another stride toward modern history. How far he departed from chronology in his order is not always perceived. The reign of the Emperor Heraclius was divided in two. Between the two parts came an enormous tract of history, including the whole of chapter 47, which began with the Christological debate of the early fifth century and ended in 1632 with the expulsion of the Jesuits from Ethiopia. An acid critic remarked that he could hardly see what the expulsion of the Jesuits in 1632 had to do with the reign of Heraclius, or even the decline and fall of the Roman Empire. The order was peculiar. In all Gibbon's volumes this was the least ideal of arrangements. But the arrangement was better than Mosheim's, because it replaced the shackle of time with the freedom of theme. Gibbon was one of the two or three historians who first saw how artificial is a "period" and therefore achieved the sense of continuity denied even to his better predecessors. Instead of dividing the European past, if not by years or by centuries then by moments (Constantine, Charlemagne, Luther), Gibbon felt the stream running through all up to the Europe of his day. He even told his readers what a difference would be made to his subject by the suppression of the Jesuits in 1773—an event almost of the day when his first volume appeared in the bookshops. This advanced perception of continuity was momentous in the treatment of church history, because Christianity was the obvious continuity from a distant Roman past.

Dr. Bowdler thought that Gibbon dragged in Christianity merely to sneer at it; that many passages of church history had nothing to do with his real theme, but were extraneous matter, pushed in like obscene footnotes to gratify an enmity if not an obsession; and that a *Decline and Fall* for young persons should omit these chapters or paragraphs. Dr. Bowdler succeeded in improving the atmosphere of the *Decline and Fall* for young readers, especially if we assume them to be masters of some rare Greek words. But he failed to understand what Gibbon was about. Gibbon not only wanted to say what happened in A.D. 476, he also wished to understand modern Europe. His chapters on ecclesiastical matters, whatever their prejudices or at times superficiality, were integral to the endeavor. Not the sneer, but the deepest and best side of his consciousness as a historian, forced him into church history.

This consciousness was not yet a search for historical development as the descendants of Vico understood it. But the attitude made that search inevitable. Gibbon stood far from the romantic historians. He could not have conceived that the romantic movement would soon metamorphose the study of the Middle Ages and make the later chapters of the history obsolete. But his work was a stage in the process which would make possible the new flowering of history.

I mentioned how Gibbon criticized Jean Le Clerc for the fault for which he and all the historians of the Enlightenment are attacked, "reducing the reason or folly of the ages to the standard of his private judgment." The charge could be justified against all his predecessors. Part of the purpose of history was moral example. From Flacius and Baronius to Mosheim or Tillemont, historians pointed the moral—not by letting their tale speak for itself, but by commenting. Mosheim had several judicious paragraphs which tried to determine who was more to blame for the passions of 431, Nestorius of Constantinople or Cyril of Alexandria, and which reached at length a verdict with which modern judges might concur. No one was yet aware—historians generally were hardly aware until they found that they disagreed with Lord Acton's last desperate longing for verdicts—how moral judgment takes a main part in "reducing the reason or folly of the ages to the standard of private judgment." The conscience cannot make allowances for mental environment. Murder is murder, and no conscience can extenuate by pleading custom, or wrong belief about heresy, or illusion about witchcraft.

This moral judgment is curiously present in Gibbon. As with Baronius's *O summa dementia!*, the note of exclamation is often a sign of moral reprobation. Gibbon[27] extracted the language of the decree of the Emperor Theodosius which condemned the Nestorians to eternal, as well as temporal, punishment: "Yet," he ended, "these were Christians! who differed only in name and shadows."

Here is the point where Gibbon most nearly reduced "the reason or folly of the ages to the standard of his private judgment." They were fighting, the ancient theologians, about nothing—names and shadows, air, words not things, an iota. Baronius did not agree; Dupin, Petau, Tillemont did not agree, but they were slaves of their cloth and their orthodoxies. The most learned and rational divines agreed, and Gibbon turned for authority to the Huguenot exiles: "The degrees of the theological hatred depend on the spirit of the war rather than the importance of the controversy."[28] "The profane of every age have derided the furious contests which the difference of a single diphthong excited," for the difference between the contending divines on the doctrine of God came at one time to rest upon the difference between the word *homoousios* ("united in essence") and *homoiousios* ("similar in essence"). Gibbon was too good a theologian not to understand what was at stake. In his *Memoirs* he wrote that he had been fond of religious disputation since he was a child. He knew well that the presence or absence of an iota could make a vital difference to meaning and that profane men who derided the fathers for quarreling over a single letter of the alphabet might be making themselves ridiculous, because "it frequently happens that the sounds and characters which approach the nearest to each other accidentally represent the most opposite ideas." But on the polemics of the fifth century he had no doubts. And because he had no doubt, he was able to hold up to an opprobrium all the more scandalous the passions of the prelates of Ephesus and Chalcedon.

He was reducing, if not the reason, at least the folly of the ages to the standard of his private judgment. "In the pursuit of a metaphysical quarrel, many thousands were slain."[29] Whether the fight touched anything important was disputed between Catholics and conservative Protestants, on one side, and radical Protestants and Deists, on the other: Gibbon took the radical side. But in the fifth century no one believed it to be other than important, and some of them believed it to be a matter of life and death. Gibbon had the attitude that all sensible men could see that they argued over nothing; how lamentable, therefore, are their passions! He has a curious piece of advice for the Emperor in Constantinople on how he ought to have handled the rival groups of bishops: "Theodosius' most effectual means were indifference and contempt."[30] The nineteenth and twentieth centuries find it hard to imagine how the Enlightenment could examine a city riot—where mobs battered at the doors of churches and even sailors from the ships in Ephesus harbor landed to join the fray— and rebuke the government for failing to act with "indifference and contempt." Again Gibbon blamed Baronius, Tillemont, "etc." for being offended by the Emperor Constantine's letter, inserted by Eusebius, which warned the contending theologians, Alexander and Arius, to moderation, for, said Gibbon, "he was yet ignorant of the difficulty of appeasing the quarrels of theologians," and lamented that men of the same religion should be divided by "inconsiderable distinctions." Gibbon suffered the same anachronism, though this time with a "perhaps" and with two "ifs" afterwards: "The indifference and contempt of the sovereign would have been, perhaps, the most effectual method of silencing the dispute, if the popular current had been less rapid and impetuous, and if Constantine himself, in the midst of faction and fanaticisms, could have preserved the calm possession of his own mind."[31] Thus Gibbon doubled the historian's sin of speculating on what might have happened if something had been different, because he speculated on what might have happened if two things had been different. The "perhaps" hints that his intellect realized they were not different and possibly could not have been different. His conscience told him that they ought to have been different. The moral judgment reduced the reason or folly of the ages to the measure of his mind.

The moral lesson, in this case, blinded the historical eyes. The Enlightenment read exhortations to itself—charity is above rubrics, Christians are Christians before they are Catholics or Protestants; agree in conduct if not in dogma, for how absurd and calamitous are the consequences if men quarrel over metaphysical niceties; abandon the spirit of the Thirty Years' War and overcome the cleavages of Reformation and Counter-Reformation. The lesson was worth reading, but it did not help in understanding the history of the early fathers which was used as evidence for it.

Let us not, in our turn, fail to understand the Enlightenment by blaming historians in the eighteenth century for *their* sense of moral reprobation. "The brutal bigotry of Baronius," wrote Gibbon, and the phrase betrayed to posterity an anachronism. But that is because the twentieth century is in small danger of burning witches or depriving men of citizenship if they reject the Athanasian Creed. The age of Enlightenment looks at first sight to be so tolerant that Gibbon's reprobations sound a little absurd. We forget that the last witch to be executed by a European government died in the last year of Gibbon's life and that in Latin America such acts continued after his death.

Toleration was insecure; perhaps it never would be secure, but it felt far less secure in 1776 than Victorian liberals imagined. The fires of Seville were close. When in his history Gibbon suddenly digressed to sing a little paean for the freedom of the mind from superstition over witches,[32] he was not merely filling space with irrelevance. The Enlightenment was reading itself another lesson. One salvo in the battery against Cardinal Baronius was a sermon on the absurdity, as well as the iniquity, of intolerance. We in our turn are guilty of anachronism if we think the lesson otiose.

This need to preach tolerance was an important part of Gibbon's sense of detachment from the Protestant tradition. Near as he stood to the writers of the Protestant left in so many respects, he wrote amid a world which reacted against the founders of the Reformation because they continued the intolerance of the centuries, burning Servetus or executing Anabaptists. "The nature of the tiger was the same," wrote Gibbon, "but he was gradually deprived of his teeth and fangs. I am more deeply scandalised," he confessed, "at the single execution of Servetus than at the hecatombs which have blazed in the Auto da Fés of Spain and Portugal."[33]

For all his quest for philosophic detachment, even Gibbon could not live quite consistently by the standard of universal toleration which his history demanded from men under circumstances where toleration was not viable. A veiled reference to the "virtues of Ganganelli" in the *Memoirs of My Life and Writings* shows that Gibbon approved the suppressing of the Jesuits which took place three years before his first volume was published. Moreover, admiring and cherishing Gibbon's love of detachment, we are perturbed when he comes to give a list (or, as he termed it, a "small, but venerable synod") of historians whom he regards as wholly unprejudiced, or, if prejudiced in favor of a system, as armed with a "firm and moderate temper which enabled them to suppress their affections, and to sacrifice their resentments." This list or "synod" contained only three names: Ammianus Marcellinus, Hume, and Paolo Sarpi. Since all three are well known to modern students of history as having particular attitudes, or "prejudices," and since Sarpi is renowned for partiality in his presentation of evidence, we can see that in enlightened history the notion of independence was turned into a way of sharing, not eradicating, bias.

Pride in his conviction that he displayed historical freedom and detachment was a small part of Gibbon's onslaught upon Baronius. Much more weighty was the defense of fragile toleration, fragile even within Gibbon himself. But if pride meant fancying that he owed nothing to his predecessors, Gibbon was not guilty. No one was more scrupulous in giving credit where it was due. This is plainest in his attitude to the historian who was the chief link between Baronius and himself, the Catholic Tillemont. Gibbon reserved his noblest tribute for a Catholic historian. His last farewell to Tillemont is well known: "Here I must take leave forever of that incomparable guide whose bigotry is overbalanced by the merits of erudition, diligence, veracity and scrupulous minuteness."[34] Though characteristically assailing as it praises, this passage contains so generous a gratitude that it has misled commentators. When I was an undergraduate, I was taught that Gibbon owed all his historical (as distinct from literary) excellence to Tillemont and that from the moment he was forced to bid Tillemont adieu his history collapsed and was no longer worth reading. This belief was—and is—widespread. Men overlook that Gibbon started it himself. He started it partly by grateful footnotes and this sad farewell. These notes were no more grateful than Tillemont deserved, but not all great authors acknowledge debts so scrupulously as Gibbon did. He started it also by quoting a review in the *Bibliotheca Historica* by a German, Meusel, who pointed out how Gibbon's history declined after Tillemont left him as a guide. He quoted this review, not in the *Decline and Fall*, of course, but in the *Memoirs of My Life and Writings*. Gibbon enjoyed quoting attacks upon himself if they were sufficiently foolish or if they contained praise. The verdict of Meusel contained true and just praise, placing Gibbon among the great historians. Even so, Gibbon was too modest, too sensitive, to translate for English readers, and he quoted the criticism in the decent obscurity of a learned language: *Sine Tillemontio duce, ubi scilicet hujus historia finitur, saepius noster titubat atque hallucinatur* especially, wrote this informed reviewer, when he treated the history of the church or the history of Roman law. Certainly the history declined after Tillemont's help had ended. But my old teachers were nevertheless wrong when they gave credit to Tillemont alone for Gibbon's stature as a historian.

What concerns us here, however, is Gibbon's sense that he owed something to past tradition and a Catholic tradition—a sense which could hardly have been expressed more strongly than by his quoting of Meusel's review and thus declaring to the world as forcibly as anyone could, and more forcibly than most would have dared, his debt to Tillemont.

If we inquire what portrait of Tillemont, the historian and the man, could be gleaned solely from Gibbon's pages, we find that the likeness was close to the real man. As Gibbon described him, he was a maker of "immense compilations,"[35] useless perhaps as narrative or synthesis, but infinitely careful and complete, a wonderful source book to which Gibbon is not ashamed to confess several times his deep indebtedness. Gibbon had neither time nor patience to plough through the long sermons of the fathers in search of rare nuggets of historical information. Tillemont had and brought forth the results in a form easy to use. He won Gibbon's heart, not only by so great a service but by his complete reliability, the never failing accuracy of his research, so that, as once Gibbon described him, "the patient and sure-footed mule of the Alps may be trusted in the most slippery paths."[36] Gibbon admired the "incredible patience"[37] which made this precision possible and saw that it was a "religious accuracy"—applied to Tillemont, the epithet carries the meaning of "pious" as well as "dedicated." He realized that he himself had no desire to write history as Tillemont wrote it. The phrase "the patient and sure-footed mule" implies a criticism as well as a compliment. He conceived of Tillemont less as a historian than as a collector who made possible the work of a historian. One of Tillemont's leading virtues was humility. When Gibbon calls him "the humble Tillemont," the phrase is also a high compliment but implies the same criticism as the word "mule"—steady, careful, persevering, with a modest, limited goal, not intruding his own person or judgment. Noting his complete array of information about an early heresy, Gibbon called Tillemont "an useful scavenger."[38]

Certainly Gibbon recorded Tillemont's Catholic attitudes. He poked a little fun at his perplexity over the hesitations of the early popes,[39] his willingness to hope that an early miracle might be true, his sense of scandal in finding virtues among infidels, and the Jansenism which led to special self-dedication when he came to treat of St. Augustine, whom Gibbon called "the founder of his sect."[40] The most delicious of these little shafts of humor may be found when Tillemont treated Cyril of Jerusalem "with tenderness and respect"; and Gibbon remarked that Tillemont threw Cyril's "virtues into the text, and his faults into the notes, in decent obscurity, at the end of the volume." The effect, in total, is one of dependence and respect, occasionally more than respect, nearer to reverence, for this unpretentious, quiet, self-effacing, trustworthy guide.

Gibbon's attitude to Tillemont has some similarity to his attitude to the older, and much more papal, Baronius. No sense here of independence from the past: in attitude of mind, a philosophic detachment, but in historical investigation, a reliance upon a tradition. Gibbon poked gentle fun at Tillemont's Catholicism and crude humor at Baronius's Catholicism. The gentle fun was compatible with a profound obligation and sense of obligation. Even the stabs at Baronius were compatible with a rueful obligation. Gibbon not only referred to Baronius constantly, but frequently recommended that readers use his *Annals*. Once he paid him a compliment without backhanded subtlety: "Baronius has treated the African rebellion with skill and learning."[41] Once he praised the Cardinal's honor and integrity in treating his evidence.[42]

To contemplate Gibbon's attitude toward the learned divines among his predecessors is not, therefore, to contemplate scorn or arrogance. He went to his sources and read the originals, especially those before A.D. 500. But he knew that he could not handle so large a mass of evidence without using guides, and, for all his shafts and sallies, he was grateful when he found useful guidance—grateful whether the guides were Catholic or Protestant: "In the contemplation of a minute or remote object," he summarized his gratitude, "I am not ashamed to borrow the aid of the strongest glasses."[43] But he gave no list of those "glasses," and we cannot think that he numbered Baronius among the strongest.

An oddity remains: Gibbon harped in his footnotes on the absurdities and intolerance of the Cardinal. To keep assailing a predecessor is for any historian a waste of time; when that predecessor wrote more than a century and a half earlier, the harping becomes an obsessive waste of time. Gibbon stabbed at Baronius to amuse, but so often that the reader begins to ask whether the motive was only amusement, and to wonder whether it mattered, deep down in his historical attitude, that once Gibbon was converted to Catholicism, and whether the onslaught grew to excess because the historian needed to reassure himself about a youthful past which so long ago he thought himself to have exorcised.

REFERENCES

[1]Edward Gibbon, *The History of the Decline and Fall of the Roman Empire* (hereafter cited as *DF*), ed. J. B. Bury, 7 volumes (London, 1899-1901), chap. 23, p. 469 n.; all subsequent references are to chapter and page of this edition.

[2]*DF*, chap. 47, p. 110.

[3]*Annals* (Lucca, 1741), VII, pp. 62-64.

[4]*Annals*, VII, p. 319.

[5]*DF*, chap. 47, p. 124.

[6]*DF*, chap. 24, p. 502.

[7]*DF*, chap. 58, p. 266.

[8]*DF*, chap. 57, p. 243.

[9]*DF*, chap. 47, p. 96.

[10]*DF*, chap. 49, p. 276.

[11]*DF*, chap. 14, p. 8.

[12]*Ibid.*, p. 3.

[13]*Ibid.*, p. 7.

[14]*DF*, chap. 16, p. 71.

[15]*DF*, "General Observations on the Fall of the Roman Empire in the West" (following chapter 38), p. 163.

[16]*DF*, chap. 14, p. 4.

[17]*DF*, chap. 49, p. 251.

[18]*DF*, chap. 33, p. 407.

[19]*DF*, chap. 56, p. 187.

[20]*DF*, chap. 49, pp. 246-47; chap. 47, p. 137.

[21]*DF*, chap. 47, p. 157.

[22]*DF*, chap. 49, p. 298.

[23]*Ibid.*, p. 283.

[24]*DF*, chap. 45, p. 23.

[25]*DF*, chap. 58, p. 287.

[26]*Vindication*, in *Miscellaneous Works*, IV, pp. 388-89.

[27]*DF*, chap. 47, p. 125.

[28]*DF*, chap. 21, p. 349.

[29]*DF*, chap. 47, p. 128.

[30]*Ibid.*, p. 116.

[31]*DF*, chap. 50, p. 355.

[32]*DF*, chap. 25, p. 16.

[33]*DF*, chap. 54, p. 127.

[34]*DF*, chap. 47, p. 132.

[35]*DF*, chap. 25, p. 26.

[36]*Ibid.*, p. 48.

[37]*DF*, chap. 32, p. 374.

[38]*DF*, chap. 27, p. 153.

[39]*Ibid.*, p. 149.

[40]*DF*, chap. 33, p. 406.

[41]*DF*, chap. 29, p. 231.

[42]*Vindication*, in *Miscellaneous Works*, IV, p. 635.

[43]*DF*, chap. 47, p. 96.

GIUSEPPE GIARRIZZO

Toward the *Decline and Fall*: Gibbon's Other Historical Interests

AT THE PRECOCIOUS AGE OF SEVENTEEN, Gibbon wrote the "Age of Sesostris," in which for the first time he attempted to systematize his scholarly interests. The work is no longer extant: its author burned it along with his other youthful writings in a great bonfire in 1772. Thirty years later, Gibbon wrote a summary of it in his *Memoirs*, but it is a rather ambiguous one: he writes that the work was not intended to reconstruct the times of Sesostris, but "to investigate the probable date of the life and reign of the Conqueror of Asia."[1] However, it was precisely by means of a critical examination of chronological events of this kind that European scholars of the previous century had tried to construct models of universal history which would not be strictly bibliocentric, and in nearly all these models Sesostris and his time were obligatory points of reference.

In dealing with the "Conqueror of Asia," Gibbon concentrates on a period of universal history in which the Scythians and Egyptians are the principal actors and the Jewish and Greek worlds are still in their infancy: "In my childish balance I presumed to weigh the system of Scaliger and Petavius, of Marsham and Newton, which I could seldom study in the originals . . . , and my sleep has been disturbed by the difficulty of reconciling the Septuagint with the Hebrew computation."[2] Besides Scaliger and Petavius, Marsham and Newton, Spencer and Bochard are also to be considered, and, after them, the Italian Giambattista Vico,. who in *De Constantia* and the *Scienza Nuova* locates Sesostris at the very beginning of "human" time. This marks a radical departure in biblical studies: by placing ancient Hebrew history in a much broader context, the Rome-oriented approach typical of Augustinian historiography—of which Bossuet, at the end of the seventeenth century, was the most authoritative exponent—was swept aside. But this radical shift was not exploited to the full by historians and politicians in the Age of Reason. The explanation for this partial failure has yet to be found: the crisis that hit Mediterranean Europe in the seventeenth century generated alternative "universalist" cultural models whose development the profound Europe-oriented movements of the eighteenth century would prevent. As Gibbon was to say in his *Memoirs*, "At a riper age, I no longer presume to connect the Greek, the Jewish, and the Egyptian antiquities, which are lost in a distant cloud."[3]

It is not easy to say to what extent Gibbon's conversion to Catholicism in 1753 influenced this spirit of renunciation. It was Bossuet's "noble" hand that had caused this fall and had directed his curiosity and interest—which had previously striven for a more comprehensive form of anthropology and sociology—toward the Romano-

Christian culture of Europe. His reconversion to Anglicanism perpetrated by a Calvinist minister had the effect of stimulating deeper reflection rather than signaling a withdrawal. The result was agreement with the conservative Pyrrhonist skeptic Bayle, who, Gibbon said, "proves that neither the way of authority nor the way of examination can afford the multitude any test of religious truth, and dextrously concludes, that custom and education must be the sole grounds of popular belief."[4] The European orientation of Gibbon's sociology and anthropology became even more marked as he continued to study under Vicat, Grotius, Puffendorf (using Barbeyrac's translation and commentary), Locke, and Montesquieu.

Between 1755 and 1758, contemplations about politics were foremost in Gibbon's mind, and they reflected much more than simply the process of growing up. The Seven Years' War had already begun, and the Age of Enlightenment had gone into a period of crisis with the rather unsettling rediscovery that Europe was a continent composed of separate nations. Gibbon wrote in 1758: "No my dear friend, I don't wish to be a cosmopolitan. Such a pompous ostentatious title is not for me, for our philosophers use it to conceal an indifference for the whole human race. I wish to love my country, and to love one needs to have preferences."[5] The Swiss journal for September and October, 1755, and his letter on the Bern regime bear witness to these new interests and preferences. They were strengthened when, on his return to England, he read the post-revolutionary English writers and proudly realized the superior stability and equilibrium of the English model.[6]

The results of these new attitudes (earlier he had cause to say, "I . . . ceased to be an Englishman"[7]) were some very interesting historical writings in the style of a political essayist, which he wrote to support theses and arguments of a strictly political nature. Gibbon was in Bern from October 16 to October 18, 1755, and he had discovered there the oligarchical nature of bourgeois law. From the foundation of the city until the end of the seventeenth century it had been easy to become a member of the Bern bourgeoisie:

> But when at the end of the last century, the offices of the *bailliage* became desirable, a result of the new distribution through the drawing of lots and through the ownership of English stocks, the people of Bern began to appreciate the value of citizenship, and decided to keep it for themselves. They therefore imposed very strict conditions . . . and punished by the loss of citizenship even the smallest violation of the obligations imposed, and they applied the laws with the maximum severity. In this way they deprived a great number of families of citizenship, and today they grant it to no foreigner.[8]

In the process of telling about the revolutions of the Bern bourgeoisie, Gibbon also wrote the story of the bourgeois of ancient Rome: In the beginning Roman citizenship was scorned, but later it became so important that the tribes of Italy, initially subject to Rome and given the title of "allies," realized that unless one was a Roman citizen one was nothing; thus they decided to go to war to achieve citizenship or die in the attempt[9]—hence the Social War. Rome's obstinacy almost caused the death of the Republic: it was finally agreed to give the allies all they had asked for—three hundred thousand lives too late. "The people of Bern have read history: why have they not realized that the same causes produce the same effects?"[10] A narrow privileged oligarchy forces the reaction of those excluded, and this reaction can only be controlled by extending participation.

This is the time that Gibbon examines in his "Letter on the Government of Bern":

When the violence of some and the weakness of the others made civilized societies necessary, this much beloved yet so very pernicious independence had to be abandoned. It became necessary for all individual wills [*toutes les volontés particulières*] to dissolve into a general will [*une volonté générale*] with which all citizens had to comply under pain of punishment.[11]

The general will of Bern, however, rested on a corrupt and restricted base: the Grand Conseil was the only legislative body, and it was at the same time the enforcer of its own laws. Gibbon preferred a two-house system:

The legislative power must be separate. A council whose members enlighten and counterbalance each other would be a well-chosen body. . . . The basic guarantee that *Liberté* requires for its own correct functioning lies in the composition of this body. . . . Each order of citizens [*chaque ordre de citoyens*], each part of the state must have its representatives whose task it is to oppose any law that does not reflect their rights or is contrary to their happiness.[12]

He describes here a concept of power with guarantees that are typical of all forms of moderate constitutionalism. In Bern, however, there were *two* nations, distinct from each other as to rights, occupations, and customs: three hundred families born to rule and one hundred thousand families born to obey. This injustice had to be eradicated, just as the absurdity of a council with executive powers had also to be eliminated:

This union of two powers which ought never to meet makes each more formidable. When they are separate, the legislative body fears violent resolutions; they would be useless unless the power that is to carry them out is armed, and this power is always its rival and counterbalance.[13]

This whole political approach can be traced back to Montesquieu and to his judgment on the constitutions of the Italian republics:

Just examine what could be the situation of a citizen in these republics. The same body of magistrates has, as enforcer of the laws, all the power it gives itself in its capacity as legislator. It can despoil the State by virtue of its general will, and since it has the power of judgment it can destroy any citizen by virtue of its particular resolutions.[14]

The "Letter" openly pleads for a moderate constitutional regime with a two-chamber structure, one to propose laws formed by a restricted, perhaps even hereditary, body and an assembly of representatives of the people whose task would be to oppose any laws contrary to the welfare of the people and their interests. This is in fact the same argument sustained in the celebrated book 11, chapter 6 of the *Esprit des lois*, "The Constitution of England," which by then had become Gibbon's fundamental political text.

In February, 1761, Gibbon published the *Essai sur l'étude de la littérature*. The structure and methodological objectives of this work, which was written partly in Lausanne[15] and partly in Buriton, are very complex. The chapters written in Lausanne deal with the polemic against "l'esprit de système" as distinct from the "esprit philosophique," and here Gibbon espouses Montesquieu's thought. In England, however, after reading Hume's *Natural History of Religion* (1757), Gibbon wrote chapters 57 and 58, which deal with the pagan "system." On the first of these themes,

Gibbon walks again along the winding path that leads from Fontenelle to Montesquieu, from the *Mémoires de l'Académie des Inscriptions* to the *Considérations* and the *Esprit des lois*. The theme is the historical erudition that rejects the "esprit de système," when research and facts demonstrate the abstract and superficially all-embracing nature of the "system" while at the same time attempting to liberate knowledge of the past—which is necessary to legitimize or modify the present—from the tenets of Pyrrhonism.

Yet, the "esprit philosophique," which "consists in the ability to return to simple ideas to discover and connect first principles," becomes a means for defining a historical basis for anthropology and sociology:

> What a spectacle it is for a truly philosophical spirit to see the most absurd opinions welcomed in the most enlightened nations, to see savages with a knowledge of the most sublime truths; true consequences, but *peu justes*, drawn from the most erroneous principles; marvelous principles which always drew near to truth without leading there; a language based on ideas and ideas justified by the language; the sources of morality the same everywhere, the opinions of seditious metaphysics differing everywhere and usually extravagant, clear only when superficial, subtle, dark and unsure every time they sought depth.[16]

The sum of so many paradoxes and contradictions upsets the "esprit de système," but not the "esprit philosophique," which can restore sociological and historical substance to the level of reality. It deals with, and is able to pinpoint, the different operations of a principle in different social and institutional contexts:

> An Iroquois work, even though it be full of absurdity, would be a priceless piece. It would offer a unique insight into the nature of man's spirit, *in conditions which we have not experienced*, dominated by customs and religious opinions completely at variance with our own. At one time we would be shocked and instructed by the contradictoriness of the ideas that would be born from it, we would try to discover the reasons, we would follow the spirit from error to error. At another, we would recognize with pleasure our own principles, but discovered in other ways, and almost always modified and altered. We should learn not only to recognise but to feel the strength of prejudices, not to be surprised ever by what seems most absurd and to distrust often what seems to us well founded.[17]

This is Montesquieu's method, reinforced by its strict application in Fontenelle and Fréret. Fréret had outlined a philosophical history of Western culture showing the various ups and downs of the "esprit philosophique" and the "esprit de système":

> The love of systems which caught hold of men's spirits after Aristotle caused the Greeks to abandon the study of nature and so halted the progress of philosophical discovery; subtle reasoning took the place of experiment: the precise sciences, geometry, astronomy, and real philosophy disappeared almost completely: no care was taken to acquire new knowledge, and the only thing that was done was to arrange and connect the knowledge they believed they had in such a way as to create systems. The whole of life was spent studying the art of reasoning, and never in actually reasoning. . . .[18]

The distinction between these two forms of *esprit* came to the fore again in modern times in the efforts of the Royal Society in London and the Académie des Inscriptions in Paris. The aim of both was to rescue the "esprit de méthode" from the deadly grasp of the "esprit de système." "The philosophical spirit is vastly different from the spirit of the system. To the extent that the former is necessary, the latter is dangerous."[19] And this is pure Fréret.

At such a high critical and methodological level, Gibbon examines the unending circle connecting scholarship, philosophy, and history: "While philosophers are not always historians, it is to be hoped that all historians are philosophers."[20] For Gibbon, Tacitus and Montesquieu above all others embody this model of *historien philosophique*. The character of Tacitus is skillfully outlined in his definition of the character of Livy:

Livy depicts for me the abuse of power, a severity that nature, terrified, approves, revenge and love at one with liberty, and tyranny falling under their attacks: but the laws of the decemviri, their character and defects, their relationship with the genius of the Roman people, with the party of the decemviri and their ambitious designs he ignores completely. Nor do I see in his writings how these laws, drawn up for a restricted, poor, and half-savage republic, could overturn it when the strength of its institution brought it to the very peak of greatness. I would have found it in Tacitus.[21]

Later, in chapter 9 of the *Decline and Fall*, Gibbon says of Tacitus that he was "the first of historians who applied the science of philosophy to the study of facts."[22] He also attributes to him the merit of "having excited the genius and the perspicacity of the philosophical historians of our time," above all, of Montesquieu. Gibbon's style, however, mixes Montesquieu with Mably: "The corruption of all the orders of the Romans came as a result of the growth of their empire, and produced the greatness of the republic."[23] The kernel of the question is "conquest"; the spread of the Empire produces a crisis in the "orders," on the one hand, and, on the other, allows the Republic to achieve its moment of "grandeur." (Only later did Gibbon, under the influence of Hume, examine the problem of the relationship between "order" and "rank," i.e., the problem of institutionalized social stratification.) But

. . . equally incapable of liberty under Sulla and Augustus, the Romans, under the former were ignorant of the truth that the civil wars and the two most cruel proscriptions of the war had taught them by Augustus's time, namely, that the republic, weighed down by the burden of its greatness and corruption, could not survive without a master.[24]

This is a judgment that takes its origin from a different view of the chronological roots of the "corruption of the orders"; unlike Montesquieu in the *Considérations* (chapter 13), Gibbon traces back to the time of Sulla the beginning of the difficulties of Republican institutions, and this had considerable bearing on his future decision to take the decline of Rome, and not its growth, as the main subject for his historical research. Gibbon's maturity as a critic and his ability to convert contemporary "philosophical" arguments into valid approaches to historiography are also revealed in his belief that religion is often used as a means for legitimizing a particular institutional organization:

It pleases me to observe how men's judgments take on the colour of their prejudices. I like to observe them when they do not dare draw from principles they consider just the conclusions they maintain are correct. I like to surprise them detesting in the barbarian what they admire in the Greek and describing as irreligious in the Pagan what they describe as sacred in the Jew.[25]

He does this not just to point out the inconsistencies of mankind, but to attempt an understanding of his anthropological and sociological motivations. Prejudice is a historical fact that must be analyzed and judged, bearing in mind how imposture in society is exploited and also bearing in mind that neither society nor its natural history is static. Gibbon's "enlightenment" never went beyond the concepts underlying Hume's theory of the natural history of the mind and of society. The modest attempts at liberalism still to be found in the *Decline and Fall*, with its emphasis on the dynamic nature of "the middling rank of men," will disappear in his later years, when, as everyone knows, he adhered to the theories of Burke:

> It is only among the savages, whose ideas are limited by their needs and whose needs are simply those of nature, that sentiment must be most alive, even though at one and the same time it will be most confused. The savage at each moment feels an agitation that he can neither explain nor repress. Weak and ignorant, he fears everything because he is defenseless against everything. He marvels at everything because he knows nothing.[26]

This was the "admiration" that for Fourmont was at the root of the deification of the stars, great men, and even animals. But Fourmont himself stressed the element of *fear*: "No one felt it more than our missionaries in America. Do they not hear cannibals and other savages give this reply every day? Is God as good as you say? Then it is useless to fear him. You teach us that the devil tries only to work evil and so all our fear is of him and so we try to propitiate him."[27] This fear-provoked "extravagance," therefore, induces him to make sacrifices to the wind, the waves, and the tempests, and to adore crocodiles, serpents, and dragons.

Gibbon unites the two feelings into a more total "scorn of self," which enables him to attribute to God some benevolence: man prays to him to obtain favors without knowing what right he has to hope for them. Everything seems superior to him: the wind-buffeted oak dominates him and, at the same time, protects and nourishes him, for "compared to the superb tree, what was his lifespan, his height and his strength?" Man needs trees but trees do not need man: "Without the insight that teaches us how superior reason is to these necessary parts of an intelligent system," each of them seems quite superior to man. And thus it was that the savage conferred life and power on these parts and fell prostrate at the feet of his own creation.[28] Experience developed these ideas, "for nations, like individuals, owe everything to experiences," and made man aware of the common nature of different objects: "This common nature which is differentiated only by time, obliged particular natures to disappear while those that are different according to place were able to survive as parts of the common nature." As nations became enlightened and idolatry became more refined, man became increasingly more aware that the universe was governed by natural laws, and he drew nearer to the concept of an efficient cause.[29] These were also Hume's conclusions on the natural history of the mind, religion, and society.

By revising and developing the central themes of Hume and Montesquieu, Gibbon arrived at a moderate-liberal form of sociology and anthropology which enabled him to go beyond the polemically erudite limits of historical Pyrrhonism: "Let us read with order, set an aim, and use this as a reference point for our studies. Through not observing this rule, there are many ignorant people who have read much; but flitting from one subject to another, they have never been able to connect their ideas. Separate particles can never form a whole."[30] Thus in the *Essai*, too, Gibbon champions a form of historiographical construction which, as we have seen, was present when his intellectual vocation was awakened. And he searches for a theme that will organize the ideas he has gained and test the various alternative methodologies.

The first interesting note in the *Journal* belongs to April 14, 1761, a few weeks before the publication of the *Essai*:

> Having considered various subjects for an historical composition I chose Charles VIII of France's expedition to Italy, I read two memoranda of M. de Foncemagne in the "Mémoires" of the Academy . . . on this subject and I made some summaries of them. This very day I have finished a dissertation in which I examined the rights of Charles VIII to the throne of Naples and the claims of the Houses of Anjou and Aragon. There are ten folio pages with ample notes.[31]

His interest in this work, which, significantly, did not deal with the history of the ancient world, lay in the fact that it involved political arguments about royal succession, specifically, whether or not it should be hereditary. This was also a central theme of the *Esprit des lois*. Gibbon, however, did not treat the question of succession in terms of its relationship to forms of government, but concentrated on Hume's theory of consent as the *sine qua non* of political obligation. This is an important departure, and it is essential for a complete understanding of his critical judgment. What right has a sovereign to choose his heir?

In the East, a sovereign has the powers of a despot and can dispose as he pleases of the life and property of his subjects: he can hand over his estates to anyone he choses just as a shepherd can give away his sheep. But this is not the case in the West, for there a sovereign is only a chief magistrate: the people can bring pressure to bear on him to ensure their happiness, and he must answer to the people for his conduct. "Gratitude confined election to a few distinguished families and the son usually succeeded the father. However a solemn election was required and, it was thought, silence and obedience expressed the consent of the nation, but the nation always reserved the right to change the succession when the public good required it."[32] The monarchy had the use, but not the ownership, of power; power was rendered legitimate either by direct popular consent or through the provisions of the fundamental laws. Gibbon denied that the rights to elect and depose belonged to the pope: "Good philosophy would make us laugh at a claim to such a right if it did not already exist so evilly."[33] And his conclusion sweeps aside all doubts: "The right of conquest is only for fierce animals; the right of succession, no matter how well conceived of in itself, lacks fixed principles; the only right that transcends all objections is that which is born of the voice of a free people."[34] Thus the "consentement des sujets" remains "the most precious of all rights."

It is significant how these conclusions coincide with the theories and arguments of Hume,[35] which Gibbon espoused after reading post-Revolutionary English political writers: "My own inclination, and that of my century, urge me to history" (July 26, 1761).[36] The apodictic tone is not sufficient to eradicate hesitancy and procrastination: "Am I capable of undertaking a career that Tacitus believed worthy of himself and of which Pliny doubted he was capable? . . . The role of the historian is a beautiful one, that of the chronicler or gazetteer is to be despised." Gibbon considered Richard Coeur de Lion's crusade. He liked the element of the marvelous! The relevant part of Hume's *History* had not yet been published and would not be until 1762; Gibbon, who shared Voltaire's positive appraisal of Saladin, anticipates his picture of a

Richard "in whom the ferocity of the gladiator and the cruelty of the tyrant are employed without success in a cause in which superstition imposed silence on religion, justice and policy."[37]

Other characters and episodes parade through Gibbon's mind after Richard, for example, the wars of the barons against Prince John and Henry III, the great epoch of the English Middle Ages, the Magna Carta—so important in the English parliamentary tradition—and the constitutional proposals of Blackstone, which Gibbon read so eagerly in these years. Another attraction was the Black Prince, the son of Edward III, whose victories Voltaire stressed in order to underline—thus following in the long tradition of Bacon and Harrington—the superiority of the English infantry over the feudal cavalry of France. Voltaire returns to this theme in dealing with Henry V and the victory of Agincourt, but Gibbon relegated it to a secondary position in a project dealing with the same period, namely, a parallel life of the English sovereign and the Emperor Titus. Gibbon mentions this project in his *Memoirs*, but there is no trace of it in his papers, just as there is no trace of his life of Sir Philip Sidney and the Scottish Marquess of Montrose, two important figures of the Elizabethan age.

Among these various interests, only the Elizabethan period seems to have held his attention for long. The life and times of Sir Walter Raleigh occupied him for a year (July, 1761–June, 1762). The adventures of this courtier, soldier, humanist, and conspirator held all the ingredients for a historical romance. But Gibbon was more interested in the "times" than in the "life" of Raleigh, and this characteristic of his historiographical style would be evident also in the *Decline and Fall*. But, "fortunately for the public and unfortunately for me," as he recalled thirty years later, "no other period in English history had attracted so many eminent scholars, including Birch and Walpole, Hurd and Mallet, Robertson and Hume. . . . I must search for some other theme."[38]

In the summer of 1762, he was once again attracted to the subject of the independence and liberty of the Swiss as was, coincidentally, the contemporary historian William Robertson. At about the same time, the idea of a history of Medici Florence gained ground because it was one of the four "happy ages" of Voltaire's universal history, ages in which "the arts knew perfection and which, by signalling the epochs of the greatness of the human spirit, serve as examples for men of the future." Gibbon, an assiduous reader of Machiavelli, poses the conflict between Lorenzo and Savonarola as a historical problem: "The Medici used letters to reinforce their power and their enemies fought them with religion."[39] Thus Gibbon follows Hume who, in a famous essay, had already criticized Addison's equation of liberty and the arts.[40] In addition, once again following Hume, he studied the critical relationship between "enthusiasm" and liberty, and he used this theme to investigate and explain the constitutional conflict raging in seventeenth-century England.

All these projects and interests, though apparently the result of a haphazard and idle curiosity, strengthened his tenacious convictions and favored a methodological approach that enabled him to resuscitate his earlier interests in antiquity, but now on a higher level. In addition, they were undertaken in the months of 1762 and 1763 when he belonged to the militia at Winchester where general conditions, though favorable to reading, were not at all favorable to research. He appears to have read everything: Erasmus and the Arminians, Homer, Mably's *Observations sur les Grecs*, and Voltaire's *Siècle de Louis XIV*. It was also at that time that Gibbon began to find differences with Voltaire, and his criticisms frequently appear as an unbalanced mixture of attraction and repulsion. As time passed the criticism grew: "[Voltaire] is not the man to turn to dusty monastic writers for instruction; he compiles rapidly and he varnishes his writings with the magic of his style thus producing an extremely pleasing work but one which is negligent and superficial."[41]

The second part of the *Siècle* (from chapter 27 onwards), Gibbon writes, is much better than the first because that age is great not on account of the monarch but for the things that were done then. "But when Condé, Turenne, Vauban, Louvois, Colbert etc. have claimed their share of fame, the part remaining to the monarch will be his having chosen and employed those great men; I may add perhaps the merit of having persisted in his choice."[42] Here again the interest in the "times" is greater than the interest in the "life." His reading, however, presents him with the opportunity to dissociate himself from Voltaire's version of *histoire philosophique*. He is against the basically monotonous nature of Voltaire's vision of psychology: "In the infinite variety of passions and situations his characters seem to have only one method of thinking and feeling, that of the author."[43] He is against his partiality: "When chronology did not permit a moral disclosure, Plutarch scorned chronology; and Voltaire is not very demanding of his authorities when it is a question of the tricks of priests, the bizarreness of superstition, and the contradictions of the human spirit."[44] He opposes ideological tendentiousness: "When the philosophical historian sets himself a political or moral system, particular exceptions, which odious truth demonstrates to him, crush him under their disturbing weight. He weakens and dissimulates them and finally he causes them to disappear in order to see only the type of facts which suit his purpose."[45]

Gibbon was right to be distrustful: by this time, the process of first considering and then rejecting projects had turned his inquisitive mind in a more fruitful direction, and his methodological approach had been enriched with sociological models and anthropological insights. Now, finally free from military service, he went to Paris at the end of the Seven Years' War where he stayed from January to May, 1763, but his experience there, all in all, was rather disappointing.

Back in Lausanne, he filled some months compiling a *Recueil sur la géographie ancienne de l'Italie*, which was both a guide to the antiquities of the country and an outline for a method of systematizing his own direct observations. By means of this "mixture of study and observation," properly digested on his return to England, Gibbon contemplated "producing something not unworthy in the eyes of the public." It was the most recent in a long series of projects. But this time it was unequivocally of an antiquarian nature, and it would one day become by a circuitous route the plan for the *Decline and Fall*.

Gibbon's reading and notes are linked together by the antiquarian theme of the history of the great Roman roads and the plan of the city itself. The first subject, the Roman roads, follows an interest which began with Montaigne, Bergier, and Botero and was subsequently explored by Maffei and Montesquieu: the study of the complex economic and political relationship between the city and the provinces—a problem that was also at the heart of the process of social and administrative stabilization that was taking place in the seventeenth century. The history of town planning in Rome is a palimpsest for the political and social history of the Republic and the Empire:

This sovereign people—a name it so well deserved—enjoyed all the rights of sovereignty and all the pleasures of greatness. A citizen left his house only to stroll under a beautiful portico, to take his place along with 80,000 comrades in a magnificent theatre in which the rarities of all the earth were on show, or to rest in the spas where all the pleasures of the senses and of the spirit were united with the pomp of the most splendid monarchs. . . . [Here] the ambitious lavished their richness on the people, first to win their favours and then to make them forget they had ever had them.[46]

Rome in the age of the kings looked more like a Tartar camp than a European city—a confused heap of huts for shepherds and brigands—until in the age of Tarquin the Proud it embarked on a policy of magnificent public buildings, including the Circus, the Capitol, the *cloacae*, and the walls. Besides, the Romans were more "virtuous" than rich, and the Gauls occupied a badly built and poor city: "I think there has been an exaggerated idea of the extent of these barbarian sackings; from some rather hyperbolical expressions of Livy we have too hastily concluded that the whole city was destroyed in the burning by the Gauls."[47] The Curia Hostilia, where the Senate met after the barbarians had been expelled, must have been in the center of the Gallic camp, and many buildings dating from the age of the kings were not destroyed until the great fire in Nero's time. Between the two conflagrations the face of Rome gradually changed: "Generals without principles or scruples pillaged the subjects of the empire, those who still retained some trace of virtue were content to despoil its enemies."[48]

This important distinction helps us to understand the limits of seventeenth-century natural-right theory, and it also helps us to understand the moderate-liberal nature of Gibbon's constitutionalism. The writings of that year reflect the profound anguish of the European intelligentsia at the anti-cosmopolitan feeling that emerged during the Seven Years' War and the period that followed. A soundly based "internal" consent and the strengthening of social hegemonies and alliances were achieved in the European states by directing "outwards," i.e., beyond "national" boundaries, social conflict and tension. In other words, "external" enemies were the price paid for "internal" pacification, which could only be achieved by a higher level of consumption.

This was the context in which the debate on luxury must be seen, helping us as it does to understand its pros and cons.[49] Gibbon himself declaimed against the magnificent palaces "built with the blood of nations," against a form of oppression which dried up the soil of social wealth and transformed it into an unproductive desert. But, at the same time, both he and Hume extolled that luxury which derives from progress in the arts and commerce. In both cases, there is no doubt about the moral and juridical legitimacy of the progress that the "enemy" pays for. The definitions of a "just war," of legitimate conquest, and of "national" slavery are broadened, with ambiguous results.

The tension is reflected in Gibbon's description of the Roman triumph, a ceremony which he regards as more noble and uplifting than the similar but useless pomposities celebrated in European courts. The most brilliant court displays, such as the carousels of Louis XIV and the feasts of the Duke of Würtemberg, proved the magnificence, and occasionally the good taste, of the monarch, but the enormous expense served only to appease the vanity or relieve the boredom of a single individual, while flocks of indifferent or bored courtiers strove to disguise their disgust under a mask of pleasure. Outside could be heard the wailing and laments of people who had seen whole provinces devastated for the pleasure of the royal hunt, or who identified the gilded ceilings of the royal palace with a hundred or more cottage families driven to ruin by taxes. Nor could religious ceremonies, with their wholly superficial and external pomp, be compared to the ancient triumphs. To be moved by them, one must believe in the theological system from whence they came—in other words, one's spirit must be filled with superstition—otherwise such ceremonies could only be scorned as ridiculous pantomime.

Everything in the Roman triumph, in contrast, was inspiring and grand. To be caught up in the sensations these ceremonies were intended to excite, one need only be "a man and a Roman." The citizen, as he looked on, saw the embodiment, almost the reality, of his Republic. The treasures and the great monuments he admired and the still-bloody spoils of the enemy lent meaning to the fierce battles and were also a testament to the importance of the conquest: "A silent but easy language told him of the danger and of the valour of his fellow countrymen, symbols chosen with taste displayed in a natural way the cities, rivers, and mountains that were the theatre of Roman enterprises, even the Gods of the nations that they had subjected to Jupiter in the Capitol."[50] This is what Gibbon meant by the direct experience of "pageantry." The glory of the victorious *dux* was not confined to his family and friends; it embraced all citizens who could glory in the dignity newly added to the Roman name, including those who helped raise the hero to the consulship with their votes. They could pride themselves in their perspicacity in recognizing his merits and in their selflessness in choosing him over all other candidates.

Gibbon's political touchstones remain soundly based in the distinction between citizen and non-citizen and in the differences among nations. Once again, but at a higher conceptual level, he examined themes which had interested him earlier and he returned to the comparison between the regime in Rome and Bern, but this time his conclusions differed significantly:

> The 120 years that passed between the end of the second Punic War and the Social War saw the flourishing of the peoples of Italy under the gentlest of governments. They lost the accursed right to declare war and make peace since it was no longer necessary. Living peacefully under the protection of the Romans, they had nothing to fear from foreigners; when disputes arose among them, the decision of a senate which looked on them all with impartial eye, saved them from the sad necessity of a recourse to arms. In exchange for all these benefits, the whole of Italy supplied a body of infantry equal to the one recruited in Rome alone and twice the number of cavalry soldiers. This was a light tribute and one which, furthermore, inured their young men to war and so rendered these peoples worthy of respect in the eyes of the Romans themselves. They possessed in full sovereignty all those other rights, administration of justice, policing, decisions on the economy and politics, which serve to make nations happy. They did not have to suffer governors whose insolence equaled their greed, nor did they see all the affairs concentrated in the capital and a wall of bronze separating the citizen from the subject. Roman citizenship was refused to the cities but if an individual revealed an ambition justified by talent, the Republic knew its own interests too well not to grant him it.

The Social War had been caused by the inability of the *soci* to appreciate "all the general advantages," as opposed to minor disadvantages no matter how irritating, and so they threatened to weaken the external power of the Republic. Out of this arose Gibbon's warning to his Swiss friends: "I am writing in the pays de Vaud. Its inhabitants must be content with their state."[51]

After the Social War and the extension of citizenship, Rome sought through war with "nations" the safety valve for releasing the tensions of internal class conflict. No matter what the price, the fruits of victory conferred on the city a splendor which could not be acquired by the fiscal exploitation of its citizens. The devotion of its generals enriched it with new temples. Pompey, Caesar, Augustus, and Agrippa, the greed of its provincial governors, and the luxury of private citizens all contributed to filling Rome with splendid buildings. And when, in A.D. 64, "chance and perhaps Nero's vanity" lit the spectacular flames, not all those buildings were destroyed, though the ones that had been hurriedly built without plan after the Gallic invasion were all devastated. By order of Nero—an order worthy of the wisest of princes— Rome rose more beautiful than ever out of the ashes and, in spite of the horrors of three civil wars, during the reign of Vespasian, when Pliny was writing his *Natural History*, the city was more splendid than it had been before its destruction fifteen years earlier: "Physical disasters were soon repaired in a capital city that can draw on the resources of an empire."[52] From Vespasian to Marcus Aurelius all the emperors contributed to the beautification of the city, and "if the decadence of the arts prevented Severus Alexander, Aurelian and Diocletian from bringing to it as much good taste, they tried to make up for it in magnificence."[53]

When the capital was moved to Constantinople, Rome went into decline. In the Dark Ages, the splendor and greatness of the city diminished, and by the time of the Renaissance the image that met the saddened eyes of the humanist was one of death and destruction. But were the barbarians responsible for this? Gibbon has recourse to Pietro Bargeo's arguments, but he rejects Bargeo's apologetic tones. He acquits the Goths of any responsibility for the disaster, laying the blame firmly at the door of the popes: "The zeal of the Popes and especially of Gregory the Great saw in a temple only the idol to whom it was consecrated. Religion was founded on the ruins of the fine arts."[54] It is an epigram that contains all the condemnatory tones of Puritan iconoclasm: "Gregory the Great and the passing of time did more harm than Attila."[55] This is yet another way of leading to a serious study of the internal and external causes of the decline of Rome, while at the same time giving subtle reasons for absolving the barbarians. "For more than a century, numerous corps of their compatriots had served in the Roman armies; they had studied the language of the nation and embraced its customs. They had adopted its religion or at least they revered it." And so he deduces that the sacking of the city by the Goths was much less reprehensible than its sacking by the Christians in 1527.

Gibbon's Italian tour from April, 1764, to May, 1765, contrary to his expectations and perhaps even his plans, did not turn out to be an exploration of antiquity. His interest in the political institutions of the states he visited and the figurative arts of both the ancient and modern worlds canceled out all the others. Unfortunately that part of the journal covering those months stops at the gates of Rome, and the veracity of the famous episode ("it was in Rome on 15th October 1764"), which Gibbon twenty-five years later states was the moment of his final decision, can no longer be verified.

The history of the following three or four years, however, leads us to doubt the powerful and definitive nature of that experience. Rome was not the central theme of his letters dating from that time; rather it was the "gouvernement féodal," a subject which also interested Montesquieu, Robertson, and Mably in those years when the anti-European front among the European nations was emerging and gaining strength.

And so Gibbon, exploiting the favorable opportunity afforded by the visit to England of one of his Swiss friends, returns to his earlier plan of writing a history of Swiss liberty. He wrote a part of it, and the conclusion still exists:

I have just outlined with weak but impartial pen the history of an obscure revolution which changed the fate of some Alpine peasants. Nonetheless it merits the attention of the philosopher who searches for man in the cottage rather than in the palace. He knows that the sacred name of liberty has always designated the unjust prerogatives of a small number of citizens and that nations seduced or compelled by their chiefs have fought a thousand times with the utmost fury for foreign interests. He studies with attentive eye the framework of Europe in the barbarous centuries of feudal anarchy. How sad that picture is for a friend of mankind! Barons and bishops disputing with the king for the bloody spoils of the commoners, those unfortunate commoners who sometimes take up arms but whose blind and uncertain fury dishonours with excesses a liberty which they cannot enjoy; some Italian popular republics torn by ever present discord and which devote themselves with equal ardour to their tribunes or their tyrants. Here one sees however a rarer spectacle more worthy of human nature: a virtuous people who have defended the most sacred rights by the most legitimate means, who showed strength in danger and moderation in victory.[56]

The Swiss are thus added to the list of those classical nations endowed with "virtue"—Sparta and Rome. The rare examples of a people "who believe in virtue in a corrupt century,"[57] an army which fights "for what men hold most dear," liberty,[58] "a masculine, vigorous liberty which seemed the work of nature alone,"[59] certainly deserve a historian.

Gibbon believed in this project and Hume explicitly exhorted him to carry it out. But a physical breakdown in 1768, followed by the death of his father in November, 1770, led him to put it off. When he was able to return to it, Deyverdun had left England, and the sources in German once again seemed to him hostile and distant. His interest in this history dissolved completely during a very precarious political and social crisis in England; Gibbon once again turned his mind to the world of Rome, and, between 1771 and 1772, with greater determination he began to collect the material for the first part of his history.

When he finally decided on the subject and structure for his magnum opus Gibbon was thirty-five years old. He worked at it for fifteen years, the central and most intellectually vital years of his life. The formative period had been long, in spite of his early precocity, but, as we have seen, it was also extraordinarily fertile. Of all the projects considered, no matter how potentially interesting, no matter how closely they mirrored the real themes and problems of contemporary debate, none actually resulted in important independent or fruitful research. But none of these intellectual experiences was wasted either. His *Memoirs* tells of a strict continuity in his work, which even the analytic construction of his diaries seems to confirm. His erudition grows, though apparently haphazardly; but his "projects," that is, his efforts to collate and systematize the knowledge gained, do in fact supply answers to contemporary problems, and so they helped him to discover and develop, given his historical inclinations, a methodology by which to communicate his total vision of man, his social relationships, and the mutual influence of past and present.

The *Decline and Fall* absorbs and contains all this early experience in Gibbon's analysis and explanation of his themes, in the richness and completeness of his methodological approach, and in the often elusive, but never ambiguous, presentation of his ideological message. Indeed, the attentive reader will find in the text as well as in the footnotes the fruits of each and every one of his projects, both those he actually carried out and those he only courted in his imagination.

REFERENCES

[1] Edward Gibbon, *Memoirs of My Life*, ed. G. A. Bonnard (1966), pp. 55-56.

[2] *Ibid.*, p. 43.

[3] *Ibid.*, p. 56.

[4] *Ibid.*, p. 64.

[5] "Lettre sur le gouvernement de Berne," G. R. de Beer, G. A. Bonnard, L. Junod, eds., *Miscellanea Gibboniana* (1952), p. 123.

[6] *Memoirs*, p. 98: "The favourite companions of my leisure were our English writers since the Revolution: they breathe the spirit of reason and liberty. . . ."

[7] *Ibid.*, p. 86.

[8] *Miscellanea Gibboniana*, p. 63, Bern, October 16-18, 1755.

[9] *Ibid.*, pp. 53-54.

[10] *Ibid.*, p. 53.

[11] *Ibid.*, p. 125.

[12] *Ibid.*, p. 126.

[13] *Ibid.*, p. 127.

[14] *Esprit des lois* XI.6, "La constitution d'Angleterre."

[15] The French Academy prize for 1755 was just "En quoi consiste l'esprit philosophique?"

[16] *Essai sur l'étude de la littérature*, in *Miscellaneous Works* (1814-15), IV, p. 60.

[17] *Ibid.*, pp. 60-61.

[18] *Mémoires de l'Académie des Inscriptions*, VI (1729), pp. 150-51. See G. Giarrizzo, *E. Gibbon e la cultura europea del Settecento* (1954), pp. 117-18.

[19] *Mémoires de l'Académie des Inscriptions*, VI, p. 151.

[20] *Essai*, p. 66.

[21] *Ibid.*, p. 67.

[22] *The History of the Decline and Fall of the Roman Empire (DF)*, ed. J. B. Bury, 7 vols. (1909-14). chap. 9, p. 230 and chap. 12, p. 344.

[23] *Essai*, p. 92.

[24] *Ibid.*, p. 89.

[25] *Ibid.*, p. 61.

[26] *Ibid.*, p. 78.

[27] *Réflexions critiques sur les histoires des anciens peuples* (1735), I, p. 232. See *DF*, chap. 50, p. 354, note 64.

[28] *Essai*, p. 79.

[29] *Ibid.*, pp. 80-81.

[30] *Miscellaneous Works* (1796), III, p. 1.

[31] *Gibbon's Journal*, ed. Low (1929), p. 24.

[32] *Miscellaneous Works*, III, pp. 13-14.

[33] *Ibid.*, p. 9.

[34] *Ibid.*, p. 17. See *DF*, chap. 41, p. 332 and chap. 59, p. 355.

[35] *A Treatise of Human Nature* III.2.10. See Giarrizzo, *D. Hume politico e storico* (1962), pp. 19ff.; D. Forbes, *Hume's Philosophical Politics* (1975), pp. 102ff.

[36] *Miscellaneous Works*, III, p. 18.

[37] *Ibid.*, p. 19.

[38] *Gibbon's Journal*, p. 103.

[39] *Ibid.*, p. 129.

[40] Forbes (above note 35), pp. 154-56.

[41] *Gibbon's Journal*, p. 129.

[42] *Ibid.*, pp. 129-30.

[43] *Miscellaneous Works*, III, p. 126.

[44] *Ibid.*, p. 128.

[45] *Ibid.*, p. 130.

[46] *Le Journal de Gibbon à Lausanne*, ed. G. Bonnard (Lausanne, 1945), p. 62.

[47] *Miscellaneous Works*, IV, p. 221.

[48] *Le Journal de Gibbon à Lausanne*, p. 63.

[49] See C. Borghero, *La polemica sul lusso nel Settecento francese* (1974), pp. xvii ff.

[50] *Miscellaneous Works*, IV, pp. 71-72.

[51] *Le Journal de Gibbon à Lausanne*, pp. 126ff.

[52] *Miscellaneous Works*, IV, p. 223.

[53] *Ibid.*, p. 225.

[54] *Le Journal de Gibbon*, p. 83.

[55] *Miscellaneous Works*, IV, p. 224.

[56] *Miscellaneous Works*, III, pp. 282-83.

[57] *Ibid.*, p. 321.

[58] *Ibid.*, p. 278.

[59] *Ibid.*, p. 250.

REUBEN A. BROWER

With Gibbon in Puerto Rico

Reuben Brower was planning to make a major contribution to this volume, but he died before he could bring it to completion. Among his papers was found this delightful travel sketch which we are pleased to publish in his memory.

—*The Editors*

WITH MY HEAD FULL OF GIBBON, on the verge of writing a piece in celebration of the bicentennial of the *Decline and Fall*, I took a week off in Puerto Rico, on the French principle of *reculer pour mieux sauter*. One blissful day, a late-afternoon drive took us up from the sea to the hill town of San Germàn, which had been first founded on the coast in 1512, and in 1570 moved to the present site. The central part of the old town has the unmistakable feel of a Latin city and an air of some antiquity. Small wooden balconied houses line the side streets and the old plaza, which is not a square, but a long narrow ellipse with a slightly raised brick terrace for walking and sitting, and with the street surrounding the whole area—a sort of stadium or miniature Piazza Navona. The surprise and the beauty of the place is the church that rises at one end, above a broad but steep flight of brick steps that ask a steady head of the climber or would-be pilgrim. At the time we saw the square, there was not a human being in sight. The church itself, "the oldest in the hemisphere," according to the guidebook, is solid and grim, with the uncompromising bareness of a natural platform or mesa which drops away steeply at the sides and in the rear, above a great expanse of valley and hills that rise to green but rugged mountains beyond. As we saw the church, near sunset, a huge cumulus cloud edged with a silvery brightness set the dark mass off, suggesting a more than earthly setting. The name of the church—it seemed almost inevitable—was Porta Coeli. The missionary *padre* or abbot who "saw" the site and who placed his church there must have had some memory of "Gibbon's" Ara Coeli. In San Germàn the arched doorway with a window above it is reminiscent of the medieval Roman church, but there is a primitive Renaissance quality in the surrounding moldings, the pilasters, and the more generous curve of the entrance arch. There is also a hint of a cloister or monkish dormitory in the fragment of wall and window to the left of the façade. The narrow bricks in the steps and in exposed parts of the terrace, like the severe block of the building, have a distinctly Roman flavor. More than Christian centuries stand back of this "simple" mission church.

The North American century intrudes in equally characteristic expressions. The Porta Coeli is no longer a church, a well-lettered sign informed us, but "a museum of religious art"; and the crowning symbol of the age, a high anchor fence topped with barbed wire, surrounds what once had been the cloister or churchyard. (Echoes of Leningrad churches turned into anti-religious museums, of concentration camps, and American properties fortified against vandalism and break-ins.) A further touch completed the twentieth-century setting. Less than fifty yards from the church steps stood the open and lighted doorway of a news store. I stepped in to buy a postcard of the church, and stopped just short of asking: the shop, shining and neat as a pin, was an "adult" bookstore. No sleazy types here, no furtive looks as in Boston or Chicago; Latin worldliness and Spanish decorum saved any embarrassment. The smiling middle-aged proprietor, the pale young man at the adding machine, couldn't have been more polite. Was the shop, like the factories beyond the old town, one more evidence of degradation, or another instance of easy Latin acceptance, the church and sex living in cheerful harmony? The new age in San Germàn was not all bad: a newer church tower in fresh creamy stucco overshadowed the *Plaza Principal*; toward the eastern end of the town were the huge ultramodern hospital of the Immaculate Conception and the delightful verandaed buildings of the Inter-American University.

If we imagine Gibbon seated—wherever he *was* seated—"musing amid the ruins" of *this* Capitol, what could he think? The embrace of mind displayed in the *Decline and Fall*, the power of "a grave and temperate irony," which Gibbon had discovered in Pascal, could they surround this scene in all its implications? The church-museum might have evoked an ironic innuendo: a singular victory here of the Enlightenment campaign against *l'infâme*. The union of triumphant Science and the Immaculate Conception would offer an agreeable occasion for one of those sentences of paired opposites that come with almost automatic ease in the pages of the *Decline and Fall*. Gibbon could have handled without embarrassment and with a certain interest the bookshop and its late-imperial exhibits, perhaps adding a footnote on the "scarcely correct taste" of the century and a more "naked" comment buried "in the obscurity of a learned language."

But Gibbon the lover of freedom, as he saw it happily exemplified in the English constitution or in any government of "the best," whether in England or Athens or Republican Rome, would not have been happy had he reflected on the source and the consequences of this new freedom for all. The economic doctrines of Adam Smith, whom he much admired, might have seemed less palatable when translated into the actuality of American big business. In the penultimate chapter of the *Decline and Fall*, Gibbon observes in a footnote: "Dr. Adam Smith . . . proves, perhaps too severely, that the most salutary effects have flowed from the meanest and most selfish causes." The strip of luxury hotels in San Juan, the flourishing drug trade in the island, and the equally flourishing criminal activities have diminished the glamor of Munoz-Marin's "Operation Bootstrap." Factories that have "raised the standard of living" are wrecking one of the loveliest landscapes in the Carribean, the black clouds of "Rich Industry" (Pope) rise from sugar-cane refineries and the "petrochemical complex" of Ponce de Leon's once charming city. If Gibbon could see that these and other horrors were the end product of the revolution he did not take seriously, model for the French Revolution that filled him with horror and dismay, he might not have spoken so lightly of observing "the decadence of two empires" (Roman and British). The twentieth-century decline and fall, seen at close range, could hardly have been expressed in the finely tuned periods of the *Decline and Fall of the Roman Empire*. An English Augustan, with a moderate attachment to the new philosophy of France, might have been pleased to recognize an echo of Virgil on the dollar bill, *novus ordo seclorum*. He would have found little comfort in a Commonwealth—as Dryden put it—"drawn to the dregs of a Democracy."

Index

Bruni, Leonardo, 87, 90, 91, 95, 97, 104
Buckingham, Duke of, 88
Buffon, Georges de, 196
Burke, Edmund, 11, 133, 135–136, 180, 193
Bury, J. B., 40, 55, 127
Byres, James, 195
Byron, George Gordon, Lord, 57

Cabasilas, Nicolas, 54
Caesar, Gaius Julius, 125, 160, 244
Caetani, Leone, 68
Calvin, John, 96
Cantù, Cesare, 83
Caperonnier, 212
Casaubon, Isaac, 142
Cassas, 200
Cassiodorus, 78
Cassius, Avidius, 30
Cassius, Dio, 216
Castel (Jesuit), 214–215
Catherine II (of Russia), 177
Cato the Elder, 56
Cattaneo, Carlo, 81–82
Caxa de Leruela, 91, 98
Caylus, Comte de, 45, 196, 202, 212
Cecaumenus, 55
Cellorigo, González de, 91, 97
Chandler, Richard, 57
Chardin, Jean, 212
Charlemagne, 225, 226
Charles IV, 48
Charles V, 97, 132
Charles VIII, 239
Châtelet, Madame du, 147
Chelebi, Katib, 95
Chénier, André, 151
Chesterfield, Lord, 21
Chillingworth, William, 8, 222
Cicero, Marcus Tullius, 4, 21, 56, 95, 128, 160
Clairon, Mlle. (Claire Josèphe Léris), 19
Clamanges, Nicholas de, 89
Clarendon, Lord, 88
Claudius, Emperor, 128, 183
Cleopatra, 168
Clérisseau, Charles-Louis, 198–199
Clovis I, 189
Cochin, Charles Nicolas, 194, 196, 202
Colbert, J. B., 54, 241
Collingwood, R. G., 127–128
Combefis, 54, 55
Commodus, Emperor, 27, 29, 30, 31, 106, 109, 129

Comnena, Anna, see Anna Comnena
Condé, Henri II de Bourbon, 241
Condillac, E. B. de, 212
Condorcet, Marquis de, 65, 159, 161, 176, 179, 180
Connolly, Cyril, 42
Constant, Benjamin, 81
Constantine I, 47, 58, 75, 118, 226, 227; and public policy, 130; murder of Crispus by, 132; conversion of, 134; and religious history, 198
Constantius II, 28, 30
Corneille, Pierre, 5, 183
Correggio, 193
Court de Gébelin, Antoine, 175
Cowper, William, 14
Crevier, 208
Crispus, Flavius Julius, 132
Crivellucci, Amedeo, 82
Croce, Benedetto, 82, 83, 84
Cromwell, Oliver, 58, 154
Crousaz, Jean-Pierre de, 208
Curchod, Suzanne, 5, 15, 17, 18, 175
Curtius, E. R., 96
Cyprian, St., 95
Cyril, St., 55
Cyril of Alexandria, St., 220

Daillé, 222
Dangeau, Marquis de, 210
Deffand, Madame du, 148
De Herbelot, Barthélemy, see Herbelot, Barthélemy d'
Démeunier, Jean Nicholas, 163
Deschamps, Eustache, 88
Deyverdun, Georges, 127, 173, 176, 245; and Mémoires littéraires de la Grande Bretagne, 5–6; Gibbon's close relationship with, 15, 17, 20; and Freemasons, 174
Diderot, Denis, 164, 175, 176, 180, 212, 214; Vie de Sénèque, 150; on "Longinus's pigmies," 153
Dietrich of Niem, 93, 95, 96
Diocletian, 39, 47, 128, 185, 199
Domitian, 106
Doria, Paolo Mattia, 98
Du Bocage, Madame, 212
Dubos, Abbé J. B., 91, 96, 99, 164
Duclos, Charles P., 212
Dufourny, 200
Dumesnil, Marie Françoise, 19
Dupin, Louis Ellies, 222, 227
Du Resnel, Abbé, 145–146, 153

Tabari, Muhammad ibn Jarir al-, 66
Tacfarinas, 30
Tacitus, Cornelius, 29, 32, 33, 56, 151, 164, 216, 239; Gibbon's admiration for, 27; *Histories*, 28, 30, 31, 34; *Annals*, 30, 34; on decline of liberty, 95, 107; and decay of senatorial virtue, 109; Germans described by, 110, 111; *Dialogus de oratoribus*, 150; and moral history, 161; as Gibbon's ideal philosophical historian, 30, 168, 237
Tamurlane, 39, 55
Tavernier, Jean Baptiste, 212
Terrasson, 211
Tertullian, 185
Theodora, 183
Theodore the Studite, 57
Theodosius, 30, 106, 113, 128, 226
Thierry, Augustin, 153
Thomas, St., 78
Thucydides, 55, 57, 161, 164
Tiberius, Emperor, 30
Tillemont, Le Nain de, 69, 160, 211, 216, 219, 220, 227; Gibbon on, 213–214, 229–230
Tiraboschi, Girolamo, 197
Titus, Emperor, 240
Tourreil, 148
Townley, Charles, 196
Trajan, 30, 32, 33, 50, 108, 134
Treves, Piero, 84
Trevor-Roper, H., 77
Trévoux, 163, 212
Tully, *see* Cicero, Marcus Tullius
Turenne, Vicomte de, 241
Turgot, Anne Robert Jacques, 97, 178–179, 180

Ulfilas, 44, 55
Ulloa, Antonio de, 98

Valla, Lorenzo, 90, 95
Varro, Marcus Terentius, 128
Vasari, Giorgio, 87, 197, 202
Vauban, Marquis de, 241
Verdelin, Madame, 213

Vertot, Abbé de, 208, 211
Vicat, Mr., 22, 234
Vico, Giambattista, 80, 82, 83, 84, 168, 226; *Scienza Nuova*, 78, 79, 174, 233; language of, 87
Virgil, 56, 128
Vitruvius, 128
Volpe, Gioacchino, 83
Voltaire (François Marie Arouet), 5, 144, 145, 153, 180, 241; on history of Byzantium, 56; on Muhammad, 65; on four ages of the arts, 96; on four ages in history, 125–126, 240; and Augustus, 128; *The Age of Louis XIV*, 134, 212, 240; on *The Spirit of the Laws*, 148; on fate of French language, 149; *Dieu et les hommes*, 172; and Seroux d'Agincourt, 196; *Lettres philosophiques*, 207; *Annales de l'Empire*, 208; Gibbon's meeting with, 209; Gibbon on historical writing of, 211–212; on distinction between sacred and profane history, 213; and Christianity, 214, 215; and "prejudice" against Catholics, 225; his appraisal of Saladin, 239

Walpole, Horace, 6, 11, 14, 37, 193, 196, 240
Walton, Henry, 2
Waqidi, al-, 66
Warburton, Bishop William, 103
Weil, Gustav, 65
Wesley, John, 93
Wheler, Sir George, 56, 198
Wickhoff, 197
Wilde, Oscar, 11
Winckelmann, Johann Joachim, 194, 196, 198, 199, 200, 202; *Geschichte der Kunst des Altertums*, 195
Winstanley, Gerrard, 89
Wurtemberg, Duke of, 48, 242
Wyatt, James, 193

Xenophon, 57

Zacchiroli, F., 80
Zeno, 141